PostgreSQL 8.4

Official Documentation

Server Administration

Volume II

Fultus™ Books

PostgreSQL

PostgreSQL 8.4 Official Documentation

Server Administration

Volume II

ISBN 1-59682-159-0

Copyright © 1996-2009 The PostgreSQL Global Development Group

Cover design and book layout by Fultus Corporation

Published by Fultus Corporation

Publisher Web: *www.fultus.com*
Linbrary - Linux Library: *www.linbrary.com*
Online Bookstore: *store.fultus.com*
email: *production@fultus.com*

Table of Contents

List of Tables

List of Examples

License

PostgreSQL is released under the BSD license.

PostgreSQL Database Management System
(formerly known as Postgres, then as Postgres95)

Portions Copyright (c) 1996-2009, The PostgreSQL Global Development Group

Portions Copyright (c) 1994, The Regents of the University of California

Permission to use, copy, modify, and distribute this software and its documentation for any purpose, without fee, and without a written agreement is hereby granted, provided that the above copyright notice and this paragraph and the following two paragraphs appear in all copies.

IN NO EVENT SHALL THE UNIVERSITY OF CALIFORNIA BE LIABLE TO ANY PARTY FOR DIRECT, INDIRECT, SPECIAL, INCIDENTAL, OR CONSEQUENTIAL DAMAGES, INCLUDING LOST PROFITS, ARISING OUT OF THE USE OF THIS SOFTWARE AND ITS DOCUMENTATION, EVEN IF THE UNIVERSITY OF CALIFORNIA HAS BEEN ADVISED OF THE POSSIBILITY OF SUCH DAMAGE.

THE UNIVERSITY OF CALIFORNIA SPECIFICALLY DISCLAIMS ANY WARRANTIES, INCLUDING, BUT NOT LIMITED TO, THE IMPLIED WARRANTIES OF MERCHANTABILITY AND FITNESS FOR A PARTICULAR PURPOSE. THE SOFTWARE PROVIDED HEREUNDER IS ON AN "AS IS" BASIS, AND THE UNIVERSITY OF CALIFORNIA HAS NO OBLIGATIONS TO PROVIDE MAINTENANCE, SUPPORT, UPDATES, ENHANCEMENTS, OR MODIFICATIONS.

Abstract

Welcome to the *PostgreSQL 8.4 Official Documentation*! After many years of development, PostgreSQL has become feature-complete in many areas. This release shows a targeted approach to adding features (e.g., authentication, monitoring, space reuse), and adds capabilities defined in the later SQL standards.

Part III.
Server Administration

This part covers topics that are of interest to a PostgreSQL database administrator. This includes installation of the software, set up and configuration of the server, management of users and databases, and maintenance tasks. Anyone who runs a PostgreSQL server, even for personal use, but especially in production, should be familiar with the topics covered in this part.

The information in this part is arranged approximately in the order in which a new user should read it. But the chapters are self-contained and can be read individually as desired. The information in this part is presented in a narrative fashion in topical units. Readers looking for a complete description of a particular command should see *Part VI*.

The first few chapters are written so they can be understood without prerequisite knowledge, so new users who need to set up their own server can begin their exploration with this part. The rest of this part is about tuning and management; that material assumes that the reader is familiar with the general use of the PostgreSQL database system. Readers are encouraged to look at *Part I* and *Part II* for additional information.

Chapter 15.
Installation from Source Code

This chapter describes the installation of PostgreSQL using the source code distribution. (If you are installing a pre-packaged distribution, such as an RPM or Debian package, ignore this chapter and read the packager's instructions instead.)

15.1. Short Version

```
./configure
gmake
su
gmake install
adduser postgres
mkdir /usr/local/pgsql/data
chown postgres /usr/local/pgsql/data
su - postgres
/usr/local/pgsql/bin/initdb -D /usr/local/pgsql/data
/usr/local/pgsql/bin/postgres -D /usr/local/pgsql/data >logfile 2>&1 &
/usr/local/pgsql/bin/createdb test
/usr/local/pgsql/bin/psql test
```

The long version is the rest of this chapter.

15.2. Requirements

In general, a modern Unix-compatible platform should be able to run PostgreSQL. The platforms that had received specific testing at the time of release are listed in *Section 15.7* (page 38) below. In the doc subdirectory of the distribution there are several platform-specific FAQ documents you might wish to consult if you are having trouble.

The following software packages are required for building PostgreSQL:

- GNU make is required; other make programs will *not* work. GNU make is often installed under the name gmake; this document will always refer to it by that name. (On some systems GNU make is the default tool with the name make.) To test for GNU make enter:

  ```
  gmake --version
  ```

  It is recommended to use version 3.76.1 or later.

- You need an ISO/ANSI C compiler (at least C89-compliant). Recent versions of GCC are recommendable, but PostgreSQL is known to build using a wide variety of compilers from different vendors.

- tar is required to unpack the source distribution, in addition to either gzip or bzip2. In addition, gzip is required to install the documentation.

- The GNU Readline library is used by default. It allows psql (the PostgreSQL command line SQL interpreter) to remember each command you type, and allows you to use arrow keys to recall and edit previous commands. This is very helpful and is strongly recommended. If you don't want to use it then you must specify the `--without-readline` option to `configure`. As an alternative, you can often use the BSD-licensed `libedit` library, originally developed on NetBSD. The `libedit` library is GNU Readline-compatible and is used if `libreadline` is not found, or if `--with-libedit-preferred` is used as an option to `configure`. If you are using a package-based Linux distribution, be aware that you need both the `readline` and `readline-devel` packages, if those are separate in your distribution.

- The zlib compression library will be used by default. If you don't want to use it then you must specify the `--without-zlib` option to `configure`. Using this option disables support for compressed archives in pg_dump and pg_restore.

The following packages are optional. They are not required in the default configuration, but they are needed when certain build options are enabled, as explained below:

- To build the server programming language PL/Perl you need a full Perl installation, including the `libperl` library and the header files. Since PL/Perl will be a shared library, the `libperl` library must be a shared library also on most platforms. This appears to be the default in recent Perl versions, but it was not in earlier versions, and in any case it is the choice of whomever installed Perl at your site.

  If you don't have the shared library but you need one, a message like this will appear during the PostgreSQL build to point out this fact:

  ```
  *** Cannot build PL/Perl because libperl is not a shared library.
  *** You might have to rebuild your Perl installation.  Refer to
  *** the documentation for details.
  ```

(If you don't follow the on-screen output you will merely notice that the PL/Perl library object, plperl.so or similar, will not be installed.) If you see this, you will have to rebuild and install Perl manually to be able to build PL/Perl. During the configuration process for Perl, request a shared library.

- To build the PL/Python server programming language, you need a Python installation with the header files and the distutils module. The distutils module is included by default with Python 1.6 and later; users of earlier versions of Python will need to install it.

Since PL/Python will be a shared library, the `libpython` library must be a shared library also on most platforms. This is not the case in a default Python installation. If after building and installing PostgreSQL you have a file called `plpython.so` (possibly a different extension), then everything went well. Otherwise you should have seen a notice like this flying by:

```
*** Cannot build PL/Python because libpython is not a shared library.
*** You might have to rebuild your Python installation.  Refer to
*** the documentation for details.
```

That means you have to rebuild (part of) your Python installation to create this shared library.

If you have problems, run Python 2.3 or later's configure using the `--enable-shared` flag. On some operating systems you don't have to build a shared library, but you will have to convince the PostgreSQL build system of this. Consult the `Makefile` in the `src/pl/plpython` directory for details.

- If you want to build the PL/Tcl procedural language, you of course need a Tcl installation. If you are using a pre-8.4 release of Tcl, ensure that it was built without multithreading support.

- To enable Native Language Support (NLS), that is, the ability to display a program's messages in a language other than English, you need an implementation of the Gettext API. Some operating systems have this built-in (e.g., Linux, NetBSD, Solaris), for other systems you can download an add-on package from *http://developer.postgresql.org/~petere/bsd-gettext/*. If you are using the Gettext implementation in the GNU C library then you will additionally need the GNU Gettext package for some utility programs. For any of the other implementations you will not need it.

- Kerberos, OpenSSL, OpenLDAP, and/or PAM, if you want to support authentication or encryption using these services.

If you are building from a CVS tree instead of using a released source package, or if you want to do server development, you also need the following packages:

- GNU Flex and Bison are needed to build from a CVS checkout, or if you changed the actual scanner and parser definition files. If you need them, be sure to get Flex 2.5.4 or later and Bison 1.875 or later. Other lex and yacc programs cannot be used.

- Perl is also needed to build from a CVS checkout, or if you changed the input files for any of the build steps that use Perl scripts. If building on Windows you will need Perl in any case.

If you need to get a GNU package, you can find it at your local GNU mirror site (see *http://www.gnu.org/order/ftp.html* for a list) or at *ftp://ftp.gnu.org/gnu/*.

Also check that you have sufficient disk space. You will need about 65 MB for the source tree during compilation and about 15 MB for the installation directory. An empty database cluster takes about 25 MB; databases take about five times the amount of space that a flat text file with the same data would take. If you are going to run the regression tests you will temporarily need up to an extra 90 MB. Use the df command to check free disk space.

15.3. Getting The Source

The PostgreSQL 8.4.0 sources can be obtained by anonymous FTP from *ftp://ftp.postgresql.org/pub/source/v8.4.0/postgresql-8.4.0.tar.gz*. Other download options can be found on our website: *http://www.postgresql.org/download/*. After you have obtained the file, unpack it:

```
gunzip postgresql-8.4.0.tar.gz
tar xf postgresql-8.4.0.tar
```

This will create a directory postgresql-8.4.0 under the current directory with the PostgreSQL sources. Change into that directory for the rest of the installation procedure.

15.4. Upgrading

These instructions assume that your existing installation is under the /usr/local/pgsql directory, and that the data area is in /usr/local/pgsql/data. Substitute your paths appropriately.

The internal data storage format typically changes in every major release of PostgreSQL. Therefore, if you are upgrading an existing installation that does not have a version number of "8.4.x", you must back up and restore your data. If you are upgrading from PostgreSQL "8.4.x", the new version can use your current data files so you should skip the backup and restore steps below because they are unnecessary.

1. If making a backup, make sure that your database is not being updated. This does not affect the integrity of the backup, but the changed data would of course not be included. If necessary, edit the permissions in the file /usr/local/pgsql/data/pg_hba.conf (or equivalent) to disallow access from everyone except you.

   To back up your database installation, type:

   ```
   pg_dumpall > outputfile
   ```

   If you need to preserve OIDs (such as when using them as foreign keys), then use the -o option when running pg_dumpall.

   To make the backup, you can use the pg_dumpall command from the version you are currently running. For best results, however, try to use the pg_dumpall command from PostgreSQL 8.4.0, since this version contains bug fixes and improvements over older versions. While this advice might seem idiosyncratic since you haven't installed the new version yet, it is advisable to follow it if you plan to install the new version in parallel with the old version. In that case you can complete the installation normally and transfer the data later. This will also decrease the downtime.

2. Shut down the old server:

    ```
    pg_ctl stop
    ```

    On systems that have PostgreSQL started at boot time, there is probably a start-up file that will accomplish the same thing. For example, on a Red Hat Linux system one might find that this works:

    ```
    /etc/rc.d/init.d/postgresql stop
    ```

3. If restoring from backup, rename or delete the old installation directory. It is a good idea to rename the directory, rather than delete it, in case you have trouble and need to revert to it. Keep in mind the directory might consume significant disk space. To rename the directory, use a command like this:

    ```
    mv /usr/local/pgsql /usr/local/pgsql.old
    ```

4. Install the new version of PostgreSQL as outlined in *Section 15.5* (page 25).

5. Create a new database cluster if needed. Remember that you must execute these commands while logged in to the special database user account (which you already have if you are upgrading).

    ```
    /usr/local/pgsql/bin/initdb -D /usr/local/pgsql/data
    ```

6. Restore your previous pg_hba.conf and any postgresql.conf modifications.

7. Start the database server, again using the special database user account:

    ```
    /usr/local/pgsql/bin/postgres -D /usr/local/pgsql/data
    ```

8. Finally, restore your data from backup with:

    ```
    /usr/local/pgsql/bin/psql -d postgres -f outputfile
    ```

    using the *new* psql.

Further discussion appears in *Section 24.5* (page 202), including instructions on how the previous installation can continue running while the new installation is installed.

15.5. Installation Procedure

1. **Configuration**

   The first step of the installation procedure is to configure the source tree for your system and choose the options you would like. This is done by running the `configure` script. For a default installation simply enter:

   `./configure`

   This script will run a number of tests to determine values for various system dependent variables and detect any quirks of your operating system, and finally will create several files in the build tree to record what it found. (You can also run `configure` in a directory outside the source tree if you want to keep the build directory separate.)

   The default configuration will build the server and utilities, as well as all client applications and interfaces that require only a C compiler. All files will be installed under `/usr/local/pgsql` by default.

   You can customize the build and installation process by supplying one or more of the following command line options to `configure`:

   `--prefix=PREFIX`

   Install all files under the directory *PREFIX* instead of /usr/local/pgsql. The actual files will be installed into various subdirectories; no files will ever be installed directly into the *PREFIX* directory.

   If you have special needs, you can also customize the individual subdirectories with the following options. However, if you leave these with their defaults, the installation will be relocatable, meaning you can move the directory after installation. (The man and doc locations are not affected by this.)

   For relocatable installs, you might want to use configure's --disable-rpath option. Also, you will need to tell the operating system how to find the shared libraries.

   `--exec-prefix=EXEC-PREFIX`

   You can install architecture-dependent files under a different prefix, *EXEC-PREFIX*, than what *PREFIX* was set to. This can be useful to share architecture-independent files between hosts. If you omit this, then *EXEC-PREFIX* is set equal to *PREFIX* and both architecture-dependent and independent files will be installed under the same tree, which is probably what you want.

   `--bindir=DIRECTORY`

   Specifies the directory for executable programs. The default is *EXEC-PREFIX*/bin, which normally means /usr/local/pgsql/bin.

`--sysconfdir=`*DIRECTORY*

Sets the directory for various configuration files, *PREFIX*/etc by default.

`--libdir=`*DIRECTORY*

Sets the location to install libraries and dynamically loadable modules. The default is *EXEC-PREFIX*/lib.

`--includedir=`*DIRECTORY*

Sets the directory for installing C and C++ header files. The default is *PREFIX*/include.

`--datarootdir=`*DIRECTORY*

Sets the root directory for various types of read-only data files. This only sets the default for some of the following options. The default is *PREFIX*/share.

`--datadir=`*DIRECTORY*

Sets the directory for read-only data files used by the installed programs. The default is *DATAROOTDIR*. Note that this has nothing to do with where your database files will be placed.

`--localedir=`*DIRECTORY*

Sets the directory for installing locale data, in particular message translation catalog files. The default is *DATAROOTDIR*/locale.

`--mandir=`*DIRECTORY*

The man pages that come with PostgreSQL will be installed under this directory, in their respective man*x* subdirectories. The default is *DATAROOTDIR*/man.

`--docdir=`*DIRECTORY*

Sets the root directory for installing documentation files, except "man" pages. This only sets the default for the following options. The default value for this option is *DATAROOTDIR*/doc/postgresql.

`--htmldir=`*DIRECTORY*

The HTML-formatted documentation for PostgreSQL will be installed under this directory. The default is *DATAROOTDIR*.

 Note

Care has been taken to make it possible to install PostgreSQL into shared installation locations (such as `/usr/local/include`) without interfering with the namespace of the rest of the system. First, the string "/postgresql" is automatically appended to `datadir`, `sysconfdir`, and `docdir`, unless the fully expanded directory name already contains the string "postgres" or "pgsql". For example, if you choose /usr/local as prefix, the documentation will be installed in /usr/local/doc/postgresql, but if the prefix is /opt/postgres, then it will be in /opt/postgres/doc. The public C header files of the client interfaces are installed into includedir and are namespace-clean. The internal header files and the server header files are installed into private directories under includedir. See the documentation of each interface for information about how to access its header files. Finally, a private subdirectory will also be created, if appropriate, under libdir for dynamically loadable modules.

--with-includes=*DIRECTORIES*

DIRECTORIES is a colon-separated list of directories that will be added to the list the compiler searches for header files. If you have optional packages (such as GNU Readline) installed in a non-standard location, you have to use this option and probably also the corresponding --with-libraries option.

Example: --with-includes=/opt/gnu/include:/usr/sup/include.

--with-libraries=*DIRECTORIES*

DIRECTORIES is a colon-separated list of directories to search for libraries. You will probably have to use this option (and the corresponding --with-includes option) if you have packages installed in non-standard locations.

Example: --with-libraries=/opt/gnu/lib:/usr/sup/lib.

--enable-nls[=*LANGUAGES*]

Enables Native Language Support (NLS), that is, the ability to display a program's messages in a language other than English. *LANGUAGES* is an optional space-separated list of codes of the languages that you want supported, for example --enable-nls='de fr'. (The intersection between your list and the set of actually provided translations will be computed automatically.) If you do not specify a list, then all available translations are installed.

To use this option, you will need an implementation of the Gettext API; see above.

--with-pgport=*NUMBER*

Set *NUMBER* as the default port number for server and clients. The default is 5432. The port can always be changed later on, but if you specify it here then both server and clients will have the same default compiled in, which can be very convenient. Usually the only good reason to select a non-default value is if you intend to run multiple PostgreSQL servers on the same machine.

--with-perl

Build the PL/Perl server-side language.

`--with-python`

> Build the PL/Python server-side language.

`--with-tcl`

> Build the PL/Tcl server-side language.

`--with-tclconfig=`*`DIRECTORY`*

> Tcl installs the file tclConfig.sh, which contains configuration information needed to build modules interfacing to Tcl. This file is normally found automatically at a well-known location, but if you want to use a different version of Tcl you can specify the directory in which to look for it.

`--with-gssapi`

> Build with support for GSSAPI authentication. On many systems, the GSSAPI (usually a part of the Kerberos installation) system is not installed in a location that is searched by default (e.g., /usr/include, /usr/lib), so you must use the options --with-includes and --with-libraries in addition to this option. configure will check for the required header files and libraries to make sure that your GSSAPI installation is sufficient before proceeding.

`--with-krb5`

> Build with support for Kerberos 5 authentication. On many systems, the Kerberos system is not installed in a location that is searched by default (e.g., /usr/include, /usr/lib), so you must use the options --with-includes and --with-libraries in addition to this option. configure will check for the required header files and libraries to make sure that your Kerberos installation is sufficient before proceeding.

`--with-krb-srvnam=`*`NAME`*

> The default name of the Kerberos service principal (also used by GSSAPI). postgres is the default. There's usually no reason to change this unless you have a Windows environment, in which case it must be set to uppercase POSTGRES.

`--with-openssl`

> Build with support for SSL (encrypted) connections. This requires the OpenSSL package to be installed. configure will check for the required header files and libraries to make sure that your OpenSSL installation is sufficient before proceeding.

`--with-pam`

> Build with PAM (Pluggable Authentication Modules) support.

`--with-ldap`

> Build with LDAP support for authentication and connection parameter lookup (see *Section 30.16* - page 303 and *Section 19.3.7* - page 142 for more information). On Unix,

this requires the OpenLDAP package to be installed. On Windows, the default WinLDAP library is used. configure will check for the required header files and libraries to make sure that your OpenLDAP installation is sufficient before proceeding.

`--without-readline`

Prevents use of the Readline library (and libedit as well). This option disables command-line editing and history in psql, so it is not recommended.

`--with-libedit-preferred`

Favors the use of the BSD-licensed libedit library rather than GPL-licensed Readline. This option is significant only if you have both libraries installed; the default in that case is to use Readline.

`--with-bonjour`

Build with Bonjour support. This requires Bonjour support in your operating system. Recommended on Mac OS X.

`--with-ossp-uuid`

Use the *OSSP UUID library*[1] when building contrib/uuid-ossp. The library provides functions to generate UUIDs.

`--with-libxml`

Build with libxml (enables SQL/XML support). Libxml version 2.6.23 or later is required for this feature.

Libxml installs a program xml2-config that can be used to detect the required compiler and linker options. PostgreSQL will use it automatically if found. To specify a libxml installation at an unusual location, you can either set the environment variable XML2_CONFIG to point to the xml2-config program belonging to the installation, or use the options --with-includes and --with-libraries.

`--with-libxslt`

Use libxslt when building contrib/xml2. contrib/xml2 relies on this library to perform XSL transformations of XML.

`--disable-integer-datetimes`

Disable support for 64-bit integer storage for timestamps and intervals, and store datetime values as floating-point numbers instead. Floating-point datetime storage was the default in PostgreSQL releases prior to 8.4, but it is now deprecated, because

---

[1] *http://www.ossp.org/pkg/lib/uuid/*

it does not support microsecond precision for the full range of timestamp values. However, integer-based datetime storage requires a 64-bit integer type. Therefore, this option can be used when no such type is available, or for compatibility with applications written for prior versions of PostgreSQL. See *Section 8.5* - Vol.I page 148 for more information.

`--disable-float4-byval`

Disable passing float4 values "by value", causing them to be passed "by reference" instead. This option costs performance, but may be needed for compatibility with old user-defined functions that are written in C and use the "version 0" calling convention. A better long-term solution is to update any such functions to use the "version 1" calling convention.

`--disable-float8-byval`

Disable passing float8 values "by value", causing them to be passed "by reference" instead. This option costs performance, but may be needed for compatibility with old user-defined functions that are written in C and use the "version 0" calling convention. A better long-term solution is to update any such functions to use the "version 1" calling convention. Note that this option affects not only float8, but also int8 and some related types such as timestamp. On 32-bit platforms, --disable-float8-byval is the default and it is not allowed to select --enable-float8-byval.

`--with-segsize=SEGSIZE`

Set the *segment size*, in gigabytes. Large tables are divided into multiple operating-system files, each of size equal to the segment size. This avoids problems with file size limits that exist on many platforms. The default segment size, 1 gigabyte, is safe on all supported platforms. If your operating system has "largefile" support (which most do, nowadays), you can use a larger segment size. This can be helpful to reduce the number of file descriptors consumed when working with very large tables. But be careful not to select a value larger than is supported by your platform and the filesystem(s) you intend to use. Other tools you might wish to use, such as tar, could also set limits on the usable file size. It is recommended, though not absolutely required, that this value be a power of 2. Note that changing this value requires an initdb.

`--with-blocksize=BLOCKSIZE`

Set the *block size*, in kilobytes. This is the unit of storage and I/O within tables. The default, 8 kilobytes, is suitable for most situations; but other values may be useful in special cases. The value must be a power of 2 between 1 and 32 (kilobytes). Note that changing this value requires an initdb.

`--with-wal-segsize=SEGSIZE`

Set the *WAL segment size*, in megabytes. This is the size of each individual file in the WAL log. It may be useful to adjust this size to control the granularity of WAL log shipping. The default size is 16 megabytes. The value must be a power of 2 between 1 and 64 (megabytes). Note that changing this value requires an initdb.

`--with-wal-blocksize=BLOCKSIZE`

Set the *WAL block size*, in kilobytes. This is the unit of storage and I/O within the WAL log. The default, 8 kilobytes, is suitable for most situations; but other values may be useful in special cases. The value must be a power of 2 between 1 and 64 (kilobytes). Note that changing this value requires an initdb.

`--disable-spinlocks`

Allow the build to succeed even if PostgreSQL has no CPU spinlock support for the platform. The lack of spinlock support will result in poor performance; therefore, this option should only be used if the build aborts and informs you that the platform lacks spinlock support. If this option is required to build PostgreSQL on your platform, please report the problem to the PostgreSQL developers.

`--enable-thread-safety`

Make the client libraries thread-safe. This allows concurrent threads in libpq and ECPG programs to safely control their private connection handles. This option requires adequate threading support in your operating system.

`--with-system-tzdata=DIRECTORY`

PostgreSQL includes its own time zone database, which it requires for date and time operations. This time zone database is in fact compatible with the "zoneinfo" time zone database provided by many operating systems such as FreeBSD, Linux, and Solaris, so it would be redundant to install it again. When this option is used, the system-supplied time zone database in *DIRECTORY* is used instead of the one included in the PostgreSQL source distribution. *DIRECTORY* must be specified as an absolute path. /usr/share/zoneinfo is a likely directory on some operating systems. Note that the installation routine will not detect mismatching or erroneous time zone data. If you use this option, you are advised to run the regression tests to verify that the time zone data you have pointed to works correctly with PostgreSQL.

This option is mainly aimed at binary package distributors who know their target operating system well. The main advantage of using this option is that the PostgreSQL package won't need to be upgraded whenever any of the many local daylight-saving time rules change. Another advantage is that PostgreSQL can be cross-compiled more straightforwardly if the time zone database files do not need to be built during the installation.

`--without-zlib`

Prevents use of the Zlib library. This disables support for compressed archives in pg_dump and pg_restore. This option is only intended for those rare systems where this library is not available.

`--enable-debug`

Compiles all programs and libraries with debugging symbols. This means that you can run the programs in a debugger to analyze problems. This enlarges the size of the installed executables considerably, and on non-GCC compilers it usually also disables compiler optimization, causing slowdowns. However, having the symbols available is extremely helpful for dealing with any problems that might arise. Currently, this option is recommended for production installations only if you use GCC. But you should always have it on if you are doing development work or running a beta version.

`--enable-coverage`

If using GCC, all programs and libraries are compiled with code coverage testing instrumentation. When run, they generate files in the build directory with code coverage metrics. See *Section 29.4* (page 243) for more information. This option is for use only with GCC and when doing development work.

`--enable-profiling`

If using GCC, all programs and libraries are compiled so they can be profiled. On backend exit, a subdirectory will be created that contains the gmon.out file for use in profiling. This option is for use only with GCC and when doing development work.

`--enable-cassert`

Enables *assertion* checks in the server, which test for many "cannot happen" conditions. This is invaluable for code development purposes, but the tests can slow down the server significantly. Also, having the tests turned on won't necessarily enhance the stability of your server! The assertion checks are not categorized for severity, and so what might be a relatively harmless bug will still lead to server restarts if it triggers an assertion failure. This option is not recommended for production use, but you should have it on for development work or when running a beta version.

`--enable-depend`

Enables automatic dependency tracking. With this option, the makefiles are set up so that all affected object files will be rebuilt when any header file is changed. This is useful if you are doing development work, but is just wasted overhead if you intend only to compile once and install. At present, this option only works with GCC.

`--enable-dtrace`

> Compiles PostgreSQL with support for the dynamic tracing tool DTrace. See *Section 26.4 (page 219)* for more information.
>
> To point to the dtrace program, the environment variable DTRACE can be set. This will often be necessary because dtrace is typically installed under /usr/sbin, which might not be in the path.
>
> Extra command-line options for the dtrace program can be specified in the environment variable DTRACEFLAGS. On Solaris, to include DTrace support in a 64-bit binary, you must specify DTRACEFLAGS="-64" to configure. For example, using the GCC compiler:
>
> ```
> ./configure CC='gcc -m64' --enable-dtrace DTRACEFLAGS='-64' ...
> ```
>
> Using Sun's compiler:
>
> ```
> ./configure CC='/opt/SUNWspro/bin/cc -xtarget=native64' --enable-dtrace DTRACEFLAGS='-64' ...
> ```

If you prefer a C compiler different from the one `configure` picks, you can set the environment variable `CC` to the program of your choice. By default, `configure` will pick `gcc` if available, else the platform's default (usually `cc`). Similarly, you can override the default compiler flags if needed with the `CFLAGS` variable.

You can specify environment variables on the `configure` command line, for example:

```
./configure CC=/opt/bin/gcc CFLAGS='-O2 -pipe'
```

Here is a list of the significant variables that can be set in this manner:

`BISON`

> Bison program

`CC`

> C compiler

`CFLAGS`

> options to pass to the C compiler

`CPP`

> C preprocessor

`CPPFLAGS`

> options to pass to the C preprocessor

`DTRACE`

> location of the dtrace program

DTRACEFLAGS

> options to pass to the dtrace program

FLEX

> Flex program

LDFLAGS

> options to pass to the link editor

LDFLAGS_SL

> linker options for shared library linking

MSGFMT

> msgfmt program for native language support

PERL

> Full path to the Perl interpreter. This will be used to determine the dependencies for building PL/Perl.

PYTHON

> Full path to the Python interpreter. This will be used to determine the dependencies for building PL/Python.

TCLSH

> Full path to the Tcl interpreter. This will be used to determine the dependencies for building PL/Tcl, and it will be substituted into Tcl scripts.

XML2_CONFIG

> xml2-config program used to locate the libxml installation.

2. **Build**

To start the build, type:

```
gmake
```

(Remember to use GNU make.) The build will take a few minutes depending on your hardware. The last line displayed should be:

```
All of PostgreSQL is successfully made. Ready to install.
```

3. **Regression Tests**

If you want to test the newly built server before you install it, you can run the regression tests at this point. The regression tests are a test suite to verify that PostgreSQL runs on your machine in the way the developers expected it to. Type:

```
gmake check
```

(This won't work as root; do it as an unprivileged user.) *Chapter 29* (page 238) contains detailed information about interpreting the test results. You can repeat this test at any later time by issuing the same command.

4. **Installing the Files**

 Note

> If you are upgrading an existing system and are going to install the new files over the old ones, be sure to back up your data and shut down the old server before proceeding, as explained in *Section 15.4* (page 23) above.

To install PostgreSQL enter:

```
gmake install
```

This will install files into the directories that were specified in *step 1*. Make sure that you have appropriate permissions to write into that area. Normally you need to do this step as root. Alternatively, you can create the target directories in advance and arrange for appropriate permissions to be granted.

You can use `gmake install-strip` instead of `gmake install` to strip the executable files and libraries as they are installed. This will save some space. If you built with debugging support, stripping will effectively remove the debugging support, so it should only be done if debugging is no longer needed. `install-strip` tries to do a reasonable job saving space, but it does not have perfect knowledge of how to strip every unneeded byte from an executable file, so if you want to save all the disk space you possibly can, you will have to do manual work.

The standard installation provides all the header files needed for client application development as well as for server-side program development, such as custom functions or data types written in C. (Prior to PostgreSQL 8.0, a separate `gmake install-all-headers` command was needed for the latter, but this step has been folded into the standard install.)

Client-only installation: If you want to install only the client applications and interface libraries, then you can use these commands:

```
gmake -C src/bin install
gmake -C src/include install
gmake -C src/interfaces install
gmake -C doc install
```

`src/bin` has a few binaries for server-only use, but they are small.

Registering eventlog on Windows: To register a Windows eventlog library with the operating system, issue this command after installation:

```
regsvr32 pgsql_library_directory/pgevent.dll
```

This creates registry entries used by the event viewer.

Uninstallation: To undo the installation use the command gmake uninstall. However, this will not remove any created directories.

Cleaning: After the installation you can free disk space by removing the built files from the source tree with the command gmake clean. This will preserve the files made by the configure program, so that you can rebuild everything with gmake later on. To reset the source tree to the state in which it was distributed, use gmake distclean. If you are going to build for several platforms within the same source tree you must do this and re-configure for each platform. (Alternatively, use a separate build tree for each platform, so that the source tree remains unmodified.)

If you perform a build and then discover that your configure options were wrong, or if you change anything that configure investigates (for example, software upgrades), then it's a good idea to do gmake distclean before reconfiguring and rebuilding. Without this, your changes in configuration choices might not propagate everywhere they need to.

15.6. Post-Installation Setup

15.6.1. Shared Libraries

On some systems with shared libraries you need to tell the system how to find the newly installed shared libraries. The systems on which this is *not* necessary include BSD/OS, FreeBSD, HP-UX, IRIX, Linux, NetBSD, OpenBSD, Tru64 UNIX (formerly Digital UNIX), and Solaris.

The method to set the shared library search path varies between platforms, but the most widely-used method is to set the environment variable LD_LIBRARY_PATH like so: In Bourne shells (sh, ksh, bash, zsh):

```
LD_LIBRARY_PATH=/usr/local/pgsql/lib
export LD_LIBRARY_PATH
```

or in csh or tcsh:

```
setenv LD_LIBRARY_PATH /usr/local/pgsql/lib
```

Replace /usr/local/pgsql/lib with whatever you set --libdir to in *step 1*. You should put these commands into a shell start-up file such as /etc/profile or ~/.bash_profile. Some good information about the caveats associated with this method can be found at *http://www.visi.com/~barr/ldpath.html*.

On some systems it might be preferable to set the environment variable LD_RUN_PATH *before* building.

On Cygwin, put the library directory in the PATH or move the .dll files into the bin directory.

If in doubt, refer to the manual pages of your system (perhaps ld.so or rld). If you later get a message like:

```
psql: error in loading shared libraries
libpq.so.2.1: cannot open shared object file: No such file or directory
```

then this step was necessary. Simply take care of it then.

If you are on BSD/OS, Linux, or SunOS 4 and you have root access you can run:

```
/sbin/ldconfig /usr/local/pgsql/lib
```

(or equivalent directory) after installation to enable the run-time linker to find the shared libraries faster. Refer to the manual page of ldconfig for more information. On FreeBSD, NetBSD, and OpenBSD the command is:

```
/sbin/ldconfig -m /usr/local/pgsql/lib
```

instead. Other systems are not known to have an equivalent command.

15.6.2. Environment Variables

If you installed into /usr/local/pgsql or some other location that is not searched for programs by default, you should add /usr/local/pgsql/bin (or whatever you set --bindir to in *step 1*) into your PATH. Strictly speaking, this is not necessary, but it will make the use of PostgreSQL much more convenient.

To do this, add the following to your shell start-up file, such as ~/.bash_profile (or /etc/profile, if you want it to affect all users):

```
PATH=/usr/local/pgsql/bin:$PATH
export PATH
```

If you are using csh or tcsh, then use this command:

```
set path = ( /usr/local/pgsql/bin $path )
```

To enable your system to find the man documentation, you need to add lines like the following to a shell start-up file unless you installed into a location that is searched by default:

```
MANPATH=/usr/local/pgsql/man:$MANPATH
export MANPATH
```

The environment variables PGHOST and PGPORT specify to client applications the host and port of the database server, overriding the compiled-in defaults. If you are going to run client applications remotely then it is convenient if every user that plans to use the database sets PGHOST. This is not required, however; the settings can be communicated via command line options to most client programs.

15.7. Supported Platforms

A platform (that is, a CPU architecture and operating system combination) is considered supported by the PostgreSQL development community if the code contains provisions to work on that platform and it has recently been verified to build and pass its regression tests on that platform. Currently, most testing of platform compatibility is done automatically by test machines in the *PostgreSQL Build Farm*[2]. If you are interested in using PostgreSQL on a platform that is not represented in the build farm, but on which the code works or can be made to work, you are strongly encouraged to set up a build farm member machine so that continued compatibility can be assured.

In general, PostgreSQL can be expected to work on these CPU architectures: x86, x86_64, IA64, PowerPC, PowerPC 64, S/390, S/390x, Sparc, Sparc 64, Alpha, ARM, MIPS, MIPSEL, M68K, and PA-RISC. Code support exists for M32R, NS32K, and VAX, but these architectures are not known to have been tested recently. It is often possible to build on an unsupported CPU type by configuring with --disable-spinlocks, but performance will be poor.

PostgreSQL can be expected to work on these operating systems: Linux (all recent distributions), Windows (Win2000 SP4 and later), FreeBSD, OpenBSD, NetBSD, Mac OS X, AIX, HP/UX, IRIX, Solaris, Tru64 Unix, and UnixWare. Other Unix-like systems may also work but are not currently being tested. In most cases, all CPU architectures supported by a given operating system will work. Look in the *Section 15.8* (page 38) below to see if there is information specific to your operating system, particularly if using an older system.

If you have installation problems on a platform that is known to be supported according to recent build farm results, please report it to *<pgsql-bugs@postgresql.org>*. If you are interested in porting PostgreSQL to a new platform, *<pgsql-hackers@postgresql.org>* is the appropriate place to discuss that.

15.8. Platform-Specific Notes

This section documents additional platform-specific issues regarding the installation and setup of PostgreSQL. Be sure to read the installation instructions, and in particular *Section 15.2* (page 20) as well. Also, check *Chapter 29* (page 238) regarding the interpretation of regression test results.

Platforms that are not covered here have no known platform-specific installation issues.

---

[2] *http://buildfarm.postgresql.org/*

15.8.1. AIX

PostgreSQL works on AIX, but getting it installed properly can be challenging. AIX versions from 4.3.3 to 6.1 are considered supported. You can use GCC or the native IBM compiler xlc. In general, using recent versions of AIX and PostgreSQL helps. Check the build farm for up to date information about which versions of AIX are known to work.

Use the following configure flags in addition to your own if you have installed Readline or libz there: --with-includes=/usr/local/include --with-libraries=/usr/local/lib.

If you don't have a PowerPC or use GCC you might see rounding differences in the geometry regression test. There will probably be warnings about 0.0/0.0 division and duplicate symbols which you can safely ignore.

Some of the AIX tools may be "a little different" from what you may be accustomed to on other platforms. If you are looking for a version of ldd, useful for determining what object code depends on what libraries, the following URLs may help you: *http://www.faqs.org/faqs/aix-faq/part4/section-22.html, http://www.han.de/~jum/aix/ldd.c.*

Table 15-1 shows the minimum recommended fix levels for various AIX versions. To check your current fix level, use oslevel -r in AIX 4.3.3 to AIX 5.2 ML 7, or oslevel -s in later versions.

AIX version	fix level
AIX 4.3.3	Maintenance Level 11 + post ML11 bundle
AIX 5.1	Maintenance Level 9 + post ML9 bundle
AIX 5.2	Technology Level 10 Service Pack 3
AIX 5.3	Technology Level 7
AIX 6.1	Base Level

Table 15-1. Minimum recommended AIX fix levels

15.8.1.1. GCC issues

On AIX 5.3, there have been some problems getting PostgreSQL to compile and run using GCC.

You will want to use a version of GCC subsequent to 3.3.2, particularly if you use a prepackaged version. We had good success with 4.0.1. Problems with earlier versions seem to have more to do with the way IBM packaged GCC than with actual issues with GCC, so that if you compile GCC yourself, you might well have success with an earlier version of GCC.

15.8.1.2. Unix-domain sockets broken

AIX 5.3 has a problem where sockaddr_storage is not defined to be large enough. In version 5.3, IBM increased the size of sockaddr_un, the address structure for Unix-domain sockets, but did not correspondingly increase the size of sockaddr_storage. The result of this is that attempts to use Unix-domain sockets with PostgreSQL lead to libpq overflowing the data structure. TCP/IP connections work OK, but not Unix-domain sockets, which prevents the regression tests from working.

The problem was reported to IBM, and is recorded as bug report PMR29657. If you upgrade to maintenance level 5300-03 or later, that will include this fix. A quick workaround is to alter _SS_MAXSIZE to 1025 in /usr/include/sys/socket.h. In either case, recompile PostgreSQL once you have the corrected header file.

15.8.1.3. Internet address issues

PostgreSQL relies on the system's getaddrinfo function to parse IP addresses in listen_addresses, pg_hba.conf, etc. Older versions of AIX have assorted bugs in this function. If you have problems related to these settings, updating to the appropriate fix level shown in *Table 15-1* should take care of it.

One user reports:

When implementing PostgreSQL version 8.1 on AIX 5.3, we periodically ran into problems where the statistics collector would "mysteriously" not come up successfully. This appears to be the result of unexpected behaviour in the IPv6 implementation. It looks like PostgreSQL and IPv6 do not play very well together at this time on AIX.

Any of the following actions "fix" the problem.

- Delete the IPv6 address for localhost:

  (as root)
  ```
  # ifconfig lo0 inet6 ::1/0 delete
  ```
- Remove IPv6 from net services. The file /etc/netsvc.conf on AIX is roughly equivalent to /etc/nsswitch.conf on Solaris/Linux. The default, on AIX, is thus:

  ```
  hosts=local,bind
  ```

  Replace this with:

  ```
  hosts=local4,bind4
  ```

  to deactivate searching for IPv6 addresses.

15.8.1.4. Memory management

AIX can be somewhat peculiar with regards to the way it does memory management. You can have a server with many multiples of gigabytes of RAM free, but still get out of memory or address space errors when running applications. One example is createlang failing with unusual errors. For example, running as the owner of the PostgreSQL installation:

```
-bash-3.00$ createlang plpgsql template1
createlang: language installation failed: ERROR:  could not load library
"/opt/dbs/pgsql748/lib/plpgsql.so": A memory address is not in the address space for the process.
```

Running as a non-owner in the group posessing the PostgreSQL installation:

```
-bash-3.00$ createlang plpgsql template1
createlang: language installation failed: ERROR: could not load library
"/opt/dbs/pgsql748/lib/plpgsql.so": Bad address
```

Another example is out of memory errors in the PostgreSQL server logs, with every memory allocation near or greater than 256 MB failing.

The overall cause of all these problems is the default bittedness and memory model used by the server process. By default, all binaries built on AIX are 32-bit. This does not depend upon hardware type or kernel in use. These 32-bit processes are limited to 4 GB of memory laid out in 256 MB segments using one of a few models. The default allows for less than 256 MB in the heap as it shares a single segment with the stack.

In the case of the createlang example, above, check your umask and the permissions of the binaries in your PostgreSQL installation. The binaries involved in that example were 32-bit and installed as mode 750 instead of 755. Due to the permissions being set in this fashion, only the owner or a member of the possessing group can load the library. Since it isn't world-readable, the loader places the object into the process' heap instead of the shared library segments where it would otherwise be placed.

The "ideal" solution for this is to use a 64-bit build of PostgreSQL, but that is not always practical, because systems with 32-bit processors can build, but not run, 64-bit binaries.

If a 32-bit binary is desired, set LDR_CNTRL to MAXDATA=0xn0000000, where $1 <= n <= 8$, before starting the PostgreSQL server, and try different values and postgresql.conf settings to find a configuration that works satisfactorily. This use of LDR_CNTRL tells AIX that you want the server to have MAXDATA bytes set aside for the heap, allocated in 256 MB segments. When you find a workable configuration, ldedit can be used to modify the binaries so that they default to using the desired heap size. PostgreSQL can also be rebuilt, passing configure LDFLAGS="-Wl,-bmaxdata:0xn0000000" to achieve the same effect.

For a 64-bit build, set OBJECT_MODE to 64 and pass CC="gcc -maix64" and LDFLAGS="-Wl,-bbigtoc" to configure. (Options for xlc might differ.) If you omit the export of OBJECT_MODE, your build may fail with linker errors. When OBJECT_MODE is set, it tells AIX's build utilities such as ar, as, and ld what type of objects to default to handling.

By default, overcommit of paging space can happen. While we have not seen this occur, AIX will kill processes when it runs out of memory and the overcommit is accessed. The closest to this that we have seen is fork failing because the system decided that there was not enough memory for another process. Like many other parts of AIX, the paging space allocation method and out-of-memory kill is configurable on a system- or process-wide basis if this becomes a problem.

References and resources

"Large Program Support"[3], *AIX Documentation: General Programming Concepts: Writing and Debugging Programs.*

"Program Address Space Overview"[4], *AIX Documentation: General Programming Concepts: Writing and Debugging Programs.*

"Performance Overview of the Virtual Memory Manager (VMM)"[5], *AIX Documentation: Performance Management Guide.*

"Page Space Allocation"[6], *AIX Documentation: Performance Management Guide.*

"Paging-space thresholds tuning"[7], *AIX Documentation: Performance Management Guide.*

Developing and Porting C and C++ Applications on AIX[8], IBM Redbook.

15.8.2. Cygwin

PostgreSQL can be built using Cygwin, a Linux-like environment for Windows, but that method is inferior to the native Windows build (see *Chapter 16* – page 50) and is no longer recommended.

When building from source, proceed according to the normal installation procedure (i.e., ./configure; make; etc.), noting the following-Cygwin specific differences:

- Set your path to use the Cygwin bin directory before the Windows utilities. This will help prevent problems with compilation.
- The GNU make command is called "make" not "gmake".
- The adduser command is not supported; use the appropriate user management application on Windows NT, 2000, or XP. Otherwise, skip this step.
- The su command is not supported; use ssh to simulate su on Windows NT, 2000, or XP. Otherwise, skip this step.

---

[3] *http://publib.boulder.ibm.com/infocenter/pseries/topic/com.ibm.aix.doc/aixprggd/genprogc/lrg_prg_support.htm*

[4] *http://publib.boulder.ibm.com/infocenter/pseries/topic/com.ibm.aix.doc/aixprggd/genprogc/address_space.htm*

[5] *http://publib.boulder.ibm.com/infocenter/pseries/v5r3/topic/com.ibm.aix.doc/aixbman/prftungd/resmgmt2.htm*

[6] *http://publib.boulder.ibm.com/infocenter/pseries/v5r3/topic/com.ibm.aix.doc/aixbman/prftungd/memperf7.htm*

[7] *http://publib.boulder.ibm.com/infocenter/pseries/v5r3/topic/com.ibm.aix.doc/aixbman/prftungd/memperf6.htm*

[8] *http://www.redbooks.ibm.com/abstracts/sg245674.html?Open*

- OpenSSL is not supported.

- Start `cygserver` for shared memory support. To do this, enter the command `/usr/sbin/cygserver &`. This program needs to be running anytime you start the PostgreSQL server or initialize a database cluster (`initdb`). The default `cygserver` configuration may need to be changed (e.g., increase `SEMMNS`) to prevent PostgreSQL from failing due to a lack of system resources.

- The parallel regression tests (`make check`) can generate spurious regression test failures due to overflowing the `listen()` backlog queue which causes connection refused errors or hangs. You can limit the number of connections using the make variable `MAX_CONNECTIONS` thus:

```
make MAX_CONNECTIONS=5 check
```

  (On some systems you can have up to about 10 simultaneous connections).

It is possible to install cygserver and the PostgreSQL server as Windows NT services. For information on how to do this, please refer to the README document included with the PostgreSQL binary package on Cygwin. It is installed in the directory /usr/share/doc/Cygwin.

15.8.3. HP-UX

PostgreSQL 7.3+ should work on Series 700/800 PA-RISC machines running HP-UX 10.X or 11.X, given appropriate system patch levels and build tools. At least one developer routinely tests on HP-UX 10.20, and we have reports of successful installations on HP-UX 11.00 and 11.11.

Aside from the PostgreSQL source distribution, you will need GNU make (HP's make will not do), and either GCC or HP's full ANSI C compiler. If you intend to build from CVS sources rather than a distribution tarball, you will also need Flex (GNU lex) and Bison (GNU yacc). We also recommend making sure you are fairly up-to-date on HP patches. At a minimum, if you are building 64 bit binaries on on HP-UX 11.11 you may need PHSS_30966 (11.11) or a successor patch otherwise initdb may hang:

PHSS_30966 s700_800 ld(1) and linker tools cumulative patch

On general principles you should be current on libc and ld/dld patches, as well as compiler patches if you are using HP's C compiler. See HP's support sites such as *http://itrc.hp.com/* and *ftp://us-ffs.external.hp.com/* for free copies of their latest patches.

If you are building on a PA-RISC 2.0 machine and want to have 64-bit binaries using GCC, you must use GCC 64-bit version. GCC binaries for HP-UX PA-RISC and Itanium are available from *http://www.hp.com/go/gcc*. Don't forget to get and install binutils at the same time.

If you are building on a PA-RISC 2.0 machine and want the compiled binaries to run on PA-RISC 1.1 machines you will need to specify +DAportable in CFLAGS.

If you are building on a HP-UX Itanium machine, you will need the latest HP ANSI C compiler with its dependent patch or successor patches:

PHSS_30848 s700_800 HP C Compiler (A.05.57)
PHSS_30849 s700_800 u2comp/be/plugin library Patch

If you have both HP's C compiler and GCC's, then you might want to explicitly select the compiler to use when you run configure:

```
./configure CC=cc
```

for HP's C compiler, or

```
./configure CC=gcc
```

for GCC. If you omit this setting, then configure will pick gcc if it has a choice.

The default install target location is /usr/local/pgsql, which you might want to change to something under /opt. If so, use the --prefix switch to configure.

In the regression tests, there might be some low-order-digit differences in the geometry tests, which vary depending on which compiler and math library versions you use. Any other error is cause for suspicion.

15.8.4. IRIX

PostgreSQL has been reported to run successfully on MIPS r8000, r10000 (both ip25 and ip27) and r12000(ip35) processors, running IRIX 6.5.5m, 6.5.12, 6.5.13, and 6.5.26 with MIPSPro compilers version 7.30, 7.3.1.2m, 7.3, and 7.4.4m.

You will need the MIPSPro full ANSI C compiler. There are problems trying to build with GCC. It is a known GCC bug (not fixed as of version 3.0) related to using functions that return certain kinds of structures. This bug affects functions like inet_ntoa, inet_lnaof, inet_netof, inet_makeaddr, and semctl. It is supposed to be fixed by forcing code to link those functions with libgcc, but this has not been tested yet.

It is known that version 7.4.1m of the MIPSPro compiler generates incorrect code. The symptom is "invalid primary checkpoint record" when trying to start the database.) Version 7.4.4m is OK; the status of intermediate versions is uncertain.

There may be a compilation problem like the following:

```
cc-1020 cc: ERROR File = pqcomm.c, Line = 427
  The identifier "TCP_NODELAY" is undefined.

                  if (setsockopt(port->sock, IPPROTO_TCP, TCP_NODELAY,
```

Some versions include TCP definitions in sys/xti.h, so it is necessary to add #include <sys/xti.h> in src/backend/libpq/pqcomm.c and in src/interfaces/libpq/fe-connect.c. If you encounter this, please let us know so we can develop a proper fix.

In the regression tests, there might be some low-order-digit differences in the geometry tests, depending on which FPU are you using. Any other error is cause for suspicion.

15.8.5. MinGW/Native Windows

PostgreSQL for Windows can be built using MinGW, a Unix-like build environment for Microsoft operating systems, or using Microsoft's Visual C++ compiler suite. The MinGW build variant uses the normal build system described in this chapter; the Visual C++ build works completely differently and is described in *Chapter 16* (page 50). There is also a precompiled binary installer which you can find at from *http://pgfoundry.org/projects/pginstaller*. It is a fully native build and uses no additional software like MinGW. The ready-made installer files are available on the main PostgreSQL FTP servers in the binary/win32 directory.

The native Win32 port requires a 32-bit NT-based Microsoft operating system, like Windows NT 4, Windows 2000/2003, or Windows XP. (NT 4 is no longer supported.) Earlier operating systems do not have sufficient infrastructure (but Cygwin may be used on those). MinGW, the Unix-like build tools, and MSYS, a collection of Unix tools required to run shell scripts like configure, can be downloaded from *http://www.mingw.org/*. Neither is required to run the resulting binaries; they are needed only for creating the binaries.

After you have everything installed, it is suggested that you run psql under CMD.EXE, as the MSYS console has buffering issues.

15.8.6. SCO OpenServer and SCO UnixWare

PostgreSQL can be built on SCO UnixWare 7 and SCO OpenServer 5. On OpenServer, you can use either the OpenServer Development Kit or the Universal Development Kit. However, some tweaking may be needed, as described below.

15.8.6.1. Skunkware

You should locate your copy of the SCO Skunkware CD. The Skunkware CD is included with UnixWare 7 and current versions of OpenServer 5. Skunkware includes ready-to-install versions of many popular programs that are available on the Internet. For example, gzip, gunzip, GNU Make, Flex, and Bison are all included. For UnixWare 7.1, this CD is now labeled "Open License Software Supplement". If you do not have this CD, the software on it is available via anonymous FTP from *ftp://ftp.sco.com/skunkware*.

Skunkware has different versions for UnixWare and OpenServer. Make sure you install the correct version for your operating system, except as noted below.

On UnixWare 7.1.3 and beyond, the GCC compiler is included on the UDK CD as is GNU Make.

15.8.6.2. GNU Make

You need to use the GNU Make program, which is on the Skunkware CD. By default, it installs as /usr/local/bin/make. To avoid confusion with the SCO make program, you may want to rename GNU make to gmake.

As of UnixWare 7.1.3 and above, the GNU Make program is is the OSTK portion of the UDK CD, and is in /usr/gnu/bin/gmake.

15.8.6.3. Readline

The Readline library is on the Skunkware CD. But it is not included on the UnixWare 7.1 Skunkware CD. If you have the UnixWare 7.0.0 or 7.0.1 Skunkware CDs, you can install it from there. Otherwise, try *ftp://ftp.sco.com/skunkware*.

By default, Readline installs into /usr/local/lib and /usr/local/include. However, the PostgreSQL configure program will not find it there without help. If you installed Readline, then use the following options to configure:

```
./configure --with-libraries=/usr/local/lib --with-includes=/usr/local/include
```

15.8.6.4. 15.8.6.4. Using the UDK on OpenServer

If you are using the new Universal Development Kit (UDK) compiler on OpenServer, you need to specify the locations of the UDK libraries:

```
./configure --with-libraries=/udk/usr/lib --with-includes=/udk/usr/include
```

Putting these together with the Readline options from above:

```
./configure --with-libraries="/udk/usr/lib /usr/local/lib" --with-
includes="/udk/usr/include /usr/local/include"
```

15.8.6.5. Reading the PostgreSQL man pages

By default, the PostgreSQL man pages are installed into /usr/local/pgsql/man. By default, UnixWare does not look there for man pages. To be able to read them you need to modify the MANPATH variable in /etc/default/man, for example:

```
MANPATH=/usr/lib/scohelp/%L/man:/usr/dt/man:/usr/man:/usr/share/man:scohelp:/usr/
local/man:/usr/local/pgsql/man
```

On OpenServer, some extra research needs to be invested to make the man pages usable, because the man system is a bit different from other platforms. Currently, PostgreSQL will not install them at all.

15.8.6.6. C99 Issues with the 7.1.1b Feature Supplement

For compilers earlier than the one released with OpenUNIX 8.0.0 (UnixWare 7.1.2), including the 7.1.1b Feature Supplement, you may need to specify -Xb in CFLAGS or the CC environment variable. The indication of this is an error in compiling tuplesort.c referencing inline functions. Apparently there was a change in the 7.1.2(8.0.0) compiler and beyond.

15.8.6.7. --enable-thread-safety and UnixWare

If you use the configure option --enable-thread-safety, you *must* use -Kpthread on *all* libpq-using programs. libpq uses pthread_* calls, which are only available with the -Kpthread/-Kthread flag.

15.8.7. Solaris

PostgreSQL is well-supported on Solaris. The more up to date your operating system, the fewer issues you will experience; details below.

Note that PostgreSQL is bundled with Solaris 10 (from update 2). Official packages are also available on *http://pgfoundry.org/projects/solarispackages/*. Packages for older Solaris versions (8, 9) you can be obtained from *http://www.sunfreeware.com/* or *http://www.blastwave.org/*.

15.8.7.1. Required tools

You can build with either GCC or Sun's compiler suite. For better code optimization, Sun's compiler is strongly recommended on the SPARC architecture. We have heard reports of problems when using GCC 2.95.1; gcc 2.95.3 or later is recommended. If you are using Sun's compiler, be careful not to select /usr/ucb/cc; use /opt/SUNWspro/bin/cc.

You can download Sun Studio from *http://developers.sun.com/sunstudio/downloads/*. Many of GNU tools are integrated into Solaris 10, or they are present on the Solaris companion CD. If you like packages for older version of Solaris, you can find these tools at *http://www.sunfreeware.com/* or *http://www.blastwave.org/*. If you prefer sources, look at *http://www.gnu.org/order/ftp.html*.

15.8.7.2. Problems with OpenSSL

When you build PostgreSQL with OpenSSL support you might get compilation errors in the following files:

- `src/backend/libpq/crypt.c`
- `src/backend/libpq/password.c`
- `src/interfaces/libpq/fe-auth.c`
- `src/interfaces/libpq/fe-connect.c`

This is because of a namespace conflict between the standard /usr/include/crypt.h header and the header files provided by OpenSSL.

Upgrading your OpenSSL installation to version 0.9.6a fixes this problem. Solaris 9 and above has a newer version of OpenSSL.

15.8.7.3. configure complains about a failed test program

If configure complains about a failed test program, this is probably a case of the run-time linker being unable to find some library, probably libz, libreadline or some other non-standard library such as libssl. To point it to the right location, set the LDFLAGS environment variable on the configure command line, e.g.,

```
configure ... LDFLAGS="-R /usr/sfw/lib:/opt/sfw/lib:/usr/local/lib"
```

See the ld man page for more information.

15.8.7.4. 64-bit build sometimes crashes

On Solaris 7 and older, the 64-bit version of libc has a buggy vsnprintf routine, which leads to erratic core dumps in PostgreSQL. The simplest known workaround is to force PostgreSQL to use its own version of vsnprintf rather than the library copy. To do this, after you run configure edit a file produced by configure: In src/Makefile.global, change the line

```
LIBOBJS =
```

to read

```
LIBOBJS = snprintf.o
```

(There might be other files already listed in this variable. Order does not matter.) Then build as usual.

15.8.7.5. Compiling for optimal performance

On the SPARC architecture, Sun Studio is strongly recommended for compilation. Try using the -xO5 optimization flag to generate significantly faster binaries. Do not use any flags that modify behavior of floating-point operations and errno processing (e.g., -fast). These flags could raise some nonstandard PostgreSQL behavior for example in the date/time computing.

If you do not have a reason to use 64-bit binaries on SPARC, prefer the 32-bit version. The 64-bit operations are slower and 64-bit binaries are slower than the 32-bit variants. And on other hand, 32-bit code on the AMD64 CPU family is not native, and that is why 32-bit code is significant slower on this CPU family.

Some tricks for tuning PostgreSQL and Solaris for performance can be found at *http://www.sun.com/servers/coolthreads/tnb/applications_postgresql.jsp*. This article is primary focused on T2000 platform, but many of the recommendations are also useful on other hardware with Solaris.

15.8.7.6. Using DTrace for tracing PostgreSQL

Yes, using DTrace is possible. See *Section 26.4* (page 219) for further information. You can also find more information in this article:

http://blogs.sun.com/robertlor/entry/user_level_dtrace_probes_in.

If you see the linking of the postgres executable abort with an error message like:

```
Undefined                           first referenced
 symbol                                 in file
AbortTransaction                       utils/probes.o
CommitTransaction                      utils/probes.o
ld: fatal: Symbol referencing errors. No output written to postgres
collect2: ld returned 1 exit status
gmake: *** [postgres] Error 1
```

your DTrace installation is too old to handle probes in static functions. You need Solaris 10u4 or newer.

Chapter 16.

Installation from Source Code on Windows

It is recommended that most users download the binary distribution for Windows, available as a Windows Installer package from the PostgreSQL website. Building from source is only intended for people developing PostgreSQL or extensions.

There are several different ways of building PostgreSQL on Windows. The complete system can be built using MinGW or Visual C++ 2005. It can also be built for older versions of Windows using Cygwin. Finally, the client access library (libpq) can be built using Visual C++ 7.1 or Borland C++ for compatibility with statically linked applications built using these tools.

Building using MinGW or Cygwin uses the normal build system, see *Chapter 15* (page 20) and the specific notes in *Section 15.8.5* (page 45) and *Section 15.8.2* (page 42). Cygwin is not recommended and should only be used for older versions of Windows where the native build does not work, such as Windows 98.

16.1. Building with Visual C++ 2005

The tools for building using Visual C++ 2005, are in the src/tools/msvc directory. When building, make sure there are no tools from MinGW or Cygwin present in your system PATH. Also, make sure you have all the required Visual C++ tools available in the PATH, usually by starting a Visual Studio Command Prompt and running the commands from there. All commands should be run from the src\tools\msvc directory.

Before you build, edit the file config.pl to reflect the configuration options you want set, including the paths to libraries used. If you need to set any other environment variables, create a file called buildenv.pl and put the required commands there. For example, to add the path for bison when it's not in the PATH, create a file containing:

```
$ENV{PATH}=$ENV{PATH} . ';c:\some\where\bison\bin';
```

16.1.1. Requirements

PostgreSQL will build using either the professional versions (any edition) or the free Express edition of Visual Studio 2005. The following additional products are required to build the complete package. Use the config.pl file to specify which directories the libraries are available in.

ActiveState Perl

ActiveState Perl is required to run the build generation scripts. MinGW or Cygwin Perl will not work. It must also be present in the PATH. Binaries can be downloaded from *http://www.activestate.com/* (Note: version 5.8 is required, the free Standard Distribution is sufficient).

ActiveState TCL

Required for building PL/TCL (Note: version 8.4 is required, the free Standard Distribution is sufficient).

Bison and Flex

Bison and Flex are required to build from CVS, but not required when building from a release file. Note that only Bison 1.875 or versions 2.2 and later will work. Bison and Flex can be downloaded from *http://gnuwin32.sourceforge.net/*.

Diff

Diff is required to run the regression tests, and can be downloaded from *http://gnuwin32.sourceforge.net/*.

Gettext

Gettext is required to build with NLS support, and can be downloaded from *http://gnuwin32.sourceforge.net/*. Note that binaries, dependencies and developer files are all needed.

Microsoft Platform SDK

It is recommended that you upgrade to the latest available version of the Microsoft Platform SDK, available for download from *http://www.microsoft.com/downloads/*.

MIT Kerberos

Required for Kerberos authentication support. MIT Kerberos can be downloaded from *http://web.mit.edu/Kerberos/dist/index.html*.

libxml2 and libxslt

Required for XML support. Binaries can be downloaded from *http://zlatkovic.com/pub/libxml* or source from *http://xmlsoft.org/*. Note that libxml2 requires iconv, which is available from the same download location.

openssl

> Required for SSL support. Binaries can be downloaded from
> *http://www.slproweb.com/products/Win32OpenSSL.html* or source from
> *http://www.openssl.org/*.

ossp-uuid

> Required for UUID-OSSP support (contrib only). Source can be downloaded from
> *http://www.ossp.org/pkg/lib/uuid/*.

Python

> Required for building PL/Python. Binaries can be downloaded from
> *http://www.python.org/*.

zlib

> Required for compression support in pg_dump and pg_restore. Binaries can be
> downloaded from *http://www.zlib.net/*.

16.1.2. Building

To build all of PostgreSQL in release configuration (the default), run the command:

```
build
```

To build all of PostgreSQL in debug configuration, run the command:

```
build DEBUG
```

To build just a single project, for example psql, run the commands:

```
build psql
build DEBUG psql
```

To change the default build configuration to debug, put the following in the buildenv.pl file:

```
$ENV{CONFIG}="Debug";
```

It is also possible to build from inside the Visual Studio GUI. In this case, you need to run:

```
perl mkvcbuild.pl
```

from the command prompt, and then open the generated pgsql.sln (in the root directory of the source tree) in Visual Studio.

16.1.3. Cleaning and installing

Most of the time, the automatic dependency tracking in Visual Studio will handle changed files. But if there have been large changes, you may need to clean the installation. To do this, simply run the clean.bat command, which will automatically clean out all generated files.

You can also run it with the dist parameter, in which case it will behave like make distclean and remove the flex/bison output files as well.

By default, all files are written into a subdirectory of the debug or release directories. To install these files using the standard layout, and also generate the files required to initialize and use the database, run the command:

```
perl install.pl c:\destination\directory
```

16.1.4. Running the regression tests

To run the regression tests, make sure you have completed the build of all required parts first. Also, make sure that the DLLs required to load all parts of the system (such as the Perl and Python DLLs for the procedural languages) are present in the system path. If they are not, set it through the buildenv.pl file. To run the tests, run one of the following commands from the src\tools\msvc directory:

```
vcregress check
vcregress installcheck
vcregress plcheck
vcregress contribcheck
```

To change the schedule used (default is the parallel), append it to the command line like:

```
vcregress check serial
```

For more information about the regression tests, see *Chapter 29* (page 238).

16.1.5. Building the documentation

Building the PostgreSQL documentation in HTML format requires several tools and files. Create a root directory for all these files, and store them in the subdirectories in the list below.

OpenJade 1.3.1-2

Download from
http://sourceforge.net/project/downloading.php?groupname=openjade&filename=openjade-1_3_1-2-bin.zip and uncompress in the subdirectory openjade-1.3.1.

DocBook DTD 4.2

Download from *http://www.oasis-open.org/docbook/sgml/4.2/docbook-4.2.zip* and uncompress in the subdirectory docbook.

DocBook DSSSL 1.79

Download from
http://sourceforge.net/project/downloading.php?groupname=docbook&filename=docbook-dsssl-1.79.zip and uncompress in the subdirectory docbook-dsssl-1.79.

ISO character entities

> Download from *http://www.oasis-open.org/cover/ISOEnts.zip* and uncompress in the
> subdirectory docbook.

Edit the buildenv.pl file, and add a variable for the location of the root directory, for
example:

```
$ENV{DOCROOT}='c:\docbook';
```

To build the documentation, run the command builddoc.bat. Note that this will actually run
the build twice, in order to generate the indexes. The generated HTML files will be in
doc\src\sgml.

16.2. Building libpq with Visual C++ or Borland C++

Using Visual C++ 7.1-8.0 or Borland C++ to build libpq is only recommended if you need a
version with different debug/release flags, or if you need a static library to link into an
application. For normal use the MinGW or Visual Studio 2005 version is recommended.

To build the libpq client library using Visual Studio 7.1 or later, change into the src directory
and type the command:

```
nmake /f win32.mak
```

To build a 64-bit version of the libpq client library using Visual Studio 8.0 or later, change
into the src directory and type in the command:

```
nmake /f win32.mak CPU=AMD64
```

See the win32.mak file for further details about supported variables.

To build the libpq client library using Borland C++, change into the src directory and type
the command:

```
make -N -DCFG=Release /f bcc32.mak
```

16.2.1. Generated files

The following files will be built:

```
interfaces\libpq\Release\libpq.dll
```

> The dynamically linkable frontend library

```
interfaces\libpq\Release\libpqdll.lib
```

> Import library to link your programs to libpq.dll

```
interfaces\libpq\Release\libpq.lib
```

> Static version of the frontend library

Normally you do not need to install any of the client files. You should place the libpq.dll file in the same directory as your applications executable file. Do not install libpq.dll into your Windows, System or System32 directory unless absolutely necessary. If this file is installed using a setup program, it should be installed with version checking using the VERSIONINFO resource included in the file, to ensure that a newer version of the library is not overwritten.

If you are planning to do development using libpq on this machine, you will have to add the src\include and src\interfaces\libpq subdirectories of the source tree to the include path in your compiler's settings.

To use the library, you must add the libpqdll.lib file to your project. (In Visual C++, just right-click on the project and choose to add it.)

Chapter 17.
Server Setup and Operation

This chapter discusses how to set up and run the database server and its interactions with the operating system.

17.1. The PostgreSQL User Account

As with any other server daemon that is accessible to the outside world, it is advisable to run PostgreSQL under a separate user account. This user account should only own the data that is managed by the server, and should not be shared with other daemons. (For example, using the user nobody is a bad idea.) It is not advisable to install executables owned by this user because compromised systems could then modify their own binaries.

To add a Unix user account to your system, look for a command useradd or adduser. The user name postgres is often used, and is assumed throughout this book, but you can use another name if you like.

17.2. Creating a Database Cluster

Before you can do anything, you must initialize a database storage area on disk. We call this a *database cluster*. (SQL uses the term catalog cluster.) A database cluster is a collection of databases that is managed by a single instance of a running database server. After initialization, a database cluster will contain a database named postgres, which is meant as a default database for use by utilities, users and third party applications. The database server itself does not require the postgres database to exist, but many external utility programs assume it exists. Another database created within each cluster during initialization is called template1. As the name suggests, this will be used as a template for subsequently created databases; it should not be used for actual work. (See *Chapter 21* – page 151 for information about creating new databases within a cluster.)

In file system terms, a database cluster will be a single directory under which all data will be stored. We call this the *data directory* or *data area*. It is completely up to you where you choose to store your data. There is no default, although locations such as /usr/local/pgsql/data or /var/lib/pgsql/data are popular. To initialize a database cluster, use the command *initdb*, which is installed with PostgreSQL. The desired file system location of your database cluster is indicated by the -D option, for example:

```
$ initdb -D /usr/local/pgsql/data
```

Note that you must execute this command while logged into the PostgreSQL user account, which is described in the previous section.

 Tip

As an alternative to the -D option, you can set the environment variable PGDATA.

initdb will attempt to create the directory you specify if it does not already exist. It is likely that it will not have the permission to do so (if you followed our advice and created an unprivileged account). In that case you should create the directory yourself (as root) and change the owner to be the PostgreSQL user. Here is how this might be done:

```
root# mkdir /usr/local/pgsql/data
root# chown postgres /usr/local/pgsql/data
root# su postgres
postgres$ initdb -D /usr/local/pgsql/data
```

initdb will refuse to run if the data directory looks like it has already been initialized.

Because the data directory contains all the data stored in the database, it is essential that it be secured from unauthorized access. initdb therefore revokes access permissions from everyone but the PostgreSQL user.

However, while the directory contents are secure, the default client authentication setup allows any local user to connect to the database and even become the database superuser. If you do not trust other local users, we recommend you use one of initdb's -W, --pwprompt or --pwfile options to assign a password to the database superuser. Also, specify -A md5 or -A password so that the default trust authentication mode is not used; or modify the generated pg_hba.conf file after running initdb, *before* you start the server for the first time. (Other reasonable approaches include using ident authentication or file system permissions to restrict connections. See *Chapter 19* (page 129) for more information.)

initdb also initializes the default locale for the database cluster. Normally, it will just take the locale settings in the environment and apply them to the initialized database. It is possible to specify a different locale for the database; more information about that can be found in *Section 22.1* (page 158). The default sort order used within the particular database cluster is set by initdb, and while you can create new databases using different sort order, the order used in the template databases that initdb creates cannot be changed without dropping and recreating them. There is also a performance impact for using locales other than C or POSIX. Therefore, it is important to make this choice correctly the first time.

initdb also sets the default character set encoding for the database cluster. Normally this should be chosen to match the locale setting. For details see *Section 22.2* (page 161).

17.2.1. Network File Systems

Many installations create database clusters on network file systems. Sometimes this is done directly via NFS, or by using a Network Attached Storage (NAS) device that uses NFS internally. PostgreSQL does nothing special for NFS file systems, meaning it assumes NFS behaves exactly like locally-connected drives (DAS, Direct Attached Storage). If client and server NFS implementations have non-standard semantics, this can cause reliability problems (see *http://www.time-travellers.org/shane/papers/NFS_considered_harmful.html*). Specifically, delayed (asynchronous) writes to the NFS server can cause reliability problems; if possible, mount NFS file systems synchronously (without caching) to avoid this. Also, soft-mounting NFS is not recommended. (Storage Area Networks (SAN) use a low-level communication protocol rather than NFS.)

17.3. Starting the Database Server

Before anyone can access the database, you must start the database server. The database server program is called postgres. The postgres program must know where to find the data it is supposed to use. This is done with the -D option. Thus, the simplest way to start the server is:

```
$ postgres -D /usr/local/pgsql/data
```

which will leave the server running in the foreground. This must be done while logged into the PostgreSQL user account. Without -D, the server will try to use the data directory named by the environment variable PGDATA. If that variable is not provided either, it will fail.

Normally it is better to start postgres in the background. For this, use the usual shell syntax:

```
$ postgres -D /usr/local/pgsql/data >logfile 2>&1 &
```

It is important to store the server's stdout and stderr output somewhere, as shown above. It will help for auditing purposes and to diagnose problems. (See *Section 23.3* – page 177 for a more thorough discussion of log file handling.)

The postgres program also takes a number of other command-line options. For more information, see the *postgres* reference page and *Chapter 18* (page 77) below.

This shell syntax can get tedious quickly. Therefore the wrapper program pg_ctl is provided to simplify some tasks. For example:

```
pg_ctl start -l logfile
```

will start the server in the background and put the output into the named log file. The -D option has the same meaning here as for postgres. pg_ctl is also capable of stopping the server.

Normally, you will want to start the database server when the computer boots. Autostart scripts are operating-system-specific. There are a few distributed with PostgreSQL in the contrib/start-scripts directory. Installing one will require root privileges.

Different systems have different conventions for starting up daemons at boot time. Many systems have a file /etc/rc.local or /etc/rc.d/rc.local. Others use rc.d directories. Whatever you do, the server must be run by the PostgreSQL user account *and not by root* or any other user. Therefore you probably should form your commands using su -c '...' postgres. For example:

```
su -c 'pg_ctl start -D /usr/local/pgsql/data -l serverlog' postgres
```

Here are a few more operating-system-specific suggestions. (In each case be sure to use the proper installation directory and user name where we show generic values.)

- For FreeBSD, look at the file `contrib/start-scripts/freebsd` in the PostgreSQL source distribution.

- On OpenBSD, add the following lines to the file `/etc/rc.local`:

```
if [ -x /usr/local/pgsql/bin/pg_ctl -a -x /usr/local/pgsql/bin/postgres ]; then
    su - -c '/usr/local/pgsql/bin/pg_ctl start -l /var/postgresql/log -s' postgres
    echo -n ' postgresql'
fi
```

- On Linux systems either add

```
/usr/local/pgsql/bin/pg_ctl start -l logfile -D /usr/local/pgsql/data
```

  to `/etc/rc.d/rc.local` or look at the file `contrib/start-scripts/linux` in the PostgreSQL source distribution.

- On NetBSD, either use the FreeBSD or Linux start scripts, depending on preference.

- On Solaris, create a file called `/etc/init.d/postgresql` that contains the following line:

```
su - postgres -c "/usr/local/pgsql/bin/pg_ctl start -l logfile -D /usr/local/pgsql/data"
```

  Then, create a symbolic link to it in /etc/rc3.d as S99postgresql.

While the server is running, its PID is stored in the file postmaster.pid in the data directory. This is used to prevent multiple server instances from running in the same data directory and can also be used for shutting down the server.

17.3.1. Server Start-up Failures

There are several common reasons the server might fail to start. Check the server's log file, or start it by hand (without redirecting standard output or standard error) and see what error messages appear. Below we explain some of the most common error messages in more detail.

```
LOG:  could not bind IPv4 socket: Address already in use
HINT:  Is another postmaster already running on port 5432? If not, wait a few seconds and retry.
FATAL:  could not create TCP/IP listen socket
```

This usually means just what it suggests: you tried to start another server on the same port where one is already running. However, if the kernel error message is not Address already in use or some variant of that, there might be a different problem. For example, trying to start a server on a reserved port number might draw something like:

```
$ postgres -p 666
LOG:  could not bind IPv4 socket: Permission denied
HINT:  Is another postmaster already running on port 666? If not, wait a few seconds and retry.
FATAL:  could not create TCP/IP listen socket
```

A message like:

```
FATAL:  could not create shared memory segment: Invalid argument
DETAIL:  Failed system call was shmget(key=5440001, size=4011376640, 03600).
```

probably means your kernel's limit on the size of shared memory is smaller than the work area PostgreSQL is trying to create (4011376640 bytes in this example). Or it could mean that you do not have System-V-style shared memory support configured into your kernel at all. As a temporary workaround, you can try starting the server with a smaller-than-normal number of buffers (*shared_buffers*). You will eventually want to reconfigure your kernel to increase the allowed shared memory size. You might also see this message when trying to start multiple servers on the same machine, if their total space requested exceeds the kernel limit.

An error like:

```
FATAL:  could not create semaphores: No space left on device
DETAIL:  Failed system call was semget(5440126, 17, 03600).
```

does *not* mean you've run out of disk space. It means your kernel's limit on the number of System V semaphores is smaller than the number PostgreSQL wants to create. As above, you might be able to work around the problem by starting the server with a reduced number of allowed connections (*max_connections*), but you'll eventually want to increase the kernel limit.

If you get an "illegal system call" error, it is likely that shared memory or semaphores are not supported in your kernel at all. In that case your only option is to reconfigure the kernel to enable these features.

Details about configuring System V IPC facilities are given in *Section 17.4.1* (page 61).

17.3.2. Client Connection Problems

Although the error conditions possible on the client side are quite varied and application-dependent, a few of them might be directly related to how the server was started up.

Conditions other than those shown below should be documented with the respective client application.

```
psql: could not connect to server: Connection refused
        Is the server running on host "server.joe.com" and accepting
        TCP/IP connections on port 5432?
```

This is the generic "I couldn't find a server to talk to" failure. It looks like the above when TCP/IP communication is attempted. A common mistake is to forget to configure the server to allow TCP/IP connections.

Alternatively, you'll get this when attempting Unix-domain socket communication to a local server:

```
psql: could not connect to server: No such file or directory
        Is the server running locally and accepting
        connections on Unix domain socket "/tmp/.s.PGSQL.5432"?
```

The last line is useful in verifying that the client is trying to connect to the right place. If there is in fact no server running there, the kernel error message will typically be either Connection refused or No such file or directory, as illustrated. (It is important to realize that Connection refused in this context does *not* mean that the server got your connection request and rejected it. That case will produce a different message, as shown in *Section 19.4 – page 144*.) Other error messages such as Connection timed out might indicate more fundamental problems, like lack of network connectivity.

17.4. Managing Kernel Resources

A large PostgreSQL installation can quickly exhaust various operating system resource limits. (On some systems, the factory defaults are so low that you don't even need a really "large" installation.) If you have encountered this kind of problem, keep reading.

17.4.1. Shared Memory and Semaphores

Shared memory and semaphores are collectively referred to as "System V IPC" (together with message queues, which are not relevant for PostgreSQL). Almost all modern operating systems provide these features, but not all of them have them turned on or sufficiently sized by default, especially systems with BSD heritage. (On Windows, PostgreSQL provides its own replacement implementation of these facilities, and so most of this section can be disregarded.)

The complete lack of these facilities is usually manifested by an "Illegal system call" error upon server start. In that case there's nothing left to do but to reconfigure your kernel. PostgreSQL won't work without them.

When PostgreSQL exceeds one of the various hard IPC limits, the server will refuse to start and should leave an instructive error message describing the problem encountered and what to do about it. (See also *Section 17.3.1* – page 59.) The relevant kernel parameters are named consistently across different systems; *Table 17-1* gives an overview. The methods to set them, however, vary. Suggestions for some platforms are given below. Be warned that it is often necessary to reboot your machine, and possibly even recompile the kernel, to change these settings.

Name	Description	Reasonable values
SHMMAX	Maximum size of shared memory segment (bytes)	at least several megabytes (see text)
SHMMIN	Minimum size of shared memory segment (bytes)	1
SHMALL	Total amount of shared memory available (bytes or pages)	if bytes, same as SHMMAX; if pages, ceil(SHMMAX/PAGE_SIZE)
SHMSEG	Maximum number of shared memory segments per process	only 1 segment is needed, but the default is much higher
SHMMNI	Maximum number of shared memory segments system-wide	like SHMSEG plus room for other applications
SEMMNI	Maximum number of semaphore identifiers (i.e., sets)	at least ceil((max_connections + autovacuum_max_workers) / 16)
SEMMNS	Maximum number of semaphores system-wide	ceil((max_connections + autovacuum_max_workers)/16)*17 plus room for other applications
SEMMSL	Maximum number of semaphores per set	at least 17
SEMMAP	Number of entries in semaphore map	see text
SEMVMX	Maximum value of semaphore	at least 1000 (The default is often 32767, don't change unless forced to)

Table 17-1. System V IPC parameters

The most important shared memory parameter is SHMMAX, the maximum size, in bytes, of a shared memory segment. If you get an error message from shmget like "Invalid argument", it is likely that this limit has been exceeded. The size of the required shared memory segment varies depending on several PostgreSQL configuration parameters, as shown in *Table 17-2*. (Any error message you might get will include the exact size of the failed allocation request.) You can, as a temporary solution, lower some of those settings to avoid the failure. While it is possible to get PostgreSQL to run with SHMMAX as small as 2 MB, you need considerably more for acceptable performance. Desirable settings are in the tens to hundreds of megabytes.

Some systems also have a limit on the total amount of shared memory in the system (SHMALL). Make sure this is large enough for PostgreSQL plus any other applications that are using shared memory segments. (Caution: SHMALL is measured in pages rather than bytes on many systems.)

Less likely to cause problems is the minimum size for shared memory segments (SHMMIN), which should be at most approximately 500 kB for PostgreSQL (it is usually just 1). The maximum number of segments system-wide (SHMMNI) or per-process (SHMSEG) are unlikely to cause a problem unless your system has them set to zero.

PostgreSQL uses one semaphore per allowed connection (*max_connections*) and allowed autovacuum worker process (*autovacuum_max_workers*), in sets of 16. Each such set will also contain a 17th semaphore which contains a "magic number", to detect collision with semaphore sets used by other applications. The maximum number of semaphores in the system is set by SEMMNS, which consequently must be at least as high as max_connections plus autovacuum_max_workers, plus one extra for each 16 allowed connections plus workers (see the formula in *Table 17-1*). The parameter SEMMNI determines the limit on the number of semaphore sets that can exist on the system at one time. Hence this parameter must be at least ceil((max_connections + autovacuum_max_workers) / 16). Lowering the number of allowed connections is a temporary workaround for failures, which are usually confusingly worded "No space left on device", from the function semget.

In some cases it might also be necessary to increase SEMMAP to be at least on the order of SEMMNS. This parameter defines the size of the semaphore resource map, in which each contiguous block of available semaphores needs an entry. When a semaphore set is freed it is either added to an existing entry that is adjacent to the freed block or it is registered under a new map entry. If the map is full, the freed semaphores get lost (until reboot). Fragmentation of the semaphore space could over time lead to fewer available semaphores than there should be.

The SEMMSL parameter, which determines how many semaphores can be in a set, must be at least 17 for PostgreSQL.

Various other settings related to "semaphore undo", such as SEMMNU and SEMUME, are not of concern for PostgreSQL.

AIX

At least as of version 5.1, it should not be necessary to do any special configuration for such parameters as SHMMAX, as it appears this is configured to allow all memory to be used as shared memory. That is the sort of configuration commonly used for other databases such as DB/2.

It might, however, be necessary to modify the global ulimit information in /etc/security/limits, as the default hard limits for file sizes (fsize) and numbers of files (nofiles) might be too low.

BSD/OS

Shared Memory. By default, only 4 MB of shared memory is supported. Keep in mind that shared memory is not pageable; it is locked in RAM. To increase the amount of shared memory supported by your system, add something like the following to your kernel configuration file:

```
options "SHMALL=8192"
options "SHMMAX=\(SHMALL*PAGE_SIZE\)"
```

SHMALL is measured in 4 kB pages, so a value of 1024 represents 4 MB of shared memory. Therefore the above increases the maximum shared memory area to 32 MB. For those running 4.3 or later, you will probably also need to increase KERNEL_VIRTUAL_MB above the default 248. Once all changes have been made, recompile the kernel, and reboot.

For those running 4.0 and earlier releases, use bpatch to find the sysptsize value in the current kernel. This is computed dynamically at boot time.

```
$ bpatch -r sysptsize
0x9 = 9
```

Next, add SYSPTSIZE as a hard-coded value in the kernel configuration file. Increase the value you found using bpatch. Add 1 for every additional 4 MB of shared memory you desire.

```
options "SYSPTSIZE=16"
```

sysptsize cannot be changed by sysctl.

Semaphores. You will probably want to increase the number of semaphores as well; the default system total of 60 will only allow about 50 PostgreSQL connections. Set the values you want in your kernel configuration file, e.g.:

```
options "SEMMNI=40"
options "SEMMNS=240"
```

FreeBSD

The default settings are only suitable for small installations (for example, default SHMMAX is 32 MB). Changes can be made via the sysctl or loader interfaces. The following parameters can be set using sysctl:

```
$ sysctl -w kern.ipc.shmall=32768
$ sysctl -w kern.ipc.shmmax=134217728
$ sysctl -w kern.ipc.semmap=256
```

To have these settings persist over reboots, modify /etc/sysctl.conf.

The remaining semaphore settings are read-only as far as sysctl is concerned, but can be changed before boot using the loader prompt:

```
(loader) set kern.ipc.semmni=256
(loader) set kern.ipc.semmns=512
(loader) set kern.ipc.semmnu=256
```

Similarly these can be saved between reboots in /boot/loader.conf.

You might also want to configure your kernel to lock shared memory into RAM and prevent it from being paged out to swap. This can be accomplished using the sysctl setting kern.ipc.shm_use_phys.

If running in FreeBSD jails by enabling sysctl's security.jail.sysvipc_allowed, postmasters running in different jails should be run by different operating system users. This improves security because it prevents non-root users from interfering with shared memory or semaphores in a different jail, and it allows the PostgreSQL IPC cleanup code to function properly. (In FreeBSD 6.0 and later the IPC cleanup code doesn't properly detect processes in other jails, preventing the running of postmasters on the same port in different jails.)

FreeBSD versions before 4.0 work like NetBSD and OpenBSD (see below).

NetBSD
OpenBSD

The options SYSVSHM and SYSVSEM need to be enabled when the kernel is compiled. (They are by default.) The maximum size of shared memory is determined by the option SHMMAXPGS (in pages). The following shows an example of how to set the various parameters (OpenBSD uses option instead):

```
options         SYSVSHM
options         SHMMAXPGS=4096
options         SHMSEG=256

options         SYSVSEM
options         SEMMNI=256
options         SEMMNS=512
options         SEMMNU=256
options         SEMMAP=256
```

You might also want to configure your kernel to lock shared memory into RAM and prevent it from being paged out to swap. This can be accomplished using the sysctl setting kern.ipc.shm_use_phys.

HP-UX

The default settings tend to suffice for normal installations. On HP-UX 10, the factory default for SEMMNS is 128, which might be too low for larger database sites.

IPC parameters can be set in the System Administration Manager (SAM) under Kernel Configuration->Configurable Parameters. Hit Create A New Kernel when you're done.

Linux

The default maximum segment size is 32 MB, which is only adequate for small PostgreSQL installations. However, the remaining defaults are quite generously sized, and usually do not require changes. The maximum shared memory segment size can be changed via the sysctl interface. For example, to allow 128 MB, and explicitly set the maximum total shared memory size to 2097152 pages (the default):

```
$ sysctl -w kernel.shmmax=134217728
$ sysctl -w kernel.shmall=2097152
```

In addition these settings can be saved between reboots in /etc/sysctl.conf.

Older distributions might not have the sysctl program, but equivalent changes can be made by manipulating the /proc file system:

```
$ echo 134217728 >/proc/sys/kernel/shmmax
$ echo 2097152 >/proc/sys/kernel/shmall
```

MacOS X

In OS X 10.2 and earlier, edit the file /System/Library/StartupItems/SystemTuning/SystemTuning and change the values in the following commands:

```
sysctl -w kern.sysv.shmmax
sysctl -w kern.sysv.shmmin
sysctl -w kern.sysv.shmmni
sysctl -w kern.sysv.shmseg
sysctl -w kern.sysv.shmall
```

In OS X 10.3 and later, these commands have been moved to /etc/rc and must be edited there. Note that /etc/rc is usually overwritten by OS X updates (such as 10.3.6 to 10.3.7) so you should expect to have to redo your editing after each update.

In OS X 10.3.9 and later, instead of editing /etc/rc you can create a file named /etc/sysctl.conf, containing variable assignments such as:

```
kern.sysv.shmmax=4194304
kern.sysv.shmmin=1
kern.sysv.shmmni=32
kern.sysv.shmseg=8
kern.sysv.shmall=1024
```

This method is better than editing /etc/rc because your changes will be preserved across system updates. Note that *all five* shared-memory parameters must be set in /etc/sysctl.conf, else the values will be ignored.

Beware that recent releases of OS X ignore attempts to set SHMMAX to a value that isn't an exact multiple of 4096.

SHMALL is measured in 4 kB pages on this platform.

In all OS X versions, you'll need to reboot to make changes in the shared memory parameters take effect.

SCO OpenServer

In the default configuration, only 512 kB of shared memory per segment is allowed. To increase the setting, first change to the directory /etc/conf/cf.d. To display the current value of SHMMAX, run:

```
./configure -y SHMMAX
```

To set a new value for SHMMAX, run:

```
./configure SHMMAX=value
```

where *value* is the new value you want to use (in bytes). After setting SHMMAX, rebuild the kernel:

```
./link_unix
```

and reboot.

Solaris

At least in version 2.6, the default maximum size of a shared memory segment is too low for PostgreSQL. The relevant settings can be changed in /etc/system, for example:

```
set shmsys:shminfo_shmmax=0x2000000
set shmsys:shminfo_shmmin=1
set shmsys:shminfo_shmmni=256
set shmsys:shminfo_shmseg=256

set semsys:seminfo_semmap=256
set semsys:seminfo_semmni=512
set semsys:seminfo_semmns=512
set semsys:seminfo_semmsl=32
```

You need to reboot for the changes to take effect.

See also *http://sunsite.uakom.sk/sunworldonline/swol-09-1997/swol-09-insidesolaris.html* for information on shared memory under Solaris.

UnixWare

On UnixWare 7, the maximum size for shared memory segments is only 512 kB in the default configuration. To display the current value of SHMMAX, run:

```
/etc/conf/bin/idtune -g SHMMAX
```

which displays the current, default, minimum, and maximum values. To set a new value for SHMMAX, run:

```
/etc/conf/bin/idtune SHMMAX value
```

where *value* is the new value you want to use (in bytes). After setting SHMMAX, rebuild the kernel:

```
/etc/conf/bin/idbuild -B
```

and reboot.

Usage	Approximate shared memory bytes required (as of 8.3)
Connections	(1800 + 270 * *max_locks_per_transaction*) * *max_connections*
Autovacuum workers	(1800 + 270 * *max_locks_per_transaction*) * *autovacuum_max_workers*
Prepared transactions	(770 + 270 * *max_locks_per_transaction*) * *max_prepared_transactions*
Shared disk buffers	(*block_size* + 208) * *shared_buffers*
WAL buffers	(*wal_block_size* + 8) * *wal_buffers*
Fixed space requirements	770 kB

Table 17-2. PostgreSQL shared memory usage

17.4.2. Resource Limits

Unix-like operating systems enforce various kinds of resource limits that might interfere with the operation of your PostgreSQL server. Of particular importance are limits on the number of processes per user, the number of open files per process, and the amount of memory available to each process. Each of these have a "hard" and a "soft" limit. The soft limit is what actually counts but it can be changed by the user up to the hard limit. The hard limit can only be changed by the root user. The system call setrlimit is responsible for setting these parameters. The shell's built-in command ulimit (Bourne shells) or limit (csh) is used to control the resource limits from the command line. On BSD-derived systems the file /etc/login.conf controls the various resource limits set during login. See the operating system documentation for details. The relevant parameters are maxproc, openfiles, and datasize. For example:

```
default:\
...
        :datasize-cur=256M:\
        :maxproc-cur=256:\
        :openfiles-cur=256:\
...
```

(-cur is the soft limit. Append -max to set the hard limit.)

Kernels can also have system-wide limits on some resources.

- On Linux /proc/sys/fs/file-max determines the maximum number of open files that the kernel will support. It can be changed by writing a different number into the file or by adding an assignment in /etc/sysctl.conf. The maximum limit of files

per process is fixed at the time the kernel is compiled; see
`/usr/src/linux/Documentation/proc.txt` for more information.

The PostgreSQL server uses one process per connection so you should provide for at least as many processes as allowed connections, in addition to what you need for the rest of your system. This is usually not a problem but if you run several servers on one machine things might get tight.

The factory default limit on open files is often set to "socially friendly" values that allow many users to coexist on a machine without using an inappropriate fraction of the system resources. If you run many servers on a machine this is perhaps what you want, but on dedicated servers you might want to raise this limit.

On the other side of the coin, some systems allow individual processes to open large numbers of files; if more than a few processes do so then the system-wide limit can easily be exceeded. If you find this happening, and you do not want to alter the system-wide limit, you can set PostgreSQL's *max_files_per_process* configuration parameter to limit the consumption of open files.

17.4.3. Linux Memory Overcommit

In Linux 2.4 and later, the default virtual memory behavior is not optimal for PostgreSQL. Because of the way that the kernel implements memory overcommit, the kernel might terminate the PostgreSQL server (the master server process) if the memory demands of another process cause the system to run out of virtual memory.

If this happens, you will see a kernel message that looks like this (consult your system documentation and configuration on where to look for such a message):

`Out of Memory: Killed process 12345 (postgres).`

This indicates that the postgres process has been terminated due to memory pressure. Although existing database connections will continue to function normally, no new connections will be accepted. To recover, PostgreSQL will need to be restarted.

One way to avoid this problem is to run PostgreSQL on a machine where you can be sure that other processes will not run the machine out of memory. If memory is tight, increasing the swap space of the operating system can help avoiding the problem, because the out-of-memory (OOM) killer is invoked whenever physical memory and swap space are exhausted.

On Linux 2.6 and later, an additional measure is to modify the kernel's behavior so that it will not "overcommit" memory. Although this setting will not prevent the *OOM killer*[1] from

---

[1] *http://lwn.net/Articles/104179/*

being invoked altogether, it will lower the chances significantly and will therefore lead to more robust system behavior. This is done by selecting strict overcommit mode via sysctl:

```
sysctl -w vm.overcommit_memory=2
```

or placing an equivalent entry in /etc/sysctl.conf. You might also wish to modify the related setting vm.overcommit_ratio. For details see the kernel documentation file Documentation/vm/overcommit-accounting.

Some vendors' Linux 2.4 kernels are reported to have early versions of the 2.6 overcommit sysctl parameter. However, setting vm.overcommit_memory to 2 on a kernel that does not have the relevant code will make things worse not better. It is recommended that you inspect the actual kernel source code (see the function vm_enough_memory in the file mm/mmap.c) to verify what is supported in your copy before you try this in a 2.4 installation. The presence of the overcommit-accounting documentation file should *not* be taken as evidence that the feature is there. If in any doubt, consult a kernel expert or your kernel vendor.

17.5. Shutting Down the Server

There are several ways to shut down the database server. You control the type of shutdown by sending different signals to the master postgres process.

SIGTERM

> This is the *Smart Shutdown* mode. After receiving SIGTERM, the server disallows new connections, but lets existing sessions end their work normally. It shuts down only after all of the sessions terminate. If the server is in online backup mode, it additionally waits until online backup mode is no longer active. While backup mode is active, new connections will still be allowed, but only to superusers (this exception allows a superuser to connect to terminate online backup mode).

SIGINT

> This is the *Fast Shutdown* mode. The server disallows new connections and sends all existing server processes SIGTERM, which will cause them to abort their current transactions and exit promptly. It then waits for the server processes to exit and finally shuts down. If the server is in online backup mode, backup mode will be terminated, rendering the backup useless.

SIGQUIT

> This is the *Immediate Shutdown* mode. The master postgres process will send a SIGQUIT to all child processes and exit immediately, without properly shutting itself down. The child processes likewise exit immediately upon receiving SIGQUIT. This will lead to

recovery (by replaying the WAL log) upon next start-up. This is recommended only in emergencies.

The *pg_ctl* program provides a convenient interface for sending these signals to shut down the server. Alternatively, you can send the signal directly using kill on non-Windows systems. The PID of the postgres process can be found using the ps program, or from the file postmaster.pid in the data directory. For example, to do a fast shutdown:

```
$ kill -INT `head -1 /usr/local/pgsql/data/postmaster.pid`
```

Important

It is best not to use SIGKILL to shut down the server. Doing so will prevent the server from releasing shared memory and semaphores, which might then have to be done manually before a new server can be started. Furthermore, SIGKILL kills the postgres process without letting it relay the signal to its subprocesses, so it will be necessary to kill the individual subprocesses by hand as well.

To terminate an individual session while allowing other sessions to continue, use pg_terminate_backend() (see *Table 9-55*) or send a SIGTERM signal to the child process associated with the session.

17.6. Preventing Server Spoofing

While the server is running, it is not possible for a malicious user to take the place of the normal database server. However, when the server is down it is possible for a local user to spoof the normal server by starting their own server. The spoof server could read passwords and queries sent by clients, but could not return any data because the PGDATA directory would still be secure because of directory permissions. Spoofing is possible because any user can start a database server; a client cannot identify an invalid server unless it is specially configured.

The simplest way to prevent invalid servers for local connections is to use a Unix domain socket directory (*unix_socket_directory*) that has write permission only for a trusted local user. This prevents a malicious user from creating their own socket file in that directory. If you are concerned that some applications might still reference /tmp for the socket file and hence be vulnerable to spoofing, during operating system startup create symbolic link /tmp/.s.PGSQL.5432 that points to the relocated socket file. You also might need to modify your /tmp cleanup script to preserve the symbolic link.

For TCP connections the server must accept only hostssl connections (*Section 19.1* – page 129) and have SSL server.key (key) and server.crt (certificate) files (*Section 17.8* – page 73). The TCP client must connect using sslmode='verify-ca' or 'verify-full' and have the required certificate files present (*Section 30.1* – page 246).

17.7. Encryption Options

PostgreSQL offers encryption at several levels, and provides flexibility in protecting data from disclosure due to database server theft, unscrupulous administrators, and insecure networks. Encryption might also be required to secure sensitive data such as medical records or financial transactions.

Password Storage Encryption

> By default, database user passwords are stored as MD5 hashes, so the administrator cannot determine the actual password assigned to the user. If MD5 encryption is used for client authentication, the unencrypted password is never even temporarily present on the server because the client MD5 encrypts it before being sent across the network.

Encryption For Specific Columns

> The contrib function library pgcrypto allows certain fields to be stored encrypted. This is useful if only some of the data is sensitive. The client supplies the decryption key and the data is decrypted on the server and then sent to the client.

> The decrypted data and the decryption key are present on the server for a brief time while it is being decrypted and communicated between the client and server. This presents a brief moment where the data and keys can be intercepted by someone with complete access to the database server, such as the system administrator.

Data Partition Encryption

> On Linux, encryption can be layered on top of a file system mount using a "loopback device". This allows an entire file system partition be encrypted on disk, and decrypted by the operating system. On FreeBSD, the equivalent facility is called GEOM Based Disk Encryption, or gbde.

> This mechanism prevents unencrypted data from being read from the drives if the drives or the entire computer is stolen. This does not protect against attacks while the file system is mounted, because when mounted, the operating system provides an unencrypted view of the data. However, to mount the file system, you need some way for the encryption key to be passed to the operating system, and sometimes the key is stored somewhere on the host that mounts the disk.

Encrypting Passwords Across A Network

> The MD5 authentication method double-encrypts the password on the client before sending it to the server. It first MD5 encrypts it based on the user name, and then encrypts it based on a random salt sent by the server when the database connection was made. It is this double-encrypted value that is sent over the network to the server. Double-encryption not only prevents the password from being discovered, it also

prevents another connection from using the same encrypted password to connect to the database server at a later time.

Encrypting Data Across A Network

SSL connections encrypt all data sent across the network: the password, the queries, and the data returned. The pg_hba.conf file allows administrators to specify which hosts can use non-encrypted connections (host) and which require SSL-encrypted connections (hostssl). Also, clients can specify that they connect to servers only via SSL. Stunnel or SSH can also be used to encrypt transmissions.

SSL Host Authentication

It is possible for both the client and server to provide SSL certificates to each other. It takes some extra configuration on each side, but this provides stronger verification of identity than the mere use of passwords. It prevents a computer from pretending to be the server just long enough to read the password send by the client. It also helps prevent "man in the middle" attacks where a computer between the client and server pretends to be the server and reads and passes all data between the client and server.

Client-Side Encryption

If the system administrator cannot be trusted, it is necessary for the client to encrypt the data; this way, unencrypted data never appears on the database server. Data is encrypted on the client before being sent to the server, and database results have to be decrypted on the client before being used.

17.8. Secure TCP/IP Connections with SSL

PostgreSQL has native support for using SSL connections to encrypt client/server communications for increased security. This requires that OpenSSL is installed on both client and server systems and that support in PostgreSQL is enabled at build time (see *Chapter 15* – page 20).

With SSL support compiled in, the PostgreSQL server can be started with SSL enabled by setting the parameter *ssl* to on in postgresql.conf. The server will listen for both standard and SSL connections on the same TCP port, and will negotiate with any connecting client on whether to use SSL. By default, this is at the client's option; see *Section 19.1* (page 129) about how to set up the server to require use of SSL for some or all connections.

PostgreSQL reads the system-wide OpenSSL configuration file. By default, this file is named openssl.cnf and is located in the directory reported by openssl version -d. This default can be overridden by setting environment variable OPENSSL_CONF to the name of the desired configuration file.

OpenSSL supports a wide range of ciphers and authentication algorithms, of varying strength. While a list of ciphers can be specified in the OpenSSL configuration file, you can specify ciphers specifically for use by the database server by modifying *ssl_ciphers* in postgresql.conf.

 Note

> It is possible to have authentication without encryption overhead by using NULL-SHA or NULL-MD5 ciphers. However, a man-in-the-middle could read and pass communications between client and server. Also, encryption overhead is minimal compared to the overhead of authentication. For these reasons NULL ciphers are not recommended.

To start in SSL mode, the files server.crt and server.key must exist in the server's data directory. These files should contain the server certificate and private key, respectively. On Unix systems, the permissions on server.key must disallow any access to world or group; achieve this by the command chmod 0600 server.key. If the private key is protected with a passphrase, the server will prompt for the passphrase and will not start until it has been entered.

17.8.1. Using client certificates

To require the client to supply a trusted certificate, place certificates of the certificate authorities (CA) you trust in the file root.crt in the data directory, and set the clientcert parameter to 1 on the appropriate line(s) in pg_hba.conf. A certificate will then be requested from the client during SSL connection startup. (See *Section 30.17* – page 304 for a description of how to set up certificates on the client.) The server will verify that the client's certificate is signed by one of the trusted certificate authorities. Certificate Revocation List (CRL) entries are also checked if the file root.crl exists.
(See *http://h71000.www7.hp.com/DOC/83final/BA554_90007/ch04s02.html* for diagrams showing SSL certificate usage.)

The clientcert option in pg_hba.conf is available for all authentication methods, but only for rows specified as hostssl. Unless specified, the default is not to verify the client certificate.

You can use the authentication method cert to use the client certificate for authenticating users. See *Section 19.3.8* (page 143) for details.

17.8.2. SSL Server File Usage

The files server.key, server.crt, root.crt, and root.crl are only examined during server start; so you must restart the server for changes in them to take effect.

File	Contents	Effect
server.crt	server certificate	requested by client
server.key	server private key	proves server certificate sent by owner; does not indicate certificate owner is trustworthy
root.crt	trusted certificate authorities	checks that client certificate is signed by a trusted certificate authority
root.crl	certificates revoked by certificate authorities	client certificate must not be on this list

Table 17-3. SSL Server File Usage

17.8.3. Creating a Self-Signed Certificate

To create a quick self-signed certificate for the server, use the following OpenSSL command:

```
openssl req -new -text -out server.req
```

Fill out the information that openssl asks for. Make sure you enter the local host name as "Common Name"; the challenge password can be left blank. The program will generate a key that is passphrase protected; it will not accept a passphrase that is less than four characters long. To remove the passphrase (as you must if you want automatic start-up of the server), run the commands:

```
openssl rsa -in privkey.pem -out server.key
rm privkey.pem
```

Enter the old passphrase to unlock the existing key. Now do:

```
openssl req -x509 -in server.req -text -key server.key -out server.crt
```

to turn the certificate into a self-signed certificate and to copy the key and certificate to where the server will look for them. Finally do:

```
chmod og-rwx server.key
```

because the server will reject the file if its permissions are more liberal than this. For more details on how to create your server private key and certificate, refer to the OpenSSL documentation.

A self-signed certificate can be used for testing, but a certificate signed by a certificate authority (CA) (either one of the global CAs or a local one) should be used in production so the client can verify the server's identity. If all the clients are local to the organization, using a local CA is recommended.

17.9. Secure TCP/IP Connections with SSH Tunnels

One can use SSH to encrypt the network connection between clients and a PostgreSQL server. Done properly, this provides an adequately secure network connection, even for non-SSL-capable clients.

First make sure that an SSH server is running properly on the same machine as the PostgreSQL server and that you can log in using ssh as some user. Then you can establish a secure tunnel with a command like this from the client machine:

```
ssh -L 63333:localhost:5432 joe@foo.com
```

The first number in the -L argument, 63333, is the port number of your end of the tunnel; it can be chosen freely. (IANA reserves ports 49152 through 65535 for private use.) The second number, 5432, is the remote end of the tunnel: the port number your server is using. The name or IP address between the port numbers is the host with the database server you are going to connect to, as seen from the host you are logging in to, which is foo.com in this example. In order to connect to the database server using this tunnel, you connect to port 63333 on the local machine:

```
psql -h localhost -p 63333 postgres
```

To the database server it will then look as though you are really user joe on host foo.com connecting to localhost in that context, and it will use whatever authentication procedure was configured for connections from this user and host. Note that the server will not think the connection is SSL-encrypted, since in fact it is not encrypted between the SSH server and the PostgreSQL server. This should not pose any extra security risk as long as they are on the same machine.

In order for the tunnel setup to succeed you must be allowed to connect via ssh as joe@foo.com, just as if you had attempted to use ssh to set up a terminal session.

You could also have set up the port forwarding as

```
ssh -L 63333:foo.com:5432 joe@foo.com
```

but then the database server will see the connection as coming in on its foo.com interface, which is not opened by the default setting listen_addresses = 'localhost'. This is usually not what you want.

If you have to "hop" to the database server via some login host, one possible setup could look like this:

```
ssh -L 63333:db.foo.com:5432 joe@shell.foo.com
```

Note that this way the connection from shell.foo.com to db.foo.com will not be encrypted by the SSH tunnel. SSH offers quite a few configuration possibilities when the network is restricted in various ways. Please refer to the SSH documentation for details.

 Tip

> Several other applications exist that can provide secure tunnels using a procedure similar in concept to the one just described.

Chapter 18.
Server Configuration

There are many configuration parameters that affect the behavior of the database system. In the first section of this chapter, we describe how to set configuration parameters. The subsequent sections discuss each parameter in detail.

18.1. Setting Parameters

All parameter names are case-insensitive. Every parameter takes a value of one of five types: Boolean, integer, floating point, string or enum. Boolean values can be written as ON, OFF, TRUE, FALSE, YES, NO, 1, 0 (all case-insensitive) or any unambiguous prefix of these.

Some settings specify a memory or time value. Each of these has an implicit unit, which is either kilobytes, blocks (typically eight kilobytes), milliseconds, seconds, or minutes. Default units can be found by referencing pg_settings.unit. For convenience, a different unit can also be specified explicitly. Valid memory units are kB (kilobytes), MB (megabytes), and GB (gigabytes); valid time units are ms (milliseconds), s (seconds), min (minutes), h (hours), and d (days). Note that the multiplier for memory units is 1024, not 1000.

Parameters of type "enum" are specified in the same way as string parameters, but are restricted to a limited set of values. The allowed values can be found from pg_settings.enumvals. Enum parameter values are case-insensitive.

One way to set these parameters is to edit the file postgresql.conf, which is normally kept in the data directory. (initdb installs a default copy there.) An example of what this file might look like is:

```
# This is a comment
log_connections = yes
log_destination = 'syslog'
search_path = '"$user", public'
shared_buffers = 128MB
```

One parameter is specified per line. The equal sign between name and value is optional. Whitespace is insignificant and blank lines are ignored. Hash marks (#) introduce comments anywhere. Parameter values that are not simple identifiers or numbers must be single-quoted. To embed a single quote in a parameter value, write either two quotes (preferred) or backslash-quote.

In addition to parameter settings, the postgresql.conf file can contain *include directives*, which specify another file to read and process as if it were inserted into the configuration file at this point. Include directives simply look like:

```
include 'filename'
```

If the file name is not an absolute path, it is taken as relative to the directory containing the referencing configuration file. Inclusions can be nested.

The configuration file is reread whenever the main server process receives a SIGHUP signal (which is most easily sent by means of pg_ctl reload). The main server process also propagates this signal to all currently running server processes so that existing sessions also get the new value. Alternatively, you can send the signal to a single server process directly. Some parameters can only be set at server start; any changes to their entries in the configuration file will be ignored until the server is restarted.

A second way to set these configuration parameters is to give them as a command-line option to the postgres command, such as:

```
postgres -c log_connections=yes -c log_destination='syslog'
```

Command-line options override any conflicting settings in postgresql.conf. Note that this means you won't be able to change the value on-the-fly by editing postgresql.conf, so while the command-line method might be convenient, it can cost you flexibility later.

Occasionally it is useful to give a command line option to one particular session only. The environment variable PGOPTIONS can be used for this purpose on the client side:

```
env PGOPTIONS='-c geqo=off' psql
```

(This works for any libpq-based client application, not just psql.) Note that this won't work for parameters that are fixed when the server is started or that must be specified in postgresql.conf.

Furthermore, it is possible to assign a set of parameter settings to a user or a database. Whenever a session is started, the default settings for the user and database involved are loaded. The commands ALTER USER and ALTER DATABASE, respectively, are used to configure these settings. Per-database settings override anything received from the postgres command-line or the configuration file, and in turn are overridden by per-user settings; both are overridden by per-session settings.

Some parameters can be changed in individual SQL sessions with the SET command, for example:

```
SET ENABLE_SEQSCAN TO OFF;
```

If SET is allowed, it overrides all other sources of values for the parameter. Some parameters cannot be changed via SET: for example, if they control behavior that cannot be changed without restarting the entire PostgreSQL server. Also, some parameters can be modified via SET or ALTER by superusers, but not by ordinary users.

The SHOW command allows inspection of the current values of all parameters.

The virtual table pg_settings (described in *Section 44.53*) also allows displaying and updating session run-time parameters. It is equivalent to SHOW and SET, but can be more convenient to use because it can be joined with other tables, or selected from using any desired selection condition. It also contains more information about what values are allowed for the parameters.

18.2. File Locations

In addition to the postgresql.conf file already mentioned, PostgreSQL uses two other manually-edited configuration files, which control client authentication (their use is discussed in *Chapter 19* – page 129). By default, all three configuration files are stored in the database cluster's data directory. The parameters described in this section allow the configuration files to be placed elsewhere. (Doing so can ease administration. In particular it is often easier to ensure that the configuration files are properly backed-up when they are kept separate.)

data_directory (string)

Specifies the directory to use for data storage. This parameter can only be set at server start.

config_file (string)

Specifies the main server configuration file (customarily called postgresql.conf). This parameter can only be set on the postgres command line.

hba_file (string)

Specifies the configuration file for host-based authentication (customarily called pg_hba.conf). This parameter can only be set at server start.

ident_file (string)

Specifies the configuration file for ident authentication (customarily called pg_ident.conf). This parameter can only be set at server start.

external_pid_file (string)

Specifies the name of an additional process-id (PID) file that the server should create for use by server administration programs. This parameter can only be set at server start.

In a default installation, none of the above parameters are set explicitly. Instead, the data directory is specified by the -D command-line option or the PGDATA environment variable, and the configuration files are all found within the data directory.

If you wish to keep the configuration files elsewhere than the data directory, the postgres -D command-line option or PGDATA environment variable must point to the directory containing the configuration files, and the data_directory parameter must be set in postgresql.conf (or on the command line) to show where the data directory is actually located. Notice that data_directory overrides -D and PGDATA for the location of the data directory, but not for the location of the configuration files.

If you wish, you can specify the configuration file names and locations individually using the parameters config_file, hba_file and/or ident_file. config_file can only be specified on the postgres command line, but the others can be set within the main configuration file. If all three parameters plus data_directory are explicitly set, then it is not necessary to specify -D or PGDATA.

When setting any of these parameters, a relative path will be interpreted with respect to the directory in which postgres is started.

18.3. Connections and Authentication

18.3.1. Connection Settings

listen_addresses (string)

Specifies the TCP/IP address(es) on which the server is to listen for connections from client applications. The value takes the form of a comma-separated list of host names and/or numeric IP addresses. The special entry * corresponds to all available IP interfaces. If the list is empty, the server does not listen on any IP interface at all, in which case only Unix-domain sockets can be used to connect to it. The default value is localhost, which allows only local "loopback" connections to be made. This parameter can only be set at server start.

port (integer)

The TCP port the server listens on; 5432 by default. Note that the same port number is used for all IP addresses the server listens on. This parameter can only be set at server start.

max_connections (integer)

Determines the maximum number of concurrent connections to the database server. The default is typically 100 connections, but might be less if your kernel settings will not support it (as determined during initdb). This parameter can only be set at server start.

Increasing this parameter might cause PostgreSQL to request more System V shared memory or semaphores than your operating system's default configuration allows. See *Section 17.4.1 (page 61)* for information on how to adjust those parameters, if necessary.

`superuser_reserved_connections` (`integer`)

Determines the number of connection "slots" that are reserved for connections by PostgreSQL superusers. At most *max_connections* connections can ever be active simultaneously. Whenever the number of active concurrent connections is at least max_connections minus superuser_reserved_connections, new connections will be accepted only for superusers.

The default value is three connections. The value must be less than the value of max_connections. This parameter can only be set at server start.

`unix_socket_directory` (`string`)

Specifies the directory of the Unix-domain socket on which the server is to listen for connections from client applications. The default is normally /tmp, but can be changed at build time. This parameter can only be set at server start.

`unix_socket_group` (`string`)

Sets the owning group of the Unix-domain socket. (The owning user of the socket is always the user that starts the server.) In combination with the parameter unix_socket_permissions this can be used as an additional access control mechanism for Unix-domain connections. By default this is the empty string, which selects the default group for the current user. This parameter can only be set at server start.

`unix_socket_permissions` (`integer`)

Sets the access permissions of the Unix-domain socket. Unix-domain sockets use the usual Unix file system permission set. The parameter value is expected to be a numeric mode specification in the form accepted by the chmod and umask system calls. (To use the customary octal format the number must start with a 0 (zero).)

The default permissions are 0777, meaning anyone can connect. Reasonable alternatives are 0770 (only user and group, see also unix_socket_group) and 0700 (only user). (Note that for a Unix-domain socket, only write permission matters and so there is no point in setting or revoking read or execute permissions.)

This access control mechanism is independent of the one described in *Chapter 19* (page 129).

This parameter can only be set at server start.

`bonjour_name` (`string`)

Specifies the Bonjour broadcast name. The computer name is used if this parameter is set to the empty string " (which is the default). This parameter is ignored if the server was not compiled with Bonjour support. This parameter can only be set at server start.

`tcp_keepalives_idle` (integer)

On systems that support the TCP_KEEPIDLE socket option, specifies the number of seconds between sending keepalives on an otherwise idle connection. A value of zero uses the system default. If TCP_KEEPIDLE is not supported, this parameter must be zero. This parameter is ignored for connections made via a Unix-domain socket.

`tcp_keepalives_interval` (integer)

On systems that support the TCP_KEEPINTVL socket option, specifies how long, in seconds, to wait for a response to a keepalive before retransmitting. A value of zero uses the system default. If TCP_KEEPINTVL is not supported, this parameter must be zero. This parameter is ignored for connections made via a Unix-domain socket.

`tcp_keepalives_count` (integer)

On systems that support the TCP_KEEPCNT socket option, specifies how many keepalives can be lost before the connection is considered dead. A value of zero uses the system default. If TCP_KEEPCNT is not supported, this parameter must be zero. This parameter is ignored for connections made via a Unix-domain socket.

18.3.2. Security and Authentication

`authentication_timeout` (integer)

Maximum time to complete client authentication, in seconds. If a would-be client has not completed the authentication protocol in this much time, the server breaks the connection. This prevents hung clients from occupying a connection indefinitely. The default is one minute (1m). This parameter can only be set in the postgresql.conf file or on the server command line.

`ssl` (boolean)

Enables SSL connections. Please read *Section 17.8* (page 73) before using this. The default is off. This parameter can only be set at server start. SSL communication is only possible with TCP/IP connections.

`ssl_ciphers` (string)

Specifies a list of SSL ciphers that are allowed to be used on secure connections. See the openssl manual page for a list of supported ciphers.

`password_encryption` (boolean)

When a password is specified in CREATE USER or ALTER USER without writing either ENCRYPTED or UNENCRYPTED, this parameter determines whether the password is to be encrypted. The default is on (encrypt the password).

`krb_server_keyfile` (string)

Sets the location of the Kerberos server key file. See *Section 19.3.5* (page 139) or *Section 19.3.3* (page 138) for details. This parameter can only be set in the postgresql.conf file or on the server command line.

`krb_srvname` (string)

Sets the Kerberos service name. See *Section 19.3.5* (page 139) for details. This parameter can only be set in the postgresql.conf file or on the server command line.

`krb_caseins_users` (boolean)

Sets whether Kerberos and GSSAPI user names should be treated case-insensitively. The default is off (case sensitive). This parameter can only be set in the postgresql.conf file or on the server command line.

`db_user_namespace` (boolean)

This parameter enables per-database user names. It is off by default. This parameter can only be set in the postgresql.conf file or on the server command line.

If this is on, you should create users as username@dbname. When username is passed by a connecting client, @ and the database name are appended to the user name and that database-specific user name is looked up by the server. Note that when you create users with names containing @ within the SQL environment, you will need to quote the user name.

With this parameter enabled, you can still create ordinary global users. Simply append @ when specifying the user name in the client. The @ will be stripped off before the user name is looked up by the server.

db_user_namespace causes the client's and server's user name representation to differ. Authentication checks are always done with the server's user name so authentication methods must be configured for the server's user name, not the client's. Because md5 uses the user name as salt on both the client and server, md5 cannot be used with db_user_namespace.

 Note

This feature is intended as a temporary measure until a complete solution is found. At that time, this option will be removed.

18.4. Resource Consumption

18.4.1. Memory

`shared_buffers` (integer)

Sets the amount of memory the database server uses for shared memory buffers. The default is typically 32 megabytes (32MB), but might be less if your kernel settings will not support it (as determined during initdb). This setting must be at least 128 kilobytes. (Non-default values of BLCKSZ change the minimum.) However, settings significantly higher than the minimum are usually needed for good performance. Several tens of megabytes are recommended for production installations. This parameter can only be set at server start.

Increasing this parameter might cause PostgreSQL to request more System V shared memory than your operating system's default configuration allows. See *Section 17.4.1* (page 61) for information on how to adjust those parameters, if necessary.

`temp_buffers` (`integer`)

Sets the maximum number of temporary buffers used by each database session. These are session-local buffers used only for access to temporary tables. The default is eight megabytes (8MB). The setting can be changed within individual sessions, but only up until the first use of temporary tables within a session; subsequent attempts to change the value will have no effect on that session.

A session will allocate temporary buffers as needed up to the limit given by temp_buffers. The cost of setting a large value in sessions that do not actually need a lot of temporary buffers is only a buffer descriptor, or about 64 bytes, per increment in temp_buffers. However if a buffer is actually used an additional 8192 bytes will be consumed for it (or in general, BLCKSZ bytes).

`max_prepared_transactions` (`integer`)

Sets the maximum number of transactions that can be in the "prepared" state simultaneously (see PREPARE TRANSACTION). Setting this parameter to zero (which is the default) disables the prepared-transaction feature. This parameter can only be set at server start.

If you are not planning to use prepared transactions, this parameter should be set to zero to prevent accidental creation of prepared transactions. If you are using prepared transactions, you will probably want max_prepared_transactions to be at least as large as *max_connections*, so that every session can have a prepared transaction pending.

Increasing this parameter might cause PostgreSQL to request more System V shared memory than your operating system's default configuration allows. See *Section 17.4.1* (page 61) for information on how to adjust those parameters, if necessary.

`work_mem` (`integer`)

Specifies the amount of memory to be used by internal sort operations and hash tables before switching to temporary disk files. The value defaults to one megabyte (1MB). Note that for a complex query, several sort or hash operations might be running in parallel; each one will be allowed to use as much memory as this value specifies before it starts to put data into temporary files. Also, several running sessions could be doing such operations concurrently. So the total memory used could be many times the value of work_mem; it is necessary to keep this fact in mind when choosing the value. Sort operations are used for ORDER BY, DISTINCT, and merge joins. Hash tables are used in hash joins, hash-based aggregation, and hash-based processing of IN subqueries.

maintenance_work_mem (integer)

Specifies the maximum amount of memory to be used in maintenance operations, such as VACUUM, CREATE INDEX, and ALTER TABLE ADD FOREIGN KEY. It defaults to 16 megabytes (16MB). Since only one of these operations can be executed at a time by a database session, and an installation normally doesn't have many of them running concurrently, it's safe to set this value significantly larger than work_mem. Larger settings might improve performance for vacuuming and for restoring database dumps.

Note that when autovacuum runs, up to *autovacuum_max_workers* times this memory may be allocated, so be careful not to set the default value too high.

max_stack_depth (integer)

Specifies the maximum safe depth of the server's execution stack. The ideal setting for this parameter is the actual stack size limit enforced by the kernel (as set by ulimit -s or local equivalent), less a safety margin of a megabyte or so. The safety margin is needed because the stack depth is not checked in every routine in the server, but only in key potentially-recursive routines such as expression evaluation. The default setting is two megabytes (2MB), which is conservatively small and unlikely to risk crashes. However, it might be too small to allow execution of complex functions. Only superusers can change this setting.

Setting max_stack_depth higher than the actual kernel limit will mean that a runaway recursive function can crash an individual backend process. On platforms where PostgreSQL can determine the kernel limit, it will not let you set this variable to an unsafe value. However, not all platforms provide the information, so caution is recommended in selecting a value.

18.4.2. Kernel Resource Usage

max_files_per_process (integer)

Sets the maximum number of simultaneously open files allowed to each server subprocess. The default is one thousand files. If the kernel is enforcing a safe per-process limit, you don't need to worry about this setting. But on some platforms (notably, most BSD systems), the kernel will allow individual processes to open many more files than the system can really support when a large number of processes all try to open that many files. If you find yourself seeing "Too many open files" failures, try reducing this setting. This parameter can only be set at server start.

`shared_preload_libraries` (`string`)

This variable specifies one or more shared libraries that are to be preloaded at server start. If more than one library is to be loaded, separate their names with commas. For example, '$libdir/mylib' would cause mylib.so (or on some platforms, mylib.sl) to be preloaded from the installation's standard library directory. This parameter can only be set at server start.

PostgreSQL procedural language libraries can be preloaded in this way, typically by using the syntax '$libdir/plXXX' where XXX is pgsql, perl, tcl, or python.

By preloading a shared library, the library startup time is avoided when the library is first used. However, the time to start each new server process might increase slightly, even if that process never uses the library. So this parameter is recommended only for libraries that will be used in most sessions.

Note

On Windows hosts, preloading a library at server start will not reduce the time required to start each new server process; each server process will re-load all preload libraries. However, shared_preload_libraries is still useful on Windows hosts because some shared libraries may need to perform certain operations that only take place at postmaster start (for example, a shared library may need to reserve lightweight locks or shared memory and you can't do that after the postmaster has started).

If a specified library is not found, the server will fail to start.

Every PostgreSQL-supported library has a "magic block" that is checked to guarantee compatibility. For this reason, non-PostgreSQL libraries cannot be loaded in this way.

18.4.3. Cost-Based Vacuum Delay

During the execution of VACUUM and ANALYZE commands, the system maintains an internal counter that keeps track of the estimated cost of the various I/O operations that are performed. When the accumulated cost reaches a limit (specified by vacuum_cost_limit), the process performing the operation will sleep for a while (specified by vacuum_cost_delay). Then it will reset the counter and continue execution.

The intent of this feature is to allow administrators to reduce the I/O impact of these commands on concurrent database activity. There are many situations in which it is not very important that maintenance commands like VACUUM and ANALYZE finish quickly;

however, it is usually very important that these commands do not significantly interfere with the ability of the system to perform other database operations. Cost-based vacuum delay provides a way for administrators to achieve this.

This feature is disabled by default for manually issued VACUUM commands. To enable it, set the vacuum_cost_delay variable to a nonzero value.

`vacuum_cost_delay` (integer)

> The length of time, in milliseconds, that the process will sleep when the cost limit has been exceeded. The default value is zero, which disables the cost-based vacuum delay feature. Positive values enable cost-based vacuuming. Note that on many systems, the effective resolution of sleep delays is 10 milliseconds; setting vacuum_cost_delay to a value that is not a multiple of 10 might have the same results as setting it to the next higher multiple of 10.
>
> When using cost-based vacuuming, appropriate values for vacuum_cost_delay are usually quite small, perhaps 10 or 20 milliseconds. Adjusting vacuum's resource consumption is best done by changing the other vacuum cost parameters.

`vacuum_cost_page_hit` (integer)

> The estimated cost for vacuuming a buffer found in the shared buffer cache. It represents the cost to lock the buffer pool, lookup the shared hash table and scan the content of the page. The default value is one.

`vacuum_cost_page_miss` (integer)

> The estimated cost for vacuuming a buffer that has to be read from disk. This represents the effort to lock the buffer pool, lookup the shared hash table, read the desired block in from the disk and scan its content. The default value is 10.

`vacuum_cost_page_dirty` (integer)

> The estimated cost charged when vacuum modifies a block that was previously clean. It represents the extra I/O required to flush the dirty block out to disk again. The default value is 20.

`vacuum_cost_limit` (integer)

> The accumulated cost that will cause the vacuuming process to sleep. The default value is 200.

 Note

> There are certain operations that hold critical locks and should therefore complete as quickly as possible. Cost-based vacuum delays do not occur during such operations.

Therefore it is possible that the cost accumulates far higher than the specified limit. To avoid uselessly long delays in such cases, the actual delay is calculated as vacuum_cost_delay * accumulated_balance / vacuum_cost_limit with a maximum of vacuum_cost_delay * 4.

18.4.4. Background Writer

There is a separate server process called the *background writer*, whose function is to issue writes of "dirty" shared buffers. The intent is that server processes handling user queries should seldom or never have to wait for a write to occur, because the background writer will do it. However there is a net overall increase in I/O load, because a repeatedly-dirtied page might otherwise be written only once per checkpoint interval, but the background writer might write it several times in the same interval. The parameters discussed in this subsection can be used to tune the behavior for local needs.

bgwriter_delay (integer)

Specifies the delay between activity rounds for the background writer. In each round the writer issues writes for some number of dirty buffers (controllable by the following parameters). It then sleeps for bgwriter_delay milliseconds, and repeats. The default value is 200 milliseconds (200ms). Note that on many systems, the effective resolution of sleep delays is 10 milliseconds; setting bgwriter_delay to a value that is not a multiple of 10 might have the same results as setting it to the next higher multiple of 10. This parameter can only be set in the postgresql.conf file or on the server command line.

bgwriter_lru_maxpages (integer)

In each round, no more than this many buffers will be written by the background writer. Setting this to zero disables background writing (except for checkpoint activity). The default value is 100 buffers. This parameter can only be set in the postgresql.conf file or on the server command line.

bgwriter_lru_multiplier (floating point)

The number of dirty buffers written in each round is based on the number of new buffers that have been needed by server processes during recent rounds. The average recent need is multiplied by bgwriter_lru_multiplier to arrive at an estimate of the number of buffers that will be needed during the next round. Dirty buffers are written until there are that many clean, reusable buffers available. (However, no more than bgwriter_lru_maxpages buffers will be written per round.) Thus, a setting of 1.0 represents a "just in time" policy of writing exactly the number of buffers predicted to be needed. Larger values provide some cushion against spikes in demand, while smaller values intentionally leave writes to be done by server processes. The default is 2.0. This parameter can only be set in the postgresql.conf file or on the server command line.

Smaller values of bgwriter_lru_maxpages and bgwriter_lru_multiplier reduce the extra I/O load caused by the background writer, but make it more likely that server processes will have to issue writes for themselves, delaying interactive queries.

18.4.5. Asynchronous Behavior

effective_io_concurrency (integer)

Sets the number of concurrent disk I/O operations that PostgreSQL expects can be executed simultaneously. Raising this value will increase the number of I/O operations that any individual PostgreSQL session attempts to initiate in parallel. The allowed range is 1 to 1000, or zero to disable issuance of asynchronous I/O requests.

A good starting point for this setting is the number of separate drives comprising a RAID 0 stripe or RAID 1 mirror being used for the database. (For RAID 5 the parity drive should not be counted.) However, if the database is often busy with multiple queries issued in concurrent sessions, lower values may be sufficient to keep the disk array busy. A value higher than needed to keep the disks busy will only result in extra CPU overhead.

For more exotic systems, such as memory-based storage or a RAID array that is limited by bus bandwidth, the correct value might be the number of I/O paths available. Some experimentation may be needed to find the best value.

Asynchronous I/O depends on an effective posix_fadvise function, which some operating systems lack. If the function is not present then setting this parameter to anything but zero will result in an error. On some operating systems (e.g., Solaris), the function is present but does not actually do anything.

18.5. Write Ahead Log

See also *Section 28.4* (page 234) for details on WAL and checkpoint tuning.

18.5.1. Settings

fsync (boolean)

If this parameter is on, the PostgreSQL server will try to make sure that updates are physically written to disk, by issuing fsync() system calls or various equivalent methods (see *wal_sync_method*). This ensures that the database cluster can recover to a consistent state after an operating system or hardware crash.

However, using fsync results in a performance penalty: when a transaction is committed, PostgreSQL must wait for the operating system to flush the write-ahead log to disk. When fsync is disabled, the operating system is allowed to do its best in buffering, ordering, and delaying writes. This can result in significantly improved performance. However, if the system crashes, the results of the last few committed transactions might be lost in part or whole. In the worst case, unrecoverable data corruption might occur. (Crashes of the database software itself are *not* a risk factor here. Only an operating-system-level crash creates a risk of corruption.)

Due to the risks involved, there is no universally correct setting for fsync. Some administrators always disable fsync, while others only turn it off during initial bulk data loads, where there is a clear restart point if something goes wrong. Others always leave fsync enabled. The default is to enable fsync, for maximum reliability. If you trust your operating system, your hardware, and your utility company (or your battery backup), you can consider disabling fsync.

In many situations, turning off *synchronous_commit* for noncritical transactions can provide much of the potential performance benefit of turning off fsync, without the attendant risks of data corruption.

This parameter can only be set in the postgresql.conf file or on the server command line. If you turn this parameter off, also consider turning off *full_page_writes*.

`synchronous_commit` (`boolean`)

Specifies whether transaction commit will wait for WAL records to be written to disk before the command returns a "success" indication to the client. The default, and safe, setting is on. When off, there can be a delay between when success is reported to the client and when the transaction is really guaranteed to be safe against a server crash. (The maximum delay is three times *wal_writer_delay*.) Unlike *fsync*, setting this parameter to off does not create any risk of database inconsistency: a crash might result in some recent allegedly-committed transactions being lost, but the database state will be just the same as if those transactions had been aborted cleanly. So, turning synchronous_commit off can be a useful alternative when performance is more important than exact certainty about the durability of a transaction. For more discussion see *Section 28.3* (page 232).

This parameter can be changed at any time; the behavior for any one transaction is determined by the setting in effect when it commits. It is therefore possible, and useful, to have some transactions commit synchronously and others asynchronously. For example, to make a single multi-statement transaction commit asynchronously when the default is the opposite, issue SET LOCAL synchronous_commit TO OFF within the transaction.

`wal_sync_method` (`enum`)

Method used for forcing WAL updates out to disk. If fsync is off then this setting is irrelevant, since updates will not be forced out at all. Possible values are:

- open_datasync (write WAL files with open() option O_DSYNC)
- fdatasync (call fdatasync() at each commit)
- fsync_writethrough (call fsync() at each commit, forcing write-through of any disk write cache)
- fsync (call fsync() at each commit)
- open_sync (write WAL files with open() option O_SYNC)

Not all of these choices are available on all platforms. The default is the first method in the above list that is supported by the platform. The open_* options also use O_DIRECT if available. This parameter can only be set in the postgresql.conf file or on the server command line.

full_page_writes (boolean)

When this parameter is on, the PostgreSQL server writes the entire content of each disk page to WAL during the first modification of that page after a checkpoint. This is needed because a page write that is in process during an operating system crash might be only partially completed, leading to an on-disk page that contains a mix of old and new data. The row-level change data normally stored in WAL will not be enough to completely restore such a page during post-crash recovery. Storing the full page image guarantees that the page can be correctly restored, but at a price in increasing the amount of data that must be written to WAL. (Because WAL replay always starts from a checkpoint, it is sufficient to do this during the first change of each page after a checkpoint. Therefore, one way to reduce the cost of full-page writes is to increase the checkpoint interval parameters.)

Turning this parameter off speeds normal operation, but might lead to a corrupt database after an operating system crash or power failure. The risks are similar to turning off fsync, though smaller. It might be safe to turn off this parameter if you have hardware (such as a battery-backed disk controller) or file-system software that reduces the risk of partial page writes to an acceptably low level (e.g., ReiserFS 4).

Turning off this parameter does not affect use of WAL archiving for point-in-time recovery (PITR) (see *Section 24.3 – page 184*).

This parameter can only be set in the postgresql.conf file or on the server command line. The default is on.

wal_buffers (integer)

The amount of memory used in shared memory for WAL data. The default is 64 kilobytes (64kB). The setting need only be large enough to hold the amount of WAL data generated by one typical transaction, since the data is written out to disk at every transaction commit. This parameter can only be set at server start.

Increasing this parameter might cause PostgreSQL to request more System V shared memory than your operating system's default configuration allows. See *Section 17.4.1* (page 61) for information on how to adjust those parameters, if necessary.

`wal_writer_delay` (`integer`)

Specifies the delay between activity rounds for the WAL writer. In each round the writer will flush WAL to disk. It then sleeps for wal_writer_delay milliseconds, and repeats. The default value is 200 milliseconds (200ms). Note that on many systems, the effective resolution of sleep delays is 10 milliseconds; setting wal_writer_delay to a value that is not a multiple of 10 might have the same results as setting it to the next higher multiple of 10. This parameter can only be set in the postgresql.conf file or on the server command line.

`commit_delay` (`integer`)

Time delay between writing a commit record to the WAL buffer and flushing the buffer out to disk, in microseconds. A nonzero delay can allow multiple transactions to be committed with only one fsync() system call, if system load is high enough that additional transactions become ready to commit within the given interval. But the delay is just wasted if no other transactions become ready to commit. Therefore, the delay is only performed if at least commit_siblings other transactions are active at the instant that a server process has written its commit record. The default is zero (no delay).

`commit_siblings` (`integer`)

Minimum number of concurrent open transactions to require before performing the commit_delay delay. A larger value makes it more probable that at least one other transaction will become ready to commit during the delay interval. The default is five transactions.

18.5.2. Checkpoints

`checkpoint_segments` (`integer`)

Maximum number of log file segments between automatic WAL checkpoints (each segment is normally 16 megabytes). The default is three segments. Increasing this parameter can increase the amount of time needed for crash recovery. This parameter can only be set in the postgresql.conf file or on the server command line.

`checkpoint_timeout` (`integer`)

Maximum time between automatic WAL checkpoints, in seconds. The default is five minutes (5min). Increasing this parameter can increase the amount of time needed for crash recovery. This parameter can only be set in the postgresql.conf file or on the server command line.

`checkpoint_completion_target` (`floating point`)

Specifies the target length of checkpoints, as a fraction of the checkpoint interval. The default is 0.5. This parameter can only be set in the postgresql.conf file or on the server command line.

`checkpoint_warning` (`integer`)

Write a message to the server log if checkpoints caused by the filling of checkpoint segment files happen closer together than this many seconds (which suggests that checkpoint_segments ought to be raised). The default is 30 seconds (30s). Zero disables the warning. This parameter can only be set in the postgresql.conf file or on the server command line.

18.5.3. Archiving

`archive_mode` (`boolean`)

When archive_mode is enabled, completed WAL segments can be sent to archive storage by setting *archive_command*. archive_mode and archive_command are separate variables so that archive_command can be changed without leaving archiving mode. This parameter can only be set at server start.

`archive_command` (`string`)

The shell command to execute to archive a completed segment of the WAL file series. Any %p in the string is replaced by the path name of the file to archive, and any %f is replaced by the file name only. (The path name is relative to the working directory of the server, i.e., the cluster's data directory.) Use %% to embed an actual % character in the command. For more information see *Section 24.3.1* (page 185). This parameter can only be set in the postgresql.conf file or on the server command line. It is ignored unless archive_mode was enabled at server start. If archive_command is an empty string (the default) while archive_mode is enabled, then WAL archiving is temporarily disabled, but the server continues to accumulate WAL segment files in the expectation that a command will soon be provided.

It is important for the command to return a zero exit status if and only if it succeeds. Examples:

```
archive_command = 'cp "%p" /mnt/server/archivedir/"%f"'
archive_command = 'copy "%p" "C:\\server\\archivedir\\%f"'  # Windows
```

`archive_timeout` (`integer`)

The *archive_command* is only invoked on completed WAL segments. Hence, if your server generates little WAL traffic (or has slack periods where it does so), there could be a long delay between the completion of a transaction and its safe recording in archive storage. To put a limit on how old unarchived data can be, you can set archive_timeout to force the server to switch to a new WAL segment file periodically. When this parameter is greater than zero, the server will switch to a new segment file whenever this many seconds have elapsed since the last segment file switch. Note that archived files that are closed early due to a forced switch are still the same length as completely full files. Therefore, it is unwise to use a very short archive_timeout — it will bloat your archive storage. archive_timeout settings of a minute or so are usually reasonable. This parameter can only be set in the postgresql.conf file or on the server command line.

18.6. Query Planning

18.6.1. Planner Method Configuration

These configuration parameters provide a crude method of influencing the query plans chosen by the query optimizer. If the default plan chosen by the optimizer for a particular query is not optimal, a temporary solution can be found by using one of these configuration parameters to force the optimizer to choose a different plan. Turning one of these settings off permanently is seldom a good idea, however. Better ways to improve the quality of the plans chosen by the optimizer include adjusting the *Planner Cost Constants*, running ANALYZE more frequently, increasing the value of the *default_statistics_target* configuration parameter, and increasing the amount of statistics collected for specific columns using ALTER TABLE SET STATISTICS.

enable_bitmapscan (boolean)

> Enables or disables the query planner's use of bitmap-scan plan types. The default is on.

enable_hashagg (boolean)

> Enables or disables the query planner's use of hashed aggregation plan types. The default is on.

enable_hashjoin (boolean)

> Enables or disables the query planner's use of hash-join plan types. The default is on.

enable_indexscan (boolean)

> Enables or disables the query planner's use of index-scan plan types. The default is on.

enable_mergejoin (boolean)

> Enables or disables the query planner's use of merge-join plan types. The default is on.

enable_nestloop (boolean)

> Enables or disables the query planner's use of nested-loop join plans. It's not possible to suppress nested-loop joins entirely, but turning this variable off discourages the planner from using one if there are other methods available. The default is on.

enable_seqscan (boolean)

> Enables or disables the query planner's use of sequential scan plan types. It's not possible to suppress sequential scans entirely, but turning this variable off discourages the planner from using one if there are other methods available. The default is on.

enable_sort (boolean)

> Enables or disables the query planner's use of explicit sort steps. It's not possible to suppress explicit sorts entirely, but turning this variable off discourages the planner from using one if there are other methods available. The default is on.

enable_tidscan (boolean)

> Enables or disables the query planner's use of TID scan plan types. The default is on.

18.6.2. Planner Cost Constants

The *cost* variables described in this section are measured on an arbitrary scale. Only their relative values matter, hence scaling them all up or down by the same factor will result in no change in the planner's choices. Traditionally, these variables have been referenced to sequential page fetches as the unit of cost; that is, seq_page_cost is conventionally set to 1.0 and the other cost variables are set with reference to that. But you can use a different scale if you prefer, such as actual execution times in milliseconds on a particular machine.

Note

> Unfortunately, there is no well-defined method for determining ideal values for the cost variables. They are best treated as averages over the entire mix of queries that a particular installation will get. This means that changing them on the basis of just a few experiments is very risky.

seq_page_cost (floating point)

> Sets the planner's estimate of the cost of a disk page fetch that is part of a series of sequential fetches. The default is 1.0.

random_page_cost (floating point)

> Sets the planner's estimate of the cost of a non-sequentially-fetched disk page. The default is 4.0. Reducing this value relative to seq_page_cost will cause the system to prefer index scans; raising it will make index scans look relatively more expensive. You can raise or lower both values together to change the importance of disk I/O costs relative to CPU costs, which are described by the following parameters.

Tip

> Although the system will let you set random_page_cost to less than seq_page_cost, it is not physically sensible to do so. However, setting them equal

makes sense if the database is entirely cached in RAM, since in that case there is no
penalty for touching pages out of sequence. Also, in a heavily-cached database you
should lower both values relative to the CPU parameters, since the cost of fetching a
page already in RAM is much smaller than it would normally be.

cpu_tuple_cost (floating point)

Sets the planner's estimate of the cost of processing each row during a query. The default
is 0.01.

cpu_index_tuple_cost (floating point)

Sets the planner's estimate of the cost of processing each index entry during an index
scan. The default is 0.005.

cpu_operator_cost (floating point)

Sets the planner's estimate of the cost of processing each operator or function executed
during a query. The default is 0.0025.

effective_cache_size (integer)

Sets the planner's assumption about the effective size of the disk cache that is available
to a single query. This is factored into estimates of the cost of using an index; a higher
value makes it more likely index scans will be used, a lower value makes it more likely
sequential scans will be used. When setting this parameter you should consider both
PostgreSQL's shared buffers and the portion of the kernel's disk cache that will be used
for PostgreSQL data files. Also, take into account the expected number of concurrent
queries on different tables, since they will have to share the available space. This
parameter has no effect on the size of shared memory allocated by PostgreSQL, nor does
it reserve kernel disk cache; it is used only for estimation purposes. The default is 128
megabytes (128MB).

18.6.3. Genetic Query Optimizer

The genetic query optimizer (GEQO) is an algorithm that does query planning using
heuristic searching. This reduces planning time for complex queries (those joining many
relations), at the cost of producing plans that are sometimes inferior to those found by the
normal exhaustive-search algorithm. Also, GEQO's searching is randomized and therefore
its plans may vary nondeterministically. For more information see *Chapter 49*.

geqo (boolean)

Enables or disables genetic query optimization. This is on by default. It is usually best
not to turn it off in production; the geqo_threshold variable provides a more granular
way to control use of GEQO.

`geqo_threshold` (`integer`)

Use genetic query optimization to plan queries with at least this many FROM items involved. (Note that a FULL OUTER JOIN construct counts as only one FROM item.) The default is 12. For simpler queries it is usually best to use the deterministic, exhaustive planner, but for queries with many tables the deterministic planner takes too long.

`geqo_effort` (`integer`)

Controls the trade-off between planning time and query plan quality in GEQO. This variable must be an integer in the range from 1 to 10. The default value is five. Larger values increase the time spent doing query planning, but also increase the likelihood that an efficient query plan will be chosen.

geqo_effort doesn't actually do anything directly; it is only used to compute the default values for the other variables that influence GEQO behavior (described below). If you prefer, you can set the other parameters by hand instead.

`geqo_pool_size` (`integer`)

Controls the pool size used by GEQO, that is the number of individuals in the genetic population. It must be at least two, and useful values are typically 100 to 1000. If it is set to zero (the default setting) then a suitable value is chosen based on geqo_effort and the number of tables in the query.

`geqo_generations` (`integer`)

Controls the number of generations used by GEQO, that is the number of iterations of the algorithm. It must be at least one, and useful values are in the same range as the pool size. If it is set to zero (the default setting) then a suitable value is chosen based on geqo_pool_size.

`geqo_selection_bias` (`floating point`)

Controls the selection bias used by GEQO. The selection bias is the selective pressure within the population. Values can be from 1.50 to 2.00; the latter is the default.

18.6.4. Other Planner Options

`default_statistics_target` (`integer`)

Sets the default statistics target for table columns that have not had a column-specific target set via ALTER TABLE SET STATISTICS. Larger values increase the time needed to do ANALYZE, but might improve the quality of the planner's estimates. The default is 100. For more information on the use of statistics by the PostgreSQL query planner, refer to *Section 14.2* - Vol.I page 380.

constraint_exclusion (enum)

> Controls the query planner's use of table constraints to optimize queries. The allowed values of constraint_exclusion are on (examine constraints for all tables), off (never examine constraints), and partition (examine constraints only for inheritance child tables and UNION ALL subqueries). partition is the default setting.
>
> When this parameter allows it for a particular table, the planner compares query conditions with the table's CHECK constraints, and omits scanning tables for which the conditions contradict the constraints. For example:
>
> ```
> CREATE TABLE parent(key integer, ...);
> CREATE TABLE child1000(check (key between 1000 and 1999)) INHERITS(parent);
> CREATE TABLE child2000(check (key between 2000 and 2999)) INHERITS(parent);
> ...
> SELECT * FROM parent WHERE key = 2400;
> ```
>
> With constraint exclusion enabled, this SELECT will not scan child1000 at all. This can improve performance when inheritance is used to build partitioned tables.
>
> Currently, constraint exclusion is enabled by default only for cases that are often used to implement table partitioning. Turning it on for all tables imposes extra planning overhead that is quite noticeable on simple queries, and most often will yield no benefit for simple queries. If you have no partitioned tables you might prefer to turn it off entirely.
>
> Refer to *Section 5.9.4* - Vol.I page 107 for more information on using constraint exclusion and partitioning.

cursor_tuple_fraction (floating point)

> Sets the planner's estimate of the fraction of a cursor's rows that will be retrieved. The default is 0.1. Smaller values of this setting bias the planner towards using "fast start" plans for cursors, which will retrieve the first few rows quickly while perhaps taking a long time to fetch all rows. Larger values put more emphasis on the total estimated time. At the maximum setting of 1.0, cursors are planned exactly like regular queries, considering only the total estimated time and not how soon the first rows might be delivered.

from_collapse_limit (integer)

> The planner will merge sub-queries into upper queries if the resulting FROM list would have no more than this many items. Smaller values reduce planning time but might yield inferior query plans. The default is eight. For more information see *Section 14.3* - Vol.I page 381.
>
> Setting this value to *geqo_threshold* or more may trigger use of the GEQO planner, resulting in nondeterministic plans. See *Section 18.6.3* (page 96).

`join_collapse_limit` (`integer`)

The planner will rewrite explicit `JOIN` constructs (except `FULL JOIN`s) into lists of `FROM` items whenever a list of no more than this many items would result. Smaller values reduce planning time but might yield inferior query plans.

By default, this variable is set the same as `from_collapse_limit`, which is appropriate for most uses. Setting it to 1 prevents any reordering of explicit `JOIN`s. Thus, the explicit join order specified in the query will be the actual order in which the relations are joined. The query planner does not always choose the optimal join order; advanced users can elect to temporarily set this variable to 1, and then specify the join order they desire explicitly. For more information see *Section 14.3 - Vol.I page 381*.

Setting this value to *geqo_threshold* or more may trigger use of the GEQO planner, resulting in nondeterministic plans. See *Section 18.6.3* (page 96).

18.7. Error Reporting and Logging

18.7.1. Where To Log

`log_destination` (`string`)

PostgreSQL supports several methods for logging server messages, including stderr, csvlog and syslog. On Windows, eventlog is also supported. Set this parameter to a list of desired log destinations separated by commas. The default is to log to stderr only. This parameter can only be set in the postgresql.conf file or on the server command line.

If csvlog is included in log_destination, log entries are output in "comma separated value" format, which is convenient for loading them into programs. See *Section 18.7.4* (page 107) for details. logging_collector must be enabled to generate CSV-format log output.

 Note

> On most Unix systems, you will need to alter the configuration of your system's syslog daemon in order to make use of the syslog option for log_destination. PostgreSQL can log to syslog facilities LOCAL0 through LOCAL7 (see *syslog_facility*), but the default syslog configuration on most platforms will discard all such messages. You will need to add something like
>
> ```
> local0.*    /var/log/postgresql
> ```
> to the syslog daemon's configuration file to make it work.

`logging_collector` (`boolean`)

This parameter allows messages sent to stderr, and CSV-format log output, to be captured and redirected into log files. This approach is often more useful than logging to syslog, since some types of messages might not appear in syslog output (a common example is dynamic-linker failure messages). This parameter can only be set at server start.

log_directory (string)

When logging_collector is enabled, this parameter determines the directory in which log files will be created. It can be specified as an absolute path, or relative to the cluster data directory. This parameter can only be set in the postgresql.conf file or on the server command line.

log_filename (string)

When logging_collector is enabled, this parameter sets the file names of the created log files. The value is treated as a strftime pattern, so %-escapes can be used to specify time-varying file names. (Note that if there are any time-zone-dependent %-escapes, the computation is done in the zone specified by *log_timezone*.) Note that the system's strftime is not used directly, so platform-specific (nonstandard) extensions do not work.

If you specify a file name without escapes, you should plan to use a log rotation utility to avoid eventually filling the entire disk. In releases prior to 8.4, if no % escapes were present, PostgreSQL would append the epoch of the new log file's creation time, but this is no longer the case.

If CSV-format output is enabled in log_destination, .csv will be appended to the timestamped log file name to create the file name for CSV-format output. (If log_filename ends in .log, the suffix is replaced instead.) In the case of the example above, the CSV file name will be server_log.1093827753.csv.

This parameter can only be set in the postgresql.conf file or on the server command line.

log_rotation_age (integer)

When logging_collector is enabled, this parameter determines the maximum lifetime of an individual log file. After this many minutes have elapsed, a new log file will be created. Set to zero to disable time-based creation of new log files. This parameter can only be set in the postgresql.conf file or on the server command line.

log_rotation_size (integer)

When logging_collector is enabled, this parameter determines the maximum size of an individual log file. After this many kilobytes have been emitted into a log file, a new log file will be created. Set to zero to disable size-based creation of new log files. This parameter can only be set in the postgresql.conf file or on the server command line.

log_truncate_on_rotation (boolean)

When logging_collector is enabled, this parameter will cause PostgreSQL to truncate (overwrite), rather than append to, any existing log file of the same name. However, truncation will occur only when a new file is being opened due to time-based rotation, not during server startup or size-based rotation. When off, pre-existing files will be appended to in all cases. For example, using this setting in combination with a log_filename like postgresql-%H.log would result in generating twenty-four hourly log files and then cyclically overwriting them. This parameter can only be set in the postgresql.conf file or on the server command line.

Example: To keep 7 days of logs, one log file per day named server_log.Mon, server_log.Tue, etc, and automatically overwrite last week's log with this week's log, set log_filename to server_log.%a, log_truncate_on_rotation to on, and log_rotation_age to 1440.

Example: To keep 24 hours of logs, one log file per hour, but also rotate sooner if the log file size exceeds 1GB, set log_filename to server_log.%H%M, log_truncate_on_rotation to on, log_rotation_age to 60, and log_rotation_size to 1000000. Including %M in log_filename allows any size-driven rotations that might occur to select a file name different from the hour's initial file name.

syslog_facility (enum)

When logging to syslog is enabled, this parameter determines the syslog "facility" to be used. You can choose from LOCAL0, LOCAL1, LOCAL2, LOCAL3, LOCAL4, LOCAL5, LOCAL6, LOCAL7; the default is LOCAL0. See also the documentation of your system's syslog daemon. This parameter can only be set in the postgresql.conf file or on the server command line.

syslog_ident (string)

When logging to syslog is enabled, this parameter determines the program name used to identify PostgreSQL messages in syslog logs. The default is postgres. This parameter can only be set in the postgresql.conf file or on the server command line.

18.7.2. When To Log

client_min_messages (enum)

Controls which message levels are sent to the client. Valid values are DEBUG5, DEBUG4, DEBUG3, DEBUG2, DEBUG1, LOG, NOTICE, WARNING, ERROR, FATAL, and PANIC. Each level includes all the levels that follow it. The later the level, the fewer messages are sent. The default is NOTICE. Note that LOG has a different rank here than in log_min_messages.

log_min_messages (enum)

Controls which message levels are written to the server log. Valid values are DEBUG5, DEBUG4, DEBUG3, DEBUG2, DEBUG1, INFO, NOTICE, WARNING, ERROR, LOG,

FATAL, and PANIC. Each level includes all the levels that follow it. The later the level, the fewer messages are sent to the log. The default is WARNING. Note that LOG has a different rank here than in client_min_messages. Only superusers can change this setting.

`log_error_verbosity` (enum)

Controls the amount of detail written in the server log for each message that is logged. Valid values are TERSE, DEFAULT, and VERBOSE, each adding more fields to displayed messages. Only superusers can change this setting.

`log_min_error_statement` (enum)

Controls whether or not the SQL statement that causes an error condition will be recorded in the server log. The current SQL statement is included in the log entry for any message of the specified severity or higher. Valid values are DEBUG5, DEBUG4, DEBUG3, DEBUG2, DEBUG1, INFO, NOTICE, WARNING, ERROR, LOG, FATAL, and PANIC. The default is ERROR, which means statements causing errors, log messages, fatal errors, or panics will be logged. To effectively turn off logging of failing statements, set this parameter to PANIC. Only superusers can change this setting.

`log_min_duration_statement` (integer)

Causes the duration of each completed statement to be logged if the statement ran for at least the specified number of milliseconds. Setting this to zero prints all statement durations. Minus-one (the default) disables logging statement durations. For example, if you set it to 250ms then all SQL statements that run 250ms or longer will be logged. Enabling this parameter can be helpful in tracking down unoptimized queries in your applications. Only superusers can change this setting.

For clients using extended query protocol, durations of the Parse, Bind, and Execute steps are logged independently.

 Note

When using this option together with *log_statement*, the text of statements that are logged because of `log_statement` will not be repeated in the duration log message. If you are not using syslog, it is recommended that you log the PID or session ID using *log_line_prefix* so that you can link the statement message to the later duration message using the process ID or session ID.

`silent_mode` (boolean)

Runs the server silently. If this parameter is set, the server will automatically run in background and any controlling terminals are disassociated. The server's standard output and standard error are redirected to /dev/null, so any messages sent to them will be lost. Unless syslog logging is selected or `logging_collector` is enabled, using this parameter is discouraged because it makes it impossible to see error messages. This parameter can only be set at server start.

Table 18-1 explains the message severity levels used by PostgreSQL. If logging output is sent to syslog or Windows' eventlog, the severity levels are translated as shown in the table.

Severity	Usage	syslog	eventlog
DEBUG1..DEBUG5	Provides successively-more-detailed information for use by developers.	DEBUG	INFORMATION
INFO	Provides information implicitly requested by the user, e.g., output from VACUUM VERBOSE.	INFO	INFORMATION
NOTICE	Provides information that might be helpful to users, e.g., notice of truncation of long identifiers.	NOTICE	INFORMATION
WARNING	Provides warnings of likely problems, e.g., COMMIT outside a transaction block.	NOTICE	WARNING
ERROR	Reports an error that caused the current command to abort.	WARNING	ERROR
LOG	Reports information of interest to administrators, e.g., checkpoint activity.	INFO	INFORMATION
FATAL	Reports an error that caused the current session to abort.	ERR	ERROR
PANIC	Reports an error that caused all database sessions to abort.	CRIT	ERROR

Table 18-1. Message severity levels

18.7.3. What To Log

`debug_print_parse` (boolean)
`debug_print_rewritten` (boolean)
`debug_print_plan` (boolean)

These parameters enable various debugging output to be emitted. When set, they print the resulting parse tree, the query rewriter output, or the execution plan for each executed query. These messages are emitted at LOG message level, so by default they will appear in the server log but will not be sent to the client. You can change that by adjusting *client_min_messages* and/or *log_min_messages*. These parameters are off by default.

`debug_pretty_print` (boolean)

When set, debug_pretty_print indents the messages produced by debug_print_parse, debug_print_rewritten, or debug_print_plan. This results in more readable but much longer output than the "compact" format used when it is off. It is on by default.

`log_checkpoints` (`boolean`)

> Causes checkpoints to be logged in the server log. Some statistics about each checkpoint are included in the log messages, including the number of buffers written and the time spent writing them. This parameter can only be set in the postgresql.conf file or on the server command line. The default is off.

`log_connections` (`boolean`)

> Causes each attempted connection to the server to be logged, as well as successful completion of client authentication. This parameter can only be set in the `postgresql.conf` file or on the server command line. The default is off.

 Note

> Some client programs, like psql, attempt to connect twice while determining if a password is required, so duplicate "connection received" messages do not necessarily indicate a problem.

`log_disconnections` (`boolean`)

> This outputs a line in the server log similar to log_connections but at session termination, and includes the duration of the session. This is off by default. This parameter can only be set in the postgresql.conf file or on the server command line.

`log_duration` (`boolean`)

> Causes the duration of every completed statement to be logged. The default is `off`. Only superusers can change this setting.

> For clients using extended query protocol, durations of the Parse, Bind, and Execute steps are logged independently.

 Note

> The difference between setting this option and setting *log_min_duration_statement* to zero is that exceeding `log_min_duration_statement` forces the text of the query to be logged, but this option doesn't. Thus, if `log_duration` is on and `log_min_duration_statement` has a positive value, all durations are logged but the query text is included only for statements exceeding the threshold. This behavior can be useful for gathering statistics in high-load installations.

`log_hostname` (`boolean`)

> By default, connection log messages only show the IP address of the connecting host. Turning on this parameter causes logging of the host name as well. Note that depending on your host name resolution setup this might impose a non-negligible performance

penalty. This parameter can only be set in the postgresql.conf file or on the server command line.

`log_line_prefix` (string)

This is a printf-style string that is output at the beginning of each log line. % characters begin "escape sequences" that are replaced with status information as outlined below. Unrecognized escapes are ignored. Other characters are copied straight to the log line. Some escapes are only recognized by session processes, and do not apply to background processes such as the main server process. This parameter can only be set in the postgresql.conf file or on the server command line. The default is an empty string.

Escape	Effect	Session only
%u	User name	yes
%d	Database name	yes
%r	Remote host name or IP address, and remote port	yes
%h	Remote host name or IP address	yes
%p	Process ID	no
%t	Time stamp without milliseconds	no
%m	Time stamp with milliseconds	no
%i	Command tag: type of session's current command	yes
%c	Session ID: see below	no
%l	Number of the log line for each session or process, starting at 1	no
%s	Process start time stamp	no
%v	Virtual transaction ID (backendID/localXID)	no
%x	Transaction ID (0 if none is assigned)	no
%q	Produces no output, but tells non-session processes to stop at this point in the string; ignored by session processes	no
%%	Literal %	no

The %c escape prints a quasi-unique session identifier, consisting of two 4-byte hexadecimal numbers (without leading zeros) separated by a dot. The numbers are the process start time and the process ID, so %c can also be used as a space saving way of printing those items. For example, to generate the session identifier from pg_stat_activity, use this query:

```
SELECT to_hex(EXTRACT(EPOCH FROM backend_start)::integer) || '.' ||
       to_hex(procpid)
FROM pg_stat_activity;
```

Tip

If you set a nonempty value for `log_line_prefix`, you should usually make its last character be a space, to provide visual separation from the rest of the log line. A punctuation character could be used too.

Tip

Syslog produces its own time stamp and process ID information, so you probably do not want to use those escapes if you are logging to syslog.

`log_lock_waits` (`boolean`)

Controls whether a log message is produced when a session waits longer than *deadlock_timeout* to acquire a lock. This is useful in determining if lock waits are causing poor performance. The default is off.

`log_statement` (`enum`)

Controls which SQL statements are logged. Valid values are none, ddl, mod, and all. ddl logs all data definition statements, such as CREATE, ALTER, and DROP statements. mod logs all ddl statements, plus data-modifying statements such as INSERT, UPDATE, DELETE, TRUNCATE, and COPY FROM. PREPARE, EXECUTE, and EXPLAIN ANALYZE statements are also logged if their contained command is of an appropriate type. For clients using extended query protocol, logging occurs when an Execute message is received, and values of the Bind parameters are included (with any embedded single-quote marks doubled).

The default is none. Only superusers can change this setting.

Note

Statements that contain simple syntax errors are not logged even by the `log_statement` = `all` setting, because the log message is emitted only after basic parsing has been done to determine the statement type. In the case of extended query protocol, this setting likewise does not log statements that fail before the Execute phase (i.e., during parse analysis or planning). Set `log_min_error_statement` to ERROR (or lower) to log such statements.

`log_temp_files` (`integer`)

Controls logging of use of temporary files. Temporary files can be created for sorts, hashes, and temporary query results. A log entry is made for each temporary file when it is deleted. A value of zero logs all temporary files, while positive values log only files whose size is greater than or equal to the specified number of kilobytes. The default setting is -1, which disables such logging. Only superusers can change this setting.

log_timezone (string)

> Sets the time zone used for timestamps written in the log. Unlike *timezone*, this value is cluster-wide, so that all sessions will report timestamps consistently. The default is unknown, which means to use whatever the system environment specifies as the time zone. See *Section 8.5.3* - Vol.I page 154 for more information. This parameter can only be set in the postgresql.conf file or on the server command line.

18.7.4. Using CSV-Format Log Output

Including csvlog in the log_destination list provides a convenient way to import log files into a database table. This option emits log lines in comma-separated-value format, with these columns: timestamp with milliseconds, user name, database name, process ID, host:port number, session ID, per-session or -process line number, command tag, session start time, virtual transaction ID, regular transaction id, error severity, SQL state code, error message, error message detail, hint, internal query that led to the error (if any), character count of the error position thereof, error context, user query that led to the error (if any and enabled by log_min_error_statement), character count of the error position thereof, location of the error in the PostgreSQL source code (if log_error_verbosity is set to verbose). Here is a sample table definition for storing CSV-format log output:

```
CREATE TABLE postgres_log
(
  log_time timestamp(3) with time zone,
  user_name text,
  database_name text,
  process_id integer,
  connection_from text,
  session_id text,
  session_line_num bigint,
  command_tag text,
  session_start_time timestamp with time zone,
  virtual_transaction_id text,
  transaction_id bigint,
  error_severity text,
  sql_state_code text,
  message text,
  detail text,
  hint text,
  internal_query text,
  internal_query_pos integer,
  context text,
  query text,
  query_pos integer,
  location text,
  PRIMARY KEY (session_id, session_line_num)
);
```

To import a log file into this table, use the COPY FROM command:

```
COPY postgres_log FROM '/full/path/to/logfile.csv' WITH csv;
```

There are a few things you need to do to simplify importing CSV log files easily and automatically:

1. Set `log_filename` and `log_rotation_age` to provide a consistent, predictable naming scheme for your log files. This lets you predict what the file name will be and know when an individual log file is complete and therefore ready to be imported.

2. Set `log_rotation_size` to 0 to disable size-based log rotation, as it makes the log file name difficult to predict.

3. Set `log_truncate_on_rotation` to on so that old log data isn't mixed with the new in the same file.

4. The table definition above includes a primary key specification. This is useful to protect against accidentally importing the same information twice. The COPY command commits all of the data it imports at one time, so any error will cause the entire import to fail. If you import a partial log file and later import the file again when it is complete, the primary key violation will cause the import to fail. Wait until the log is complete and closed before importing. This procedure will also protect against accidentally importing a partial line that hasn't been completely written, which would also cause COPY to fail.

18.8. Run-Time Statistics

18.8.1. Query and Index Statistics Collector

These parameters control server-wide statistics collection features. When statistics collection is enabled, the data that is produced can be accessed via the pg_stat and pg_statio family of system views. Refer to *Chapter 26* (page 210) for more information.

`track_activities` (boolean)

Enables the collection of information on the currently executing command of each session, along with the time at which that command began execution. This parameter is on by default. Note that even when enabled, this information is not visible to all users, only to superusers and the user owning the session being reported on; so it should not represent a security risk. Only superusers can change this setting.

`track_activity_query_size` (integer)

Specifies the number of bytes reserved to track the currently executing command for each active session, for the pg_stat_activity.current_query field. The default value is 1024. This parameter can only be set at server start.

track_counts (boolean)

> Enables collection of statistics on database activity. This parameter is on by default, because the autovacuum daemon needs the collected information. Only superusers can change this setting.

track_functions (enum)

> Enables tracking of function call counts and time used. Specify pl to track only procedural-language functions, all to also track SQL and C language functions. The default is none, which disables function statistics tracking. Only superusers can change this setting.

 Note

> SQL-language functions that are simple enough to be "inlined" into the calling query will not be tracked, regardless of this setting.

update_process_title (boolean)

> Enables updating of the process title every time a new SQL command is received by the server. The process title is typically viewed by the ps command, or in Windows by using the Process Explorer. Only superusers can change this setting.

stats_temp_directory (string)

> Sets the directory to store temporary statistics data in. This can be a path relative to the data directory or an absolute path. The default is pg_stat_tmp. Pointing this at a RAM based filesystem will decrease physical I/O requirements and can lead to improved performance. This parameter can only be set in the postgresql.conf file or on the server command line.

18.8.2. Statistics Monitoring

log_statement_stats (boolean)
log_parser_stats (boolean)
log_planner_stats (boolean)
log_executor_stats (boolean)

> For each query, write performance statistics of the respective module to the server log. This is a crude profiling instrument. log_statement_stats reports total statement statistics, while the others report per-module statistics. log_statement_stats cannot be enabled together with any of the per-module options. All of these options are disabled by default. Only superusers can change these settings.

18.9. Automatic Vacuuming

These settings control the behavior of the *autovacuum* feature. Refer to *Section 23.1.5* (page 175) for more information.

autovacuum (boolean)

> Controls whether the server should run the autovacuum launcher daemon. This is on by default; however, *track_counts* must also be turned on for autovacuum to work. This parameter can only be set in the postgresql.conf file or on the server command line.
>
> Note that even when this parameter is disabled, the system will launch autovacuum processes if necessary to prevent transaction ID wraparound. See *Section 23.1.4* – page 172 for more information.

log_autovacuum_min_duration (integer)

> Causes each action executed by autovacuum to be logged if it ran for at least the specified number of milliseconds. Setting this to zero logs all autovacuum actions. Minus-one (the default) disables logging autovacuum actions. For example, if you set this to 250ms then all automatic vacuums and analyzes that run 250ms or longer will be logged. Enabling this parameter can be helpful in tracking autovacuum activity. This setting can only be set in the postgresql.conf file or on the server command line.

autovacuum_max_workers (integer)

> Specifies the maximum number of autovacuum processes (other than the autovacuum launcher) which may be running at any one time. The default is three. This parameter can only be set in the postgresql.conf file or on the server command line.

autovacuum_naptime (integer)

> Specifies the minimum delay between autovacuum runs on any given database. In each round the daemon examines the database and issues VACUUM and ANALYZE commands as needed for tables in that database. The delay is measured in seconds, and the default is one minute (1m). This parameter can only be set in the postgresql.conf file or on the server command line.

autovacuum_vacuum_threshold (integer)

> Specifies the minimum number of updated or deleted tuples needed to trigger a VACUUM in any one table. The default is 50 tuples. This parameter can only be set in the postgresql.conf file or on the server command line. This setting can be overridden for individual tables by changing storage parameters.

autovacuum_analyze_threshold (integer)

> Specifies the minimum number of inserted, updated or deleted tuples needed to trigger an ANALYZE in any one table. The default is 50 tuples. This parameter can only be set

in the postgresql.conf file or on the server command line. This setting can be overridden for individual tables by changing storage parameters.

`autovacuum_vacuum_scale_factor` (floating point)

Specifies a fraction of the table size to add to autovacuum_vacuum_threshold when deciding whether to trigger a VACUUM. The default is 0.2 (20% of table size). This parameter can only be set in the postgresql.conf file or on the server command line. This setting can be overridden for individual tables by changing storage parameters.

`autovacuum_analyze_scale_factor` (floating point)

Specifies a fraction of the table size to add to autovacuum_analyze_threshold when deciding whether to trigger an ANALYZE. The default is 0.1 (10% of table size). This parameter can only be set in the postgresql.conf file or on the server command line. This setting can be overridden for individual tables by changing storage parameters.

`autovacuum_freeze_max_age` (integer)

Specifies the maximum age (in transactions) that a table's pg_class.relfrozenxid field can attain before a VACUUM operation is forced to prevent transaction ID wraparound within the table. Note that the system will launch autovacuum processes to prevent wraparound even when autovacuum is otherwise disabled. The default is 200 million transactions. This parameter can only be set at server start, but the setting can be reduced for individual tables by changing storage parameters. For more information see *Section 23.1.4* (page 172).

`autovacuum_vacuum_cost_delay` (integer)

Specifies the cost delay value that will be used in automatic VACUUM operations. If -1 is specified, the regular *vacuum_cost_delay* value will be used. The default value is 20 milliseconds. This parameter can only be set in the postgresql.conf file or on the server command line. This setting can be overridden for individual tables by changing storage parameters.

`autovacuum_vacuum_cost_limit` (integer)

Specifies the cost limit value that will be used in automatic VACUUM operations. If -1 is specified (which is the default), the regular *vacuum_cost_limit* value will be used. Note that the value is distributed proportionally among the running autovacuum workers, if there is more than one, so that the sum of the limits of each worker never exceeds the limit on this variable. This parameter can only be set in the postgresql.conf file or on the server command line. This setting can be overridden for individual tables by changing storage parameters.

18.10. Client Connection Defaults

18.10.1. Statement Behavior

search_path (string)

This variable specifies the order in which schemas are searched when an object (table, data type, function, etc.) is referenced by a simple name with no schema component. When there are objects of identical names in different schemas, the one found first in the search path is used. An object that is not in any of the schemas in the search path can only be referenced by specifying its containing schema with a qualified (dotted) name.

The value for search_path has to be a comma-separated list of schema names. If one of the list items is the special value $user, then the schema having the name returned by SESSION_USER is substituted, if there is such a schema. (If not, $user is ignored.)

The system catalog schema, pg_catalog, is always searched, whether it is mentioned in the path or not. If it is mentioned in the path then it will be searched in the specified order. If pg_catalog is not in the path then it will be searched *before* searching any of the path items.

Likewise, the current session's temporary-table schema, pg_temp_*nnn*, is always searched if it exists. It can be explicitly listed in the path by using the alias pg_temp. If it is not listed in the path then it is searched first (before even pg_catalog). However, the temporary schema is only searched for relation (table, view, sequence, etc) and data type names. It will never be searched for function or operator names.

When objects are created without specifying a particular target schema, they will be placed in the first schema listed in the search path. An error is reported if the search path is empty.

The default value for this parameter is '"$user", public' (where the second part will be ignored if there is no schema named public). This supports shared use of a database (where no users have private schemas, and all share use of public), private per-user schemas, and combinations of these. Other effects can be obtained by altering the default search path setting, either globally or per-user.

The current effective value of the search path can be examined via the SQL function current_schemas(). This is not quite the same as examining the value of search_path, since current_schemas() shows how the requests appearing in search_path were resolved.

For more information on schema handling, see *Section 5.7*- Vol.I page 93.

default_tablespace (string)

This variable specifies the default tablespace in which to create objects (tables and indexes) when a CREATE command does not explicitly specify a tablespace.

The value is either the name of a tablespace, or an empty string to specify using the default tablespace of the current database. If the value does not match the name of any existing tablespace, PostgreSQL will automatically use the default tablespace of the current database. If a nondefault tablespace is specified, the user must have CREATE privilege for it, or creation attempts will fail.

This variable is not used for temporary tables; for them, *temp_tablespaces* is consulted instead.

For more information on tablespaces, see *Section 21.6* – page 155.

temp_tablespaces (string)

This variable specifies tablespace(s) in which to create temporary objects (temp tables and indexes on temp tables) when a CREATE command does not explicitly specify a tablespace. Temporary files for purposes such as sorting large data sets are also created in these tablespace(s).

The value is a list of names of tablespaces. When there is more than one name in the list, PostgreSQL chooses a random member of the list each time a temporary object is to be created; except that within a transaction, successively created temporary objects are placed in successive tablespaces from the list. If the selected element of the list is an empty string, PostgreSQL will automatically use the default tablespace of the current database instead.

When temp_tablespaces is set interactively, specifying a nonexistent tablespace is an error, as is specifying a tablespace for which the user does not have CREATE privilege. However, when using a previously set value, nonexistent tablespaces are ignored, as are tablespaces for which the user lacks CREATE privilege. In particular, this rule applies when using a value set in postgresql.conf.

The default value is an empty string, which results in all temporary objects being created in the default tablespace of the current database.

See also default_tablespace.

check_function_bodies (boolean)

This parameter is normally on. When set to off, it disables validation of the function body string during CREATE FUNCTION. Disabling validation is occasionally useful to avoid problems such as forward references when restoring function definitions from a dump.

default_transaction_isolation (enum)

Each SQL transaction has an isolation level, which can be either "read uncommitted", "read committed", "repeatable read", or "serializable". This parameter controls the default isolation level of each new transaction. The default is "read committed".

Consult *Chapter 13* - Vol.I page 361 and SET TRANSACTION for more information.

`default_transaction_read_only` (boolean)

A read-only SQL transaction cannot alter non-temporary tables. This parameter controls the default read-only status of each new transaction. The default is `off` (read/write).

Consult SET TRANSACTION for more information.

`session_replication_role` (enum)

Controls firing of replication-related triggers and rules for the current session. Setting this variable requires superuser privilege and results in discarding any previously cached query plans. Possible values are origin (the default), replica and local. See ALTER TABLE for more information.

`statement_timeout` (integer)

Abort any statement that takes over the specified number of milliseconds, starting from the time the command arrives at the server from the client. If `log_min_error_statement` is set to ERROR or lower, the statement that timed out will also be logged. A value of zero (the default) turns off the limitation.

Setting statement_timeout in postgresql.conf is not recommended because it affects all sessions.

`vacuum_freeze_table_age` (integer)

VACUUM performs a whole-table scan if the table's pg_class.relfrozenxid field has reached the age specified by this setting. The default is 150 million transactions. Although users can set this value anywhere from zero to one billion, VACUUM will silently limit the effective value to 95% of *autovacuum_freeze_max_age*, so that a periodical manual VACUUM has a chance to run before an anti-wraparound autovacuum is launched for the table. For more information see *Section 23.1.4* (page 172).

`vacuum_freeze_min_age` (integer)

Specifies the cutoff age (in transactions) that VACUUM should use to decide whether to replace transaction IDs with FrozenXID while scanning a table. The default is 50 million transactions. Although users can set this value anywhere from zero to one billion, VACUUM will silently limit the effective value to half the value of *autovacuum_freeze_max_age*, so that there is not an unreasonably short time between forced autovacuums. For more information see *Section 23.1.4* (page 172).

`xmlbinary` (enum)

Sets how binary values are to be encoded in XML. This applies for example when bytea values are converted to XML by the functions xmlelement or xmlforest. Possible values are base64 and hex, which are both defined in the XML Schema standard. The default is base64. For further information about XML-related functions, see *Section 9.14* - Vol.I page 250.

The actual choice here is mostly a matter of taste, constrained only by possible restrictions in client applications. Both methods support all possible values, although the hex encoding will be somewhat larger than the base64 encoding.

`xmloption (enum)`

Sets whether DOCUMENT or CONTENT is implicit when converting between XML and character string values. See *Section 8.13* - Vol.I page 171 for a description of this. Valid values are DOCUMENT and CONTENT. The default is CONTENT.

According to the SQL standard, the command to set this option is

```
SET XML OPTION { DOCUMENT | CONTENT };
```

This syntax is also available in PostgreSQL.

18.10.2. Locale and Formatting

`DateStyle (string)`

Sets the display format for date and time values, as well as the rules for interpreting ambiguous date input values. For historical reasons, this variable contains two independent components: the output format specification (ISO, Postgres, SQL, or German) and the input/output specification for year/month/day ordering (DMY, MDY, or YMD). These can be set separately or together. The keywords Euro and European are synonyms for DMY; the keywords US, NonEuro, and NonEuropean are synonyms for MDY. See *Section 8.5* - Vol.I page 148 for more information. The built-in default is ISO, MDY, but initdb will initialize the configuration file with a setting that corresponds to the behavior of the chosen lc_time locale.

`IntervalStyle (enum)`

Sets the display format for interval values. The value `sql_standard` will produce output matching SQL standard interval literals. The value `postgres` (which is the default) will produce output matching PostgreSQL releases prior to 8.4 when the *DateStyle* parameter was set to ISO. The value `postgres_verbose` will produce output matching PostgreSQL releases prior to 8.4 when the `DateStyle` parameter was set to non-ISO output. The value `iso_8601` will produce output matching the time interval "format with designators" defined in section 4.4.3.2 of ISO 8601.

The IntervalStyle parameter also affects the interpretation of ambiguous interval input. See *Section 8.5.4* - Vol.I page 156 for more information.

`timezone` (`string`)

Sets the time zone for displaying and interpreting time stamps. The default is unknown, which means to use whatever the system environment specifies as the time zone. See *Section 8.5.3* - Vol.I page 154 for more information.

`timezone_abbreviations` (`string`)

Sets the collection of time zone abbreviations that will be accepted by the server for datetime input. The default is 'Default', which is a collection that works in most of the world; there are also 'Australia' and 'India', and other collections can be defined for a particular installation. See *Appendix B* for more information.

`extra_float_digits` (`integer`)

This parameter adjusts the number of digits displayed for floating-point values, including float4, float8, and geometric data types. The parameter value is added to the standard number of digits (FLT_DIG or DBL_DIG as appropriate). The value can be set as high as 2, to include partially-significant digits; this is especially useful for dumping float data that needs to be restored exactly. Or it can be set negative to suppress unwanted digits.

`client_encoding` (`string`)

Sets the client-side encoding (character set). The default is to use the database encoding.

`lc_messages` (`string`)

Sets the language in which messages are displayed. Acceptable values are system-dependent; see *Section 22.1* – page 158 for more information. If this variable is set to the empty string (which is the default) then the value is inherited from the execution environment of the server in a system-dependent way.

On some systems, this locale category does not exist. Setting this variable will still work, but there will be no effect. Also, there is a chance that no translated messages for the desired language exist. In that case you will continue to see the English messages.

Only superusers can change this setting, because it affects the messages sent to the server log as well as to the client.

`lc_monetary` (`string`)

Sets the locale to use for formatting monetary amounts, for example with the to_char family of functions. Acceptable values are system-dependent; see *Section 22.1* (page 158) for more information. If this variable is set to the empty string (which is the default) then the value is inherited from the execution environment of the server in a system-dependent way.

`lc_numeric` (string)

Sets the locale to use for formatting numbers, for example with the to_char family of functions. Acceptable values are system-dependent; see *Section 22.1* (page 158) for more information. If this variable is set to the empty string (which is the default) then the value is inherited from the execution environment of the server in a system-dependent way.

`lc_time` (string)

Sets the locale to use for formatting dates and times, for example with the to_char family of functions. Acceptable values are system-dependent; see *Section 22.1* (page 158)for more information. If this variable is set to the empty string (which is the default) then the value is inherited from the execution environment of the server in a system-dependent way.

`default_text_search_config` (string)

Selects the text search configuration that is used by those variants of the text search functions that do not have an explicit argument specifying the configuration. See *Chapter 12 - Vol.I page 321* for further information. The built-in default is pg_catalog.simple, but initdb will initialize the configuration file with a setting that corresponds to the chosen lc_ctype locale, if a configuration matching that locale can be identified.

18.10.3. Other Defaults

`dynamic_library_path` (string)

If a dynamically loadable module needs to be opened and the file name specified in the CREATE FUNCTION or LOAD command does not have a directory component (i.e., the name does not contain a slash), the system will search this path for the required file.

The value for dynamic_library_path has to be a list of absolute directory paths separated by colons (or semi-colons on Windows). If a list element starts with the special string $libdir, the compiled-in PostgreSQL package library directory is substituted for $libdir. This is where the modules provided by the standard PostgreSQL distribution are installed. (Use pg_config --pkglibdir to find out the name of this directory.) For example:

```
dynamic_library_path = '/usr/local/lib/postgresql:/home/my_project/lib:$libdir'
```

or, in a Windows environment:

```
dynamic_library_path = 'C:\tools\postgresql;H:\my_project\lib;$libdir'
```

The default value for this parameter is `'$libdir'`. If the value is set to an empty string, the automatic path search is turned off.

This parameter can be changed at run time by superusers, but a setting done that way will only persist until the end of the client connection, so this method should be reserved for development purposes. The recommended way to set this parameter is in the postgresql.conf configuration file.

`gin_fuzzy_search_limit` (`integer`)

Soft upper limit of the size of the set returned by GIN index. For more information see *Section 52.4*.

`local_preload_libraries` (`string`)

This variable specifies one or more shared libraries that are to be preloaded at connection start. If more than one library is to be loaded, separate their names with commas. This parameter cannot be changed after the start of a particular session.

Because this is not a superuser-only option, the libraries that can be loaded are restricted to those appearing in the `plugins` subdirectory of the installation's standard library directory. (It is the database administrator's responsibility to ensure that only "safe" libraries are installed there.) Entries in `local_preload_libraries` can specify this directory explicitly, for example `$libdir/plugins/mylib`, or just specify the library name — `mylib` would have the same effect as `$libdir/plugins/mylib`.

There is no performance advantage to loading a library at session start rather than when it is first used. Rather, the intent of this feature is to allow debugging or performance-measurement libraries to be loaded into specific sessions without an explicit LOAD command being given. For example, debugging could be enabled for all sessions under a given user name by setting this parameter with ALTER USER SET.

If a specified library is not found, the connection attempt will fail.

Every PostgreSQL-supported library has a "magic block" that is checked to guarantee compatibility. For this reason, non-PostgreSQL libraries cannot be loaded in this way.

18.11. Lock Management

`deadlock_timeout` (`integer`)

This is the amount of time, in milliseconds, to wait on a lock before checking to see if there is a deadlock condition. The check for deadlock is relatively slow, so the server doesn't run it every time it waits for a lock. We optimistically assume that deadlocks are not common in production applications and just wait on the lock for a while before starting the check for a deadlock. Increasing this value reduces the amount of time wasted in needless deadlock checks, but slows down reporting of real deadlock errors. The default is one second (1s), which is probably about the smallest value you would want in practice. On a heavily loaded server you might want to raise it. Ideally the setting should exceed your typical transaction time, so as to improve the odds that a lock will be released before the waiter decides to check for deadlock.

When *log_lock_waits* is set, this parameter also determines the length of time to wait before a log message is issued about the lock wait. If you are trying to investigate locking delays you might want to set a shorter than normal deadlock_timeout.

max_locks_per_transaction (integer)

The shared lock table is created to track locks on max_locks_per_transaction * (*max_connections* + *max_prepared_transactions*) objects (e.g., tables); hence, no more than this many distinct objects can be locked at any one time. This parameter controls the average number of object locks allocated for each transaction; individual transactions can lock more objects as long as the locks of all transactions fit in the lock table. This is *not* the number of rows that can be locked; that value is unlimited. The default, 64, has historically proven sufficient, but you might need to raise this value if you have clients that touch many different tables in a single transaction. This parameter can only be set at server start.

Increasing this parameter might cause PostgreSQL to request more System V shared memory than your operating system's default configuration allows. See *Section 17.4.1* (page 61) for information on how to adjust those parameters, if necessary.

18.12. Version and Platform Compatibility

18.12.1. Previous PostgreSQL Versions

add_missing_from (boolean)

When on, tables that are referenced by a query will be automatically added to the FROM clause if not already present. This behavior does not comply with the SQL standard and many people dislike it because it can mask mistakes (such as referencing a table where you should have referenced its alias). The default is off. This variable can be enabled for compatibility with releases of PostgreSQL prior to 8.1, where this behavior was allowed by default.

Note that even when this variable is enabled, a warning message will be emitted for each implicit FROM entry referenced by a query. Users are encouraged to update their applications to not rely on this behavior, by adding all tables referenced by a query to the query's FROM clause (or its USING clause in the case of DELETE).

array_nulls (boolean)

This controls whether the array input parser recognizes unquoted NULL as specifying a null array element. By default, this is on, allowing array values containing null values to be entered. However, PostgreSQL versions before 8.2 did not support null values in arrays, and therefore would treat NULL as specifying a normal array element with the string value "NULL". For backwards compatibility with applications that require the old behavior, this variable can be turned off.

Note that it is possible to create array values containing null values even when this variable is off.

backslash_quote (enum)

This controls whether a quote mark can be represented by \' in a string literal. The preferred, SQL-standard way to represent a quote mark is by doubling it ('') but PostgreSQL has historically also accepted \'. However, use of \' creates security risks because in some client character set encodings, there are multibyte characters in which the last byte is numerically equivalent to ASCII \. If client-side code does escaping incorrectly then a SQL-injection attack is possible. This risk can be prevented by making the server reject queries in which a quote mark appears to be escaped by a backslash. The allowed values of backslash_quote are on (allow \' always), off (reject always), and safe_encoding (allow only if client encoding does not allow ASCII \ within a multibyte character). safe_encoding is the default setting.

Note that in a standard-conforming string literal, \ just means \ anyway. This parameter affects the handling of non-standard-conforming literals, including escape string syntax (E'...').

default_with_oids (boolean)

This controls whether CREATE TABLE and CREATE TABLE AS include an OID column in newly-created tables, if neither WITH OIDS nor WITHOUT OIDS is specified. It also determines whether OIDs will be included in tables created by SELECT INTO. In PostgreSQL 8.1 default_with_oids is off by default; in prior versions of PostgreSQL, it was on by default.

The use of OIDs in user tables is considered deprecated, so most installations should leave this variable disabled. Applications that require OIDs for a particular table should specify WITH OIDS when creating the table. This variable can be enabled for compatibility with old applications that do not follow this behavior.

escape_string_warning (boolean)

When on, a warning is issued if a backslash (\) appears in an ordinary string literal ('...' syntax) and standard_conforming_strings is off. The default is on.

Applications that wish to use backslash as escape should be modified to use escape string syntax (E'...'), because the default behavior of ordinary strings will change in a future release for SQL compatibility. This variable can be enabled to help detect applications that will break.

regex_flavor (enum)

The regular expression "flavor" can be set to advanced, extended, or basic. The default is advanced. The extended setting might be useful for exact backwards compatibility with pre-7.4 releases of PostgreSQL. See *Section 9.7.3.1 - Vol.I page 213* for details.

sql_inheritance (boolean)

This controls the inheritance semantics. If turned off, subtables are not included by various commands by default; basically an implied ONLY key word. This was added for compatibility with releases prior to 7.1. See *Section 5.8 - Vol.I page 98* for more information.

standard_conforming_strings (boolean)

This controls whether ordinary string literals ('...') treat backslashes literally, as specified in the SQL standard. The default is currently off, causing PostgreSQL to have its historical behavior of treating backslashes as escape characters. The default will change to on in a future release to improve compatibility with the standard. Applications can check this parameter to determine how string literals will be processed. The presence of this parameter can also be taken as an indication that the escape string syntax (E'...') is supported. Escape string syntax should be used if an application desires backslashes to be treated as escape characters.

synchronize_seqscans (boolean)

This allows sequential scans of large tables to synchronize with each other, so that concurrent scans read the same block at about the same time and hence share the I/O workload. When this is enabled, a scan might start in the middle of the table and then "wrap around" the end to cover all rows, so as to synchronize with the activity of scans already in progress. This can result in unpredictable changes in the row ordering returned by queries that have no ORDER BY clause. Setting this parameter to off ensures the pre-8.3 behavior in which a sequential scan always starts from the beginning of the table. The default is on.

18.12.2. Platform and Client Compatibility

transform_null_equals (boolean)

When on, expressions of the form *expr* = NULL (or NULL = *expr*) are treated as *expr* IS NULL, that is, they return true if *expr* evaluates to the null value, and false otherwise. The correct SQL-spec-compliant behavior of *expr* = NULL is to always return null (unknown). Therefore this parameter defaults to off.

However, filtered forms in Microsoft Access generate queries that appear to use *expr* = NULL to test for null values, so if you use that interface to access the database you might want to turn this option on. Since expressions of the form *expr* = NULL always return the null value (using the correct interpretation) they are not very useful and do not appear often in normal applications, so this option does little harm in practice. But new users are frequently confused about the semantics of expressions involving null values, so this option is not on by default.

Note that this option only affects the exact form = NULL, not other comparison operators or other expressions that are computationally equivalent to some expression involving the equals operator (such as IN). Thus, this option is not a general fix for bad programming.

Refer to *Section 9.2* - Vol.I page 191 for related information.

18.13. Preset Options

The following "parameters" are read-only, and are determined when PostgreSQL is compiled or when it is installed. As such, they have been excluded from the sample postgresql.conf file. These options report various aspects of PostgreSQL behavior that might be of interest to certain applications, particularly administrative front-ends.

block_size (integer)

Reports the size of a disk block. It is determined by the value of BLCKSZ when building the server. The default value is 8192 bytes. The meaning of some configuration variables (such as *shared_buffers*) is influenced by block_size. See *Section 18.4* (page 83) for information.

integer_datetimes (boolean)

Reports whether PostgreSQL was built with support for 64-bit-integer dates and times. This can be disabled by configuring with --disable-integer-datetimes when building PostgreSQL. The default value is on.

lc_collate (string)

Reports the locale in which sorting of textual data is done. See *Section 22.1* (page 158) for more information. This value is determined when a database is created.

lc_ctype (string)

Reports the locale that determines character classifications. See *Section 22.1* (page 158) for more information. This value is determined when a database is created. Ordinarily this will be the same as lc_collate, but for special applications it might be set differently.

`max_function_args` (`integer`)

Reports the maximum number of function arguments. It is determined by the value of FUNC_MAX_ARGS when building the server. The default value is 100 arguments.

`max_identifier_length` (`integer`)

Reports the maximum identifier length. It is determined as one less than the value of NAMEDATALEN when building the server. The default value of NAMEDATALEN is 64; therefore the default max_identifier_length is 63 bytes.

`max_index_keys` (`integer`)

Reports the maximum number of index keys. It is determined by the value of INDEX_MAX_KEYS when building the server. The default value is 32 keys.

`segment_size` (`integer`)

Reports the number of blocks (pages) that can be stored within a file segment. It is determined by the value of RELSEG_SIZE when building the server. The maximum size of a segment file in bytes is equal to segment_size multiplied by block_size; by default this is 1GB.

`server_encoding` (`string`)

Reports the database encoding (character set). It is determined when the database is created. Ordinarily, clients need only be concerned with the value of *client_encoding*.

`server_version` (`string`)

Reports the version number of the server. It is determined by the value of PG_VERSION when building the server.

`server_version_num` (`integer`)

Reports the version number of the server as an integer. It is determined by the value of PG_VERSION_NUM when building the server.

`wal_block_size` (`integer`)

Reports the size of a WAL disk block. It is determined by the value of XLOG_BLCKSZ when building the server. The default value is 8192 bytes.

`wal_segment_size` (`integer`)

Reports the number of blocks (pages) in a WAL segment file. The total size of a WAL segment file in bytes is equal to wal_segment_size multiplied by wal_block_size; by default this is 16MB. See *Section 28.4* (page 234) for more information.

18.14. Customized Options

This feature was designed to allow parameters not normally known to PostgreSQL to be added by add-on modules (such as procedural languages). This allows add-on modules to be configured in the standard ways.

`custom_variable_classes` (`string`)

> This variable specifies one or several class names to be used for custom variables, in the form of a comma-separated list. A custom variable is a variable not normally known to PostgreSQL proper but used by some add-on module. Such variables must have names consisting of a class name, a dot, and a variable name. custom_variable_classes specifies all the class names in use in a particular installation. This parameter can only be set in the postgresql.conf file or on the server command line.

The difficulty with setting custom variables in postgresql.conf is that the file must be read before add-on modules have been loaded, and so custom variables would ordinarily be rejected as unknown. When custom_variable_classes is set, the server will accept definitions of arbitrary variables within each specified class. These variables will be treated as placeholders and will have no function until the module that defines them is loaded. When a module for a specific class is loaded, it will add the proper variable definitions for its class name, convert any placeholder values according to those definitions, and issue warnings for any placeholders of its class that remain (which presumably would be misspelled configuration variables).

Here is an example of what postgresql.conf might contain when using custom variables:

```
custom_variable_classes = 'plr,plperl'
plr.path = '/usr/lib/R'
plperl.use_strict = true
plruby.use_strict = true              # generates error: unknown class name
```

18.15. Developer Options

The following parameters are intended for work on the PostgreSQL source, and in some cases to assist with recovery of severely damaged databases. There should be no reason to use them in a production database setup. As such, they have been excluded from the sample postgresql.conf file. Note that many of these parameters require special source compilation flags to work at all.

`allow_system_table_mods` (`boolean`)

> Allows modification of the structure of system tables. This is used by initdb. This parameter can only be set at server start.

`debug_assertions` (`boolean`)

> Turns on various assertion checks. This is a debugging aid. If you are experiencing strange problems or crashes you might want to turn this on, as it might expose

programming mistakes. To use this parameter, the macro USE_ASSERT_CHECKING must be defined when PostgreSQL is built (accomplished by the configure option --enable-cassert). Note that debug_assertions defaults to on if PostgreSQL has been built with assertions enabled.

ignore_system_indexes (boolean)

Ignore system indexes when reading system tables (but still update the indexes when modifying the tables). This is useful when recovering from damaged system indexes. This parameter cannot be changed after session start.

post_auth_delay (integer)

If nonzero, a delay of this many seconds occurs when a new server process is started, after it conducts the authentication procedure. This is intended to give an opportunity to attach to the server process with a debugger. This parameter cannot be changed after session start.

pre_auth_delay (integer)

If nonzero, a delay of this many seconds occurs just after a new server process is forked, before it conducts the authentication procedure. This is intended to give an opportunity to attach to the server process with a debugger to trace down misbehavior in authentication. This parameter can only be set in the postgresql.conf file or on the server command line.

trace_notify (boolean)

Generates a great amount of debugging output for the LISTEN and NOTIFY commands. *client_min_messages* or *log_min_messages* must be DEBUG1 or lower to send this output to the client or server log, respectively.

trace_sort (boolean)

If on, emit information about resource usage during sort operations. This parameter is only available if the TRACE_SORT macro was defined when PostgreSQL was compiled. (However, TRACE_SORT is currently defined by default.)

trace_locks (boolean)

If on, emit information about lock usage. Information dumped includes the type of lock operation, the type of lock and the unique identifier of the object being locked or unlocked. Also included are bitmasks for the lock types already granted on this object as well as for the lock types awaited on this object. For each lock type a count of the number of granted locks and waiting locks is also dumped as well as the totals. An example of the log file output is shown here:

LOG: LockAcquire: new: lock(0xb7acd844) id(24688,24696,0,0,0,1) grantMask(0)
req(0,0,0,0,0,0,0)=0 grant(0,0,0,0,0,0,0)=0 wait(0) type(AccessShareLock)

LOG: GrantLock: lock(0xb7acd844) id(24688,24696,0,0,0,1) grantMask(2)
req(1,0,0,0,0,0,0)=1 grant(1,0,0,0,0,0,0)=1 wait(0) type(AccessShareLock)

LOG: UnGrantLock: updated: lock(0xb7acd844) id(24688,24696,0,0,0,1) grantMask(0)
req(0,0,0,0,0,0,0)=0 grant(0,0,0,0,0,0,0)=0 wait(0) type(AccessShareLock)

LOG: CleanUpLock: deleting: lock(0xb7acd844) id(24688,24696,0,0,0,1) grantMask(0)
req(0,0,0,0,0,0,0)=0 grant(0,0,0,0,0,0,0)=0 wait(0) type(INVALID)

Details of the structure being dumped may be found in src/include/storage/lock.h

This parameter is only available if the LOCK_DEBUG macro was defined when
PostgreSQL was compiled.

`trace_lwlocks` (boolean)

If on, emit information about lightweight lock usage. Lightweight locks are intended
primarily to provide mutual exclusion of access to shared-memory data structures.

This parameter is only available if the LOCK_DEBUG macro was defined when
PostgreSQL was compiled.

`trace_userlocks` (boolean)

If on, emit information about user lock usage. Output is the same as for trace_locks, only
for user locks.

User locks were removed as of PostgreSQL version 8.2. This option currently has no
effect.

This parameter is only available if the LOCK_DEBUG macro was defined when
PostgreSQL was compiled.

`trace_lock_oidmin` (integer)

If set, do not trace locks for tables below this OID. (use to avoid output on system tables)

This parameter is only available if the LOCK_DEBUG macro was defined when
PostgreSQL was compiled.

`trace_lock_table` (integer)

Unconditionally trace locks on this table (OID).

This parameter is only available if the LOCK_DEBUG macro was defined when
PostgreSQL was compiled.

`debug_deadlocks` (boolean)

If set, dumps information about all current locks when a DeadLockTimeout occurs.

This parameter is only available if the LOCK_DEBUG macro was defined when PostgreSQL was compiled.

`log_btree_build_stats` (boolean)

If set, logs system resource usage statistics (memory and CPU) on various btree operations.

This parameter is only available if the BTREE_BUILD_STATS macro was defined when PostgreSQL was compiled.

`wal_debug` (boolean)

If on, emit WAL-related debugging output. This parameter is only available if the WAL_DEBUG macro was defined when PostgreSQL was compiled.

`zero_damaged_pages` (boolean)

Detection of a damaged page header normally causes PostgreSQL to report an error, aborting the current command. Setting zero_damaged_pages to on causes the system to instead report a warning, zero out the damaged page, and continue processing. This behavior *will destroy data*, namely all the rows on the damaged page. But it allows you to get past the error and retrieve rows from any undamaged pages that might be present in the table. So it is useful for recovering data if corruption has occurred due to hardware or software error. You should generally not set this on until you have given up hope of recovering data from the damaged page(s) of a table. The default setting is off, and it can only be changed by a superuser.

18.16. Short Options

For convenience there are also single letter command-line option switches available for some parameters. They are described in *Table 18-2*. Some of these options exist for historical reasons, and their presence as a single-letter option does not necessarily indicate an endorsement to use the option heavily.

Short option	Equivalent
-A x	debug_assertions = x
-B x	shared_buffers = x
-d x	log_min_messages = DEBUGx
-e	datestyle = euro
-fb, -fh, -fi, -fm,	enable_bitmapscan = off, enable_hashjoin = off, enable_indexscan = off,

Short option	Equivalent
-fn,-fs,-ft	enable_mergejoin = off, enable_nestloop = off, enable_seqscan = off, enable_tidscan = off
-F	fsync = off
-h x	listen_addresses = x
-i	listen_addresses = '*'
-k x	unix_socket_directory = x
-l	ssl = on
-N x	max_connections = x
-O	allow_system_table_mods = on
-p x	port = x
-P	ignore_system_indexes = on
-s	log_statement_stats = on
-S x	work_mem = x
-tpa,-tpl,-te	log_parser_stats = on, log_planner_stats = on, log_executor_stats = on
-W x	post_auth_delay = x

Table 18-2. Short option key

Chapter 19.
Client Authentication

When a client application connects to the database server, it specifies which PostgreSQL database user name it wants to connect as, much the same way one logs into a Unix computer as a particular user. Within the SQL environment the active database user name determines access privileges to database objects — see *Chapter 20* (page 145) for more information. Therefore, it is essential to restrict which database users can connect.

 Note

As explained in *Chapter 20* (page 145), PostgreSQL actually does privilege management in terms of "roles". In this chapter, we consistently use *database user* to mean "role with the LOGIN privilege".

Authentication is the process by which the database server establishes the identity of the client, and by extension determines whether the client application (or the user who runs the client application) is permitted to connect with the database user name that was requested.

PostgreSQL offers a number of different client authentication methods. The method used to authenticate a particular client connection can be selected on the basis of (client) host address, database, and user.

PostgreSQL database user names are logically separate from user names of the operating system in which the server runs. If all the users of a particular server also have accounts on the server's machine, it makes sense to assign database user names that match their operating system user names. However, a server that accepts remote connections might have many database users who have no local operating system account, and in such cases there need be no connection between database user names and OS user names.

19.1. The `pg_hba.conf` file

Client authentication is controlled by a configuration file, which traditionally is named pg_hba.conf and is stored in the database cluster's data directory. (HBA stands for host-based authentication.) A default pg_hba.conf file is installed when the data directory is initialized by initdb. It is possible to place the authentication configuration file elsewhere, however; see the *hba_file* configuration parameter.

The general format of the pg_hba.conf file is a set of records, one per line. Blank lines are ignored, as is any text after the # comment character. A record is made up of a number of fields which are separated by spaces and/or tabs. Fields can contain white space if the field value is quoted. Records cannot be continued across lines.

Each record specifies a connection type, a client IP address range (if relevant for the connection type), a database name, a user name, and the authentication method to be used for connections matching these parameters. The first record with a matching connection type, client address, requested database, and user name is used to perform authentication. There is no "fall-through" or "backup": if one record is chosen and the authentication fails, subsequent records are not considered. If no record matches, access is denied.

A record can have one of the seven formats

```
local      database   user   auth-method   [auth-options]
host       database   user   CIDR-address   auth-method   [auth-options]
hostssl    database   user   CIDR-address   auth-method   [auth-options]
hostnossl  database   user   CIDR-address   auth-method   [auth-options]
host       database   user   IP-address   IP-mask   auth-method   [auth-options]
hostssl    database   user   IP-address   IP-mask   auth-method   [auth-options]
hostnossl  database   user   IP-address   IP-mask   auth-method   [auth-options]
```

The meaning of the fields is as follows:

local

> This record matches connection attempts using Unix-domain sockets. Without a record of this type, Unix-domain socket connections are disallowed.

host

> This record matches connection attempts made using TCP/IP. host records match either SSL or non-SSL connection attempts.

 Note

> Remote TCP/IP connections will not be possible unless the server is started with an appropriate value for the *listen_addresses* configuration parameter, since the default behavior is to listen for TCP/IP connections only on the local loopback address localhost.

hostssl

> This record matches connection attempts made using TCP/IP, but only when the connection is made with SSL encryption.

> To make use of this option the server must be built with SSL support. Furthermore, SSL must be enabled at server start time by setting the *ssl* configuration parameter (see *Section 17.8* – page 73 for more information).

`hostnossl`

> This record type has the opposite logic to hostssl: it only matches connection attempts made over TCP/IP that do not use SSL.

database

> Specifies which database name(s) this record matches. The value all specifies that it matches all databases. The value sameuser specifies that the record matches if the requested database has the same name as the requested user. The value samerole specifies that the requested user must be a member of the role with the same name as the requested database. (samegroup is an obsolete but still accepted spelling of samerole.) Otherwise, this is the name of a specific PostgreSQL database. Multiple database names can be supplied by separating them with commas. A separate file containing database names can be specified by preceding the file name with @.

user

> Specifies which database user name(s) this record matches. The value all specifies that it matches all users. Otherwise, this is either the name of a specific database user, or a group name preceded by +. (Recall that there is no real distinction between users and groups in PostgreSQL; a + mark really means "match any of the roles that are directly or indirectly members of this role", while a name without a + mark matches only that specific role.) Multiple user names can be supplied by separating them with commas. A separate file containing user names can be specified by preceding the file name with @.

CIDR-address

> Specifies the client machine IP address range that this record matches. This field contains an IP address in standard dotted decimal notation and a CIDR mask length. (IP addresses can only be specified numerically, not as domain or host names.) The mask length indicates the number of high-order bits of the client IP address that must match. Bits to the right of this must be zero in the given IP address. There must not be any white space between the IP address, the /, and the CIDR mask length.

> Typical examples of a *CIDR-address* are 172.20.143.89/32 for a single host, or 172.20.143.0/24 for a small network, or 10.6.0.0/16 for a larger one. To specify a single host, use a CIDR mask of 32 for IPv4 or 128 for IPv6. In a network address, do not omit trailing zeroes.

> An IP address given in IPv4 format will match IPv6 connections that have the corresponding address, for example 127.0.0.1 will match the IPv6 address ::ffff:127.0.0.1. An entry given in IPv6 format will match only IPv6 connections, even if the represented address is in the IPv4-in-IPv6 range. Note that entries in IPv6 format will be rejected if the system's C library does not have support for IPv6 addresses.

> This field only applies to host, hostssl, and hostnossl records.

`IP-address`
`IP-mask`

These fields can be used as an alternative to the *CIDR-address* notation. Instead of specifying the mask length, the actual mask is specified in a separate column. For example, 255.0.0.0 represents an IPv4 CIDR mask length of 8, and 255.255.255.255 represents a CIDR mask length of 32.

These fields only apply to host, hostssl, and hostnossl records.

`auth-method`

Specifies the authentication method to use when a connection matches this record. The possible choices are summarized here; details are in *Section 19.3* (page 137).

> `trust`
>
> > Allow the connection unconditionally. This method allows anyone that can connect to the PostgreSQL database server to login as any PostgreSQL user they like, without the need for a password. See *Section 19.3.1* (page 137) for details.
>
> `reject`
>
> > Reject the connection unconditionally. This is useful for "filtering out" certain hosts from a group.
>
> `md5`
>
> > Require the client to supply an MD5-encrypted password for authentication. See *Section 19.3.2* (page 137) for details.
>
> `password`
>
> > Require the client to supply an unencrypted password for authentication. Since the password is sent in clear text over the network, this should not be used on untrusted networks. See *Section 19.3.2* (page 137) for details.
>
> `gss`
>
> > Use GSSAPI to authenticate the user. This is only available for TCP/IP connections. See *Section 19.3.3* (page 138) for details.
>
> `sspi`
>
> > Use SSPI to authenticate the user. This is only available on Windows. See *Section 19.3.4* (page 138) for details.
>
> `krb5`
>
> > Use Kerberos V5 to authenticate the user. This is only available for TCP/IP connections. See *Section 19.3.5* (page 139) for details.

ident

> Obtain the operating system user name of the client (for TCP/IP connections by
> contacting the ident server on the client, for local connections by getting it from
> the operating system) and check if it matches the requested database user name.
> See *Section 19.3.6* (page 141) for details.

ldap

> Authenticate using an LDAP server. See *Section 19.3.7* (page 142) for details.

cert

> Authenticate using SSL client certificates. See *Section 19.3.8* (page 143) for details.

pam

> Authenticate using the Pluggable Authentication Modules (PAM) service
> provided by the operating system. See *Section 19.3.9* (page 143) for details.

auth-options

> After the *auth-method* field, there can be field(s) of the form *name=value* that specify
> options for the authentication method. Details about which options are available for
> which authentication method appear below.

Files included by @ constructs are read as lists of names, which can be separated by either
whitespace or commas. Comments are introduced by #, just as in pg_hba.conf, and nested @
constructs are allowed. Unless the file name following @ is an absolute path, it is taken to be
relative to the directory containing the referencing file.

Since the pg_hba.conf records are examined sequentially for each connection attempt, the
order of the records is significant. Typically, earlier records will have tight connection match
parameters and weaker authentication methods, while later records will have looser match
parameters and stronger authentication methods. For example, one might wish to use trust
authentication for local TCP/IP connections but require a password for remote TCP/IP
connections. In this case a record specifying trust authentication for connections from
127.0.0.1 would appear before a record specifying password authentication for a wider
range of allowed client IP addresses.

The pg_hba.conf file is read on start-up and when the main server process receives a
SIGHUP signal. If you edit the file on an active system, you will need to signal the server
(using pg_ctl reload or kill -HUP) to make it re-read the file.

 Tip

> To connect to a particular database, a user must not only pass the pg_hba.conf
> checks, but must have the CONNECT privilege for the database. If you wish to restrict

which users can connect to which databases, it's usually easier to control this by granting/revoking CONNECT privilege than to put the rules into pg_hba.conf entries.

Some examples of pg_hba.conf entries are shown in *Example 19-1*. See the next section for details on the different authentication methods.

```
# Allow any user on the local system to connect to any database under
# any database user name using Unix-domain sockets (the default for local
# connections).
#
# TYPE   DATABASE     USER          CIDR-ADDRESS             METHOD
local    all          all                                    trust

# The same using local loopback TCP/IP connections.
#
# TYPE   DATABASE     USER          CIDR-ADDRESS             METHOD
host     all          all           127.0.0.1/32             trust

# The same as the previous line, but using a separate netmask column
#
# TYPE   DATABASE     USER          IP-ADDRESS     IP-MASK            METHOD
host     all          all           127.0.0.1      255.255.255.255   trust

# Allow any user from any host with IP address 192.168.93.x to connect
# to database "postgres" as the same user name that ident reports for
# the connection (typically the Unix user name).
#
# TYPE   DATABASE     USER          CIDR-ADDRESS             METHOD
host     postgres     all           192.168.93.0/24          ident

# Allow any user from host 192.168.12.10 to connect to database
# "postgres" if the user's password is correctly supplied.
#
# TYPE   DATABASE     USER          CIDR-ADDRESS             METHOD
host     postgres     all           192.168.12.10/32         md5

# In the absence of preceding "host" lines, these two lines will
# reject all connections from 192.168.54.1 (since that entry will be
# matched first), but allow Kerberos 5 connections from anywhere else
# on the Internet.  The zero mask means that no bits of the host IP
# address are considered so it matches any host.
#
# TYPE   DATABASE     USER          CIDR-ADDRESS             METHOD
host     all          all           192.168.54.1/32          reject
host     all          all           0.0.0.0/0                krb5

# Allow users from 192.168.x.x hosts to connect to any database, if
# they pass the ident check.  If, for example, ident says the user is
# "bryanh" and he requests to connect as PostgreSQL user "guest1", the
# connection is allowed if there is an entry in pg_ident.conf for map
# "omicron" that says "bryanh" is allowed to connect as "guest1".
#
```

```
# TYPE   DATABASE      USER         CIDR-ADDRESS          METHOD
host     all           all          192.168.0.0/16        ident map=omicron

# If these are the only three lines for local connections, they will
# allow local users to connect only to their own databases (databases
# with the same name as their database user name) except for administrators
# and members of role "support", who can connect to all databases.  The file
# $PGDATA/admins contains a list of names of administrators.  Passwords
# are required in all cases.
#
# TYPE   DATABASE      USER         CIDR-ADDRESS          METHOD
local    sameuser      all                                md5
local    all           @admins                            md5
local    all           +support                           md5

# The last two lines above can be combined into a single line:
local    all           @admins,+support                   md5

# The database column can also use lists and file names:
local    db1,db2,@demodbs  all                            md5
```

Example 19-1. Example pg_hba.conf entries

19.2. Username maps

When using an external authentication system like Ident or GSSAPI, the name of the operating system user that initiated the connection might not be the same as the database user he needs to connect as. In this case, a user name map can be applied to map the operating system username to a database user. To use username mapping, specify map=*map-name* in the options field in pg_hba.conf. This option is supported for all authentication methods that receive external usernames. Since different mappings might be needed for different connections, the name of the map to be used is specified in the *map-name* parameter in pg_hba.conf to indicate which map to use for each individual connection.

Username maps are defined in the ident map file, which by default is named pg_ident.conf and is stored in the cluster's data directory. (It is possible to place the map file elsewhere, however; see the *ident_file* configuration parameter.) The ident map file contains lines of the general form:

map-name system-username database-username

Comments and whitespace are handled in the same way as in pg_hba.conf. The *map-name* is an arbitrary name that will be used to refer to this mapping in pg_hba.conf. The other two fields specify an operating system user name and a matching database user name. The same *map-name* can be used repeatedly to specify multiple user-mappings within a single map.

There is no restriction regarding how many database users a given operating system user can correspond to, nor vice versa. Thus, entries in a map should be thought of as meaning "this operating system user is allowed to connect as this database user", rather than implying that they are equivalent. The connection will be allowed if there is any map entry that matches the user name obtained from the external authentication system to the database user name that the user has requested to connect as.

If the *system-username* field starts with a slash (/), the remainder of the field is treated as a regular expression. (See *Section 9.7.3.1* – Vol.I page 213 for details of PostgreSQL's regular expression syntax. Regular expressions in username maps are always treated as being "advanced" flavor.) The regular expression can include a single capture, or parenthesized subexpression, which can then be referenced in the *database-username* field as \1 (backslash-one). This allows the mapping of multiple usernames in a single line, which is particularly useful for simple syntax substitutions. For example, these entries

```
mymap     /^(.*)@mydomain\.com$        \1
mymap     /^(.*)@otherdomain\.com$     guest
```

will remove the domain part for users with system usernames that end with @mydomain.com, and allow any user whose system name ends with @otherdomain.com to log in as guest.

 Tip

Keep in mind that by default, a regular expression can match just part of a string. It's usually wise to use ^ and $, as shown in the above example, to force the match to be to the entire system username.

The pg_ident.conf file is read on start-up and when the main server process receives a SIGHUP signal. If you edit the file on an active system, you will need to signal the server (using pg_ctl reload or kill -HUP) to make it re-read the file.

A `pg_ident.conf` file that could be used in conjunction with the `pg_hba.conf` file in *Example 19-1* is shown in *Example 19-2*. In this example setup, anyone logged in to a machine on the 192.168 network that does not have the Unix user name bryanh, ann, or robert would not be granted access. Unix user robert would only be allowed access when he tries to connect as PostgreSQL user bob, not as robert or anyone else. ann would only be allowed to connect as ann. User bryanh would be allowed to connect as either bryanh himself or as guest1.

```
# MAPNAME       SYSTEM-USERNAME     PG-USERNAME

omicron        bryanh              bryanh
omicron        ann                 ann
# bob has user name robert on these machines
omicron        robert              bob
```

```
# bryanh can also connect as guest1
omicron         bryanh              guest1
```

Example 19-2. An example pg_ident.conf file

19.3. Authentication methods

The following subsections describe the authentication methods in more detail.

19.3.1. Trust authentication

When trust authentication is specified, PostgreSQL assumes that anyone who can connect to the server is authorized to access the database with whatever database user name they specify (even superuser names). Of course, restrictions made in the database and user columns still apply. This method should only be used when there is adequate operating-system-level protection on connections to the server.

trust authentication is appropriate and very convenient for local connections on a single-user workstation. It is usually *not* appropriate by itself on a multiuser machine. However, you might be able to use trust even on a multiuser machine, if you restrict access to the server's Unix-domain socket file using file-system permissions. To do this, set the unix_socket_permissions (and possibly unix_socket_group) configuration parameters as described in *Section 18.3* – page 80. Or you could set the unix_socket_directory configuration parameter to place the socket file in a suitably restricted directory.

Setting file-system permissions only helps for Unix-socket connections. Local TCP/IP connections are not restricted by file-system permissions. Therefore, if you want to use file-system permissions for local security, remove the host ... 127.0.0.1 ... line from pg_hba.conf, or change it to a non-trust authentication method.

trust authentication is only suitable for TCP/IP connections if you trust every user on every machine that is allowed to connect to the server by the pg_hba.conf lines that specify trust. It is seldom reasonable to use trust for any TCP/IP connections other than those from localhost (127.0.0.1).

19.3.2. Password authentication

The password-based authentication methods are md5 and password. These methods operate similarly except for the way that the password is sent across the connection: respectively, MD5-hashed and clear-text.

If you are at all concerned about password "sniffing" attacks then md5 is preferred. Plain password should always be avoided if possible. However, md5 cannot be used with the *db_user_namespace* feature. If the connection is protected by SSL encryption then password can be used safely (though SSL certificate authentication might be a better choice if one is depending on using SSL).

PostgreSQL database passwords are separate from operating system user passwords. The password for each database user is stored in the pg_authid system catalog. Passwords can be managed with the SQL commands CREATE USER and ALTER USER, e.g., CREATE USER foo WITH PASSWORD 'secret';. By default, that is, if no password has been set up, the stored password is null and password authentication will always fail for that user.

19.3.3. GSSAPI authentication

GSSAPI is an industry-standard protocol for secure authentication defined in RFC 2743. PostgreSQL supports GSSAPI with Kerberos authentication according to RFC 1964. GSSAPI provides automatic authentication (single sign-on) for systems that support it. The authentication itself is secure, but the data sent over the database connection will be in clear unless SSL is used.

When GSSAPI uses Kerberos, it uses a standard principal in the format `servicename/hostname@realm`. For information about the parts of the principal, and how to set up the required keys, see *Section 19.3.5* –page 139. GSSAPI support has to be enabled when PostgreSQL is built; see *Chapter 15* – page 20 for more information.

The following configuration options are supported for GSSAPI:

`map`

> Allows for mapping between system and database usernames. See *Section 19.2* – page 135 for details.

`include_realm`

> If set to 1, the realm name from the authenticated user principal is included in the system user name that's passed through username mapping (*Section 19.2* – page 135). This is useful for handling users from multiple realms.

`krb_realm`

> Sets the realm to match user principal names against. If this parameter is set, only users of that realm will be accepted. If it is not set, users of any realm can connect, subject to whatever username mapping is done.

19.3.4. SSPI authentication

SSPI is a Windows technology for secure authentication with single sign-on. PostgreSQL will use SSPI in negotiate mode, which will use Kerberos when possible and automatically fall back to NTLM in other cases. SSPI authentication only works when both server and client are running Windows.

When using Kerberos authentication, SSPI works the same way GSSAPI does. See *Section 19.3.3* - page 138 for details.

The following configuration options are supported for SSPI:

map

> Allows for mapping between system and database usernames. See *Section 19.2* - page 135 for details.

include_realm

> If set to 1, the realm name from the authenticated user principal is included in the system user name that's passed through username mapping (*Section 19.2*- page 135). This is useful for handling users from multiple realms.

krb_realm

> Sets the realm to match user principal names against. If this parameter is set, only users of that realm will be accepted. If it is not set, users of any realm can connect, subject to whatever username mapping is done.

19.3.5. Kerberos authentication

 Note

> Native Kerberos authentication has been deprecated and should be used only for backward compatibility. New and upgraded installations are encouraged to use the industry-standard GSSAPI authentication (see *Section 19.3.3* - page 138) instead.

Kerberos is an industry-standard secure authentication system suitable for distributed computing over a public network. A description of the Kerberos system is far beyond the scope of this document; in full generality it can be quite complex (yet powerful). The *Kerberos FAQ*[1] or *MIT Kerberos page*[2] can be good starting points for exploration. Several sources for Kerberos distributions exist. Kerberos provides secure authentication but does not encrypt queries or data passed over the network; for that use SSL.

PostgreSQL supports Kerberos version 5. Kerberos support has to be enabled when PostgreSQL is built; see *Chapter 15* - page 20 for more information.

PostgreSQL operates like a normal Kerberos service. The name of the service principal is *servicename/hostname@realm*.

servicename can be set on the server side using the *krb_srvname* configuration parameter, and on the client side using the krbsrvname connection parameter. (See also *Section 30.1.* - page 246) The installation default can be changed from the default postgres at build time using

---

[1] *http://www.nrl.navy.mil/CCS/people/kenh/kerberos-faq.html*
[2] *http://web.mit.edu/kerberos/www/*

./configure --with-krb-srvnam=*whatever*. In most environments, this parameter never needs to be changed. However, to support multiple PostgreSQL installations on the same host it is necessary. Some Kerberos implementations might also require a different service name, such as Microsoft Active Directory which requires the service name to be in uppercase (POSTGRES).

hostname is the fully qualified host name of the server machine. The service principal's realm is the preferred realm of the server machine.

Client principals must have their PostgreSQL database user name as their first component, for example pgusername@realm. Alternatively, you can use a username mapping to map from the first component of the principal name to the database user name. By default, the realm of the client is not checked by PostgreSQL. If you have cross-realm authentication enabled and need to verify the realm, use the krb_realm parameter, or enable include_realm and use username mapping to check the realm.

Make sure that your server keytab file is readable (and preferably only readable) by the PostgreSQL server account. (See also *Section 17.1.* - page 56) The location of the key file is specified by the *krb_server_keyfile* configuration parameter. The default is /usr/local/pgsql/etc/krb5.keytab (or whichever directory was specified as sysconfdir at build time).

The keytab file is generated by the Kerberos software; see the Kerberos documentation for details. The following example is for MIT-compatible Kerberos 5 implementations:

```
kadmin% ank -randkey postgres/server.my.domain.org
kadmin% ktadd -k krb5.keytab postgres/server.my.domain.org
```

When connecting to the database make sure you have a ticket for a principal matching the requested database user name. For example, for database user name fred, both principal fred@EXAMPLE.COM and fred/users.example.com@EXAMPLE.COM could be used to authenticate to the database server.

If you use mod_auth_kerb[3] and mod_perl on your Apache web server, you can use AuthType KerberosV5SaveCredentials with a mod_perl script. This gives secure database access over the web, no extra passwords required.

The following configuration options are supported for Kerberos:

map

> Allows for mapping between system and database usernames. See *Section 19.2* - page 135 for details.

---

[3] *http://modauthkerb.sf.net/*

`include_realm`

> If set to 1, the realm name from the authenticated user principal is included in the system user name that's passed through username mapping (*Section 19.2* - page 135). This is useful for handling users from multiple realms.

`krb_realm`

> Sets the realm to match user principal names against. If this parameter is set, only users of that realm will be accepted. If it is not set, users of any realm can connect, subject to whatever username mapping is done.

`krb_server_hostname`

> Sets the host name part of the service principal. This, combined with krb_srvname, is used to generate the complete service principal, that is krb_srvname/krb_server_hostname@REALM. If not set, the default is the server host name.

19.3.6. Ident-based authentication

The ident authentication method works by obtaining the client's operating system user name and using it as the allowed database user name (with an optional username mapping). The determination of the client's user name is the security-critical point, and it works differently depending on the connection type.

The following configuration options are supported for ident:

`map`

> Allows for mapping between system and database usernames. See *Section 19.2* - page 135 for details.

19.3.6.1. Ident Authentication over TCP/IP

The "Identification Protocol" is described in RFC 1413. Virtually every Unix-like operating system ships with an ident server that listens on TCP port 113 by default. The basic functionality of an ident server is to answer questions like "What user initiated the connection that goes out of your port X and connects to my port Y?". Since PostgreSQL knows both X and Y when a physical connection is established, it can interrogate the ident server on the host of the connecting client and could theoretically determine the operating system user for any given connection this way.

The drawback of this procedure is that it depends on the integrity of the client: if the client machine is untrusted or compromised an attacker could run just about any program on port 113 and return any user name he chooses. This authentication method is therefore only appropriate for closed networks where each client machine is under tight control and where the database and system administrators operate in close contact. In other words, you must trust the machine running the ident server. Heed the warning:

The Identification Protocol is not intended as an authorization or access control protocol.

--RFC 1413

Some ident servers have a nonstandard option that causes the returned user name to be encrypted, using a key that only the originating machine's administrator knows. This option *must not* be used when using the ident server with PostgreSQL, since PostgreSQL does not have any way to decrypt the returned string to determine the actual user name.

19.3.6.2. Ident Authentication over Local Sockets

On systems supporting SO_PEERCRED requests for Unix-domain sockets (currently Linux, FreeBSD, NetBSD, OpenBSD, BSD/OS, and Solaris), ident authentication can also be applied to local connections. In this case, no security risk is added by using ident authentication; indeed it is a preferable choice for local connections on such systems.

On systems without SO_PEERCRED requests, ident authentication is only available for TCP/IP connections. As a work-around, it is possible to specify the localhost address 127.0.0.1 and make connections to this address. This method is trustworthy to the extent that you trust the local ident server.

19.3.7. LDAP authentication

This authentication method operates similarly to password except that it uses LDAP as the password verification method. LDAP is used only to validate the user name/password pairs. Therefore the user must already exist in the database before LDAP can be used for authentication.

The server will bind to the distinguished name constructed as *prefix username suffix*. Typically, the *prefix* parameter is used to specify cn=, or *DOMAIN* in an Active Directory environment. *suffix* is used to specify the remaining part of the DN in a non-Active Directory environment.

The following configuration options are supported for LDAP:

ldapserver

Name or IP of LDAP server to connect to.

ldapprefix

String to prepend to the username when forming the DN to bind as.

ldapsuffix

String to append to the username when forming the DN to bind as.

`ldapport`

> Port number on LDAP server to connect to. If no port is specified, the default port in the LDAP library will be used.

`ldaptls`

> Set to 1 to make the connection between PostgreSQL and the LDAP server use TLS encryption. Note that this only encrypts the traffic to the LDAP server — the connection to the client will still be unencrypted unless SSL is used.

 Note

> Since LDAP often uses commas and spaces to separate the different parts of a DN, it is often necessary to use double-quoted parameter values when configuring LDAP options, for example:

```
ldapserver=ldap.example.net ldapprefix="cn=" ldapsuffix=", dc=example, dc=net"
```

19.3.8. Certificate authentication

This authentication method uses SSL client certificates to perform authentication. It is therefore only available for SSL connections. When using this authentication method, the server will require that the client provide a valid certificate. No password prompt will be sent to the client. The cn attribute of the certificate will be compared to the requested database username, and if they match the login will be allowed. Username mapping can be used to allow cn to be different from the database username.

The following configuration options are supported for SSL certificate authentication:

`map`

> Allows for mapping between system and database usernames. See *Section 19.2* - page 135 for details.

19.3.9. PAM authentication

This authentication method operates similarly to password except that it uses PAM (Pluggable Authentication Modules) as the authentication mechanism. The default PAM service name is postgresql. PAM is used only to validate user name/password pairs. Therefore the user must already exist in the database before PAM can be used for authentication. For more information about PAM, please read the *Linux-PAM Page*[4] and the *Solaris PAM Page*[5].

---

[4] *http://www.kernel.org/pub/linux/libs/pam/*
[5] *http://www.sun.com/software/solaris/pam/*

The following configuration options are supported for PAM:

`pamservice`

PAM service name.

 Note

If PAM is set up to read /etc/shadow, authentication will fail because the PostgreSQL server is started by a non-root user. However, this is not an issue when PAM is configured to use LDAP or other authentication methods.

19.4. Authentication problems

Authentication failures and related problems generally manifest themselves through error messages like the following:

`FATAL:  no pg_hba.conf entry for host "123.123.123.123", user "andym", database "testdb"`

This is what you are most likely to get if you succeed in contacting the server, but it does not want to talk to you. As the message suggests, the server refused the connection request because it found no matching entry in its pg_hba.conf configuration file.

`FATAL:  Password authentication failed for user "andym"`

Messages like this indicate that you contacted the server, and it is willing to talk to you, but not until you pass the authorization method specified in the pg_hba.conf file. Check the password you are providing, or check your Kerberos or ident software if the complaint mentions one of those authentication types.

`FATAL:  user "andym" does not exist`

The indicated database user name was not found.

`FATAL:  database "testdb" does not exist`

The database you are trying to connect to does not exist. Note that if you do not specify a database name, it defaults to the database user name, which might or might not be the right thing.

 Tip

The server log might contain more information about an authentication failure than is reported to the client. If you are confused about the reason for a failure, check the log.

Chapter 20.
Database Roles and Privileges

PostgreSQL manages database access permissions using the concept of *roles*. A role can be thought of as either a database user, or a group of database users, depending on how the role is set up. Roles can own database objects (for example, tables) and can assign privileges on those objects to other roles to control who has access to which objects. Furthermore, it is possible to grant *membership* in a role to another role, thus allowing the member role use of privileges assigned to the role it is a member of.

The concept of roles subsumes the concepts of "users" and "groups". In PostgreSQL versions before 8.1, users and groups were distinct kinds of entities, but now there are only roles. Any role can act as a user, a group, or both.

This chapter describes how to create and manage roles and introduces the privilege system. More information about the various types of database objects and the effects of privileges can be found in *Chapter 5* - Vol.I page 77.

20.1. Database Roles

Database roles are conceptually completely separate from operating system users. In practice it might be convenient to maintain a correspondence, but this is not required. Database roles are global across a database cluster installation (and not per individual database). To create a role use the CREATE ROLE SQL command:

```
CREATE ROLE name;
```

name follows the rules for SQL identifiers: either unadorned without special characters, or double-quoted. (In practice, you will usually want to add additional options, such as LOGIN, to the command. More details appear below.) To remove an existing role, use the analogous DROP ROLE command:

```
DROP ROLE name;
```

For convenience, the programs *createuser* and *dropuser* are provided as wrappers around these SQL commands that can be called from the shell command line:

```
createuser name
dropuser name
```

To determine the set of existing roles, examine the pg_roles system catalog, for example

```
SELECT rolname FROM pg_roles;
```

The *psql* program's \du meta-command is also useful for listing the existing roles.

In order to bootstrap the database system, a freshly initialized system always contains one predefined role. This role is always a "superuser", and by default (unless altered when running initdb) it will have the same name as the operating system user that initialized the database cluster. Customarily, this role will be named postgres. In order to create more roles you first have to connect as this initial role.

Every connection to the database server is made in the name of some particular role, and this role determines the initial access privileges for commands issued on that connection. The role name to use for a particular database connection is indicated by the client that is initiating the connection request in an application-specific fashion. For example, the psql program uses the -U command line option to indicate the role to connect as. Many applications assume the name of the current operating system user by default (including createuser and psql). Therefore it is often convenient to maintain a naming correspondence between roles and operating system users.

The set of database roles a given client connection can connect as is determined by the client authentication setup, as explained in *Chapter 19* - page 129. (Thus, a client is not necessarily limited to connect as the role with the same name as its operating system user, just as a person's login name need not match her real name.) Since the role identity determines the set of privileges available to a connected client, it is important to carefully configure this when setting up a multiuser environment.

20.2. Role Attributes

A database role can have a number of attributes that define its privileges and interact with the client authentication system.

login privilege

> Only roles that have the LOGIN attribute can be used as the initial role name for a database connection. A role with the LOGIN attribute can be considered the same thing as a "database user". To create a role with login privilege, use either:

```
CREATE ROLE name LOGIN;
CREATE USER name;
```

> (CREATE USER is equivalent to CREATE ROLE except that CREATE USER assumes LOGIN by default, while CREATE ROLE does not.)

superuser status

> A database superuser bypasses all permission checks. This is a dangerous privilege and should not be used carelessly; it is best to do most of your work as a role that is not a

superuser. To create a new database superuser, use CREATE ROLE *name* SUPERUSER. You must do this as a role that is already a superuser.

database creation

A role must be explicitly given permission to create databases (except for superusers, since those bypass all permission checks). To create such a role, use CREATE ROLE *name* CREATEDB.

role creation

A role must be explicitly given permission to create more roles (except for superusers, since those bypass all permission checks). To create such a role, use CREATE ROLE *name* CREATEROLE. A role with CREATEROLE privilege can alter and drop other roles, too, as well as grant or revoke membership in them. However, to create, alter, drop, or change membership of a superuser role, superuser status is required; CREATEROLE is not sufficient for that.

password

A password is only significant if the client authentication method requires the user to supply a password when connecting to the database. The password and md5 authentication methods make use of passwords. Database passwords are separate from operating system passwords. Specify a password upon role creation with CREATE ROLE *name* PASSWORD '*string*'.

A role's attributes can be modified after creation with ALTER ROLE. See the reference pages for the CREATE ROLE and ALTER ROLE commands for details.

 Tip

It is good practice to create a role that has the CREATEDB and CREATEROLE privileges, but is not a superuser, and then use this role for all routine management of databases and roles. This approach avoids the dangers of operating as a superuser for tasks that do not really require it.

A role can also have role-specific defaults for many of the run-time configuration settings described in *Chapter 18* - page 77. For example, if for some reason you want to disable index scans (hint: not a good idea) anytime you connect, you can use:

```
ALTER ROLE myname SET enable_indexscan TO off;
```

This will save the setting (but not set it immediately). In subsequent connections by this role it will appear as though SET enable_indexscan TO off; had been executed just before the session started. You can still alter this setting during the session; it will only be the default. To remove a role-specific default setting, use ALTER ROLE *rolename* RESET *varname*;. Note that role-specific defaults attached to roles without LOGIN privilege are fairly useless, since they will never be invoked.

20.3. Privileges

When an object is created, it is assigned an owner. The owner is normally the role that executed the creation statement. For most kinds of objects, the initial state is that only the owner (or a superuser) can do anything with the object. To allow other roles to use it, *privileges* must be granted. There are several different kinds of privilege: SELECT, INSERT, UPDATE, DELETE, TRUNCATE, REFERENCES, TRIGGER, CREATE, CONNECT, TEMPORARY, EXECUTE, and USAGE. For more information on the different types of privileges supported by PostgreSQL, see the GRANT reference page.

To assign privileges, the GRANT command is used. So, if joe is an existing role, and accounts is an existing table, the privilege to update the table can be granted with:

```
GRANT UPDATE ON accounts TO joe;
```

The special name PUBLIC can be used to grant a privilege to every role on the system. Writing ALL in place of a specific privilege specifies that all privileges that apply to the object will be granted.

To revoke a privilege, use the fittingly named REVOKE command:

```
REVOKE ALL ON accounts FROM PUBLIC;
```

The special privileges of an object's owner (i.e., the right to modify or destroy the object) are always implicit in being the owner, and cannot be granted or revoked. But the owner can choose to revoke his own ordinary privileges, for example to make a table read-only for himself as well as others.

An object can be assigned to a new owner with an ALTER command of the appropriate kind for the object. Superusers can always do this; ordinary roles can only do it if they are both the current owner of the object (or a member of the owning role) and a member of the new owning role.

20.4. Role Membership

It is frequently convenient to group users together to ease management of privileges: that way, privileges can be granted to, or revoked from, a group as a whole. In PostgreSQL this is done by creating a role that represents the group, and then granting *membership* in the group role to individual user roles.

To set up a group role, first create the role:

```
CREATE ROLE name;
```

Typically a role being used as a group would not have the LOGIN attribute, though you can set it if you wish.

Once the group role exists, you can add and remove members using the GRANT and
REVOKE commands:

```
GRANT group_role TO role1, ... ;
REVOKE group_role FROM role1, ... ;
```

You can grant membership to other group roles, too (since there isn't really any distinction
between group roles and non-group roles). The database will not let you set up circular
membership loops. Also, it is not permitted to grant membership in a role to PUBLIC.

The members of a role can use the privileges of the group role in two ways. First, every
member of a group can explicitly do SET ROLE to temporarily "become" the group role. In
this state, the database session has access to the privileges of the group role rather than the
original login role, and any database objects created are considered owned by the group role
not the login role. Second, member roles that have the INHERIT attribute automatically
have use of privileges of roles they are members of. As an example, suppose we have done:

```
CREATE ROLE joe LOGIN INHERIT;
CREATE ROLE admin NOINHERIT;
CREATE ROLE wheel NOINHERIT;
GRANT admin TO joe;
GRANT wheel TO admin;
```

Immediately after connecting as role joe, a database session will have use of privileges
granted directly to joe plus any privileges granted to admin, because joe "inherits" admin's
privileges. However, privileges granted to wheel are not available, because even though joe
is indirectly a member of wheel, the membership is via admin which has the NOINHERIT
attribute. After:

```
SET ROLE admin;
```

the session would have use of only those privileges granted to admin, and not those granted
to joe. After:

```
SET ROLE wheel;
```

the session would have use of only those privileges granted to wheel, and not those granted
to either joe or admin. The original privilege state can be restored with any of:

```
SET ROLE joe;
SET ROLE NONE;
RESET ROLE;
```

 Note

> The SET ROLE command always allows selecting any role that the original login role
> is directly or indirectly a member of. Thus, in the above example, it is not necessary
> to become admin before becoming wheel.

Note

In the SQL standard, there is a clear distinction between users and roles, and users do not automatically inherit privileges while roles do. This behavior can be obtained in PostgreSQL by giving roles being used as SQL roles the INHERIT attribute, while giving roles being used as SQL users the NOINHERIT attribute. However, PostgreSQL defaults to giving all roles the INHERIT attribute, for backwards compatibility with pre-8.1 releases in which users always had use of permissions granted to groups they were members of.

The role attributes LOGIN, SUPERUSER, CREATEDB, and CREATEROLE can be thought of as special privileges, but they are never inherited as ordinary privileges on database objects are. You must actually SET ROLE to a specific role having one of these attributes in order to make use of the attribute. Continuing the above example, we might well choose to grant CREATEDB and CREATEROLE to the admin role. Then a session connecting as role joe would not have these privileges immediately, only after doing SET ROLE admin.

To destroy a group role, use DROP ROLE:

```
DROP ROLE name;
```

Any memberships in the group role are automatically revoked (but the member roles are not otherwise affected). Note however that any objects owned by the group role must first be dropped or reassigned to other owners; and any permissions granted to the group role must be revoked.

20.5. Functions and Triggers

Functions and triggers allow users to insert code into the backend server that other users might execute unintentionally. Hence, both mechanisms permit users to "Trojan horse" others with relative ease. The only real protection is tight control over who can define functions.

Functions run inside the backend server process with the operating system permissions of the database server daemon. If the programming language used for the function allows unchecked memory accesses, it is possible to change the server's internal data structures. Hence, among many other things, such functions can circumvent any system access controls. Function languages that allow such access are considered "untrusted", and PostgreSQL allows only superusers to create functions written in those languages.

Chapter 21.
Managing Databases

Every instance of a running PostgreSQL server manages one or more databases. Databases are therefore the topmost hierarchical level for organizing SQL objects ("database objects"). This chapter describes the properties of databases, and how to create, manage, and destroy them.

21.1. Overview

A database is a named collection of SQL objects ("database objects"). Generally, every database object (tables, functions, etc.) belongs to one and only one database. (But there are a few system catalogs, for example pg_database, that belong to a whole cluster and are accessible from each database within the cluster.) More accurately, a database is a collection of schemas and the schemas contain the tables, functions, etc. So the full hierarchy is: server, database, schema, table (or some other kind of object, such as a function).

When connecting to the database server, a client must specify in its connection request the name of the database it wants to connect to. It is not possible to access more than one database per connection. (But an application is not restricted in the number of connections it opens to the same or other databases.) Databases are physically separated and access control is managed at the connection level. If one PostgreSQL server instance is to house projects or users that should be separate and for the most part unaware of each other, it is therefore recommendable to put them into separate databases. If the projects or users are interrelated and should be able to use each other's resources they should be put in the same database, but possibly into separate schemas. Schemas are a purely logical structure and who can access what is managed by the privilege system. More information about managing schemas is in *Section 5.7* - Vol.I page 93.

Databases are created with the CREATE DATABASE command (see *Section 21.2* - page 152) and destroyed with the DROP DATABASE command (see *Section 21.5* - page 155). To determine the set of existing databases, examine the pg_database system catalog, for example

```
SELECT datname FROM pg_database;
```

The *psql* program's \l meta-command and -l command-line option are also useful for listing the existing databases.

Note

The SQL standard calls databases "catalogs", but there is no difference in practice.

21.2. Creating a Database

In order to create a database, the PostgreSQL server must be up and running (see *Section 17.3* - page 58).

Databases are created with the SQL command CREATE DATABASE:

```
CREATE DATABASE name;
```

where *name* follows the usual rules for SQL identifiers. The current role automatically becomes the owner of the new database. It is the privilege of the owner of a database to remove it later on (which also removes all the objects in it, even if they have a different owner).

The creation of databases is a restricted operation. See *Section 20.2* - page 146 for how to grant permission.

Since you need to be connected to the database server in order to execute the CREATE DATABASE command, the question remains how the *first* database at any given site can be created. The first database is always created by the initdb command when the data storage area is initialized. (See *Section 17.2* - page 56.) This database is called postgres. So to create the first "ordinary" database you can connect to postgres.

A second database, template1, is also created by initdb. Whenever a new database is created within the cluster, template1 is essentially cloned. This means that any changes you make in template1 are propagated to all subsequently created databases. Therefore it is unwise to use template1 for real work, but when used judiciously this feature can be convenient. More details appear in *Section 21.3* - page 153.

As a convenience, there is a program that you can execute from the shell to create new databases, createdb.

```
createdb dbname
```

createdb does no magic. It connects to the postgres database and issues the CREATE DATABASE command, exactly as described above. The *createdb* reference page contains the invocation details. Note that createdb without any arguments will create a database with the current user name, which might or might not be what you want.

Note

Chapter 19 - page 129 contains information about how to restrict who can connect to a given database.

Sometimes you want to create a database for someone else. That role should become the owner of the new database, so he can configure and manage it himself. To achieve that, use one of the following commands:

```
CREATE DATABASE dbname OWNER rolename;
```

from the SQL environment, or:

```
createdb -O rolename dbname
```

from the shell. You must be a superuser to be allowed to create a database for someone else (that is, for a role you are not a member of).

21.3. Template Databases

CREATE DATABASE actually works by copying an existing database. By default, it copies the standard system database named template1. Thus that database is the "template" from which new databases are made. If you add objects to template1, these objects will be copied into subsequently created user databases. This behavior allows site-local modifications to the standard set of objects in databases. For example, if you install the procedural language PL/pgSQL in template1, it will automatically be available in user databases without any extra action being taken when those databases are made.

There is a second standard system database named template0. This database contains the same data as the initial contents of template1, that is, only the standard objects predefined by your version of PostgreSQL. template0 should never be changed after initdb. By instructing CREATE DATABASE to copy template0 instead of template1, you can create a "virgin" user database that contains none of the site-local additions in template1. This is particularly handy when restoring a pg_dump dump: the dump script should be restored in a virgin database to ensure that one recreates the correct contents of the dumped database, without any conflicts with objects that might have been added to template1 later on.

Another common reason for copying template0 instead of template1 is that new encoding and locale settings can be specified when copying template0, whereas a copy of template1 must use the same settings it does. This is because template1 might contain encoding-specific or locale-specific data, while template0 is known not to.

To create a database by copying template0, use:

```
CREATE DATABASE dbname TEMPLATE template0;
```

from the SQL environment, or:

```
createdb -T template0 dbname
```

from the shell.

It is possible to create additional template databases, and indeed one can copy any database in a cluster by specifying its name as the template for CREATE DATABASE. It is important to understand, however, that this is not (yet) intended as a general-purpose "COPY DATABASE" facility. The principal limitation is that no other sessions can be connected to the source database while it is being copied. CREATE DATABASE will fail if any other connection exists when it starts; otherwise, new connections to the source database are locked out until CREATE DATABASE completes.

Two useful flags exist in pg_database for each database: the columns datistemplate and datallowconn. datistemplate can be set to indicate that a database is intended as a template for CREATE DATABASE. If this flag is set, the database can be cloned by any user with CREATEDB privileges; if it is not set, only superusers and the owner of the database can clone it. If datallowconn is false, then no new connections to that database will be allowed (but existing sessions are not killed simply by setting the flag false). The template0 database is normally marked datallowconn = false to prevent modification of it. Both template0 and template1 should always be marked with datistemplate = true.

 Note

> template1 and template0 do not have any special status beyond the fact that the name template1 is the default source database name for CREATE DATABASE. For example, one could drop template1 and recreate it from template0 without any ill effects. This course of action might be advisable if one has carelessly added a bunch of junk in template1. (To delete template1, it must have pg_database.datistemplate = false.)
>
> The postgres database is also created when a database cluster is initialized. This database is meant as a default database for users and applications to connect to. It is simply a copy of template1 and can be dropped and recreated if required.

21.4. Database Configuration

Recall from *Chapter 18* - page 77 that the PostgreSQL server provides a large number of run-time configuration variables. You can set database-specific default values for many of these settings.

For example, if for some reason you want to disable the GEQO optimizer for a given database, you'd ordinarily have to either disable it for all databases or make sure that every connecting client is careful to issue SET geqo TO off;. To make this setting the default within a particular database, you can execute the command:

```
ALTER DATABASE mydb SET geqo TO off;
```

This will save the setting (but not set it immediately). In subsequent connections to this database it will appear as though SET geqo TO off; had been executed just before the session started. Note that users can still alter this setting during their sessions; it will only be the default. To undo any such setting, use ALTER DATABASE *dbname* RESET *varname*;.

21.5. Destroying a Database

Databases are destroyed with the command DROP DATABASE:

```
DROP DATABASE name;
```

Only the owner of the database, or a superuser, can drop a database. Dropping a database removes all objects that were contained within the database. The destruction of a database cannot be undone.

You cannot execute the DROP DATABASE command while connected to the victim database. You can, however, be connected to any other database, including the template1 database. template1 would be the only option for dropping the last user database of a given cluster.

For convenience, there is also a shell program to drop databases, *dropdb*:

```
dropdb dbname
```

(Unlike createdb, it is not the default action to drop the database with the current user name.)

21.6. Tablespaces

Tablespaces in PostgreSQL allow database administrators to define locations in the file system where the files representing database objects can be stored. Once created, a tablespace can be referred to by name when creating database objects.

By using tablespaces, an administrator can control the disk layout of a PostgreSQL installation. This is useful in at least two ways. First, if the partition or volume on which the cluster was initialized runs out of space and cannot be extended, a tablespace can be created on a different partition and used until the system can be reconfigured.

Second, tablespaces allow an administrator to use knowledge of the usage pattern of database objects to optimize performance. For example, an index which is very heavily used can be placed on a very fast, highly available disk, such as an expensive solid state device. At the same time a table storing archived data which is rarely used or not performance critical could be stored on a less expensive, slower disk system.

To define a tablespace, use the CREATE TABLESPACE command, for example::

```
CREATE TABLESPACE fastspace LOCATION '/mnt/sda1/postgresql/data';
```

The location must be an existing, empty directory that is owned by the PostgreSQL system user. All objects subsequently created within the tablespace will be stored in files underneath this directory.

Note

There is usually not much point in making more than one tablespace per logical file system, since you cannot control the location of individual files within a logical file system. However, PostgreSQL does not enforce any such limitation, and indeed it is not directly aware of the file system boundaries on your system. It just stores files in the directories you tell it to use.

Creation of the tablespace itself must be done as a database superuser, but after that you can allow ordinary database users to make use of it. To do that, grant them the CREATE privilege on it.

Tables, indexes, and entire databases can be assigned to particular tablespaces. To do so, a user with the CREATE privilege on a given tablespace must pass the tablespace name as a parameter to the relevant command. For example, the following creates a table in the tablespace space1:

```
CREATE TABLE foo(i int) TABLESPACE space1;
```

Alternatively, use the *default_tablespace* parameter:

```
SET default_tablespace = space1;
CREATE TABLE foo(i int);
```

When default_tablespace is set to anything but an empty string, it supplies an implicit TABLESPACE clause for CREATE TABLE and CREATE INDEX commands that do not have an explicit one.

There is also a *temp_tablespaces* parameter, which determines the placement of temporary tables and indexes, as well as temporary files that are used for purposes such as sorting large data sets. This can be a list of tablespace names, rather than only one, so that the load associated with temporary objects can be spread over multiple tablespaces. A random member of the list is picked each time a temporary object is to be created.

The tablespace associated with a database is used to store the system catalogs of that database. Furthermore, it is the default tablespace used for tables, indexes, and temporary files created within the database, if no TABLESPACE clause is given and no other selection is specified by default_tablespace or temp_tablespaces (as appropriate). If a database is created without specifying a tablespace for it, it uses the same tablespace as the template database it is copied from.

Two tablespaces are automatically created by initdb. The pg_global tablespace is used for shared system catalogs. The pg_default tablespace is the default tablespace of the template1 and template0 databases (and, therefore, will be the default tablespace for other databases as well, unless overridden by a TABLESPACE clause in CREATE DATABASE).

Once created, a tablespace can be used from any database, provided the requesting user has sufficient privilege. This means that a tablespace cannot be dropped until all objects in all databases using the tablespace have been removed.

To remove an empty tablespace, use the DROP TABLESPACE command.

To determine the set of existing tablespaces, examine the pg_tablespace system catalog, for example

```
SELECT spcname FROM pg_tablespace;
```

The *psql* program's \db meta-command is also useful for listing the existing tablespaces.

PostgreSQL makes use of symbolic links to simplify the implementation of tablespaces. This means that tablespaces can be used *only* on systems that support symbolic links.

The directory $PGDATA/pg_tblspc contains symbolic links that point to each of the non-built-in tablespaces defined in the cluster. Although not recommended, it is possible to adjust the tablespace layout by hand by redefining these links. Two warnings: do not do so while the server is running; and after you restart the server, update the pg_tablespace catalog to show the new locations. (If you do not, pg_dump will continue to show the old tablespace locations.)

Chapter 22.
Localization

This chapter describes the available localization features from the point of view of the administrator. PostgreSQL supports localization with two approaches:

- Using the locale features of the operating system to provide locale-specific collation order, number formatting, translated messages, and other aspects.
- Providing a number of different character sets to support storing text in all kinds of languages, and providing character set translation between client and server.

22.1. Locale Support

Locale support refers to an application respecting cultural preferences regarding alphabets, sorting, number formatting, etc. PostgreSQL uses the standard ISO C and POSIX locale facilities provided by the server operating system. For additional information refer to the documentation of your system.

22.1.1. Overview

Locale support is automatically initialized when a database cluster is created using initdb. initdb will initialize the database cluster with the locale setting of its execution environment by default, so if your system is already set to use the locale that you want in your database cluster then there is nothing else you need to do. If you want to use a different locale (or you are not sure which locale your system is set to), you can instruct initdb exactly which locale to use by specifying the --locale option. For example:

```
initdb --locale=sv_SE
```

This example for Unix systems sets the locale to Swedish (sv) as spoken in Sweden (SE). Other possibilities might be en_US (U.S. English) and fr_CA (French Canadian). If more than one character set can be useful for a locale then the specifications look like this: cs_CZ.ISO8859-2. What locales are available under what names on your system depends on what was provided by the operating system vendor and what was installed. On most Unix systems, the command locale -a will provide a list of available locales. Windows uses more verbose locale names, such as German_Germany or Swedish_Sweden.1252, but the principles are the same.

Occasionally it is useful to mix rules from several locales, e.g., use English collation rules but Spanish messages. To support that, a set of locale subcategories exist that control only a certain aspect of the localization rules:

LC_COLLATE	String sort order
LC_CTYPE	Character classification (What is a letter? Its upper-case equivalent?)
LC_MESSAGES	Language of messages
LC_MONETARY	Formatting of currency amounts
LC_NUMERIC	Formatting of numbers
LC_TIME	Formatting of dates and times

The category names translate into names of `initdb` options to override the locale choice for a specific category. For instance, to set the locale to French Canadian, but use U.S. rules for formatting currency, use `initdb --locale=fr_CA --lc-monetary=en_US`.

If you want the system to behave as if it had no locale support, use the special locale C or POSIX.

The nature of some locale categories is that their value has to be fixed when the database is created. You can use different settings for different databases, but once a database is created, you cannot change them for that database anymore. LC_COLLATE and LC_CTYPE are these categories. They affect the sort order of indexes, so they must be kept fixed, or indexes on text columns will become corrupt. The default values for these categories are determined when initdb is run, and those values are used when new databases are created, unless specified otherwise in the CREATE DATABASE command.

The other locale categories can be changed whenever desired by setting the server configuration parameters that have the same name as the locale categories (see *Section 18.10.2 - page 115* for details). The values that are chosen by initdb are actually only written into the configuration file postgresql.conf to serve as defaults when the server is started. If you delete these assignments from postgresql.conf then the server will inherit the settings from its execution environment.

Note that the locale behavior of the server is determined by the environment variables seen by the server, not by the environment of any client. Therefore, be careful to configure the correct locale settings before starting the server. A consequence of this is that if client and server are set up in different locales, messages might appear in different languages depending on where they originated.

 Note

> When we speak of inheriting the locale from the execution environment, this means the following on most operating systems: For a given locale category, say the

collation, the following environment variables are consulted in this order until one is found to be set: LC_ALL, LC_COLLATE (or the variable corresponding to the respective category), LANG. If none of these environment variables are set then the locale defaults to C.

Some message localization libraries also look at the environment variable LANGUAGE which overrides all other locale settings for the purpose of setting the language of messages. If in doubt, please refer to the documentation of your operating system, in particular the documentation about gettext, for more information.

To enable messages to be translated to the user's preferred language, NLS must have been selected at build time (configure --enable-nls). All other locale support is built in automatically.

22.1.2. Behavior

The locale settings influence the following SQL features:

- Sort order in queries using ORDER BY or the standard comparison operators on textual data
- The ability to use indexes with LIKE clauses
- The upper, lower, and initcap functions
- The to_char family of functions

The drawback of using locales other than C or POSIX in PostgreSQL is its performance impact. It slows character handling and prevents ordinary indexes from being used by LIKE. For this reason use locales only if you actually need them.

As a workaround to allow PostgreSQL to use indexes with LIKE clauses under a non-C locale, several custom operator classes exist. These allow the creation of an index that performs a strict character-by-character comparison, ignoring locale comparison rules. Refer to *Section 11.9* - Vol.I page 318 for more information.

22.1.3. Problems

If locale support doesn't work according to the explanation above, check that the locale support in your operating system is correctly configured. To check what locales are installed on your system, you can use the command locale -a if your operating system provides it.

Check that PostgreSQL is actually using the locale that you think it is. The LC_COLLATE and LC_CTYPE settings are determined when a database is created, and cannot be changed except by creating a new database. Other locale settings including LC_MESSAGES and LC_MONETARY are initially determined by the environment the server is started in, but can be changed on-the-fly. You can check the active locale settings using the SHOW command.

The directory src/test/locale in the source distribution contains a test suite for PostgreSQL's locale support.

Client applications that handle server-side errors by parsing the text of the error message will obviously have problems when the server's messages are in a different language. Authors of such applications are advised to make use of the error code scheme instead.

Maintaining catalogs of message translations requires the on-going efforts of many volunteers that want to see PostgreSQL speak their preferred language well. If messages in your language are currently not available or not fully translated, your assistance would be appreciated. If you want to help, refer to *Chapter 47* or write to the developers' mailing list.

22.2. Character Set Support

The character set support in PostgreSQL allows you to store text in a variety of character sets (also called encodings), including single-byte character sets such as the ISO 8859 series and multiple-byte character sets such as EUC (Extended Unix Code), UTF-8, and Mule internal code. All supported character sets can be used transparently by clients, but a few are not supported for use within the server (that is, as a server-side encoding). The default character set is selected while initializing your PostgreSQL database cluster using initdb. It can be overridden when you create a database, so you can have multiple databases each with a different character set.

An important restriction, however, is that each database's character set must be compatible with the database's LC_CTYPE and LC_COLLATE locale settings. For C or POSIX locale, any character set is allowed, but for other locales there is only one character set that will work correctly. (On Windows, however, UTF-8 encoding can be used with any locale.)

22.2.1. Supported Character Sets

Table 22-1 shows the character sets available for use in PostgreSQL.

Name	Description	Language	Server?	Bytes/Char	Aliases
BIG5	Big Five	Traditional Chinese	No	1-2	WIN950, Windows950
EUC_CN	Extended UNIX Code-CN	Simplified Chinese	Yes	1-3	
EUC_JP	Extended UNIX Code-JP	Japanese	Yes	1-3	
EUC_JIS_2004	Extended UNIX Code-JP, JIS X 0213	Japanese	Yes	1-3	

Name	Description	Language	Server?	Bytes/Char	Aliases
EUC_KR	Extended UNIX Code-KR	Korean	Yes	1-3	
EUC_TW	Extended UNIX Code-TW	Traditional Chinese, Taiwanese	Yes	1-3	
GB18030	National Standard	Chinese	No	1-2	
GBK	Extended National Standard	Simplified Chinese	No	1-2	WIN936, Windows936
ISO_8859_5	ISO 8859-5, ECMA 113	Latin/Cyrillic	Yes	1	
ISO_8859_6	ISO 8859-6, ECMA 114	Latin/Arabic	Yes	1	
ISO_8859_7	ISO 8859-7, ECMA 118	Latin/Greek	Yes	1	
ISO_8859_8	ISO 8859-8, ECMA 121	Latin/Hebrew	Yes	1	
JOHAB	JOHAB	Korean (Hangul)	No	1-3	
KOI8R	KOI8-R	Cyrillic (Russian)	Yes	1	KOI8
KOI8U	KOI8-U	Cyrillic (Ukrainian)	Yes	1	
LATIN1	ISO 8859-1, ECMA 94	Western European	Yes	1	ISO88591
LATIN2	ISO 8859-2, ECMA 94	Central European	Yes	1	ISO88592
LATIN3	ISO 8859-3, ECMA 94	South European	Yes	1	ISO88593
LATIN4	ISO 8859-4, ECMA 94	North European	Yes	1	ISO88594
LATIN5	ISO 8859-9, ECMA 128	Turkish	Yes	1	ISO88599
LATIN6	ISO 8859-10, ECMA 144	Nordic	Yes	1	ISO885910
LATIN7	ISO 8859-13	Baltic	Yes	1	ISO885913
LATIN8	ISO 8859-14	Celtic	Yes	1	ISO885914
LATIN9	ISO 8859-15	LATIN1 with Euro and accents	Yes	1	ISO885915
LATIN10	ISO 8859-16, ASRO SR 14111	Romanian	Yes	1	ISO885916
MULE_INTERNAL	Mule internal code	Multilingual Emacs	Yes	1-4	

Name	Description	Language	Server?	Bytes/Char	Aliases
SJIS	Shift JIS	Japanese	No	1-2	Mskanji, ShiftJIS, WIN932, Windows932
SHIFT_JIS_2004	Shift JIS, JIS X 0213	Japanese	No	1-2	
SQL_ASCII	unspecified (see text)	*any*	Yes	1	
UHC	Unified Hangul Code	Korean	No	1-2	WIN949, Windows949
UTF8	Unicode, 8-bit	*all*	Yes	1-4	Unicode
WIN866	Windows CP866	Cyrillic	Yes	1	ALT
WIN874	Windows CP874	Thai	Yes	1	
WIN1250	Windows CP1250	Central European	Yes	1	
WIN1251	Windows CP1251	Cyrillic	Yes	1	WIN
WIN1252	Windows CP1252	Western European	Yes	1	
WIN1253	Windows CP1253	Greek	Yes	1	
WIN1254	Windows CP1254	Turkish	Yes	1	
WIN1255	Windows CP1255	Hebrew	Yes	1	
WIN1256	Windows CP1256	Arabic	Yes	1	
WIN1257	Windows CP1257	Baltic	Yes	1	
WIN1258	Windows CP1258	Vietnamese	Yes	1	ABC, TCVN, TCVN5712, VSCII

Table 22-1. PostgreSQL Character Sets

Not all APIs support all the listed character sets. For example, the PostgreSQL JDBC driver does not support MULE_INTERNAL, LATIN6, LATIN8, and LATIN10.

The SQL_ASCII setting behaves considerably differently from the other settings. When the server character set is SQL_ASCII, the server interprets byte values 0-127 according to the ASCII standard, while byte values 128-255 are taken as uninterpreted characters. No encoding conversion will be done when the setting is SQL_ASCII. Thus, this setting is not so much a declaration that a specific encoding is in use, as a declaration of ignorance about the encoding. In most cases, if you are working with any non-ASCII data, it is unwise to use the SQL_ASCII setting, because PostgreSQL will be unable to help you by converting or validating non-ASCII characters.

22.2.2. Setting the Character Set

initdb defines the default character set for a PostgreSQL cluster. For example,

```
initdb -E EUC_JP
```

sets the default character set (encoding) to EUC_JP (Extended Unix Code for Japanese). You can use --encoding instead of -E if you prefer to type longer option strings. If no -E or --encoding option is given, initdb attempts to determine the appropriate encoding to use based on the specified or default locale.

You can specify a non-default encoding at database creation time, provided that the encoding is compatible with the selected locale:

```
createdb -E EUC_KR -T template0 --lc-collate=ko_KR.euckr --lc-ctype=ko_KR.euckr korean
```

This will create a database named korean that uses the character set EUC_KR, and locale ko_KR. Another way to accomplish this is to use this SQL command:

```
CREATE DATABASE korean WITH ENCODING 'EUC_KR' LC_COLLATE='ko_KR.euckr'
LC_CTYPE='ko_KR.euckr' TEMPLATE=template0;
```

Notice that the above commands specify copying the template0 database. When copying any other database, the encoding and locale settings cannot be changed from those of the source database, because that might result in corrupt data. For more information see *Section 21.3* - page 153.

The encoding for a database is stored in the system catalog pg_database. You can see it by using the -l option or the \l command of psql.

```
$ psql -l
                          List of databases
    Name    |  Owner   |  Encoding  |   Collation   |    Ctype     |    Access Privileges
------------+----------+------------+---------------+--------------+----------------------
 clocaledb  | hlinnaka | SQL_ASCII  | C             | C            |
 englishdb  | hlinnaka | UTF8       | en_GB.UTF8    | en_GB.UTF8   |
 japanese   | hlinnaka | UTF8       | ja_JP.UTF8    | ja_JP.UTF8   |
 korean     | hlinnaka | EUC_KR     | ko_KR.euckr   | ko_KR.euckr  |
 postgres   | hlinnaka | UTF8       | fi_FI.UTF8    | fi_FI.UTF8   |
 template0  | hlinnaka | UTF8       | fi_FI.UTF8    | fi_FI.UTF8   | {=c/hlinnaka,hlinnaka=CTc/hlinnaka}
 template1  | hlinnaka | UTF8       | fi_FI.UTF8    | fi_FI.UTF8   | {=c/hlinnaka,hlinnaka=CTc/hlinnaka}
(7 rows)
```

 Important

On most modern operating systems, PostgreSQL can determine which character set is implied by an LC_CTYPE setting, and it will enforce that only the matching database encoding is used. On older systems it is your responsibility to ensure that you use the encoding expected by the locale you have selected. A mistake in this area is likely to lead to strange misbehavior of locale-dependent operations such as sorting.

PostgreSQL will allow superusers to create databases with SQL_ASCII encoding even when LC_CTYPE is not C or POSIX. As noted above, SQL_ASCII does not enforce that the data stored in the database has any particular encoding, and so this choice poses risks of locale-dependent misbehavior. Using this combination of settings is deprecated and may someday be forbidden altogether.

22.2.3. Automatic Character Set Conversion Between Server and Client

PostgreSQL supports automatic character set conversion between server and client for certain character set combinations. The conversion information is stored in the pg_conversion system catalog. PostgreSQL comes with some predefined conversions, as shown in *Table 22-2*. You can create a new conversion using the SQL command CREATE CONVERSION.

Server Character Set	Available Client Character Sets
BIG5	*not supported as a server encoding*
EUC_CN	*EUC_CN*, MULE_INTERNAL, UTF8
EUC_JP	*EUC_JP*, MULE_INTERNAL, SJIS, UTF8
EUC_KR	*EUC_KR*, MULE_INTERNAL, UTF8
EUC_TW	*EUC_TW*, BIG5, MULE_INTERNAL, UTF8
GB18030	*not supported as a server encoding*
GBK	*not supported as a server encoding*
ISO_8859_5	*ISO_8859_5*, KOI8R, MULE_INTERNAL, UTF8, WIN866, WIN1251
ISO_8859_6	*ISO_8859_6*, UTF8
ISO_8859_7	*ISO_8859_7*, UTF8
ISO_8859_8	*ISO_8859_8*, UTF8
JOHAB	*JOHAB*, UTF8
KOI8R	*KOI8R*, ISO_8859_5, MULE_INTERNAL, UTF8, WIN866, WIN1251
KOI8U	*KOI8U*, UTF8
LATIN1	*LATIN1*, MULE_INTERNAL, UTF8
LATIN2	*LATIN2*, MULE_INTERNAL, UTF8, WIN1250
LATIN3	*LATIN3*, MULE_INTERNAL, UTF8
LATIN4	*LATIN4*, MULE_INTERNAL, UTF8
LATIN5	*LATIN5*, UTF8
LATIN6	*LATIN6*, UTF8
LATIN7	*LATIN7*, UTF8
LATIN8	*LATIN8*, UTF8
LATIN9	*LATIN9*, UTF8
LATIN10	*LATIN10*, UTF8
MULE_INTERNAL	*MULE_INTERNAL*, BIG5, EUC_CN, EUC_JP, EUC_KR, EUC_TW, ISO_8859_5, KOI8R, LATIN1 to LATIN4, SJIS, WIN866, WIN1250, WIN1251
SJIS	*not supported as a server encoding*

Server Character Set	Available Client Character Sets
SQL_ASCII	*any (no conversion will be performed)*
UHC	*not supported as a server encoding*
UTF8	*all supported encodings*
WIN866	*WIN866,* ISO_8859_5, KOI8R, MULE_INTERNAL, UTF8, WIN1251
WIN874	*WIN874,* UTF8
WIN1250	*WIN1250,* LATIN2, MULE_INTERNAL, UTF8
WIN1251	*WIN1251,* ISO_8859_5, KOI8R, MULE_INTERNAL, UTF8, WIN866
WIN1252	*WIN1252,* UTF8
WIN1253	*WIN1253,* UTF8
WIN1254	*WIN1254,* UTF8
WIN1255	*WIN1255,* UTF8
WIN1256	*WIN1256,* UTF8
WIN1257	*WIN1257,* UTF8
WIN1258	*WIN1258,* UTF8

Table 22-2. Client/Server Character Set Conversions

To enable automatic character set conversion, you have to tell PostgreSQL the character set (encoding) you would like to use in the client. There are several ways to accomplish this:

- Using the \encoding command in psql. \encoding allows you to change client encoding on the fly. For example, to change the encoding to SJIS, type:

  \encoding SJIS

- libpq (*Section 30.9* - page 288) has functions to control the client encoding.

- Using SET client_encoding TO. Setting the client encoding can be done with this SQL command:

  SET CLIENT_ENCODING TO 'value';

  Also you can use the standard SQL syntax SET NAMES for this purpose:

  SET NAMES 'value';

  To query the current client encoding:

  SHOW client_encoding;

  To return to the default encoding:

  RESET client_encoding;

- Using PGCLIENTENCODING. If the environment variable PGCLIENTENCODING is defined in the client's environment, that client encoding is automatically selected when a connection to the server is made. (This can subsequently be overridden using any of the other methods mentioned above.)

- Using the configuration variable *client_encoding*. If the `client_encoding` variable is set, that client encoding is automatically selected when a connection to the server is made. (This can subsequently be overridden using any of the other methods mentioned above.)

If the conversion of a particular character is not possible — suppose you chose `EUC_JP` for the server and `LATIN1` for the client, then some Japanese characters do not have a representation in `LATIN1` — then an error is reported.

If the client character set is defined as SQL_ASCII, encoding conversion is disabled, regardless of the server's character set. Just as for the server, use of SQL_ASCII is unwise unless you are working with all-ASCII data.

22.2.4. Further Reading

These are good sources to start learning about various kinds of encoding systems.

http://www.i18ngurus.com/docs/984813247.html

An extensive collection of documents about character sets, encodings, and code pages.

ftp://ftp.ora.com/pub/examples/nutshell/ujip/doc/cjk.inf

Detailed explanations of EUC_JP, EUC_CN, EUC_KR, EUC_TW appear in section 3.2.

http://www.unicode.org/

The web site of the Unicode Consortium.

RFC 3629

UTF-8 is defined here.

Chapter 23.
Routine Database Maintenance Tasks

PostgreSQL, like any database software, requires that certain tasks be performed regularly to achieve optimum performance. The tasks discussed here are *required*, but they are repetitive in nature and can easily be automated using standard tools such as cron scripts or Windows' Task Scheduler. But it is the database administrator's responsibility to set up appropriate scripts, and to check that they execute successfully.

One obvious maintenance task is creation of backup copies of the data on a regular schedule. Without a recent backup, you have no chance of recovery after a catastrophe (disk failure, fire, mistakenly dropping a critical table, etc.). The backup and recovery mechanisms available in PostgreSQL are discussed at length in *Chapter 24* - page 179.

The other main category of maintenance task is periodic "vacuuming" of the database. This activity is discussed in *Section 23.1* - page 168. Closely related to this is updating the statistics that will be used by the query planner, as discussed in *Section 23.1.3* - page 171.

Another task that might need periodic attention is log file management. This is discussed in *Section 23.3* - page 177.

check_postgres.pl[1] is available for monitoring database health and reporting unusual conditions. check_postgres.pl integrates with Nagios and MRTG, but can be run standalone too.

PostgreSQL is low-maintenance compared to some other database management systems. Nonetheless, appropriate attention to these tasks will go far towards ensuring a pleasant and productive experience with the system.

23.1. Routine Vacuuming

PostgreSQL databases require periodic maintenance known as *vacuuming*. For many installations, it is sufficient to let vacuuming be performed by the *autovacuum daemon*, which is described in *Section 23.1.5* - page 175. You might need to adjust the autovacuuming parameters described there to obtain best results for your situation. Some database

---

[1] *http://bucardo.org/check_postgres/*

administrators will want to supplement or replace the daemon's activities with manually-managed VACUUM commands, which typically are executed according to a schedule by cron or Task Scheduler scripts. To set up manually-managed vacuuming properly, it is essential to understand the issues discussed in the next few subsections. Administrators who rely on autovacuuming may still wish to skim this material to help them understand and adjust autovacuuming.

23.1.1. Vacuuming Basics

PostgreSQL's VACUUM command has to process each table on a regular basis for several reasons:

1.   To recover or reuse disk space occupied by updated or deleted rows.
2.   To update data statistics used by the PostgreSQL query planner.
3.   To protect against loss of very old data due to *transaction ID wraparound.*

Each of these reasons dictates performing VACUUM operations of varying frequency and scope, as explained in the following subsections.

There are two variants of VACUUM: standard VACUUM and VACUUM FULL. VACUUM FULL can reclaim more disk space but runs much more slowly. Also, the standard form of VACUUM can run in parallel with production database operations. (Commands such as SELECT, INSERT, UPDATE, and DELETE will continue to function as normal, though you will not be able to modify the definition of a table with commands such as ALTER TABLE while it is being vacuumed.) VACUUM FULL requires exclusive lock on the table it is working on, and therefore cannot be done in parallel with other use of the table. Another disadvantage of VACUUM FULL is that while it reduces table size, it does not reduce index size proportionally; in fact it can make indexes *larger.* Generally, therefore, administrators should strive to use standard VACUUM and avoid VACUUM FULL.

VACUUM creates a substantial amount of I/O traffic, which can cause poor performance for other active sessions. There are configuration parameters that can be adjusted to reduce the performance impact of background vacuuming — see *Section 18.4.3* - page 86.

23.1.2. Recovering Disk Space

In PostgreSQL, an UPDATE or DELETE of a row does not immediately remove the old version of the row. This approach is necessary to gain the benefits of multiversion concurrency control (see *Chapter 13* - Vol.I page 361): the row version must not be deleted while it is still potentially visible to other transactions. But eventually, an outdated or deleted row version is no longer of interest to any transaction. The space it occupies must then be reclaimed for reuse by new rows, to avoid infinite growth of disk space requirements. This is done by running VACUUM.

The standard form of VACUUM removes dead row versions in tables and indexes and marks the space available for future reuse. However, it will not return the space to the operating system, except in the special case where one or more pages at the end of a table become entirely free and an exclusive table lock can be easily obtained. In contrast, VACUUM FULL actively compacts tables by moving row versions to earlier pages. It is thus able to force pages at the end of the table to become entirely free, whereupon it will return them to the operating system. However, if many rows must be moved, this can take a long time. Also, moving a row requires transiently making duplicate index entries for it (the entry pointing to its new location must be made before the old entry can be removed); so moving a lot of rows this way causes severe index bloat.

The usual goal of routine vacuuming is to do standard VACUUMs often enough to avoid needing VACUUM FULL. The autovacuum daemon attempts to work this way, and in fact will never issue VACUUM FULL. In this approach, the idea is not to keep tables at their minimum size, but to maintain steady-state usage of disk space: each table occupies space equivalent to its minimum size plus however much space gets used up between vacuumings. Although VACUUM FULL can be used to shrink a table back to its minimum size and return the disk space to the operating system, there is not much point in this if the table will just grow again in the future. Thus, moderately-frequent standard VACUUM runs are a better approach than infrequent VACUUM FULL runs for maintaining heavily-updated tables.

Some administrators prefer to schedule vacuuming themselves, for example doing all the work at night when load is low. The difficulty with doing vacuuming according to a fixed schedule is that if a table has an unexpected spike in update activity, it may get bloated to the point that VACUUM FULL is really necessary to reclaim space. Using the autovacuum daemon alleviates this problem, since the daemon schedules vacuuming dynamically in response to update activity. It is unwise to disable the daemon completely unless you have an extremely predictable workload. One possible compromise is to set the daemon's parameters so that it will only react to unusually heavy update activity, thus keeping things from getting out of hand, while scheduled VACUUMs are expected to do the bulk of the work when the load is typical.

For those not using autovacuum, a typical approach is to schedule a database-wide VACUUM once a day during a low-usage period, supplemented by more frequent vacuuming of heavily-updated tables as necessary. (Some installations with extremely high update rates vacuum their busiest tables as often as once every few minutes.) If you have multiple databases in a cluster, don't forget to VACUUM each one; the program *vacuumdb* might be helpful.

 Tip

Neither form of VACUUM is entirely satisfactory when a table contains large numbers of dead row versions as a result of massive update or delete activity. If you have such a table and you need to reclaim the excess disk space it occupies, the best way is to use CLUSTER or one of the table-rewriting variants of ALTER TABLE. These commands rewrite an entire new copy of the table and build new indexes for it. Like VACUUM FULL, they require exclusive lock. Note that they also temporarily use extra disk space, since the old copies of the table and indexes can't be released until the new ones are complete. In the worst case where your disk is nearly full, VACUUM FULL may be the only workable alternative.

 Tip

If you have a table whose entire contents are deleted on a periodic basis, consider doing it with TRUNCATE rather than using DELETE followed by VACUUM. TRUNCATE removes the entire content of the table immediately, without requiring a subsequent VACUUM or VACUUM FULL to reclaim the now-unused disk space. The disadvantage is that strict MVCC semantics are violated.

23.1.3. Updating Planner Statistics

The PostgreSQL query planner relies on statistical information about the contents of tables in order to generate good plans for queries. These statistics are gathered by the ANALYZE command, which can be invoked by itself or as an optional step in VACUUM. It is important to have reasonably accurate statistics, otherwise poor choices of plans might degrade database performance.

The autovacuum daemon, if enabled, will automatically issue ANALYZE commands whenever the content of a table has changed sufficiently. However, administrators might prefer to rely on manually-scheduled ANALYZE operations, particularly if it is known that update activity on a table will not affect the statistics of "interesting" columns. The daemon schedules ANALYZE strictly as a function of the number of rows inserted or updated; it has no knowledge of whether that will lead to meaningful statistical changes.

As with vacuuming for space recovery, frequent updates of statistics are more useful for heavily-updated tables than for seldom-updated ones. But even for a heavily-updated table, there might be no need for statistics updates if the statistical distribution of the data is not changing much. A simple rule of thumb is to think about how much the minimum and maximum values of the columns in the table change. For example, a timestamp column that contains the time of row update will have a constantly-increasing maximum value as rows are added and updated; such a column will probably need more frequent statistics updates than, say, a column containing URLs for pages accessed on a website. The URL column might receive changes just as often, but the statistical distribution of its values probably changes relatively slowly.

It is possible to run ANALYZE on specific tables and even just specific columns of a table, so the flexibility exists to update some statistics more frequently than others if your application requires it. In practice, however, it is usually best to just analyze the entire database, because it is a fast operation. ANALYZE uses a statistical random sampling of the rows of a table rather than reading every single row.

 Tip

> Although per-column tweaking of ANALYZE frequency might not be very productive, you might well find it worthwhile to do per-column adjustment of the level of detail of the statistics collected by ANALYZE. Columns that are heavily used in WHERE clauses and have highly irregular data distributions might require a finer-grain data histogram than other columns. See ALTER TABLE SET STATISTICS, or change the database-wide default using the *default_statistics_target* configuration parameter.

23.1.4. Preventing Transaction ID Wraparound Failures

PostgreSQL's MVCC transaction semantics depend on being able to compare transaction ID (XID) numbers: a row version with an insertion XID greater than the current transaction's XID is "in the future" and should not be visible to the current transaction. But since transaction IDs have limited size (32 bits at this writing) a cluster that runs for a long time (more than 4 billion transactions) would suffer *transaction ID wraparound*: the XID counter wraps around to zero, and all of a sudden transactions that were in the past appear to be in the future — which means their outputs become invisible. In short, catastrophic data loss. (Actually the data is still there, but that's cold comfort if you cannot get at it.) To avoid this, it is necessary to vacuum every table in every database at least once every two billion transactions.

The reason that periodic vacuuming solves the problem is that PostgreSQL distinguishes a special XID FrozenXID. This XID is always considered older than every normal XID. Normal XIDs are compared using modulo-2^{31} arithmetic. This means that for every normal XID, there are two billion XIDs that are "older" and two billion that are "newer"; another way to say it is that the normal XID space is circular with no endpoint. Therefore, once a row version has been created with a particular normal XID, the row version will appear to be "in the past" for the next two billion transactions, no matter which normal XID we are talking about. If the row version still exists after more than two billion transactions, it will suddenly appear to be in the future. To prevent data loss, old row versions must be reassigned the XID FrozenXID sometime before they reach the two-billion-transactions-old mark. Once they are assigned this special XID, they will appear to be "in the past" to all normal transactions regardless of wraparound issues, and so such row versions will be good until deleted, no matter how long that is. This reassignment of old XIDs is handled by VACUUM.

vacuum_freeze_min_age controls how old an XID value has to be before it's replaced with FrozenXID. Larger values of this setting preserve transactional information longer, while smaller values increase the number of transactions that can elapse before the table must be vacuumed again.

VACUUM normally skips pages that don't have any dead row versions, but those pages might still have row versions with old XID values. To ensure all old XIDs have been replaced by FrozenXID, a scan of the whole table is needed. *vacuum_freeze_table_age* controls when VACUUM does that: a whole table sweep is forced if the table hasn't been fully scanned for vacuum_freeze_table_age minus vacuum_freeze_min_age transactions. Setting it to 0 forces VACUUM to always scan all pages, effectively ignoring the visibility map.

The maximum time that a table can go unvacuumed is two billion transactions minus the vacuum_freeze_min_age that was used when VACUUM last scanned the whole table. If it were to go unvacuumed for longer than that, data loss could result. To ensure that this does not happen, autovacuum is invoked on any table that might contain XIDs older than the age specified by the configuration parameter *autovacuum_freeze_max_age*. (This will happen even if autovacuum is otherwise disabled.)

This implies that if a table is not otherwise vacuumed, autovacuum will be invoked on it approximately once every autovacuum_freeze_max_age minus vacuum_freeze_min_age transactions. For tables that are regularly vacuumed for space reclamation purposes, this is of little importance. However, for static tables (including tables that receive inserts, but no updates or deletes), there is no need for vacuuming for space reclamation, and so it can be useful to try to maximize the interval between forced autovacuums on very large static tables. Obviously one can do this either by increasing autovacuum_freeze_max_age or by decreasing vacuum_freeze_min_age.

The effective maximum for `vacuum_freeze_table_age` is 0.95 * `autovacuum_freeze_max_age`; a setting higher than that will be capped to the maximum. A value higher than `autovacuum_freeze_max_age` wouldn't make sense because an anti-wraparound autovacuum would be triggered at that point anyway, and the 0.95 multiplier leaves some breathing room to run a manual VACUUM before that happens. As a rule of thumb, `vacuum_freeze_table_age` should be set to a value somewhat below `autovacuum_freeze_max_age`, leaving enough gap so that a regularly scheduled VACUUM or an autovacuum triggered by normal delete and update activity is run in that window. Setting it too close could lead to anti-wraparound autovacuums, even though the table was recently vacuumed to reclaim space, whereas lower values lead to more frequent whole-table scans.

The sole disadvantage of increasing `autovacuum_freeze_max_age` (and `vacuum_freeze_table_age` along with it) is that the `pg_clog` subdirectory of the database cluster will take more space, because it must store the commit status for all transactions back to the `autovacuum_freeze_max_age` horizon. The commit status uses two bits per transaction, so if `autovacuum_freeze_max_age` has its maximum allowed value of a little less than two billion, `pg_clog` can be expected to grow to about half a gigabyte. If this is trivial compared to your total database size, setting `autovacuum_freeze_max_age` to its maximum allowed value is recommended. Otherwise, set it depending on what you are willing to allow for `pg_clog` storage. (The default, 200 million transactions, translates to about 50MB of `pg_clog` storage.)

One disadvantage of decreasing `vacuum_freeze_min_age` is that it might cause VACUUM to do useless work: changing a table row's XID to `FrozenXID` is a waste of time if the row is modified soon thereafter (causing it to acquire a new XID). So the setting should be large enough that rows are not frozen until they are unlikely to change any more. Another disadvantage of decreasing this setting is that details about exactly which transaction inserted or modified a row will be lost sooner. This information sometimes comes in handy, particularly when trying to analyze what went wrong after a database failure. For these two reasons, decreasing this setting is not recommended except for completely static tables.

To track the age of the oldest XIDs in a database, VACUUM stores XID statistics in the system tables `pg_class` and `pg_database`. In particular, the `relfrozenxid` column of a table's `pg_class` row contains the freeze cutoff XID that was used by the last whole-table VACUUM for that table. All normal XIDs older than this cutoff XID are guaranteed to have been replaced by `FrozenXID` within the table. Similarly, the `datfrozenxid` column of a database's `pg_database` row is a lower bound on the normal XIDs appearing in that database — it is just the minimum of the per-table `relfrozenxid` values within the database. A convenient way to examine this information is to execute queries such as:

```
SELECT relname, age(relfrozenxid) FROM pg_class WHERE relkind = 'r';
SELECT datname, age(datfrozenxid) FROM pg_database;
```

The `age` column measures the number of transactions from the cutoff XID to the current transaction's XID.

VACUUM normally only scans pages that have been modified since the last vacuum, but `relfrozenxid` can only be advanced when the whole table is scanned. The whole table is scanned when `relfrozenxid` is more than `vacuum_freeze_table_age` transactions old, when the VACUUM FREEZE command is used, or when all pages happen to require vacuuming to remove dead row versions. When VACUUM scans the whole table, after it's finished `age(relfrozenxid)` should be a little more than the `vacuum_freeze_min_age` setting that was used (more by the number of transactions started since the VACUUM started). If no whole-table-scanning VACUUM is issued on the table until `autovacuum_freeze_max_age` is reached, an autovacuum will soon be forced for the table.

If for some reason autovacuum fails to clear old XIDs from a table, the system will begin to emit warning messages like this when the database's oldest XIDs reach ten million transactions from the wraparound point:

```
WARNING:  database "mydb" must be vacuumed within 177009986 transactions
HINT:  To avoid a database shutdown, execute a database-wide VACUUM in "mydb".
```

(A manual VACUUM should fix the problem, as suggested by the hint; but note that the VACUUM must be performed by a superuser, else it will fail to process system catalogs and thus not be able to advance the database's datfrozenxid.) If these warnings are ignored, the system will shut down and refuse to execute any new transactions once there are fewer than 1 million transactions left until wraparound:

```
ERROR:  database is not accepting commands to avoid wraparound data loss in database "mydb"
HINT:  Stop the postmaster and use a standalone backend to VACUUM in "mydb".
```

The 1-million-transaction safety margin exists to let the administrator recover without data loss, by manually executing the required VACUUM commands. However, since the system will not execute commands once it has gone into the safety shutdown mode, the only way to do this is to stop the server and use a single-user backend to execute VACUUM. The shutdown mode is not enforced by a single-user backend. See the *postgres* reference page for details about using a single-user backend.

23.1.5. The Autovacuum Daemon

PostgreSQL has an optional but highly recommended feature called *autovacuum*, whose purpose is to automate the execution of VACUUM and ANALYZE commands. When enabled, autovacuum checks for tables that have had a large number of inserted, updated or deleted tuples. These checks use the statistics collection facility; therefore, autovacuum cannot be used unless *track_counts* is set to true. In the default configuration, autovacuuming is enabled and the related configuration parameters are appropriately set.

The "autovacuum daemon" actually consists of multiple processes. There is a persistent daemon process, called the *autovacuum launcher*, which is in charge of starting *autovacuum worker* processes for all databases. The launcher will distribute the work across time, attempting to start one worker on each database every *autovacuum_naptime* seconds. One worker will be launched for each database, with a maximum of *autovacuum_max_workers* processes running at the same time. If there are more than *autovacuum_max_workers* databases to be processed, the next database will be processed as soon as the first worker finishes. Each worker process will check each table within its database and execute VACUUM and/or ANALYZE as needed.

The *autovacuum_max_workers* setting limits how many workers may be running at any time. If several large tables all become eligible for vacuuming in a short amount of time, all autovacuum workers may become occupied with vacuuming those tables for a long period. This would result in other tables and databases not being vacuumed until a worker became available. There is not a limit on how many workers might be in a single database, but workers do try to avoid repeating work that has already been done by other workers. Note that the number of running workers does not count towards the *max_connections* nor the *superuser_reserved_connections* limits.

Tables whose relfrozenxid value is more than *autovacuum_freeze_max_age* transactions old are always vacuumed (this also applies to those tables whose freeze max age has been modified via storage parameters; see below). Otherwise, if the number of tuples obsoleted since the last VACUUM exceeds the "vacuum threshold", the table is vacuumed. The vacuum threshold is defined as:

```
vacuum threshold = vacuum base threshold + vacuum scale factor * number of tuples
```

where the vacuum base threshold is *autovacuum_vacuum_threshold*, the vacuum scale factor is *autovacuum_vacuum_scale_factor*, and the number of tuples is pg_class.reltuples. The number of obsolete tuples is obtained from the statistics collector; it is a semi-accurate count updated by each UPDATE and DELETE operation. (It is only semi-accurate because some information might be lost under heavy load.) If the relfrozenxid value of the table is more than vacuum_freeze_table_age transactions old, the whole table is scanned to freeze old tuples and advance relfrozenxid, otherwise only pages that have been modified since the last vacuum are scanned.

For analyze, a similar condition is used: the threshold, defined as:

```
analyze threshold = analyze base threshold + analyze scale factor * number of tuples
```

is compared to the total number of tuples inserted or updated since the last ANALYZE.

The default thresholds and scale factors are taken from postgresql.conf, but it is possible to override them on a table-by-table basis; see *Storage Parameters* for more information. If a setting has been changed via storage parameters, that value is used; otherwise the global settings are used. See *Section 18.9* - page 110 for more details on the global settings.

Besides the base threshold values and scale factors, there are six more autovacuum parameters that can be set for each table via storage parameters. The first parameter, autovacuum_enabled, can be set to false to instruct the autovacuum daemon to skip that particular table entirely. In this case autovacuum will only touch the table if it must do so to prevent transaction ID wraparound. Another two parameters, autovacuum_vacuum_cost_delay and autovacuum_vacuum_cost_limit, are used to set table-specific values for the *Cost-Based Vacuum Delay* feature. autovacuum_freeze_min_age, autovacuum_freeze_max_age and autovacuum_freeze_table_age are used to set values for *vacuum_freeze_min_age*, *autovacuum_freeze_max_age* and *vacuum_freeze_table_age* respectively.

When multiple workers are running, the cost limit is "balanced" among all the running workers, so that the total impact on the system is the same, regardless of the number of workers actually running.

23.2. Routine Reindexing

In some situations it is worthwhile to rebuild indexes periodically with the REINDEX command.

In PostgreSQL releases before 7.4, periodic reindexing was frequently necessary to avoid "index bloat", due to lack of internal space reclamation in B-tree indexes. Any situation in which the range of index keys changed over time — for example, an index on timestamps in a table where old entries are eventually deleted — would result in bloat, because index pages for no-longer-needed portions of the key range were not reclaimed for re-use. Over time, the index size could become indefinitely much larger than the amount of useful data in it.

In PostgreSQL 7.4 and later, index pages that have become completely empty are reclaimed for re-use. There is still a possibility for inefficient use of space: if all but a few index keys on a page have been deleted, the page remains allocated. So a usage pattern in which all but a few keys in each range are eventually deleted will see poor use of space. For such usage patterns, periodic reindexing is recommended.

The potential for bloat in non-B-tree indexes has not been well characterized. It is a good idea to keep an eye on the index's physical size when using any non-B-tree index type.

Also, for B-tree indexes a freshly-constructed index is somewhat faster to access than one that has been updated many times, because logically adjacent pages are usually also physically adjacent in a newly built index. (This consideration does not currently apply to non-B-tree indexes.) It might be worthwhile to reindex periodically just to improve access speed.

23.3. Log File Maintenance

It is a good idea to save the database server's log output somewhere, rather than just routing it to /dev/null. The log output is invaluable when it comes time to diagnose problems. However, the log output tends to be voluminous (especially at higher debug levels) and you won't want to save it indefinitely. You need to "rotate" the log files so that new log files are started and old ones removed after a reasonable period of time.

If you simply direct the stderr of postgres into a file, you will have log output, but the only way to truncate the log file is to stop and restart the server. This might be OK if you are using PostgreSQL in a development environment, but few production servers would find this behavior acceptable.

A better approach is to send the server's stderr output to some type of log rotation program. There is a built-in log rotation program, which you can use by setting the configuration parameter logging_collector to true in postgresql.conf. The control parameters for this program are described in *Section 18.7.1* - page 99. You can also use this approach to capture the log data in machine readable CSV format.

Alternatively, you might prefer to use an external log rotation program, if you have one that you are already using with other server software. For example, the rotatelogs tool included in the Apache distribution can be used with PostgreSQL. To do this, just pipe the server's stderr output to the desired program. If you start the server with pg_ctl, then stderr is already redirected to stdout, so you just need a pipe command, for example:

```
pg_ctl start | rotatelogs /var/log/pgsql_log 86400
```

Another production-grade approach to managing log output is to send it all to syslog and let syslog deal with file rotation. To do this, set the configuration parameter log_destination to syslog (to log to syslog only) in postgresql.conf. Then you can send a SIGHUP signal to the syslog daemon whenever you want to force it to start writing a new log file. If you want to automate log rotation, the logrotate program can be configured to work with log files from syslog.

On many systems, however, syslog is not very reliable, particularly with large log messages; it might truncate or drop messages just when you need them the most. Also, on Linux, syslog will sync each message to disk, yielding poor performance. (You can use a - at the start of the file name in the syslog configuration file to disable syncing.)

Note that all the solutions described above take care of starting new log files at configurable intervals, but they do not handle deletion of old, no-longer-interesting log files. You will probably want to set up a batch job to periodically delete old log files. Another possibility is to configure the rotation program so that old log files are overwritten cyclically.

Chapter 24.
Backup and Restore

As with everything that contains valuable data, PostgreSQL databases should be backed up regularly. While the procedure is essentially simple, it is important to have a clear understanding of the underlying techniques and assumptions.

There are three fundamentally different approaches to backing up PostgreSQL data:

- SQL dump
- File system level backup
- Continuous archiving

Each has its own strengths and weaknesses. Each is discussed in turn below.

24.1. SQL Dump

The idea behind this dump method is to generate a text file with SQL commands that, when fed back to the server, will recreate the database in the same state as it was at the time of the dump. PostgreSQL provides the utility program *pg_dump* for this purpose. The basic usage of this command is:

```
pg_dump dbname > outfile
```

As you see, pg_dump writes its results to the standard output. We will see below how this can be useful.

pg_dump is a regular PostgreSQL client application (albeit a particularly clever one). This means that you can do this backup procedure from any remote host that has access to the database. But remember that pg_dump does not operate with special permissions. In particular, it must have read access to all tables that you want to back up, so in practice you almost always have to run it as a database superuser.

To specify which database server pg_dump should contact, use the command line options -h *host* and -p *port*. The default host is the local host or whatever your PGHOST environment variable specifies. Similarly, the default port is indicated by the PGPORT environment variable or, failing that, by the compiled-in default. (Conveniently, the server will normally have the same compiled-in default.)

Like any other PostgreSQL client application, pg_dump will by default connect with the database user name that is equal to the current operating system user name. To override this, either specify the -U option or set the environment variable PGUSER. Remember that pg_dump connections are subject to the normal client authentication mechanisms (which are described in *Chapter 19* - page 129).

Dumps created by pg_dump are internally consistent, that is, the dump represents a snapshot of the database as of the time pg_dump begins running. pg_dump does not block other operations on the database while it is working. (Exceptions are those operations that need to operate with an exclusive lock, such as most forms of ALTER TABLE.)

 Important

> If your database schema relies on OIDs (for instance as foreign keys) you must instruct pg_dump to dump the OIDs as well. To do this, use the -o command line option.

24.1.1. Restoring the dump

The text files created by pg_dump are intended to be read in by the psql program. The general command form to restore a dump is

```
psql dbname < infile
```

where *infile* is what you used as *outfile* for the pg_dump command. The database *dbname* will not be created by this command, so you must create it yourself from template0 before executing psql (e.g., with createdb -T template0 *dbname*). psql supports options similar to pg_dump's for specifying the database server to connect to and the user name to use. See the *psql* reference page for more information.

Before restoring a SQL dump, all the users who own objects or were granted permissions on objects in the dumped database must already exist. If they do not, then the restore will fail to recreate the objects with the original ownership and/or permissions. (Sometimes this is what you want, but usually it is not.)

By default, the psql script will continue to execute after an SQL error is encountered. You might wish to use the following command at the top of the script to alter that behaviour and have psql exit with an exit status of 3 if an SQL error occurs:

```
\set ON_ERROR_STOP
```

Either way, you will have an only partially restored database. Alternatively, you can specify that the whole dump should be restored as a single transaction, so the restore is either fully completed or fully rolled back. This mode can be specified by passing the -1 or --single-transaction command-line options to psql. When using this mode, be aware that even the smallest of errors can rollback a restore that has already run for many hours. However, that might still be preferable to manually cleaning up a complex database after a partially restored dump.

The ability of pg_dump and psql to write to or read from pipes makes it possible to dump a database directly from one server to another, for example:

```
pg_dump -h host1 dbname | psql -h host2 dbname
```

 Important

> The dumps produced by pg_dump are relative to template0. This means that any languages, procedures, etc. added via template1 will also be dumped by pg_dump. As a result, when restoring, if you are using a customized template1, you must create the empty database from template0, as in the example above.

After restoring a backup, it is wise to run ANALYZE on each database so the query optimizer has useful statistics. An easy way to do this is to run vacuumdb -a -z; this is equivalent to running VACUUM ANALYZE on each database manually. For more advice on how to load large amounts of data into PostgreSQL efficiently, refer to *Section 14.4 - Vol.I* page 384.

24.1.2. Using `pg_dumpall`

pg_dump dumps only a single database at a time, and it does not dump information about roles or tablespaces (because those are cluster-wide rather than per-database). To support convenient dumping of the entire contents of a database cluster, the *pg_dumpall* program is provided. pg_dumpall backs up each database in a given cluster, and also preserves cluster-wide data such as role and tablespace definitions. The basic usage of this command is:

```
pg_dumpall > outfile
```

The resulting dump can be restored with psql:

```
psql -f infile postgres
```

(Actually, you can specify any existing database name to start from, but if you are reloading into an empty cluster then postgres should usually be used.) It is always necessary to have database superuser access when restoring a pg_dumpall dump, as that is required to restore the role and tablespace information. If you use tablespaces, be careful that the tablespace paths in the dump are appropriate for the new installation.

pg_dumpall works by emitting commands to re-create roles, tablespaces, and empty databases, then invoking pg_dump for each database. This means that while each database will be internally consistent, the snapshots of different databases might not be exactly in-sync.

24.1.3. Handling large databases

Since PostgreSQL allows tables larger than the maximum file size on your system, it can be problematic to dump such a table to a file, since the resulting file will likely be larger than the maximum size allowed by your system. Since pg_dump can write to the standard output, you can use standard Unix tools to work around this possible problem. There are several ways to do it:

Use compressed dumps. You can use your favorite compression program, for example gzip:

```
pg_dump dbname | gzip > filename.gz
```

Reload with:

```
gunzip -c filename.gz | psql dbname
```

or:

```
cat filename.gz | gunzip | psql dbname
```

Use split. The split command allows you to split the output into pieces that are acceptable in size to the underlying file system. For example, to make chunks of 1 megabyte:

```
pg_dump dbname | split -b 1m - filename
```

Reload with:

```
cat filename* | psql dbname
```

Use pg_dump's custom dump format. If PostgreSQL was built on a system with the zlib compression library installed, the custom dump format will compress data as it writes it to the output file. This will produce dump file sizes similar to using gzip, but it has the added advantage that tables can be restored selectively. The following command dumps a database using the custom dump format:

```
pg_dump -Fc dbname > filename
```

A custom-format dump is not a script for psql, but instead must be restored with pg_restore, for example:

```
pg_restore -d dbname filename
```

See the *pg_dump* and *pg_restore* reference pages for details.

For very large databases, you might need to combine split with one of the other two approaches.

24.2. File System Level Backup

An alternative backup strategy is to directly copy the files that PostgreSQL uses to store the data in the database. In *Section 17.2 - page 56* it is explained where these files are located, but you have probably found them already if you are interested in this method. You can use whatever method you prefer for doing usual file system backups, for example:

```
tar -cf backup.tar /usr/local/pgsql/data
```

There are two restrictions, however, which make this method impractical, or at least inferior to the pg_dump method:

1. The database server *must* be shut down in order to get a usable backup. Half-way measures such as disallowing all connections will *not* work (in part because `tar` and similar tools do not take an atomic snapshot of the state of the file system, but also because of internal buffering within the server). Information about stopping the server can be found in *Section 17.5 - page 70*. Needless to say that you also need to shut down the server before restoring the data.

2. If you have dug into the details of the file system layout of the database, you might be tempted to try to back up or restore only certain individual tables or databases from their respective files or directories. This will *not* work because the information contained in these files contains only half the truth. The other half is in the commit log files `pg_clog/*`, which contain the commit status of all transactions. A table file is only usable with this information. Of course it is also impossible to restore only a table and the associated `pg_clog` data because that would render all other tables in the database cluster useless. So file system backups only work for complete backup and restoration of an entire database cluster.

An alternative file-system backup approach is to make a "consistent snapshot" of the data directory, if the file system supports that functionality (and you are willing to trust that it is implemented correctly). The typical procedure is to make a "frozen snapshot" of the volume containing the database, then copy the whole data directory (not just parts, see above) from the snapshot to a backup device, then release the frozen snapshot. This will work even while the database server is running. However, a backup created in this way saves the database files in a state where the database server was not properly shut down; therefore, when you start the database server on the backed-up data, it will think the previous server instance had crashed and replay the WAL log. This is not a problem, just be aware of it (and be sure to include the WAL files in your backup).

If your database is spread across multiple file systems, there might not be any way to obtain exactly-simultaneous frozen snapshots of all the volumes. For example, if your data files and WAL log are on different disks, or if tablespaces are on different file systems, it might not be possible to use snapshot backup because the snapshots *must* be simultaneous. Read your file system documentation very carefully before trusting to the consistent-snapshot technique in such situations.

If simultaneous snapshots are not possible, one option is to shut down the database server long enough to establish all the frozen snapshots. Another option is perform a continuous archiving base backup (*Section 24.3.2* - page 188) because such backups are immune to file system changes during the backup. This requires enabling continuous archiving just during the backup process; restore is done using continuous archive recovery (*Section 24.3.3* - page 190).

Another option is to use rsync to perform a file system backup. This is done by first running rsync while the database server is running, then shutting down the database server just long enough to do a second rsync. The second rsync will be much quicker than the first, because it has relatively little data to transfer, and the end result will be consistent because the server was down. This method allows a file system backup to be performed with minimal downtime.

Note that a file system backup will not necessarily be smaller than an SQL dump. On the contrary, it will most likely be larger. (pg_dump does not need to dump the contents of indexes for example, just the commands to recreate them.) However, taking a file system backup might be faster.

24.3. Continuous Archiving and Point-In-Time Recovery (PITR)

At all times, PostgreSQL maintains a *write ahead log* (WAL) in the pg_xlog/ subdirectory of the cluster's data directory. The log describes every change made to the database's data files. This log exists primarily for crash-safety purposes: if the system crashes, the database can be restored to consistency by "replaying" the log entries made since the last checkpoint. However, the existence of the log makes it possible to use a third strategy for backing up databases: we can combine a file-system-level backup with backup of the WAL files. If recovery is needed, we restore the backup and then replay from the backed-up WAL files to bring the backup up to current time. This approach is more complex to administer than either of the previous approaches, but it has some significant benefits:

- We do not need a perfectly consistent backup as the starting point. Any internal inconsistency in the backup will be corrected by log replay (this is not significantly different from what happens during crash recovery). So we don't need file system snapshot capability, just tar or a similar archiving tool.

- Since we can string together an indefinitely long sequence of WAL files for replay, continuous backup can be achieved simply by continuing to archive the WAL files. This is particularly valuable for large databases, where it might not be convenient to take a full backup frequently.

- There is nothing that says we have to replay the WAL entries all the way to the end. We could stop the replay at any point and have a consistent snapshot of the database as it was at that time. Thus, this technique supports *point-in-time recovery*: it is possible to restore the database to its state at any time since your base backup was taken.

- If we continuously feed the series of WAL files to another machine that has been loaded with the same base backup file, we have a *warm standby* system: at any point we can bring up the second machine and it will have a nearly-current copy of the database.

As with the plain file-system-backup technique, this method can only support restoration of an entire database cluster, not a subset. Also, it requires a lot of archival storage: the base backup might be bulky, and a busy system will generate many megabytes of WAL traffic that have to be archived. Still, it is the preferred backup technique in many situations where high reliability is needed.

To recover successfully using continuous archiving (also called "online backup" by many database vendors), you need a continuous sequence of archived WAL files that extends back at least as far as the start time of your backup. So to get started, you should set up and test your procedure for archiving WAL files *before* you take your first base backup. Accordingly, we first discuss the mechanics of archiving WAL files.

24.3.1. Setting up WAL archiving

In an abstract sense, a running PostgreSQL system produces an indefinitely long sequence of WAL records. The system physically divides this sequence into WAL *segment files*, which are normally 16MB apiece (although the segment size can be altered when building PostgreSQL). The segment files are given numeric names that reflect their position in the abstract WAL sequence. When not using WAL archiving, the system normally creates just a few segment files and then "recycles" them by renaming no-longer-needed segment files to higher segment numbers. It's assumed that a segment file whose contents precede the checkpoint-before-last is no longer of interest and can be recycled.

When archiving WAL data, we need to capture the contents of each segment file once it is filled, and save that data somewhere before the segment file is recycled for reuse. Depending on the application and the available hardware, there could be many different ways of "saving the data somewhere": we could copy the segment files to an NFS-mounted directory on another machine, write them onto a tape drive (ensuring that you have a way of identifying the original name of each file), or batch them together and burn them onto CDs, or something else entirely. To provide the database administrator with as much flexibility as possible, PostgreSQL tries not to make any assumptions about how the archiving will be done. Instead, PostgreSQL lets the administrator specify a shell command to be executed to copy a completed segment file to wherever it needs to go. The command could be as simple as a cp, or it could invoke a complex shell script — it's all up to you.

To enable WAL archiving, set the *archive_mode* configuration parameter to on, and specify the shell command to use in the *archive_command* configuration parameter. In practice these settings will always be placed in the postgresql.conf file. In archive_command, any %p is replaced by the path name of the file to archive, while any %f is replaced by the file name only. (The path name is relative to the current working directory, i.e., the cluster's data directory.) Write %% if you need to embed an actual % character in the command. The simplest useful command is something like:

```
archive_command = 'cp -i %p /mnt/server/archivedir/%f </dev/null'
```

which will copy archivable WAL segments to the directory /mnt/server/archivedir. (This is an example, not a recommendation, and might not work on all platforms.) After the %p and %f parameters have been replaced, the actual command executed might look like this:

```
cp -i pg_xlog/00000001000000A900000065 /mnt/server/archivedir/00000001000000A900000065 </dev/null
```

A similar command will be generated for each new file to be archived.

The archive command will be executed under the ownership of the same user that the PostgreSQL server is running as. Since the series of WAL files being archived contains effectively everything in your database, you will want to be sure that the archived data is protected from prying eyes; for example, archive into a directory that does not have group or world read access.

It is important that the archive command return zero exit status if and only if it succeeded. Upon getting a zero result, PostgreSQL will assume that the file has been successfully archived, and will remove or recycle it. However, a nonzero status tells PostgreSQL that the file was not archived; it will try again periodically until it succeeds.

The archive command should generally be designed to refuse to overwrite any pre-existing archive file. This is an important safety feature to preserve the integrity of your archive in case of administrator error (such as sending the output of two different servers to the same archive directory). It is advisable to test your proposed archive command to ensure that it indeed does not overwrite an existing file, *and that it returns nonzero status in this case*. We have found that cp -i does this correctly on some platforms but not others. If the chosen command does not itself handle this case correctly, you should add a command to test for pre-existence of the archive file. For example, something like:

```
archive_command = 'test ! -f .../%f && cp %p .../%f'
```

works correctly on most Unix variants.

While designing your archiving setup, consider what will happen if the archive command fails repeatedly because some aspect requires operator intervention or the archive runs out of space. For example, this could occur if you write to tape without an autochanger; when the tape fills, nothing further can be archived until the tape is swapped. You should ensure that any error condition or request to a human operator is reported appropriately so that the situation can be resolved reasonably quickly. The pg_xlog/ directory will continue to fill with WAL segment files until the situation is resolved. (If the filesystem containing pg_xlog/ fills up, PostgreSQL will do a PANIC shutdown. No prior transactions will be lost, but the database will be unavailable until you free some space.)

The speed of the archiving command is not important, so long as it can keep up with the average rate at which your server generates WAL data. Normal operation continues even if the archiving process falls a little behind. If archiving falls significantly behind, this will increase the amount of data that would be lost in the event of a disaster. It will also mean that the pg_xlog/ directory will contain large numbers of not-yet-archived segment files, which could eventually exceed available disk space. You are advised to monitor the archiving process to ensure that it is working as you intend.

In writing your archive command, you should assume that the file names to be archived can be up to 64 characters long and can contain any combination of ASCII letters, digits, and dots. It is not necessary to remember the original relative path (%p) but it is necessary to remember the file name (%f).

Note that although WAL archiving will allow you to restore any modifications made to the data in your PostgreSQL database, it will not restore changes made to configuration files (that is, postgresql.conf, pg_hba.conf and pg_ident.conf), since those are edited manually rather than through SQL operations. You might wish to keep the configuration files in a location that will be backed up by your regular file system backup procedures. See *Section 18.2 - page 79* for how to relocate the configuration files.

The archive command is only invoked on completed WAL segments. Hence, if your server generates only little WAL traffic (or has slack periods where it does so), there could be a long delay between the completion of a transaction and its safe recording in archive storage. To put a limit on how old unarchived data can be, you can set *archive_timeout* to force the server to switch to a new WAL segment file at least that often. Note that archived files that are ended early due to a forced switch are still the same length as completely full files. It is therefore unwise to set a very short archive_timeout — it will bloat your archive storage. archive_timeout settings of a minute or so are usually reasonable.

Also, you can force a segment switch manually with pg_switch_xlog, if you want to ensure that a just-finished transaction is archived as soon as possible. Other utility functions related to WAL management are listed in *Table 9-56*.

When archive_mode is off some SQL commands are optimized to avoid WAL logging, as described in *Section 14.4.7 - Vol.I page 385*. If archiving were turned on during execution of one of these statements, WAL would not contain enough information for archive recovery. (Crash recovery is unaffected.) For this reason, archive_mode can only be changed at server start. However, archive_command can be changed with a configuration file reload. If you wish to temporarily stop archiving, one way to do it is to set archive_command to the empty string (''). This will cause WAL files to accumulate in pg_xlog/ until a working archive_command is re-established.

24.3.2. Making a Base Backup

The procedure for making a base backup is relatively simple:

1. Ensure that WAL archiving is enabled and working.

2. Connect to the database as a superuser, and issue the command:

   ```
   SELECT pg_start_backup('label');
   ```

   where label is any string you want to use to uniquely identify this backup operation. (One good practice is to use the full path where you intend to put the backup dump file.) pg_start_backup creates a *backup label* file, called backup_label, in the cluster directory with information about your backup.

   It does not matter which database within the cluster you connect to to issue this command. You can ignore the result returned by the function; but if it reports an error, deal with that before proceeding.

   By default, pg_start_backup can take a long time to finish. This is because it performs a checkpoint, and the I/O required for the checkpoint will be spread out over a significant period of time, by default half your inter-checkpoint interval (see the configuration parameter *checkpoint_completion_target*). Usually this is what you want, because it minimizes the impact on query processing. If you just want to start the backup as soon as possible, use:

   ```
   SELECT pg_start_backup('label', true);
   ```

   This forces the checkpoint to be done as quickly as possible.

3. Perform the backup, using any convenient file-system-backup tool such as tar or cpio. It is neither necessary nor desirable to stop normal operation of the database while you do this.

4. Again connect to the database as a superuser, and issue the command:

   ```
   SELECT pg_stop_backup();
   ```

   This terminates the backup mode and performs an automatic switch to the next WAL segment. The reason for the switch is to arrange that the last WAL segment file written during the backup interval is immediately ready to archive.

5. Once the WAL segment files used during the backup are archived, you are done. The file identified by pg_stop_backup's result is the last segment that is required to form

a complete set of backup files. pg_stop_backup does not return until the last segment has been archived. Archiving of these files happens automatically since you have already configured archive_command. In most cases this happens quickly, but you are advised to monitor your archive system to ensure there are no delays. If the archive process has fallen behind because of failures of the archive command, it will keep retrying until the archive succeeds and the backup is complete. If you wish to place a time limit on the execution of pg_stop_backup, set an appropriate statement_timeout value.

Some backup tools that you might wish to use emit warnings or errors if the files they are trying to copy change while the copy proceeds. This situation is normal, and not an error, when taking a base backup of an active database; so you need to ensure that you can distinguish complaints of this sort from real errors. For example, some versions of rsync return a separate exit code for "vanished source files", and you can write a driver script to accept this exit code as a non-error case. Also, some versions of GNU tar return an error code indistinguishable from a fatal error if a file was truncated while tar was copying it. Fortunately, GNU tar versions 1.16 and later exit with 1 if a file was changed during the backup, and 2 for other errors.

It is not necessary to be very concerned about the amount of time elapsed between pg_start_backup and the start of the actual backup, nor between the end of the backup and pg_stop_backup; a few minutes' delay won't hurt anything. (However, if you normally run the server with full_page_writes disabled, you might notice a drop in performance between pg_start_backup and pg_stop_backup, since full_page_writes is effectively forced on during backup mode.) You must ensure that these steps are carried out in sequence without any possible overlap, or you will invalidate the backup.

Be certain that your backup dump includes all of the files underneath the database cluster directory (e.g., /usr/local/pgsql/data). If you are using tablespaces that do not reside underneath this directory, be careful to include them as well (and be sure that your backup dump archives symbolic links as links, otherwise the restore will mess up your tablespaces).

You can, however, omit from the backup dump the files within the pg_xlog/ subdirectory of the cluster directory. This slight complication is worthwhile because it reduces the risk of mistakes when restoring. This is easy to arrange if pg_xlog/ is a symbolic link pointing to someplace outside the cluster directory, which is a common setup anyway for performance reasons.

To make use of the backup, you will need to keep around all the WAL segment files generated during and after the file system backup. To aid you in doing this, the pg_stop_backup function creates a *backup history file* that is immediately stored into the WAL archive area. This file is named after the first WAL segment file that you need to have to make use of the backup. For example, if the starting WAL file is

000000010000123400055CD the backup history file will be named something like 000000010000123400055CD.007C9330.backup. (The second part of the file name stands for an exact position within the WAL file, and can ordinarily be ignored.) Once you have safely archived the file system backup and the WAL segment files used during the backup (as specified in the backup history file), all archived WAL segments with names numerically less are no longer needed to recover the file system backup and can be deleted. However, you should consider keeping several backup sets to be absolutely certain that you can recover your data.

The backup history file is just a small text file. It contains the label string you gave to pg_start_backup, as well as the starting and ending times and WAL segments of the backup. If you used the label to identify where the associated dump file is kept, then the archived history file is enough to tell you which dump file to restore, should you need to do so.

Since you have to keep around all the archived WAL files back to your last base backup, the interval between base backups should usually be chosen based on how much storage you want to expend on archived WAL files. You should also consider how long you are prepared to spend recovering, if recovery should be necessary — the system will have to replay all those WAL segments, and that could take awhile if it has been a long time since the last base backup.

It's also worth noting that the pg_start_backup function makes a file named backup_label in the database cluster directory, which is then removed again by pg_stop_backup. This file will of course be archived as a part of your backup dump file. The backup label file includes the label string you gave to pg_start_backup, as well as the time at which pg_start_backup was run, and the name of the starting WAL file. In case of confusion it will therefore be possible to look inside a backup dump file and determine exactly which backup session the dump file came from.

It is also possible to make a backup dump while the server is stopped. In this case, you obviously cannot use pg_start_backup or pg_stop_backup, and you will therefore be left to your own devices to keep track of which backup dump is which and how far back the associated WAL files go. It is generally better to follow the continuous archiving procedure above.

24.3.3. Recovering using a Continuous Archive Backup

Okay, the worst has happened and you need to recover from your backup. Here is the procedure:

1. Stop the server, if it's running.

2. If you have the space to do so, copy the whole cluster data directory and any tablespaces to a temporary location in case you need them later. Note that this

precaution will require that you have enough free space on your system to hold two copies of your existing database. If you do not have enough space, you need at the least to copy the contents of the pg_xlog subdirectory of the cluster data directory, as it might contain logs which were not archived before the system went down.

3. Clean out all existing files and subdirectories under the cluster data directory and under the root directories of any tablespaces you are using.

4. Restore the database files from your base backup. Be careful that they are restored with the right ownership (the database system user, not root!) and with the right permissions. If you are using tablespaces, you should verify that the symbolic links in pg_tblspc/ were correctly restored.

5. Remove any files present in pg_xlog/; these came from the backup dump and are therefore probably obsolete rather than current. If you didn't archive pg_xlog/ at all, then recreate it, being careful to ensure that you re-establish it as a symbolic link if you had it set up that way before.

6. If you had unarchived WAL segment files that you saved in step 2, copy them into pg_xlog/. (It is best to copy them, not move them, so that you still have the unmodified files if a problem occurs and you have to start over.)

7. Create a recovery command file recovery.conf in the cluster data directory (see *Recovery Settings* – page 184). You might also want to temporarily modify pg_hba.conf to prevent ordinary users from connecting until you are sure the recovery has worked.

8. Start the server. The server will go into recovery mode and proceed to read through the archived WAL files it needs. Should the recovery be terminated because of an external error, the server can simply be restarted and it will continue recovery. Upon completion of the recovery process, the server will rename recovery.conf to recovery.done (to prevent accidentally re-entering recovery mode in case of a crash later) and then commence normal database operations.

9. Inspect the contents of the database to ensure you have recovered to where you want to be. If not, return to step 1. If all is well, let in your users by restoring pg_hba.conf to normal.

The key part of all this is to set up a recovery command file that describes how you want to recover and how far the recovery should run. You can use recovery.conf.sample (normally installed in the installation share/ directory) as a prototype. The one thing that you absolutely must specify in recovery.conf is the restore_command, which tells PostgreSQL how to get back archived WAL file segments. Like the archive_command, this is a shell command string. It can contain %f, which is replaced by the name of the desired log file, and

%p, which is replaced by the path name to copy the log file to. (The path name is relative to the current working directory, i.e., the cluster's data directory.) Write %% if you need to embed an actual % character in the command. The simplest useful command is something like:

```
restore_command = 'cp /mnt/server/archivedir/%f %p'
```

which will copy previously archived WAL segments from the directory /mnt/server/archivedir. You could of course use something much more complicated, perhaps even a shell script that requests the operator to mount an appropriate tape.

It is important that the command return nonzero exit status on failure. The command *will* be asked for files that are not present in the archive; it must return nonzero when so asked. This is not an error condition. Not all of the requested files will be WAL segment files; you should also expect requests for files with a suffix of .backup or .history. Also be aware that the base name of the %p path will be different from %f; do not expect them to be interchangeable.

WAL segments that cannot be found in the archive will be sought in pg_xlog/; this allows use of recent un-archived segments. However segments that are available from the archive will be used in preference to files in pg_xlog/. The system will not overwrite the existing contents of pg_xlog/ when retrieving archived files.

Normally, recovery will proceed through all available WAL segments, thereby restoring the database to the current point in time (or as close as we can get given the available WAL segments). So a normal recovery will end with a "file not found" message, the exact text of the error message depending upon your choice of restore_command. You may also see an error message at the start of recovery for a file named something like 00000001.history. This is also normal and does not indicate a problem in simple recovery situations. See *Section 24.3.4 - page 194* for discussion.

If you want to recover to some previous point in time (say, right before the junior DBA dropped your main transaction table), just specify the required stopping point in recovery.conf. You can specify the stop point, known as the "recovery target", either by date/time or by completion of a specific transaction ID. As of this writing only the date/time option is very usable, since there are no tools to help you identify with any accuracy which transaction ID to use.

 Note

> The stop point must be after the ending time of the base backup, i.e., the end time of pg_stop_backup. You cannot use a base backup to recover to a time when that backup was still going on. (To recover to such a time, you must go back to your previous base backup and roll forward from there.)

If recovery finds a corruption in the WAL data then recovery will complete at that point and the server will not start. In such a case the recovery process could be re-run from the beginning, specifying a "recovery target" before the point of corruption so that recovery can complete normally. If recovery fails for an external reason, such as a system crash or if the WAL archive has become inaccessible, then the recovery can simply be restarted and it will restart almost from where it failed. Recovery restart works much like checkpointing in normal operation: the server periodically forces all its state to disk, and then updates the pg_control file to indicate that the already-processed WAL data need not be scanned again.

24.3.3.1. Recovery Settings

These settings can only be made in the recovery.conf file, and apply only for the duration of the recovery. They must be reset for any subsequent recovery you wish to perform. They cannot be changed once recovery has begun.

restore_command (string)

> The shell command to execute to retrieve an archived segment of the WAL file series. This parameter is required. Any %f in the string is replaced by the name of the file to retrieve from the archive, and any %p is replaced by the path name to copy it to on the server. (The path name is relative to the current working directory, i.e., the cluster's data directory.) Any %r is replaced by the name of the file containing the last valid restart point. That is the earliest file that must be kept to allow a restore to be restartable, so this information can be used to truncate the archive to just the minimum required to support restart from the current restore. %r would typically be used in a warm-standby configuration (see *Section 24.4* - page 198). Write %% to embed an actual % character in the command.

> It is important for the command to return a zero exit status if and only if it succeeds. The command *will* be asked for file names that are not present in the archive; it must return nonzero when so asked. Examples:

```
restore_command = 'cp /mnt/server/archivedir/%f "%p"'
restore_command = 'copy "C:\\server\\archivedir\\%f" "%p"'  # Windows
```

recovery_end_command (string)

> This parameter specifies a shell command that will be executed once only at the end of recovery. This parameter is optional. The purpose of the recovery_end_command is to provide a mechanism for cleanup following replication or recovery. Any %r is replaced by the name of the file containing the last valid restart point. That is the earliest file that must be kept to allow a restore to be restartable, so this information can be used to truncate the archive to just the minimum required to support restart from the current restore. %r would typically be used in a warm-standby configuration (see *Section 24.4* - page 198). Write %% to embed an actual % character in the command.

If the command returns a non-zero exit status then a WARNING log message will be written and the database will proceed to start up anyway. An exception is that if the command was terminated by a signal, the database will not proceed with startup.

recovery_target_time (timestamp)

This parameter specifies the time stamp up to which recovery will proceed. At most one of recovery_target_time and *recovery_target_xid* can be specified. The default is to recover to the end of the WAL log. The precise stopping point is also influenced by *recovery_target_inclusive*.

recovery_target_xid (string)

This parameter specifies the transaction ID up to which recovery will proceed. Keep in mind that while transaction IDs are assigned sequentially at transaction start, transactions can complete in a different numeric order. The transactions that will be recovered are those that committed before (and optionally including) the specified one. At most one of recovery_target_xid and *recovery_target_time* can be specified. The default is to recover to the end of the WAL log. The precise stopping point is also influenced by *recovery_target_inclusive*.

recovery_target_inclusive (boolean)

Specifies whether we stop just after the specified recovery target (true), or just before the recovery target (false). Applies to both *recovery_target_time* and *recovery_target_xid*, whichever one is specified for this recovery. This indicates whether transactions having exactly the target commit time or ID, respectively, will be included in the recovery. Default is true.

recovery_target_timeline (string)

Specifies recovering into a particular timeline. The default is to recover along the same timeline that was current when the base backup was taken. You would only need to set this parameter in complex re-recovery situations, where you need to return to a state that itself was reached after a point-in-time recovery. See *Section 24.3.4* - page 194 for discussion.

24.3.4. Timelines

The ability to restore the database to a previous point in time creates some complexities that are akin to science-fiction stories about time travel and parallel universes. In the original history of the database, perhaps you dropped a critical table at 5:15PM on Tuesday evening, but didn't realize your mistake until Wednesday noon. Unfazed, you get out your backup, restore to the point-in-time 5:14PM Tuesday evening, and are up and running. In *this* history of the database universe, you never dropped the table at all. But suppose you later realize this wasn't such a great idea after all, and would like to return to sometime Wednesday morning in the original history. You won't be able to if, while your database was up-and-running, it overwrote some of the sequence of WAL segment files that led up to the time you now wish you could get back to. So you really want to distinguish the series of WAL records generated after you've done a point-in-time recovery from those that were generated in the original database history.

To deal with these problems, PostgreSQL has a notion of *timelines*. Whenever an archive recovery is completed, a new timeline is created to identify the series of WAL records generated after that recovery. The timeline ID number is part of WAL segment file names, and so a new timeline does not overwrite the WAL data generated by previous timelines. It is in fact possible to archive many different timelines. While that might seem like a useless feature, it's often a lifesaver. Consider the situation where you aren't quite sure what point-in-time to recover to, and so have to do several point-in-time recoveries by trial and error until you find the best place to branch off from the old history. Without timelines this process would soon generate an unmanageable mess. With timelines, you can recover to *any* prior state, including states in timeline branches that you later abandoned.

Each time a new timeline is created, PostgreSQL creates a "timeline history" file that shows which timeline it branched off from and when. These history files are necessary to allow the system to pick the right WAL segment files when recovering from an archive that contains multiple timelines. Therefore, they are archived into the WAL archive area just like WAL segment files. The history files are just small text files, so it's cheap and appropriate to keep them around indefinitely (unlike the segment files which are large). You can, if you like, add comments to a history file to make your own notes about how and why this particular timeline came to be. Such comments will be especially valuable when you have a thicket of different timelines as a result of experimentation.

The default behavior of recovery is to recover along the same timeline that was current when the base backup was taken. If you want to recover into some child timeline (that is, you want to return to some state that was itself generated after a recovery attempt), you need to specify the target timeline ID in recovery.conf. You cannot recover into timelines that branched off earlier than the base backup.

24.3.5. Tips and Examples

Some tips for configuring continuous archiving are given here.

24.3.5.1. Standalone hot backups

It is possible to use PostgreSQL's backup facilities to produce standalone hot backups. These are backups that cannot be used for point-in-time recovery, yet are typically much faster to backup and restore than pg_dump dumps. (They are also much larger than pg_dump dumps, so in some cases the speed advantage could be negated.)

To prepare for standalone hot backups, set archive_mode to on, and set up an archive_command that performs archiving only when a "switch file" exists. For example:

```
archive_command = 'test ! -f /var/lib/pgsql/backup_in_progress || cp -i %p
/var/lib/pgsql/archive/%f < /dev/null'
```

This command will perform archiving when /var/lib/pgsql/backup_in_progress exists, and otherwise silently return zero exit status (allowing PostgreSQL to recycle the unwanted WAL file).

With this preparation, a backup can be taken using a script like the following:

```
touch /var/lib/pgsql/backup_in_progress
psql -c "select pg_start_backup('hot_backup');"
tar -cf /var/lib/pgsql/backup.tar /var/lib/pgsql/data/
psql -c "select pg_stop_backup();"
rm /var/lib/pgsql/backup_in_progress
tar -rf /var/lib/pgsql/backup.tar /var/lib/pgsql/archive/
```

The switch file /var/lib/pgsql/backup_in_progress is created first, enabling archiving of completed WAL files to occur. After the backup the switch file is removed. Archived WAL files are then added to the backup so that both base backup and all required WAL files are part of the same tar file. Please remember to add error handling to your backup scripts.

If archive storage size is a concern, use pg_compresslog, *http://pglesslog.projects.postgresql.org/*, to remove unnecessary *full_page_writes* and trailing space from the WAL files. You can then use gzip to further compress the output of pg_compresslog:

```
archive_command = 'pg_compresslog %p - | gzip > /var/lib/pgsql/archive/%f'
```

You will then need to use gunzip and pg_decompresslog during recovery:

```
restore_command = 'gunzip < /mnt/server/archivedir/%f | pg_decompresslog - %p'
```

24.3.5.2. archive_command scripts

Many people choose to use scripts to define their archive_command, so that their postgresql.conf entry looks very simple:

```
archive_command = 'local_backup_script.sh'
```

Using a separate script file is advisable any time you want to use more than a single command in the archiving process. This allows all complexity to be managed within the script, which can be written in a popular scripting language such as bash or perl. Any messages written to stderr from the script will appear in the database server log, allowing complex configurations to be diagnosed easily if they fail.

Examples of requirements that might be solved within a script include:

- Copying data to secure off-site data storage

- Batching WAL files so that they are transferred every three hours, rather than one at a time

- Interfacing with other backup and recovery software

- Interfacing with monitoring software to report errors

24.3.6. Caveats

At this writing, there are several limitations of the continuous archiving technique. These will probably be fixed in future releases:

- Operations on hash indexes are not presently WAL-logged, so replay will not update these indexes. The recommended workaround is to manually REINDEX each such index after completing a recovery operation.

- If a CREATE DATABASE command is executed while a base backup is being taken, and then the template database that the CREATE DATABASE copied is modified while the base backup is still in progress, it is possible that recovery will cause those modifications to be propagated into the created database as well. This is of course undesirable. To avoid this risk, it is best not to modify any template databases while taking a base backup.

- CREATE TABLESPACE commands are WAL-logged with the literal absolute path, and will therefore be replayed as tablespace creations with the same absolute path. This might be undesirable if the log is being replayed on a different machine. It can be dangerous even if the log is being replayed on the same machine, but into a new data directory: the replay will still overwrite the contents of the original tablespace. To avoid potential gotchas of this sort, the best practice is to take a new base backup after creating or dropping tablespaces.

It should also be noted that the default WAL format is fairly bulky since it includes many disk page snapshots. These page snapshots are designed to support crash recovery, since we might need to fix partially-written disk pages. Depending on your system hardware and software, the risk of partial writes might be small enough to ignore, in which case you can significantly reduce the total volume of archived logs by turning off page snapshots using the *full_page_writes* parameter. (Read the notes and warnings in *Chapter 28* - page 230 before you do so.) Turning off page snapshots does not prevent use of the logs for PITR operations. An area for future development is to compress archived WAL data by removing unnecessary page copies even when full_page_writes is on. In the meantime, administrators might wish to reduce the number of page snapshots included in WAL by increasing the checkpoint interval parameters as much as feasible.

24.4. Warm Standby Servers for High Availability

Continuous archiving can be used to create a *high availability* (HA) cluster configuration with one or more *standby servers* ready to take over operations if the primary server fails. This capability is widely referred to as *warm standby* or *log shipping*.

The primary and standby server work together to provide this capability, though the servers are only loosely coupled. The primary server operates in continuous archiving mode, while each standby server operates in continuous recovery mode, reading the WAL files from the primary. No changes to the database tables are required to enable this capability, so it offers low administration overhead in comparison with some other replication approaches. This configuration also has relatively low performance impact on the primary server.

Directly moving WAL records from one database server to another is typically described as log shipping. PostgreSQL implements file-based log shipping, which means that WAL records are transferred one file (WAL segment) at a time. WAL files (16MB) can be shipped easily and cheaply over any distance, whether it be to an adjacent system, another system on the same site or another system on the far side of the globe. The bandwidth required for this technique varies according to the transaction rate of the primary server. Record-based log shipping is also possible with custom-developed procedures, as discussed in *Section 24.4.4 - - page 202.*

It should be noted that the log shipping is asynchronous, i.e., the WAL records are shipped after transaction commit. As a result there is a window for data loss should the primary server suffer a catastrophic failure: transactions not yet shipped will be lost. The length of the window of data loss can be limited by use of the archive_timeout parameter, which can be set as low as a few seconds if required. However such low settings will substantially increase the bandwidth requirements for file shipping. If you need a window of less than a minute or so, it's probably better to look into record-based log shipping.

The standby server is not available for access, since it is continually performing recovery processing. Recovery performance is sufficiently good that the standby will typically be only moments away from full availability once it has been activated. As a result, we refer to this capability as a warm standby configuration that offers high availability. Restoring a server from an archived base backup and rollforward will take considerably longer, so that technique only offers a solution for disaster recovery, not high availability.

24.4.1. Planning

It is usually wise to create the primary and standby servers so that they are as similar as possible, at least from the perspective of the database server. In particular, the path names associated with tablespaces will be passed across as-is, so both primary and standby servers must have the same mount paths for tablespaces if that feature is used. Keep in mind that if

CREATE TABLESPACE is executed on the primary, any new mount point needed for it must be created on both the primary and all standby servers before the command is executed. Hardware need not be exactly the same, but experience shows that maintaining two identical systems is easier than maintaining two dissimilar ones over the lifetime of the application and system. In any case the hardware architecture must be the same − shipping from, say, a 32-bit to a 64-bit system will not work.

In general, log shipping between servers running different major PostgreSQL release levels will not be possible. It is the policy of the PostgreSQL Global Development Group not to make changes to disk formats during minor release upgrades, so it is likely that running different minor release levels on primary and standby servers will work successfully. However, no formal support for that is offered and you are advised to keep primary and standby servers at the same release level as much as possible. When updating to a new minor release, the safest policy is to update the standby servers first − a new minor release is more likely to be able to read WAL files from a previous minor release than vice versa.

There is no special mode required to enable a standby server. The operations that occur on both primary and standby servers are entirely normal continuous archiving and recovery tasks. The only point of contact between the two database servers is the archive of WAL files that both share: primary writing to the archive, standby reading from the archive. Care must be taken to ensure that WAL archives for separate primary servers do not become mixed together or confused. The archive need not be large, if it is only required for the standby operation.

The magic that makes the two loosely coupled servers work together is simply a restore_command used on the standby that, when asked for the next WAL file, waits for it to become available from the primary. The restore_command is specified in the recovery.conf file on the standby server. Normal recovery processing would request a file from the WAL archive, reporting failure if the file was unavailable. For standby processing it is normal for the next WAL file to be unavailable, so we must be patient and wait for it to appear. For files ending in .backup or .history there is no need to wait, and a non-zero return code must be returned. A waiting restore_command can be written as a custom script that loops after polling for the existence of the next WAL file. There must also be some way to trigger failover, which should interrupt the restore_command, break the loop and return a file-not-found error to the standby server. This ends recovery and the standby will then come up as a normal server.

Pseudocode for a suitable restore_command is:

```
triggered = false;
while (!NextWALFileReady() && !triggered)
{
    sleep(100000L);            /* wait for ~0.1 sec */
```

```
    if (CheckForExternalTrigger())
        triggered = true;
}
if (!triggered)
        CopyWALFileForRecovery();
```

A working example of a waiting restore_command is provided as a contrib module named pg_standby. It should be used as a reference on how to correctly implement the logic described above. It can also be extended as needed to support specific configurations or environments.

PostgreSQL does not provide the system software required to identify a failure on the primary and notify the standby system and then the standby database server. Many such tools exist and are well integrated with other aspects required for successful failover, such as IP address migration.

The means for triggering failover is an important part of planning and design. The restore_command is executed in full once for each WAL file. The process running the restore_command is therefore created and dies for each file, so there is no daemon or server process and so we cannot use signals and a signal handler. A more permanent notification is required to trigger the failover. It is possible to use a simple timeout facility, especially if used in conjunction with a known archive_timeout setting on the primary. This is somewhat error prone since a network problem or busy primary server might be sufficient to initiate failover. A notification mechanism such as the explicit creation of a trigger file is less error prone, if this can be arranged.

The size of the WAL archive can be minimized by using the %r option of the restore_command. This option specifies the last archive file name that needs to be kept to allow the recovery to restart correctly. This can be used to truncate the archive once files are no longer required, if the archive is writable from the standby server.

24.4.2. Implementation

The short procedure for configuring a standby server is as follows. For full details of each step, refer to previous sections as noted.

1. Set up primary and standby systems as near identically as possible, including two identical copies of PostgreSQL at the same release level.

2. Set up continuous archiving from the primary to a WAL archive located in a directory on the standby server. Ensure that *archive_mode*, *archive_command* and *archive_timeout* are set appropriately on the primary (see *Section 24.3.1 - page 185*).

3. Make a base backup of the primary server (see *Section 24.3.2 - page 188*), and load this data onto the standby.

4. Begin recovery on the standby server from the local WAL archive, using a `recovery.conf` that specifies a `restore_command` that waits as described previously (see *Section 24.3.3* - page 190).

Recovery treats the WAL archive as read-only, so once a WAL file has been copied to the standby system it can be copied to tape at the same time as it is being read by the standby database server. Thus, running a standby server for high availability can be performed at the same time as files are stored for longer term disaster recovery purposes.

For testing purposes, it is possible to run both primary and standby servers on the same system. This does not provide any worthwhile improvement in server robustness, nor would it be described as HA.

24.4.3. Failover

If the primary server fails then the standby server should begin failover procedures.

If the standby server fails then no failover need take place. If the standby server can be restarted, even some time later, then the recovery process can also be immediately restarted, taking advantage of restartable recovery. If the standby server cannot be restarted, then a full new standby server instance should be created.

If the primary server fails and then immediately restarts, you must have a mechanism for informing it that it is no longer the primary. This is sometimes known as STONITH (Shoot the Other Node In The Head), which is necessary to avoid situations where both systems think they are the primary, which will lead to confusion and ultimately data loss.

Many failover systems use just two systems, the primary and the standby, connected by some kind of heartbeat mechanism to continually verify the connectivity between the two and the viability of the primary. It is also possible to use a third system (called a witness server) to prevent some cases of inappropriate failover, but the additional complexity might not be worthwhile unless it is set up with sufficient care and rigorous testing.

Once failover to the standby occurs, we have only a single server in operation. This is known as a degenerate state. The former standby is now the primary, but the former primary is down and might stay down. To return to normal operation we must fully recreate a standby server, either on the former primary system when it comes up, or on a third, possibly new, system. Once complete the primary and standby can be considered to have switched roles. Some people choose to use a third server to provide backup to the new primary until the new standby server is recreated, though clearly this complicates the system configuration and operational processes.

So, switching from primary to standby server can be fast but requires some time to re-prepare the failover cluster. Regular switching from primary to standby is useful, since it allows regular downtime on each system for maintenance. This also serves as a test of the failover mechanism to ensure that it will really work when you need it. Written administration procedures are advised.

24.4.4. Record-based Log Shipping

PostgreSQL directly supports file-based log shipping as described above. It is also possible to implement record-based log shipping, though this requires custom development.

An external program can call the pg_xlogfile_name_offset() function (see *Section 9.24* - Vol.I page 289) to find out the file name and the exact byte offset within it of the current end of WAL. It can then access the WAL file directly and copy the data from the last known end of WAL through the current end over to the standby server(s). With this approach, the window for data loss is the polling cycle time of the copying program, which can be very small, but there is no wasted bandwidth from forcing partially-used segment files to be archived. Note that the standby servers' restore_command scripts still deal in whole WAL files, so the incrementally copied data is not ordinarily made available to the standby servers. It is of use only when the primary dies — then the last partial WAL file is fed to the standby before allowing it to come up. So correct implementation of this process requires cooperation of the restore_command script with the data copying program.

24.4.5. Incrementally Updated Backups

In a warm standby configuration, it is possible to offload the expense of taking periodic base backups from the primary server; instead base backups can be made by backing up a standby server's files. This concept is generally known as incrementally updated backups, log change accumulation, or more simply, change accumulation.

If we take a backup of the standby server's data directory while it is processing logs shipped from the primary, we will be able to reload that data and restart the standby's recovery process from the last restart point. We no longer need to keep WAL files from before the restart point. If we need to recover, it will be faster to recover from the incrementally updated backup than from the original base backup.

Since the standby server is not "live", it is not possible to use pg_start_backup() and pg_stop_backup() to manage the backup process; it will be up to you to determine how far back you need to keep WAL segment files to have a recoverable backup. You can do this by running pg_controldata on the standby server to inspect the control file and determine the current checkpoint WAL location, or by using the log_checkpoints option to print values to the server log.

24.5. Migration Between Releases

This section discusses how to migrate your database data from one PostgreSQL release to a newer one. The software installation procedure *per se* is not the subject of this section; those details are in *Chapter 15* - page 20.

As a general rule, the internal data storage format is subject to change between major releases of PostgreSQL (where the number after the first dot changes). This does not apply to different minor releases under the same major release (where the number after the second dot changes); these always have compatible storage formats. For example, releases 8.1.1, 8.2.3, and 8.3 are not compatible, whereas 8.2.3 and 8.2.4 are. When you update between compatible versions, you can simply replace the executables and reuse the data directory on disk. Otherwise you need to back up your data and restore it on the new server. This has to be done using pg_dump; file system level backup methods obviously won't work. There are checks in place that prevent you from using a data directory with an incompatible version of PostgreSQL, so no great harm can be done by trying to start the wrong server version on a data directory.

It is recommended that you use the pg_dump and pg_dumpall programs from the newer version of PostgreSQL, to take advantage of any enhancements that might have been made in these programs. Current releases of the dump programs can read data from any server version back to 7.0.

The least downtime can be achieved by installing the new server in a different directory and running both the old and the new servers in parallel, on different ports. Then you can use something like:

```
pg_dumpall -p 5432 | psql -d postgres -p 6543
```

to transfer your data. Or use an intermediate file if you want. Then you can shut down the old server and start the new server at the port the old one was running at. You should make sure that the old database is not updated after you begin to run pg_dumpall, otherwise you will lose that data. See *Chapter 19* - page 129 for information on how to prohibit access.

It is also possible to use replication methods, such as Slony, to create a slave server with the updated version of PostgreSQL. The slave can be on the same computer or a different computer. Once it has synced up with the master server (running the older version of PostgreSQL), you can switch masters and make the slave the master and shut down the older database instance. Such a switch-over results in only several seconds of downtime for an upgrade.

If you cannot or do not want to run two servers in parallel, you can do the backup step before installing the new version, bring down the server, move the old version out of the way, install the new version, start the new server, and restore the data. For example:

```
pg_dumpall > backup
pg_ctl stop
mv /usr/local/pgsql /usr/local/pgsql.old
cd ~/postgresql-8.4.0
gmake install
initdb -D /usr/local/pgsql/data
postgres -D /usr/local/pgsql/data
psql -f backup postgres
```

See *Chapter 17* - page 56 about ways to start and stop the server and other details. The installation instructions will advise you of strategic places to perform these steps.

 Note

When you "move the old installation out of the way" it might no longer be perfectly usable. Some of the executable programs contain absolute paths to various installed programs and data files. This is usually not a big problem, but if you plan on using two installations in parallel for a while you should assign them different installation directories at build time. (This problem is rectified in PostgreSQL 8.0 and later, so long as you move all subdirectories containing installed files together; for example if /usr/local/postgres/bin/ goes to /usr/local/postgres.old/bin/, then /usr/local/postgres/share/ must go to /usr/local/postgres.old/share/. In pre-8.0 releases moving an installation like this will not work.)

In practice you probably want to test your client applications on the new version before switching over completely. This is another reason for setting up concurrent installations of old and new versions. When testing a PostgreSQL major upgrade, consider the following categories of possible changes:

Administration

The capabilities available for administrators to monitor and control the server often change and improve in each major release.

SQL

Typically this includes new SQL command capabilities and not changes in behavior, unless specifically mentioned in the release notes.

Library API

Typically libraries like libpq only add new functionality, again unless mentioned in the release notes.

System Catalogs

System catalog changes usually only affect database management tools.

Server C-language API

This involved changes in the backend function API, which is written in the C programming language. Such changes effect code that references backend functions deep inside the server.

Chapter 25.
High Availability, Load Balancing & Replication

Database servers can work together to allow a second server to take over quickly if the primary server fails (high availability), or to allow several computers to serve the same data (load balancing). Ideally, database servers could work together seamlessly. Web servers serving static web pages can be combined quite easily by merely load-balancing web requests to multiple machines. In fact, read-only database servers can be combined relatively easily too. Unfortunately, most database servers have a read/write mix of requests, and read/write servers are much harder to combine. This is because though read-only data needs to be placed on each server only once, a write to any server has to be propagated to all servers so that future read requests to those servers return consistent results.

This synchronization problem is the fundamental difficulty for servers working together. Because there is no single solution that eliminates the impact of the sync problem for all use cases, there are multiple solutions. Each solution addresses this problem in a different way, and minimizes its impact for a specific workload.

Some solutions deal with synchronization by allowing only one server to modify the data. Servers that can modify data are called read/write or "master" servers. Servers that can reply to read-only queries are called "slave" servers. Servers that cannot be accessed until they are changed to master servers are called "standby" servers.

Some solutions are synchronous, meaning that a data-modifying transaction is not considered committed until all servers have committed the transaction. This guarantees that a failover will not lose any data and that all load-balanced servers will return consistent results no matter which server is queried. In contrast, asynchronous solutions allow some delay between the time of a commit and its propagation to the other servers, opening the possibility that some transactions might be lost in the switch to a backup server, and that load balanced servers might return slightly stale results. Asynchronous communication is used when synchronous would be too slow.

Solutions can also be categorized by their granularity. Some solutions can deal only with an entire database server, while others allow control at the per-table or per-database level.

Performance must be considered in any choice. There is usually a trade-off between functionality and performance. For example, a full synchronous solution over a slow network might cut performance by more than half, while an asynchronous one might have a minimal performance impact.

The remainder of this section outlines various failover, replication, and load balancing solutions. A *glossary*[1] is also available.

Shared Disk Failover

> Shared disk failover avoids synchronization overhead by having only one copy of the database. It uses a single disk array that is shared by multiple servers. If the main database server fails, the standby server is able to mount and start the database as though it was recovering from a database crash. This allows rapid failover with no data loss.

> Shared hardware functionality is common in network storage devices. Using a network file system is also possible, though care must be taken that the file system has full POSIX behavior (see *Section 17.2.1* - page 58). One significant limitation of this method is that if the shared disk array fails or becomes corrupt, the primary and standby servers are both nonfunctional. Another issue is that the standby server should never access the shared storage while the primary server is running.

File System (Block-Device) Replication

> A modified version of shared hardware functionality is file system replication, where all changes to a file system are mirrored to a file system residing on another computer. The only restriction is that the mirroring must be done in a way that ensures the standby server has a consistent copy of the file system — specifically, writes to the standby must be done in the same order as those on the master. DRBD is a popular file system replication solution for Linux.

Warm Standby Using Point-In-Time Recovery (PITR)

> A warm standby server (see *Section 24.4* - page 198) can be kept current by reading a stream of write-ahead log (WAL) records. If the main server fails, the warm standby contains almost all of the data of the main server, and can be quickly made the new master database server. This is asynchronous and can only be done for the entire database server.

Master-Slave Replication

> A master-slave replication setup sends all data modification queries to the master server. The master server asynchronously sends data changes to the slave server. The slave can

---

[1] *http://www.postgres-r.org/documentation/terms*

answer read-only queries while the master server is running. The slave server is ideal for data warehouse queries.

Slony-I is an example of this type of replication, with per-table granularity, and support for multiple slaves. Because it updates the slave server asynchronously (in batches), there is possible data loss during fail over.

Statement-Based Replication Middleware

With statement-based replication middleware, a program intercepts every SQL query and sends it to one or all servers. Each server operates independently. Read-write queries are sent to all servers, while read-only queries can be sent to just one server, allowing the read workload to be distributed.

If queries are simply broadcast unmodified, functions like random(), CURRENT_TIMESTAMP, and sequences would have different values on different servers. This is because each server operates independently, and because SQL queries are broadcast (and not actual modified rows). If this is unacceptable, either the middleware or the application must query such values from a single server and then use those values in write queries. Also, care must be taken that all transactions either commit or abort on all servers, perhaps using two-phase commit (PREPARE TRANSACTION and COMMIT PREPARED. Pgpool-II and Sequoia are examples of this type of replication.

Asynchronous Multimaster Replication

For servers that are not regularly connected, like laptops or remote servers, keeping data consistent among servers is a challenge. Using asynchronous multimaster replication, each server works independently, and periodically communicates with the other servers to identify conflicting transactions. The conflicts can be resolved by users or conflict resolution rules. Bucardo is an example of this type of replication.

Synchronous Multimaster Replication

In synchronous multimaster replication, each server can accept write requests, and modified data is transmitted from the original server to every other server before each transaction commits. Heavy write activity can cause excessive locking, leading to poor performance. In fact, write performance is often worse than that of a single server. Read requests can be sent to any server. Some implementations use shared disk to reduce the communication overhead. Synchronous multimaster replication is best for mostly read workloads, though its big advantage is that any server can accept write requests — there is no need to partition workloads between master and slave servers, and because the data changes are sent from one server to another, there is no problem with non-deterministic functions like random().

PostgreSQL does not offer this type of replication, though PostgreSQL two-phase commit (PREPARE TRANSACTION and COMMIT PREPARED) can be used to implement this in application code or middleware.

Commercial Solutions

Because PostgreSQL is open source and easily extended, a number of companies have taken PostgreSQL and created commercial closed-source solutions with unique failover, replication, and load balancing capabilities.

Table 25-1 summarizes the capabilities of the various solutions listed above.

Feature	Shared Disk Failover	File System Replication	Warm Standby Using PITR	Master-Slave Replication	Statement-Based Replication Middleware	Asynchronous Multimaster Replication	Synchronous Multimaster Replication
Most Common Implementation	NAS	DRBD	PITR	Slony	pgpool-II	Bucardo	
Communication Method	shared disk	disk blocks	WAL	table rows	SQL	table rows	table rows and row locks
No special hardware required		•	•	•	•	•	•
Allows multiple master servers					•	•	•
No master server overhead	•		•		•		
No waiting for multiple servers	•		•	•		•	
Master failure will never lose data	•	•			•		•
Slaves accept read-only queries				•	•	•	•
Per-table granularity				•		•	•
No conflict resolution necessary	•	•	•	•			•

Table 25-1. High Availability, Load Balancing, and Replication Feature Matrix

There are a few solutions that do not fit into the above categories:

Data Partitioning

Data partitioning splits tables into data sets. Each set can be modified by only one server. For example, data can be partitioned by offices, e.g., London and Paris, with a server in each office. If queries combining London and Paris data are necessary, an application can query both servers, or master/slave replication can be used to keep a read-only copy of the other office's data on each server.

Multiple-Server Parallel Query Execution

Many of the above solutions allow multiple servers to handle multiple queries, but none allow a single query to use multiple servers to complete faster. This solution allows multiple servers to work concurrently on a single query. It is usually accomplished by splitting the data among servers and having each server execute its part of the query and return results to a central server where they are combined and returned to the user. Pgpool-II has this capability. Also, this can be implemented using the PL/Proxy toolset.

Chapter 26.
Monitoring Database Activity

A database administrator frequently wonders, "What is the system doing right now?" This chapter discusses how to find that out.

Several tools are available for monitoring database activity and analyzing performance. Most of this chapter is devoted to describing PostgreSQL's statistics collector, but one should not neglect regular Unix monitoring programs such as ps, top, iostat, and vmstat. Also, once one has identified a poorly-performing query, further investigation might be needed using PostgreSQL's EXPLAIN command. *Section 14.1 - Vol.I page 374* discusses EXPLAIN and other methods for understanding the behavior of an individual query.

26.1. Standard Unix Tools

On most platforms, PostgreSQL modifies its command title as reported by ps, so that individual server processes can readily be identified. A sample display is

```
$ ps auxww | grep ^postgres
postgres   960 0.0 1.1 6104 1480 pts/1 SN 13:17 0:00 postgres -i
postgres   963 0.0 1.1 7084 1472 pts/1 SN 13:17 0:00 postgres: writer process
postgres   965 0.0 1.1 6152 1512 pts/1 SN 13:17 0:00 postgres: stats collector process
postgres   998 0.0 2.3 6532 2992 pts/1 SN 13:18 0:00 postgres: tgl runbug 127.0.0.1 idle
postgres  1003 0.0 2.4 6532 3128 pts/1 SN 13:19 0:00 postgres: tgl regression [local] SELECT waiting
postgres  1016 0.1 2.4 6532 3080 pts/1 SN 13:19 0:00 postgres: tgl regression [local] idle in
transaction
```

(The appropriate invocation of ps varies across different platforms, as do the details of what is shown. This example is from a recent Linux system.) The first process listed here is the master server process. The command arguments shown for it are the same ones given when it was launched. The next two processes are background worker processes automatically launched by the master process. (The "stats collector" process will not be present if you have set the system not to start the statistics collector.) Each of the remaining processes is a server process handling one client connection. Each such process sets its command line display in the form

```
postgres: user database host activity
```

The user, database, and connection source host items remain the same for the life of the client connection, but the activity indicator changes. The activity can be idle (i.e., waiting for a client command), idle in transaction (waiting for client inside a BEGIN block), or a command type name such as SELECT. Also, waiting is attached if the server process is presently waiting on a lock held by another server process. In the above example we can infer that process 1003 is waiting for process 1016 to complete its transaction and thereby release some lock or other.

If you have turned off *update_process_title* then the activity indicator is not updated; the process title is set only once when a new process is launched. On some platforms this saves a useful amount of per-command overhead, on others it's insignificant.

 Tip

> Solaris requires special handling. You must use /usr/ucb/ps, rather than /bin/ps. You also must use two w flags, not just one. In addition, your original invocation of the postgres command must have a shorter ps status display than that provided by each server process. If you fail to do all three things, the ps output for each server process will be the original postgres command line.

26.2. The Statistics Collector

PostgreSQL's *statistics collector* is a subsystem that supports collection and reporting of information about server activity. Presently, the collector can count accesses to tables and indexes in both disk-block and individual-row terms. It also tracks total numbers of rows in each table, and the last vacuum and analyze times for each table. It can also count calls to user-defined functions and the total time spent in each one.

PostgreSQL also supports determining the exact command currently being executed by other server processes. This is an independent facility that does not depend on the collector process.

26.2.1. Statistics Collection Configuration

Since collection of statistics adds some overhead to query execution, the system can be configured to collect or not collect information. This is controlled by configuration parameters that are normally set in postgresql.conf. (See *Chapter 18* - page 77 for details about setting configuration parameters.)

The parameter *track_counts* controls whether statistics are collected about table and index accesses.

The parameter *track_functions* enables tracking of usage of user-defined functions.

The parameter *track_activities* enables monitoring of the current command being executed by any server process.

Normally these parameters are set in postgresql.conf so that they apply to all server processes, but it is possible to turn them on or off in individual sessions using the SET command. (To prevent ordinary users from hiding their activity from the administrator, only superusers are allowed to change these parameters with SET.)

The statistics collector communicates with the backends needing information (including autovacuum) through temporary files. These files are stored in the pg_stat_tmp subdirectory. When the postmaster shuts down, a permanent copy of the statistics data is stored in the global subdirectory. For increased performance, the parameter *stats_temp_directory* can be pointed at a RAM based filesystem, decreasing physical I/O requirements.

26.2.2. Viewing Collected Statistics

Several predefined views, listed in *Table 26-1*, are available to show the results of statistics collection. Alternatively, one can build custom views using the underlying statistics functions.

When using the statistics to monitor current activity, it is important to realize that the information does not update instantaneously. Each individual server process transmits new statistical counts to the collector just before going idle; so a query or transaction still in progress does not affect the displayed totals. Also, the collector itself emits a new report at most once per PGSTAT_STAT_INTERVAL milliseconds (500 unless altered while building the server). So the displayed information lags behind actual activity. However, current-query information collected by track_activities is always up-to-date.

Another important point is that when a server process is asked to display any of these statistics, it first fetches the most recent report emitted by the collector process and then continues to use this snapshot for all statistical views and functions until the end of its current transaction. So the statistics will appear not to change as long as you continue the current transaction. Similarly, information about the current queries of all processes is collected when any such information is first requested within a transaction, and the same information will be displayed throughout the transaction. This is a feature, not a bug, because it allows you to perform several queries on the statistics and correlate the results without worrying that the numbers are changing underneath you. But if you want to see new results with each query, be sure to do the queries outside any transaction block. Alternatively, you can invoke pg_stat_clear_snapshot(), which will discard the current transaction's statistics snapshot (if any). The next use of statistical information will cause a new snapshot to be fetched.

View Name	Description
pg_stat_activity	One row per server process, showing database OID, database name, process ID, user OID, user name, current query, query's waiting status, time at which the current transaction and current query began execution, time at which the process

View Name	Description
	was started, and client's address and port number. The columns that report data on the current query are available unless the parameter `track_activities` has been turned off. Furthermore, these columns are only visible if the user examining the view is a superuser or the same as the user owning the process being reported on.
pg_stat_bgwriter	One row only, showing cluster-wide statistics from the background writer: number of scheduled checkpoints, requested checkpoints, buffers written by checkpoints and cleaning scans, and the number of times the background writer stopped a cleaning scan because it had written too many buffers. Also includes statistics about the shared buffer pool, including buffers written by backends (that is, not by the background writer) and total buffers allocated.
pg_stat_database	One row per database, showing database OID, database name, number of active server processes connected to that database, number of transactions committed and rolled back in that database, total disk blocks read, total buffer hits (i.e., block read requests avoided by finding the block already in buffer cache), number of rows returned, fetched, inserted, updated and deleted.
pg_stat_all_tables	For each table in the current database (including TOAST tables), the table OID, schema and table name, number of sequential scans initiated, number of live rows fetched by sequential scans, number of index scans initiated (over all indexes belonging to the table), number of live rows fetched by index scans, numbers of row insertions, updates, and deletions, number of row updates that were HOT (i.e., no separate index update), numbers of live and dead rows, the last time the table was vacuumed manually, the last time it was vacuumed by the autovacuum daemon, the last time it was analyzed manually, and the last time it was analyzed by the autovacuum daemon.
pg_stat_sys_tables	Same as `pg_stat_all_tables`, except that only system tables are shown.
pg_stat_user_tables	Same as `pg_stat_all_tables`, except that only user tables are shown.
pg_stat_all_indexes	For each index in the current database, the table and index OID, schema, table and index name, number of index scans initiated on that index, number of index entries returned by index scans, and number of live table rows fetched by simple index scans using that index.
pg_stat_sys_indexes	Same as `pg_stat_all_indexes`, except that only indexes on system tables are shown.
pg_stat_user_indexes	Same as `pg_stat_all_indexes`, except that only indexes on user tables are shown.
pg_statio_all_tables	For each table in the current database (including TOAST tables), the table OID, schema and table name, number of disk blocks read from that table, number of buffer hits, numbers of disk blocks read and buffer hits in all indexes of that table, numbers of disk blocks read and buffer hits from that table's auxiliary TOAST table (if any), and numbers of disk blocks read and buffer hits for the TOAST table's index.
pg_statio_sys_tables	Same as `pg_statio_all_tables`, except that only system tables are shown.

View Name	Description
pg_statio_user_tables	Same as pg_statio_all_tables, except that only user tables are shown.
pg_statio_all_indexes	For each index in the current database, the table and index OID, schema, table and index name, numbers of disk blocks read and buffer hits in that index.
pg_statio_sys_indexes	Same as pg_statio_all_indexes, except that only indexes on system tables are shown.
pg_statio_user_indexes	Same as pg_statio_all_indexes, except that only indexes on user tables are shown.
pg_statio_all_sequences	For each sequence object in the current database, the sequence OID, schema and sequence name, numbers of disk blocks read and buffer hits in that sequence.
pg_statio_sys_sequences	Same as pg_statio_all_sequences, except that only system sequences are shown. (Presently, no system sequences are defined, so this view is always empty.)
pg_statio_user_sequences	Same as pg_statio_all_sequences, except that only user sequences are shown.
pg_stat_user_functions	For all tracked functions, function OID, schema, name, number of calls, total time, and self time. Self time is the amount of time spent in the function itself, total time includes the time spent in functions it called. Time values are in milliseconds.

Table 26-1. Standard Statistics Views

The per-index statistics are particularly useful to determine which indexes are being used and how effective they are.

Beginning in PostgreSQL 8.1, indexes can be used either directly or via "bitmap scans". In a bitmap scan the output of several indexes can be combined via AND or OR rules; so it is difficult to associate individual heap row fetches with specific indexes when a bitmap scan is used. Therefore, a bitmap scan increments the pg_stat_all_indexes.idx_tup_read count(s) for the index(es) it uses, and it increments the pg_stat_all_tables.idx_tup_fetch count for the table, but it does not affect pg_stat_all_indexes.idx_tup_fetch.

 Note

> Before PostgreSQL 8.1, the idx_tup_read and idx_tup_fetch counts were essentially always equal. Now they can be different even without considering bitmap scans, because idx_tup_read counts index entries retrieved from the index while idx_tup_fetch counts live rows fetched from the table; the latter will be less if any dead or not-yet-committed rows are fetched using the index.

The pg_statio_ views are primarily useful to determine the effectiveness of the buffer cache. When the number of actual disk reads is much smaller than the number of buffer hits, then the cache is satisfying most read requests without invoking a kernel call. However, these statistics do not give the entire story: due to the way in which PostgreSQL handles disk I/O, data that is not in the PostgreSQL buffer cache might still reside in the kernel's I/O cache, and might therefore still be fetched without requiring a physical read. Users interested in obtaining more detailed information on PostgreSQL I/O behavior are advised to use the PostgreSQL statistics collector in combination with operating system utilities that allow insight into the kernel's handling of I/O.

Other ways of looking at the statistics can be set up by writing queries that use the same underlying statistics access functions as these standard views do. These functions are listed in *Table 26-2*. The per-database access functions take a database OID as argument to identify which database to report on. The per-table and per-index functions take a table or index OID. The functions for function-call statistics take a function OID. (Note that only tables, indexes, and functions in the current database can be seen with these functions.) The per-server-process access functions take a server process number, which ranges from one to the number of currently active server processes.

Function	Return Type	Description
pg_stat_get_db_numbackends(oid)	integer	Number of active server processes for database
pg_stat_get_db_xact_commit(oid)	bigint	Transactions committed in database
pg_stat_get_db_xact_rollback(oid)	bigint	Transactions rolled back in database
pg_stat_get_db_blocks_fetched(oid)	bigint	Number of disk block fetch requests for database
pg_stat_get_db_blocks_hit(oid)	bigint	Number of disk block fetch requests found in cache for database
pg_stat_get_db_tuples_returned(oid)	bigint	Number of tuples returned for database
pg_stat_get_db_tuples_fetched(oid)	bigint	Number of tuples fetched for database
pg_stat_get_db_tuples_inserted(oid)	bigint	Number of tuples inserted in database
pg_stat_get_db_tuples_updated(oid)	bigint	Number of tuples updated in database
pg_stat_get_db_tuples_deleted(oid)	bigint	Number of tuples deleted in database
pg_stat_get_numscans(oid)	bigint	Number of sequential scans done when argument is a table, or number of index scans done when argument is an index
pg_stat_get_tuples_returned(oid)	bigint	Number of rows read by sequential scans when argument is a table, or number of index entries returned when argument is an index
pg_stat_get_tuples_fetched(oid)	bigint	Number of table rows fetched by bitmap scans when argument is a

Function	Return Type	Description
		table, or table rows fetched by simple index scans using the index when argument is an index
pg_stat_get_tuples_inserted(oid)	bigint	Number of rows inserted into table
pg_stat_get_tuples_updated(oid)	bigint	Number of rows updated in table (includes HOT updates)
pg_stat_get_tuples_deleted(oid)	bigint	Number of rows deleted from table
pg_stat_get_tuples_hot_updated(oid)	bigint	Number of rows HOT-updated in table
pg_stat_get_live_tuples(oid)	bigint	Number of live rows in table
pg_stat_get_dead_tuples(oid)	bigint	Number of dead rows in table
pg_stat_get_blocks_fetched(oid)	bigint	Number of disk block fetch requests for table or index
pg_stat_get_blocks_hit(oid)	bigint	Number of disk block requests found in cache for table or index
pg_stat_get_last_vacuum_time(oid)	timestamptz	Time of the last vacuum initiated by the user on this table
pg_stat_get_last_autovacuum_time(oid)	timestamptz	Time of the last vacuum initiated by the autovacuum daemon on this table
pg_stat_get_last_analyze_time(oid)	timestamptz	Time of the last analyze initiated by the user on this table
pg_stat_get_last_autoanalyze_time(oid)	timestamptz	Time of the last analyze initiated by the autovacuum daemon on this table
pg_backend_pid()	integer	Process ID of the server process attached to the current session
pg_stat_get_activity(integer)	setof record	Returns a record of information about the backend with the specified pid, or one record for each active backend in the system if NULL is specified. The fields returned are the same as in the pg_stat_activity view
pg_stat_get_function_calls(oid)	bigint	Number of times the function has been called.
pg_stat_get_function_time(oid)	bigint	Total wall clock time spent in the function, in microseconds. Includes the time spent in functions called by this one.
pg_stat_get_function_self_time(oid)	bigint	Time spent in only this function. Time spent in called functions is excluded.

Function	Return Type	Description
pg_stat_get_backend_idset()	setof integer	Set of currently active server process numbers (from 1 to the number of active server processes). See usage example in the text
pg_stat_get_backend_pid(integer)	integer	Process ID of the given server process
pg_stat_get_backend_dbid(integer)	oid	Database ID of the given server process
pg_stat_get_backend_userid(integer)	oid	User ID of the given server process
pg_stat_get_backend_activity(integer)	text	Active command of the given server process, but only if the current user is a superuser or the same user as that of the session being queried (and track_activities is on)
pg_stat_get_backend_waiting(integer)	boolean	True if the given server process is waiting for a lock, but only if the current user is a superuser or the same user as that of the session being queried (and track_activities is on)
pg_stat_get_backend_activity_start (integer)	timestamp with time zone	The time at which the given server process' currently executing query was started, but only if the current user is a superuser or the same user as that of the session being queried (and track_activities is on)
pg_stat_get_backend_xact_start(integer)	timestamp with time zone	The time at which the given server process' currently executing transaction was started, but only if the current user is a superuser or the same user as that of the session being queried (and track_activities is on)
pg_stat_get_backend_start(integer)	timestamp with time zone	The time at which the given server process was started, or null if the current user is not a superuser nor the same user as that of the session being queried
pg_stat_get_backend_client_addr(integer)	inet	The IP address of the client connected to the given server process. Null if the connection is over a Unix domain socket. Also null if the current user is not a superuser nor the same user as that of the session being queried

Function	Return Type	Description
pg_stat_get_backend_client_port(integer)	integer	The IP port number of the client connected to the given server process. -1 if the connection is over a Unix domain socket. Null if the current user is not a superuser nor the same user as that of the session being queried
pg_stat_get_bgwriter_timed_checkpoints()	bigint	The number of times the background writer has started timed checkpoints (because the checkpoint_ timeout time has expired)
pg_stat_get_bgwriter_requested_checkpoints ()	bigint	The number of times the background writer has started checkpoints based on requests from backends because the checkpoint_segments has been exceeded or because the CHECKPOINT command has been issued
pg_stat_get_bgwriter_buf_written_ checkpoints()	bigint	The number of buffers written by the background writer during checkpoints
pg_stat_get_bgwriter_buf_written_clean()	bigint	The number of buffers written by the background writer for routine cleaning of dirty pages
pg_stat_get_bgwriter_maxwritten_clean()	bigint	The number of times the background writer has stopped its cleaning scan because it has written more buffers than specified in the bgwriter_ lru_maxpages parameter
pg_stat_get_buf_written_backend()	bigint	The number of buffers written by backends because they needed to allocate a new buffer
pg_stat_get_buf_alloc()	bigint	The total number of buffer allocations
pg_stat_clear_snapshot()	void	Discard the current statistics snapshot
pg_stat_reset()	void	Reset all statistics counters for the current database to zero (requires superuser privileges)

Table 26-2. Statistics Access Functions

 Note

pg_stat_get_blocks_fetched minus pg_stat_get_blocks_hit gives the number of kernel read() calls issued for the table, index, or database; the number of actual physical reads is usually lower due to kernel-level buffering. The *_blks_read statistics columns use this subtraction, i.e., fetched minus hit.

All functions to access information about backends are indexed by backend id number, except pg_stat_get_activity which is indexed by PID. The function pg_stat_get_backend_idset provides a convenient way to generate one row for each active server process. For example, to show the PIDs and current queries of all server processes:

```
SELECT pg_stat_get_backend_pid(s.backendid) AS procpid,
       pg_stat_get_backend_activity(s.backendid) AS current_query
    FROM (SELECT pg_stat_get_backend_idset() AS backendid) AS s;
```

26.3. Viewing Locks

Another useful tool for monitoring database activity is the pg_locks system table. It allows the database administrator to view information about the outstanding locks in the lock manager. For example, this capability can be used to:

- View all the locks currently outstanding, all the locks on relations in a particular database, all the locks on a particular relation, or all the locks held by a particular PostgreSQL session.
- Determine the relation in the current database with the most ungranted locks (which might be a source of contention among database clients).
- Determine the effect of lock contention on overall database performance, as well as the extent to which contention varies with overall database traffic.

Details of the pg_locks view appear in *Section 44.48*. For more information on locking and managing concurrency with PostgreSQL, refer to *Chapter 13* - Vol.I page 361.

26.4. Dynamic Tracing

PostgreSQL provides facilities to support dynamic tracing of the database server. This allows an external utility to be called at specific points in the code and thereby trace execution.

A number of probes or trace points are already inserted into the source code. These probes are intended to be used by database developers and administrators. By default the probes are not compiled into PostgreSQL; the user needs to explicitly tell the configure script to make the probes available.

Currently, only the *DTrace* utility is supported, which is available on OpenSolaris, Solaris 10, and Mac OS X Leopard. It is expected that DTrace will be available in the future on FreeBSD and possibly other operating systems. The *SystemTap* project for Linux also provides a DTrace equivalent. Supporting other dynamic tracing utilities is theoretically possible by changing the definitions for the macros in src/include/utils/probes.h.

26.4.1. Compiling for Dynamic Tracing

By default, probes are not available, so you will need to explicitly tell the configure script to make the probes available in PostgreSQL. To include DTrace support specify --enable-dtrace to configure. See *Section 15.5* - page 25 for further information.

26.4.2. Built-in Probes

A number of standard probes are provided in the source code, as shown in *Table 26-3*. More can certainly be added to enhance PostgreSQL's observability.

Name	Parameters	Description
transaction-start	(LocalTransactionId)	Probe that fires at the start of a new transaction. arg0 is the transaction id.
transaction-commit	(LocalTransactionId)	Probe that fires when a transaction completes successfully. arg0 is the transaction id.
transaction-abort	(LocalTransactionId)	Probe that fires when a transaction completes unsuccessfully. arg0 is the transaction id.
query-start	(const char *)	Probe that fires when the processing of a query is started. arg0 is the query string.
query-done	(const char *)	Probe that fires when the processing of a query is complete. arg0 is the query string.
query-parse-start	(const char *)	Probe that fires when the parsing of a query is started. arg0 is the query string.
query-parse-done	(const char *)	Probe that fires when the parsing of a query is complete. arg0 is the query string.
query-rewrite-start	(const char *)	Probe that fires when the rewriting of a query is started. arg0 is the query string.
query-rewrite-done	(const char *)	Probe that fires when the rewriting of a query is complete. arg0 is the query string.
query-plan-start	()	Probe that fires when the planning of a query is started.
query-plan-done	()	Probe that fires when the planning of a query is complete.
query-execute-start	()	Probe that fires when the execution of a query is started.
query-execute-done	()	Probe that fires when the execution of a query is complete.
statement-status	(const char *)	Probe that fires anytime the server process updates its `pg_stat_activity.current_query` status. arg0 is the new status string.
checkpoint-start	(int)	Probe that fires when a checkpoint is started. arg0 holds the bitwise flags used to distinguish different checkpoint types, such as shutdown, immediate or force.

checkpoint-done	(int, int, int, int, int)	Probe that fires when a checkpoint is complete. (The probes listed next fire in sequence during checkpoint processing.) arg0 is the number of buffers written. arg1 is the total number of buffers. arg2, arg3 and arg4 contain the number of xlog file(s) added, removed and recycled respectively.
clog-checkpoint-start	(bool)	Probe that fires when the CLOG portion of a checkpoint is started. arg0 is true for normal checkpoint, false for shutdown checkpoint.
clog-checkpoint-done	(bool)	Probe that fires when the CLOG portion of a checkpoint is complete. arg0 has the same meaning as for clog-checkpoint-start.
subtrans-checkpoint-start	(bool)	Probe that fires when the SUBTRANS portion of a checkpoint is started. arg0 is true for normal checkpoint, false for shutdown checkpoint.
subtrans-checkpoint-done	(bool)	Probe that fires when the SUBTRANS portion of a checkpoint is complete. arg0 has the same meaning as for subtrans-checkpoint-start.
multixact-checkpoint-start	(bool)	Probe that fires when the MultiXact portion of a checkpoint is started. arg0 is true for normal checkpoint, false for shutdown checkpoint.
multixact-checkpoint-done	(bool)	Probe that fires when the MultiXact portion of a checkpoint is complete. arg0 has the same meaning as for multixact-checkpoint-start.
buffer-checkpoint-start	(int)	Probe that fires when the buffer-writing portion of a checkpoint is started. arg0 holds the bitwise flags used to distinguish different checkpoint types, such as shutdown, immediate or force.
buffer-sync-start	(int, int)	Probe that fires when we begin to write dirty buffers during checkpoint (after identifying which buffers must be written). arg0 is the total number of buffers. arg1 is the number that are currently dirty and need to be written.
buffer-sync-written	(int)	Probe that fires after each buffer is written during checkpoint. arg0 is the ID number of the buffer.
buffer-sync-done	(int, int, int)	Probe that fires when all dirty buffers have been written. arg0 is the total number of buffers. arg1 is the number of buffers actually written by the checkpoint process. arg2 is the number that were expected to be written (arg1 of buffer-sync-start); any difference reflects other processes flushing buffers during the checkpoint.
buffer-checkpoint-sync-start	()	Probe that fires after dirty buffers have been written to the kernel, and before starting to issue fsync requests.
buffer-checkpoint-done	()	Probe that fires when syncing of buffers to disk is complete.

twophase-checkpoint-start	()	Probe that fires when the two-phase portion of a checkpoint is started.
twophase-checkpoint-done	()	Probe that fires when the two-phase portion of a checkpoint is complete.
buffer-read-start	(ForkNumber, BlockNumber, Oid, Oid, Oid, bool, bool)	Probe that fires when a buffer read is started. arg0 and arg1 contain the fork and block numbers of the page (but arg1 will be -1 if this is a relation extension request). arg2, arg3, and arg4 contain the tablespace, database, and relation OIDs identifying the relation. arg5 is true for a local buffer, false for a shared buffer. arg6 is true for a relation extension request, false for normal read.
buffer-read-done	(ForkNumber, BlockNumber, Oid, Oid, Oid, bool, bool, bool)	Probe that fires when a buffer read is complete. arg0 and arg1 contain the fork and block numbers of the page (if this is a relation extension request, arg1 now contains the block number of the newly added block). arg2, arg3, and arg4 contain the tablespace, database, and relation OIDs identifying the relation. arg5 is true for a local buffer, false for a shared buffer. arg6 is true for a relation extension request, false for normal read. arg7 is true if the buffer was found in the pool, false if not.
buffer-flush-start	(ForkNumber, BlockNumber, Oid, Oid, Oid)	Probe that fires before issuing any write request for a shared buffer. arg0 and arg1 contain the fork and block numbers of the page. arg2, arg3, and arg4 contain the tablespace, database, and relation OIDs identifying the relation.
buffer-flush-done	(ForkNumber, BlockNumber, Oid, Oid, Oid)	Probe that fires when a write request is complete. (Note that this just reflects the time to pass the data to the kernel; it's typically not actually been written to disk yet.) The arguments are the same as for buffer-flush-start.
buffer-write-dirty-start	(ForkNumber, BlockNumber, Oid, Oid, Oid)	Probe that fires when a server process begins to write a dirty buffer. (If this happens often, it implies that *shared_buffers* is too small or the bgwriter control parameters need adjustment.) arg0 and arg1 contain the fork and block numbers of the page. arg2, arg3, and arg4 contain the tablespace, database, and relation OIDs identifying the relation.
buffer-write-dirty-done	(ForkNumber, BlockNumber, Oid, Oid, Oid)	Probe that fires when a dirty-buffer write is complete. The arguments are the same as for buffer-write-dirty-start.
wal-buffer-write-dirty-start	()	Probe that fires when when a server process begins to write a dirty WAL buffer because no more WAL buffer space is available. (If this happens often, it implies that *wal_buffers* is too small.)
wal-buffer-write-dirty-done	()	Probe that fires when a dirty WAL buffer write is complete.
xlog-insert	(unsigned char, unsigned char)	Probe that fires when a WAL record is inserted. arg0 is the resource manager (rmid) for the record. arg1 contains the info flags.

xlog-switch	()	Probe that fires when a WAL segment switch is requested.
smgr-md-read-start	(ForkNumber, BlockNumber, Oid, Oid, Oid)	Probe that fires when beginning to read a block from a relation. arg0 and arg1 contain the fork and block numbers of the page. arg2, arg3, and arg4 contain the tablespace, database, and relation OIDs identifying the relation.
smgr-md-read-done	(ForkNumber, BlockNumber, Oid, Oid, Oid, int, int)	Probe that fires when a block read is complete. arg0 and arg1 contain the fork and block numbers of the page. arg2, arg3, and arg4 contain the tablespace, database, and relation OIDs identifying the relation. arg5 is the number of bytes actually read, while arg6 is the number requested (if these are different it indicates trouble).
smgr-md-write-start	(ForkNumber, BlockNumber, Oid, Oid, Oid)	Probe that fires when beginning to write a block to a relation. arg0 and arg1 contain the fork and block numbers of the page. arg2, arg3, and arg4 contain the tablespace, database, and relation OIDs identifying the relation.
smgr-md-write-done	(ForkNumber, BlockNumber, Oid, Oid, Oid, int, int)	Probe that fires when a block write is complete. arg0 and arg1 contain the fork and block numbers of the page. arg2, arg3, and arg4 contain the tablespace, database, and relation OIDs identifying the relation. arg5 is the number of bytes actually written, while arg6 is the number requested (if these are different it indicates trouble).
sort-start	(int, bool, int, int, bool)	Probe that fires when a sort operation is started. arg0 indicates heap, index or datum sort. arg1 is true for unique-value enforcement. arg2 is the number of key columns. arg3 is the number of kilobytes of work memory allowed. arg4 is true if random access to the sort result is required.
sort-done	(bool, long)	Probe that fires when a sort is complete. arg0 is true for external sort, false for internal sort. arg1 is the number of disk blocks used for an external sort, or kilobytes of memory used for an internal sort.
lwlock-acquire	(LWLockId, LWLockMode)	Probe that fires when an LWLock has been acquired. arg0 is the LWLock's ID. arg1 is the requested lock mode, either exclusive or shared.
lwlock-release	(LWLockId)	Probe that fires when an LWLock has been released (but note that any released waiters have not yet been awakened). arg0 is the LWLock's ID.
lwlock-wait-start	(LWLockId, LWLockMode)	Probe that fires when an LWLock was not immediately available and a server process has begun to wait for the lock to become available. arg0 is the LWLock's ID. arg1 is the requested lock mode, either exclusive or shared.
lwlock-wait-done	(LWLockId, LWLockMode)	Probe that fires when a server process has been released from its wait for an LWLock (it does not actually have the lock yet). arg0 is the LWLock's ID. arg1 is the requested lock mode, either exclusive or shared.
lwlock-condacquire	(LWLockId, LWLockMode)	Probe that fires when an LWLock was successfully acquired when the caller specified no waiting. arg0 is the LWLock's ID. arg1 is the requested lock mode, either exclusive or shared.

lwlock-condacquire-fail	(LWLockId, LWLockMode)	Probe that fires when an LWLock was not successfully acquired when the caller specified no waiting. arg0 is the LWLock's ID. arg1 is the requested lock mode, either exclusive or shared.
lock-wait-start	(unsigned int, unsigned int, unsigned int, unsigned int, unsigned int, LOCKMODE)	Probe that fires when a request for a heavyweight lock (lmgr lock) has begun to wait because the lock is not available. arg0 through arg3 are the tag fields identifying the object being locked. arg4 indicates the type of object being locked. arg5 indicates the lock type being requested.
lock-wait-done	(unsigned int, unsigned int, unsigned int, unsigned int, unsigned int, LOCKMODE)	Probe that fires when a request for a heavyweight lock (lmgr lock) has finished waiting (i.e., has acquired the lock). The arguments are the same as for lock-wait-start.
deadlock-found	()	Probe that fires when a deadlock is found by the deadlock detector.

Table 26-3. Built-in DTrace Probes

Type	Definition
LocalTransactionId	unsigned int
LWLockId	int
LWLockMode	int
LOCKMODE	int
BlockNumber	unsigned int
Oid	unsigned int
ForkNumber	int
bool	char

Table 26-4. Defined Types Used in Probe Parameters

26.4.3. Using Probes

The example below shows a DTrace script for analyzing transaction counts in the system, as an alternative to snapshotting pg_stat_database before and after a performance test:

```
#!/usr/sbin/dtrace -qs

postgresql$1:::transaction-start
{
      @start["Start"] = count();
      self->ts  = timestamp;
}

postgresql$1:::transaction-abort
{
      @abort["Abort"] = count();
}
```

```
postgresql$1:::transaction-commit
/self->ts/
{
        @commit["Commit"] = count();
        @time["Total time (ns)"] = sum(timestamp - self->ts);
        self->ts=0;
}
```

When executed, the example D script gives output such as:

```
# ./txn_count.d `pgrep -n postgres` or ./txn_count.d <PID>
^C

Start                                         71
Commit                                        70
Total time (ns)                       2312105013
```

 Note

> SystemTap uses a different notation for trace scripts than DTrace does, even though
> the underlying trace points are compatible. One point worth noting is that at this
> writing, SystemTap scripts must reference probe names using double underlines in
> place of hyphens. This is expected to be fixed in future SystemTap releases.

You should remember that DTrace scripts need to be carefully written and debugged,
otherwise the trace information collected might be meaningless. In most cases where
problems are found it is the instrumentation that is at fault, not the underlying system.
When discussing information found using dynamic tracing, be sure to enclose the script
used to allow that too to be checked and discussed.

More example scripts can be found in the PgFoundry *dtrace project*.

26.4.4. Defining New Probes

New probes can be defined within the code wherever the developer desires, though this will
require a recompilation. Below are the steps for inserting new probes:

1. Decide on probe names and data to be made available through the probes

2. Add the probe definitions to `src/backend/utils/probes.d`

3. Include `pg_trace.h` if it is not already present in the module(s) containing the probe
   points, and insert `TRACE_POSTGRESQL` probe macros at the desired locations in the
   source code

4. Recompile and verify that the new probes are available

Example: Here is an example of how you would add a probe to trace all new transactions by
transaction ID.

1. Decide that the probe will be named `transaction-start` and requires a parameter of type LocalTransactionId

2. Add the probe definition to `src/backend/utils/probes.d`:

    ```
    probe transaction__start(LocalTransactionId);
    ```

    Note the use of the double underline in the probe name. In a DTrace script using the probe, the double underline needs to be replaced with a hyphen, so transaction-start is the name to document for users.

3. At compile time, `transaction__start` is converted to a macro called `TRACE_POSTGRESQL_TRANSACTION_START` (notice the underscores are single here), which is available by including `pg_trace.h`. Add the macro call to the appropriate location in the source code. In this case, it looks like the following:

    ```
    TRACE_POSTGRESQL_TRANSACTION_START(vxid.localTransactionId);
    ```

4. After recompiling and running the new binary, check that your newly added probe is available by executing the following DTrace command. You should see similar output:

    ```
    # dtrace -ln transaction-start
       ID    PROVIDER          MODULE         FUNCTION NAME
    18705 postgresql49878     postgres     StartTransactionCommand transaction-start
    18755 postgresql49877     postgres     StartTransactionCommand transaction-start
    18805 postgresql49876     postgres     StartTransactionCommand transaction-start
    18855 postgresql49875     postgres     StartTransactionCommand transaction-start
    18986 postgresql49873     postgres     StartTransactionCommand transaction-start
    ```

There are a few things to be careful about when adding trace macros to the C code:

*   You should take care that the data types specified for a probe's parameters match the data types of the variables used in the macro. Otherwise, you will get compilation errors.

*   On most platforms, if PostgreSQL is built with `--enable-dtrace`, the arguments to a trace macro will be evaluated whenever control passes through the macro, *even if no tracing is being done*. This is usually not worth worrying about if you are just reporting the values of a few local variables. But beware of putting expensive function calls into the arguments. If you need to do that, consider protecting the macro with a check to see if the trace is actually enabled:

    ```
    if (TRACE_POSTGRESQL_TRANSACTION_START_ENABLED())
        TRACE_POSTGRESQL_TRANSACTION_START(some_function(...));
    ```

    Each trace macro has a corresponding ENABLED macro.

Chapter 27.
Monitoring Disk Usage

This chapter discusses how to monitor the disk usage of a PostgreSQL database system.

27.1. Determining Disk Usage

Each table has a primary heap disk file where most of the data is stored. If the table has any columns with potentially-wide values, there is also a TOAST file associated with the table, which is used to store values too wide to fit comfortably in the main table (see *Section 53.2*). There will be one index on the TOAST table, if present. There might also be indexes associated with the base table. Each table and index is stored in a separate disk file — possibly more than one file, if the file would exceed one gigabyte. Naming conventions for these files are described in *Section 53.1*.

You can monitor disk space from three ways: using SQL functions listed in *Table 9-57*, using VACUUM information, and from the command line using the tools in contrib/oid2name. The SQL functions are the easiest to use and report information about tables, tables with indexes and long value storage (TOAST), databases, and tablespaces.

Using psql on a recently vacuumed or analyzed database, you can issue queries to see the disk usage of any table:

```
SELECT relfilenode, relpages FROM pg_class WHERE relname = 'customer';

 relfilenode | relpages
-------------+----------
       16806 |       60
(1 row)
```

Each page is typically 8 kilobytes. (Remember, relpages is only updated by VACUUM, ANALYZE, and a few DDL commands such as CREATE INDEX.) The relfilenode value is of interest if you want to examine the table's disk file directly.

To show the space used by TOAST tables, use a query like the following:

```
SELECT relname, relpages
    FROM pg_class,
         (SELECT reltoastrelid FROM pg_class
          WHERE relname = 'customer') ss
```

```
    WHERE oid = ss.reltoastrelid
        OR oid = (SELECT reltoastidxid FROM pg_class
                        WHERE oid = ss.reltoastrelid)
    ORDER BY relname;
```

relname	relpages
pg_toast_16806	0
pg_toast_16806_index	1

You can easily display index sizes, too:

```
SELECT c2.relname, c2.relpages
    FROM pg_class c, pg_class c2, pg_index i
    WHERE c.relname = 'customer'
        AND c.oid = i.indrelid
        AND c2.oid = i.indexrelid
    ORDER BY c2.relname;
```

relname	relpages
customer_id_indexdex	26

It is easy to find your largest tables and indexes using this information:

```
SELECT relname, relpages FROM pg_class ORDER BY relpages DESC;
```

relname	relpages
bigtable	3290
customer	3144

You can also use contrib/oid2name to show disk usage. See README.oid2name in that directory for examples. It includes a script that shows disk usage for each database.

27.2. Disk Full Failure

The most important disk monitoring task of a database administrator is to make sure the disk doesn't grow full. A filled data disk will not result in data corruption, but it might prevent useful activity from occurring. If the disk holding the WAL files grows full, database server panic and consequent shutdown might occur.

If you cannot free up additional space on the disk by deleting other things, you can move some of the database files to other file systems by making use of tablespaces. See *Section 21.6 - page 155* for more information about that.

 Tip

Some file systems perform badly when they are almost full, so do not wait until the disk is completely full to take action.

If your system supports per-user disk quotas, then the database will naturally be subject to whatever quota is placed on the user the server runs as. Exceeding the quota will have the same bad effects as running out of space entirely.

Chapter 28.
Reliability and the Write-Ahead Log

This chapter explains how the Write-Ahead Log is used to obtain efficient, reliable operation.

28.1. Reliability

Reliability is an important property of any serious database system, and PostgreSQL does everything possible to guarantee reliable operation. One aspect of reliable operation is that all data recorded by a committed transaction should be stored in a nonvolatile area that is safe from power loss, operating system failure, and hardware failure (except failure of the nonvolatile area itself, of course). Successfully writing the data to the computer's permanent storage (disk drive or equivalent) ordinarily meets this requirement. In fact, even if a computer is fatally damaged, if the disk drives survive they can be moved to another computer with similar hardware and all committed transactions will remain intact.

While forcing data periodically to the disk platters might seem like a simple operation, it is not. Because disk drives are dramatically slower than main memory and CPUs, several layers of caching exist between the computer's main memory and the disk platters. First, there is the operating system's buffer cache, which caches frequently requested disk blocks and combines disk writes. Fortunately, all operating systems give applications a way to force writes from the buffer cache to disk, and PostgreSQL uses those features. (See the *wal_sync_method* parameter to adjust how this is done.)

Next, there might be a cache in the disk drive controller; this is particularly common on RAID controller cards. Some of these caches are *write-through*, meaning writes are passed along to the drive as soon as they arrive. Others are *write-back*, meaning data is passed on to the drive at some later time. Such caches can be a reliability hazard because the memory in the disk controller cache is volatile, and will lose its contents in a power failure. Better controller cards have *battery-backed* caches, meaning the card has a battery that maintains power to the cache in case of system power loss. After power is restored the data will be written to the disk drives.

And finally, most disk drives have caches. Some are write-through while some are write-back, and the same concerns about data loss exist for write-back drive caches as exist for disk controller caches. Consumer-grade IDE and SATA drives are particularly likely to have write-back caches that will not survive a power failure. To check write caching on Linux use hdparm -I; it is enabled if there is a * next to Write cache. hdparm -W to turn off write caching. On FreeBSD use atacontrol. (For SCSI disks use *sdparm*[1] to turn off WCE.) On Solaris the disk write cache is controlled by *format -e*[2]. (The Solaris ZFS file system is safe with disk write-cache enabled because it issues its own disk cache flush commands.) On Windows if wal_sync_method is open_datasync (the default), write caching is disabled by unchecking *My Computer \ Open \ {select disk drive} \ Properties \ Hardware \ Properties \ Policies \ Enable write caching on the disk*. Also on Windows, fsync and fsync_writethrough never do write caching.

When the operating system sends a write request to the disk hardware, there is little it can do to make sure the data has arrived at a truly non-volatile storage area. Rather, it is the administrator's responsibility to be sure that all storage components ensure data integrity. Avoid disk controllers that have non-battery-backed write caches. At the drive level, disable write-back caching if the drive cannot guarantee the data will be written before shutdown.

Another risk of data loss is posed by the disk platter write operations themselves. Disk platters are divided into sectors, commonly 512 bytes each. Every physical read or write operation processes a whole sector. When a write request arrives at the drive, it might be for 512 bytes, 1024 bytes, or 8192 bytes, and the process of writing could fail due to power loss at any time, meaning some of the 512-byte sectors were written, and others were not. To guard against such failures, PostgreSQL periodically writes full page images to permanent storage *before* modifying the actual page on disk. By doing this, during crash recovery PostgreSQL can restore partially-written pages. If you have a battery-backed disk controller or file-system software that prevents partial page writes (e.g., ReiserFS 4), you can turn off this page imaging by using the *full_page_writes* parameter.

28.2. Write-Ahead Logging (WAL)

Write-Ahead Logging (WAL) is a standard method for ensuring data integrity. A detailed description can be found in most (if not all) books about transaction processing. Briefly, WAL's central concept is that changes to data files (where tables and indexes reside) must be written only after those changes have been logged, that is, after log records describing the changes have been flushed to permanent storage. If we follow this procedure, we do not need to flush data pages to disk on every transaction commit, because we know that in the event of a crash we will be able to recover the database using the log: any changes that have

---

[1] *http://sg.torque.net/sg/sdparm.html*
[2] *http://www.sun.com/bigadmin/content/submitted/format_utility.jsp*

not been applied to the data pages can be redone from the log records. (This is roll-forward recovery, also known as REDO.)

 Tip

> Because WAL restores database file contents after a crash, journaled filesystems are not necessary for reliable storage of the data files or WAL files. In fact, journaling overhead can reduce performance, especially if journaling causes file system *data* to be flushed to disk. Fortunately, data flushing during journaling can often be disabled with a filesystem mount option, e.g. data=writeback on a Linux ext3 file system. Journaled file systems do improve boot speed after a crash.

Using WAL results in a significantly reduced number of disk writes, because only the log file needs to be flushed to disk to guarantee that a transaction is committed, rather than every data file changed by the transaction. The log file is written sequentially, and so the cost of syncing the log is much less than the cost of flushing the data pages. This is especially true for servers handling many small transactions touching different parts of the data store. Furthermore, when the server is processing many small concurrent transactions, one fsync of the log file may suffice to commit many transactions.

WAL also makes it possible to support on-line backup and point-in-time recovery, as described in *Section 24.3* - page 184. By archiving the WAL data we can support reverting to any time instant covered by the available WAL data: we simply install a prior physical backup of the database, and replay the WAL log just as far as the desired time. What's more, the physical backup doesn't have to be an instantaneous snapshot of the database state — if it is made over some period of time, then replaying the WAL log for that period will fix any internal inconsistencies.

28.3. Asynchronous Commit

Asynchronous commit is an option that allows transactions to complete more quickly, at the cost that the most recent transactions may be lost if the database should crash. In many applications this is an acceptable trade-off.

As described in the previous section, transaction commit is normally *synchronous*: the server waits for the transaction's WAL records to be flushed to permanent storage before returning a success indication to the client. The client is therefore guaranteed that a transaction reported to be committed will be preserved, even in the event of a server crash immediately after. However, for short transactions this delay is a major component of the total transaction time. Selecting asynchronous commit mode means that the server returns success as soon as the transaction is logically completed, before the WAL records it generated have actually made their way to disk. This can provide a significant boost in throughput for small transactions.

Asynchronous commit introduces the risk of data loss. There is a short time window between the report of transaction completion to the client and the time that the transaction is truly committed (that is, it is guaranteed not to be lost if the server crashes). Thus asynchronous commit should not be used if the client will take external actions relying on the assumption that the transaction will be remembered. As an example, a bank would certainly not use asynchronous commit for a transaction recording an ATM's dispensing of cash. But in many scenarios, such as event logging, there is no need for a strong guarantee of this kind.

The risk that is taken by using asynchronous commit is of data loss, not data corruption. If the database should crash, it will recover by replaying WAL up to the last record that was flushed. The database will therefore be restored to a self-consistent state, but any transactions that were not yet flushed to disk will not be reflected in that state. The net effect is therefore loss of the last few transactions. Because the transactions are replayed in commit order, no inconsistency can be introduced — for example, if transaction B made changes relying on the effects of a previous transaction A, it is not possible for A's effects to be lost while B's effects are preserved.

The user can select the commit mode of each transaction, so that it is possible to have both synchronous and asynchronous commit transactions running concurrently. This allows flexible trade-offs between performance and certainty of transaction durability. The commit mode is controlled by the user-settable parameter *synchronous_commit*, which can be changed in any of the ways that a configuration parameter can be set. The mode used for any one transaction depends on the value of synchronous_commit when transaction commit begins.

Certain utility commands, for instance DROP TABLE, are forced to commit synchronously regardless of the setting of synchronous_commit. This is to ensure consistency between the server's file system and the logical state of the database. The commands supporting two-phase commit, such as PREPARE TRANSACTION, are also always synchronous.

If the database crashes during the risk window between an asynchronous commit and the writing of the transaction's WAL records, then changes made during that transaction *will* be lost. The duration of the risk window is limited because a background process (the "WAL writer") flushes unwritten WAL records to disk every *wal_writer_delay* milliseconds. The actual maximum duration of the risk window is three times wal_writer_delay because the WAL writer is designed to favor writing whole pages at a time during busy periods.

 Caution

An immediate-mode shutdown is equivalent to a server crash, and will therefore cause loss of any unflushed asynchronous commits.

Asynchronous commit provides behavior different from setting *fsync* = off. fsync is a server-wide setting that will alter the behavior of all transactions. It disables all logic within PostgreSQL that attempts to synchronize writes to different portions of the database, and therefore a system crash (that is, a hardware or operating system crash, not a failure of PostgreSQL itself) could result in arbitrarily bad corruption of the database state. In many scenarios, asynchronous commit provides most of the performance improvement that could be obtained by turning off fsync, but without the risk of data corruption.

commit_delay also sounds very similar to asynchronous commit, but it is actually a synchronous commit method (in fact, commit_delay is ignored during an asynchronous commit). commit_delay causes a delay just before a synchronous commit attempts to flush WAL to disk, in the hope that a single flush executed by one such transaction can also serve other transactions committing at about the same time. Setting commit_delay can only help when there are many concurrently committing transactions, and it is difficult to tune it to a value that actually helps rather than hurting throughput.

28.4. WAL Configuration

There are several WAL-related configuration parameters that affect database performance. This section explains their use. Consult *Chapter 18 - page 77* for general information about setting server configuration parameters.

Checkpoints are points in the sequence of transactions at which it is guaranteed that the data files have been updated with all information written before the checkpoint. At checkpoint time, all dirty data pages are flushed to disk and a special checkpoint record is written to the log file. (The changes were previously flushed to the WAL files.) In the event of a crash, the crash recovery procedure looks at the latest checkpoint record to determine the point in the log (known as the redo record) from which it should start the REDO operation. Any changes made to data files before that point are guaranteed to be already on disk. Hence, after a checkpoint, log segments preceding the one containing the redo record are no longer needed and can be recycled or removed. (When WAL archiving is being done, the log segments must be archived before being recycled or removed.)

The checkpoint requirement of flushing all dirty data pages to disk can cause a significant I/O load. For this reason, checkpoint activity is throttled so I/O begins at checkpoint start and completes before the next checkpoint starts; this minimizes performance degradation during checkpoints.

The server's background writer process will automatically perform a checkpoint every so often. A checkpoint is created every *checkpoint_segments* log segments, or every *checkpoint_timeout* seconds, whichever comes first. The default settings are 3 segments and 300 seconds respectively. It is also possible to force a checkpoint by using the SQL command CHECKPOINT.

Reducing checkpoint_segments and/or checkpoint_timeout causes checkpoints to be done more often. This allows faster after-crash recovery (since less work will need to be redone). However, one must balance this against the increased cost of flushing dirty data pages more often. If *full_page_writes* is set (as is the default), there is another factor to consider. To ensure data page consistency, the first modification of a data page after each checkpoint results in logging the entire page content. In that case, a smaller checkpoint interval increases the volume of output to the WAL log, partially negating the goal of using a smaller interval, and in any case causing more disk I/O.

Checkpoints are fairly expensive, first because they require writing out all currently dirty buffers, and second because they result in extra subsequent WAL traffic as discussed above. It is therefore wise to set the checkpointing parameters high enough that checkpoints don't happen too often. As a simple sanity check on your checkpointing parameters, you can set the *checkpoint_warning* parameter. If checkpoints happen closer together than checkpoint_warning seconds, a message will be output to the server log recommending increasing checkpoint_segments. Occasional appearance of such a message is not cause for alarm, but if it appears often then the checkpoint control parameters should be increased. Bulk operations such as large COPY transfers might cause a number of such warnings to appear if you have not set checkpoint_segments high enough.

To avoid flooding the I/O system with a burst of page writes, writing dirty buffers during a checkpoint is spread over a period of time. That period is controlled by *checkpoint_completion_target*, which is given as a fraction of the checkpoint interval. The I/O rate is adjusted so that the checkpoint finishes when the given fraction of checkpoint_segments WAL segments have been consumed since checkpoint start, or the given fraction of checkpoint_timeout seconds have elapsed, whichever is sooner. With the default value of 0.5, PostgreSQL can be expected to complete each checkpoint in about half the time before the next checkpoint starts. On a system that's very close to maximum I/O throughput during normal operation, you might want to increase checkpoint_completion_target to reduce the I/O load from checkpoints. The disadvantage of this is that prolonging checkpoints affects recovery time, because more WAL segments will need to be kept around for possible use in recovery. Although checkpoint_completion_target can be set as high as 1.0, it is best to keep it less than that (perhaps 0.9 at most) since checkpoints include some other activities besides writing dirty buffers. A setting of 1.0 is quite likely to result in checkpoints not being completed on time, which would result in performance loss due to unexpected variation in the number of WAL segments needed.

There will always be at least one WAL segment file, and will normally not be more than (2 + checkpoint_completion_target) * checkpoint_segments + 1 files. Each segment file is normally 16 MB (though this size can be altered when building the server). You can use this to estimate space requirements for WAL. Ordinarily, when old log segment files are no longer needed, they are recycled (renamed to become the next segments in the numbered sequence). If, due to a short-term peak of log output rate, there are more than 3 * checkpoint_segments + 1 segment files, the unneeded segment files will be deleted instead of recycled until the system gets back under this limit.

There are two commonly used internal WAL functions: LogInsert and LogFlush. LogInsert is used to place a new record into the WAL buffers in shared memory. If there is no space for the new record, LogInsert will have to write (move to kernel cache) a few filled WAL buffers. This is undesirable because LogInsert is used on every database low level modification (for example, row insertion) at a time when an exclusive lock is held on affected data pages, so the operation needs to be as fast as possible. What is worse, writing WAL buffers might also force the creation of a new log segment, which takes even more time. Normally, WAL buffers should be written and flushed by a LogFlush request, which is made, for the most part, at transaction commit time to ensure that transaction records are flushed to permanent storage. On systems with high log output, LogFlush requests might not occur often enough to prevent LogInsert from having to do writes. On such systems one should increase the number of WAL buffers by modifying the configuration parameter *wal_buffers*. The default number of WAL buffers is 8. Increasing this value will correspondingly increase shared memory usage. When *full_page_writes* is set and the system is very busy, setting this value higher will help smooth response times during the period immediately following each checkpoint.

The *commit_delay* parameter defines for how many microseconds the server process will sleep after writing a commit record to the log with LogInsert but before performing a LogFlush. This delay allows other server processes to add their commit records to the log so as to have all of them flushed with a single log sync. No sleep will occur if *fsync* is not enabled, nor if fewer than *commit_siblings* other sessions are currently in active transactions; this avoids sleeping when it's unlikely that any other session will commit soon. Note that on most platforms, the resolution of a sleep request is ten milliseconds, so that any nonzero commit_delay setting between 1 and 10000 microseconds would have the same effect. Good values for these parameters are not yet clear; experimentation is encouraged.

The *wal_sync_method* parameter determines how PostgreSQL will ask the kernel to force WAL updates out to disk. All the options should be the same as far as reliability goes, but it's quite platform-specific which one will be the fastest. Note that this parameter is irrelevant if fsync has been turned off.

Enabling the *wal_debug* configuration parameter (provided that PostgreSQL has been compiled with support for it) will result in each LogInsert and LogFlush WAL call being logged to the server log. This option might be replaced by a more general mechanism in the future.

28.5. WAL Internals

WAL is automatically enabled; no action is required from the administrator except ensuring that the disk-space requirements for the WAL logs are met, and that any necessary tuning is done (see *Section 28.4* - page 234).

WAL logs are stored in the directory pg_xlog under the data directory, as a set of segment files, normally each 16 MB in size (but the size can be changed by altering the --with-wal-segsize configure option when building the server). Each segment is divided into pages, normally 8 kB each (this size can be changed via the --with-wal-blocksize configure option). The log record headers are described in access/xlog.h; the record content is dependent on the type of event that is being logged. Segment files are given ever-increasing numbers as names, starting at 000000010000000000000000. The numbers do not wrap, at present, but it should take a very very long time to exhaust the available stock of numbers.

It is of advantage if the log is located on another disk than the main database files. This can be achieved by moving the directory pg_xlog to another location (while the server is shut down, of course) and creating a symbolic link from the original location in the main data directory to the new location.

The aim of WAL, to ensure that the log is written before database records are altered, can be subverted by disk drives that falsely report a successful write to the kernel, when in fact they have only cached the data and not yet stored it on the disk. A power failure in such a situation might still lead to irrecoverable data corruption. Administrators should try to ensure that disks holding PostgreSQL's WAL log files do not make such false reports.

After a checkpoint has been made and the log flushed, the checkpoint's position is saved in the file pg_control. Therefore, when recovery is to be done, the server first reads pg_control and then the checkpoint record; then it performs the REDO operation by scanning forward from the log position indicated in the checkpoint record. Because the entire content of data pages is saved in the log on the first page modification after a checkpoint (assuming *full_page_writes* is not disabled), all pages changed since the checkpoint will be restored to a consistent state.

To deal with the case where pg_control is corrupted, we should support the possibility of scanning existing log segments in reverse order — newest to oldest — in order to find the latest checkpoint. This has not been implemented yet. pg_control is small enough (less than one disk page) that it is not subject to partial-write problems, and as of this writing there have been no reports of database failures due solely to inability to read pg_control itself. So while it is theoretically a weak spot, pg_control does not seem to be a problem in practice.

Chapter 29.
Regression Tests

The regression tests are a comprehensive set of tests for the SQL implementation in PostgreSQL. They test standard SQL operations as well as the extended capabilities of PostgreSQL.

29.1. Running the Tests

The regression tests can be run against an already installed and running server, or using a temporary installation within the build tree. Furthermore, there is a "parallel" and a "sequential" mode for running the tests. The sequential method runs each test script in turn, whereas the parallel method starts up multiple server processes to run groups of tests in parallel. Parallel testing gives confidence that interprocess communication and locking are working correctly. For historical reasons, the sequential test is usually run against an existing installation and the parallel method against a temporary installation, but there are no technical reasons for this.

To run the regression tests after building but before installation, type:

```
gmake check
```

in the top-level directory. (Or you can change to src/test/regress and run the command there.) This will first build several auxiliary files, such as some sample user-defined trigger functions, and then run the test driver script. At the end you should see something like:

```
=======================
 All 115 tests passed.
=======================
```

or otherwise a note about which tests failed. See *Section 29.2 - page 240* below before assuming that a "failure" represents a serious problem.

Because this test method runs a temporary server, it will not work when you are the root user (since the server will not start as root). If you already did the build as root, you do not have to start all over. Instead, make the regression test directory writable by some other user, log in as that user, and restart the tests. For example:

```
root# chmod -R a+w src/test/regress
root# su - joeuser
```

```
joeuser$ cd top-level build directory
joeuser$ gmake check
```

(The only possible "security risk" here is that other users might be able to alter the regression test results behind your back. Use common sense when managing user permissions.)

Alternatively, run the tests after installation.

If you have configured PostgreSQL to install into a location where an older PostgreSQL installation already exists, and you perform gmake check before installing the new version, you might find that the tests fail because the new programs try to use the already-installed shared libraries. (Typical symptoms are complaints about undefined symbols.) If you wish to run the tests before overwriting the old installation, you'll need to build with configure --disable-rpath. It is not recommended that you use this option for the final installation, however.

The parallel regression test starts quite a few processes under your user ID. Presently, the maximum concurrency is twenty parallel test scripts, which means forty processes: there's a server process and a psql process for each test script. So if your system enforces a per-user limit on the number of processes, make sure this limit is at least fifty or so, else you might get random-seeming failures in the parallel test. If you are not in a position to raise the limit, you can cut down the degree of parallelism by setting the MAX_CONNECTIONS parameter. For example:

```
gmake MAX_CONNECTIONS=10 check
```

runs no more than ten tests concurrently.

To run the tests after installation (see *Chapter 15* - page 20), initialize a data area and start the server, as explained in *Chapter 17* - page 56, then type:

```
gmake installcheck
```

or for a parallel test:

```
gmake installcheck-parallel
```

The tests will expect to contact the server at the local host and the default port number, unless directed otherwise by PGHOST and PGPORT environment variables.

The source distribution also contains regression tests for the optional procedural languages and for some of the contrib modules. At present, these tests can be used only against an already-installed server. To run the tests for all procedural languages that have been built and installed, change to the src/pl directory of the build tree and type:

```
gmake installcheck
```

You can also do this in any of the subdirectories of src/pl to run tests for just one procedural language. To run the tests for all contrib modules that have them, change to the contrib directory of the build tree and type:

```
gmake installcheck
```

The contrib modules must have been built and installed first. You can also do this in a subdirectory of contrib to run the tests for just one module.

29.2. Test Evaluation

Some properly installed and fully functional PostgreSQL installations can "fail" some of these regression tests due to platform-specific artifacts such as varying floating-point representation and message wording. The tests are currently evaluated using a simple diff comparison against the outputs generated on a reference system, so the results are sensitive to small system differences. When a test is reported as "failed", always examine the differences between expected and actual results; you might find that the differences are not significant. Nonetheless, we still strive to maintain accurate reference files across all supported platforms, so it can be expected that all tests pass.

The actual outputs of the regression tests are in files in the src/test/regress/results directory. The test script uses diff to compare each output file against the reference outputs stored in the src/test/regress/expected directory. Any differences are saved for your inspection in src/test/regress/regression.diffs. (Or you can run diff yourself, if you prefer.)

If for some reason a particular platform generates a "failure" for a given test, but inspection of the output convinces you that the result is valid, you can add a new comparison file to silence the failure report in future test runs. See *Section 29.3* - page 242 for details.

29.2.1. Error message differences

Some of the regression tests involve intentional invalid input values. Error messages can come from either the PostgreSQL code or from the host platform system routines. In the latter case, the messages can vary between platforms, but should reflect similar information. These differences in messages will result in a "failed" regression test that can be validated by inspection.

29.2.2. Locale differences

If you run the tests against a server that was initialized with a collation-order locale other than C, then there might be differences due to sort order and follow-up failures. The regression test suite is set up to handle this problem by providing alternative result files that together are known to handle a large number of locales.

To run the tests in a different locale when using the temporary-installation method, pass the appropriate locale-related environment variables on the make command line, for example:

```
gmake check LANG=de_DE.utf8
```

(The regression test driver unsets LC_ALL, so it does not work to choose the locale using that variable.) To use no locale, either unset all locale-related environment variables (or set them to C) or use the following special invocation:

```
gmake check NO_LOCALE=1
```

When running the tests against an existing installation, the locale setup is determined by the existing installation. To change it, initialize the database cluster with a different locale by passing the appropriate options to initdb.

In general, it is nevertheless advisable to try to run the regression tests in the locale setup that is wanted for production use, as this will exercise the locale- and encoding-related code portions that will actually be used in production. Depending on the operating system environment, you might get failures, but then you will at least know what locale-specific behaviors to expect when running real applications.

29.2.3. Date and time differences

Most of the date and time results are dependent on the time zone environment. The reference files are generated for time zone PST8PDT (Berkeley, California), and there will be apparent failures if the tests are not run with that time zone setting. The regression test driver sets environment variable PGTZ to PST8PDT, which normally ensures proper results.

29.2.4. Floating-point differences

Some of the tests involve computing 64-bit floating-point numbers (double precision) from table columns. Differences in results involving mathematical functions of double precision columns have been observed. The float8 and geometry tests are particularly prone to small differences across platforms, or even with different compiler optimization options. Human eyeball comparison is needed to determine the real significance of these differences which are usually 10 places to the right of the decimal point.

Some systems display minus zero as -0, while others just show 0.

Some systems signal errors from pow() and exp() differently from the mechanism expected by the current PostgreSQL code.

29.2.5. Row ordering differences

You might see differences in which the same rows are output in a different order than what appears in the expected file. In most cases this is not, strictly speaking, a bug. Most of the regression test scripts are not so pedantic as to use an ORDER BY for every single SELECT, and so their result row orderings are not well-defined according to the letter of the SQL specification. In practice, since we are looking at the same queries being executed on the same data by the same software, we usually get the same result ordering on all platforms, and so the lack of ORDER BY isn't a problem. Some queries do exhibit cross-platform ordering differences, however. When testing against an already-installed server, ordering differences can also be caused by non-C locale settings or non-default parameter settings, such as custom values of work_mem or the planner cost parameters.

Therefore, if you see an ordering difference, it's not something to worry about, unless the query does have an ORDER BY that your result is violating. But please report it anyway, so that we can add an ORDER BY to that particular query and thereby eliminate the bogus "failure" in future releases.

You might wonder why we don't order all the regression test queries explicitly to get rid of this issue once and for all. The reason is that that would make the regression tests less useful, not more, since they'd tend to exercise query plan types that produce ordered results to the exclusion of those that don't.

29.2.6. Insufficient stack depth

If the errors test results in a server crash at the select infinite_recurse() command, it means that the platform's limit on process stack size is smaller than the *max_stack_depth* parameter indicates. This can be fixed by running the server under a higher stack size limit (4MB is recommended with the default value of max_stack_depth). If you are unable to do that, an alternative is to reduce the value of max_stack_depth.

29.2.7. The "random" test

The random test script is intended to produce random results. In rare cases, this causes the random regression test to fail. Typing:

```
diff results/random.out expected/random.out
```

should produce only one or a few lines of differences. You need not worry unless the random test fails repeatedly.

29.3. Variant Comparison Files

Since some of the tests inherently produce environment-dependent results, we have provided ways to specify alternative "expected" result files. Each regression test can have several comparison files showing possible results on different platforms. There are two independent mechanisms for determining which comparison file is used for each test.

The first mechanism allows comparison files to be selected for specific platforms. There is a mapping file, src/test/regress/resultmap, that defines which comparison file to use for each platform. To eliminate bogus test "failures" for a particular platform, you first choose or make a variant result file, and then add a line to the resultmap file.

Each line in the mapping file is of the form

```
testname:output:platformpattern=comparisonfilename
```

The test name is just the name of the particular regression test module. The output value indicates which output file to check. For the standard regression tests, this is always out. The value corresponds to the file extension of the output file. The platform pattern is a pattern in the style of the Unix tool expr (that is, a regular expression with an implicit ^ anchor at the start). It is matched against the platform name as printed by config.guess. The comparison file name is the base name of the substitute result comparison file.

For example: some systems interpret very small floating-point values as zero, rather than reporting an underflow error. This causes a few differences in the float8 regression test. Therefore, we provide a variant comparison file, float8-small-is-zero.out, which includes the results to be expected on these systems. To silence the bogus "failure" message on OpenBSD platforms, resultmap includes:

```
float8:out:i.86-.*-openbsd=float8-small-is-zero.out
```

which will trigger on any machine for which the output of config.guess matches i.86-.*-openbsd. Other lines in resultmap select the variant comparison file for other platforms where it's appropriate.

The second selection mechanism for variant comparison files is much more automatic: it simply uses the "best match" among several supplied comparison files. The regression test driver script considers both the standard comparison file for a test, *testname*.out, and variant files named *testname_digit*.out (where the *digit* is any single digit 0-9). If any such file is an exact match, the test is considered to pass; otherwise, the one that generates the shortest diff is used to create the failure report. (If resultmap includes an entry for the particular test, then the base *testname* is the substitute name given in resultmap.)

For example, for the char test, the comparison file char.out contains results that are expected in the C and POSIX locales, while the file char_1.out contains results sorted as they appear in many other locales.

The best-match mechanism was devised to cope with locale-dependent results, but it can be used in any situation where the test results cannot be predicted easily from the platform name alone. A limitation of this mechanism is that the test driver cannot tell which variant is actually "correct" for the current environment; it will just pick the variant that seems to work best. Therefore it is safest to use this mechanism only for variant results that you are willing to consider equally valid in all contexts.

29.4. Test Coverage Examination

The PostgreSQL source code can be compiled with coverage testing instrumentation, so that it becomes possible to examine which parts of the code are covered by the regression tests or any other test suite that is run with the code. This is currently supported when compiling with GCC and requires the gcov and lcov programs.

A typical workflow would look like this:

```
./configure --enable-coverage ... OTHER OPTIONS ...
gmake
gmake check # or other test suite
gmake coverage-html
```

Then point your HTML browser to coverage/index.html.

To reset the execution counts between test runs, run:

```
gmake coverage-clean
```

Part IV.
Client Interfaces

This part describes the client programming interfaces distributed with PostgreSQL. Each of these chapters can be read independently. Note that there are many other programming interfaces for client programs that are distributed separately and contain their own documentation (*Appendix G* lists some of the more popular ones). Readers of this part should be familiar with using SQL commands to manipulate and query the database (see *Part II* - Vol.I page 54) and of course with the programming language that the interface uses.

Chapter 30.
libpq - C Library

libpq is the C application programmer's interface to PostgreSQL. libpq is a set of library functions that allow client programs to pass queries to the PostgreSQL backend server and to receive the results of these queries.

libpq is also the underlying engine for several other PostgreSQL application interfaces, including those written for C++, Perl, Python, Tcl and ECPG. So some aspects of libpq's behavior will be important to you if you use one of those packages. In particular, *Section 30.13* - page 300, *Section 30.14* - page 302 and *Section 30.17* - page 304 describe behavior that is visible to the user of any application that uses libpq.

Some short programs are included at the end of this chapter (*Section 30.20* - page 310) to show how to write programs that use libpq. There are also several complete examples of libpq applications in the directory src/test/examples in the source code distribution.

Client programs that use libpq must include the header file libpq-fe.h and must link with the libpq library.

30.1. Database Connection Control Functions

The following functions deal with making a connection to a PostgreSQL backend server. An application program can have several backend connections open at one time. (One reason to do that is to access more than one database.) Each connection is represented by a PGconn object, which is obtained from the function PQconnectdb or PQsetdbLogin. Note that these functions will always return a non-null object pointer, unless perhaps there is too little memory even to allocate the PGconn object. The PQstatus function should be called to check whether a connection was successfully made before queries are sent via the connection object.

Warning

On Unix, forking a process with open libpq connections can lead to unpredictable results because the parent and child processes share the same sockets and operating system resources. For this reason, such usage is not recommended, though doing an exec from the child process to load a new executable is safe.

Note

On Windows, there is a way to improve performance if a single database connection is repeatedly started and shutdown. Internally, libpq calls WSAStartup() and WSACleanup() for connection startup and shutdown, respectively. WSAStartup() increments an internal Windows library reference count which is decremented by WSACleanup(). When the reference count is just one, calling WSACleanup() frees all resources and all DLLs are unloaded. This is an expensive operation. To avoid this, an application can manually call WSAStartup() so resources will not be freed when the last database connection is closed.

PQconnectdb

Makes a new connection to the database server.

```
PGconn *PQconnectdb(const char *conninfo);
```

This function opens a new database connection using the parameters taken from the string conninfo. Unlike PQsetdbLogin below, the parameter set can be extended without changing the function signature, so use of this function (or its nonblocking analogues PQconnectStart and PQconnectPoll) is preferred for new application programming.

The passed string can be empty to use all default parameters, or it can contain one or more parameter settings separated by whitespace. Each parameter setting is in the form keyword = value. Spaces around the equal sign are optional. To write an empty value or a value containing spaces, surround it with single quotes, e.g., keyword = 'a value'. Single quotes and backslashes within the value must be escaped with a backslash, i.e., \' and \\.

The currently recognized parameter key words are:

host

Name of host to connect to. If this begins with a slash, it specifies Unix-domain communication rather than TCP/IP communication; the value is the name of the directory in which the socket file is stored. The default behavior when host is not specified is to connect to a Unix-domain socket in /tmp (or whatever socket directory was specified when PostgreSQL was built). On machines without Unix-domain sockets, the default is to connect to localhost.

hostaddr

Numeric IP address of host to connect to. This should be in the standard IPv4 address format, e.g., 172.28.40.9. If your machine supports IPv6, you can also use those addresses. TCP/IP communication is always used when a nonempty string is specified for this parameter.

Using `hostaddr` instead of `host` allows the application to avoid a host name lookup, which might be important in applications with time constraints. However, Kerberos and GSSAPI authentication requires the host name. The following therefore applies: If `host` is specified without `hostaddr`, a host name lookup occurs. If `hostaddr` is specified without `host`, the value for `hostaddr` gives the remote address. When Kerberos is used, a reverse name query occurs to obtain the host name for Kerberos. If both `host` and `hostaddr` are specified, the value for `hostaddr` gives the remote address; the value for `host` is ignored, unless Kerberos is used, in which case that value is used for Kerberos authentication. (Note that authentication is likely to fail if libpq is passed a host name that is not the name of the machine at `hostaddr`.) Also, `host` rather than `hostaddr` is used to identify the connection in `~/.pgpass` (see *Section 30.14* - page 302).

Without either a host name or host address, libpq will connect using a local Unix-domain socket; or on machines without Unix-domain sockets, it will attempt to connect to `localhost`.

`port`

Port number to connect to at the server host, or socket file name extension for Unix-domain connections.

`dbname`

The database name. Defaults to be the same as the user name.

`user`

PostgreSQL user name to connect as. Defaults to be the same as the operating system name of the user running the application.

`password`

Password to be used if the server demands password authentication.

`connect_timeout`

Maximum wait for connection, in seconds (write as a decimal integer string). Zero or not specified means wait indefinitely. It is not recommended to use a timeout of less than 2 seconds.

`options`

Adds command-line options to send to the server at run-time. For example, setting this to `-c geqo=off` sets the session's value of the `geqo` parameter to `off`. For a detailed discussion of the available options, consult *Chapter 18* - page 77.

`tty`

Ignored (formerly, this specified where to send server debug output).

sslmode

> This option determines whether or with what priority a SSL TCP/IP connection will be negotiated with the server. There are six modes:

Option	Description
disable	only try a non-SSL connection
allow	first try a non-SSL connection; if that fails, try an SSL connection
prefer (default)	first try an SSL connection; if that fails, try a non-SSL connection
require	only try an SSL connection
verify-ca	only try an SSL connection, and verify that the server certificate is issued by a trusted CA.
verify-full	only try an SSL connection, verify that the server certificate is issued by a trusted CA and that the server hostname matches that in the certificate.

Table 30-1. sslmode options

> See *Section 30.17* - page 304 for a detailed description of how these options work.
>
> sslmode is ignored for Unix domain socket communication. If PostgreSQL is compiled without SSL support, using option require will cause an error, while options allow and prefer will be accepted but libpq will not actually attempt an SSL connection.

requiressl

> This option is deprecated in favor of the sslmode setting.
>
> If set to 1, an SSL connection to the server is required (this is equivalent to sslmode require). libpq will then refuse to connect if the server does not accept an SSL connection. If set to 0 (default), libpq will negotiate the connection type with the server (equivalent to sslmode prefer). This option is only available if PostgreSQL is compiled with SSL support.

sslcert

> This parameter specifies the file name of the client SSL certificate.

sslkey

> This parameter specifies the location for the secret key used for the client certificate. It can either specify a filename that will be used instead of the default ~/.postgresql/postgresql.key, or can specify an external engine (engines are OpenSSL loadable modules). The external engine specification should consist of a colon-separated engine name and an engine-specific key identifier.

`sslrootcert`

This parameter specifies the file name of the root SSL certificate.

`sslcrl`

This parameter specifies the file name of the SSL certificate revocation list (CRL).

`krbsrvname`

Kerberos service name to use when authenticating with Kerberos 5 or GSSAPI. This must match the service name specified in the server configuration for Kerberos authentication to succeed. (See also *Section 19.3.5* - page 139 and *Section 19.3.3* - page 138.)

`gsslib`

GSS library to use for GSSAPI authentication. Only used on Windows. Set to `gssapi` to force libpq to use the GSSAPI library for authentication instead of the default SSPI.

`service`

Service name to use for additional parameters. It specifies a service name in `pg_service.conf` that holds additional connection parameters. This allows applications to specify only a service name so connection parameters can be centrally maintained. See *Section 30.15* - page 302.

If any parameter is unspecified, then the corresponding environment variable (see *Section 30.13* - page 300) is checked. If the environment variable is not set either, then the indicated built-in defaults are used.

`PQsetdbLogin`

Makes a new connection to the database server.

```
PGconn *PQsetdbLogin(const char *pghost,
                     const char *pgport,
                     const char *pgoptions,
                     const char *pgtty,
                     const char *dbName,
                     const char *login,
                     const char *pwd);
```

This is the predecessor of PQconnectdb with a fixed set of parameters. It has the same functionality except that the missing parameters will always take on default values. Write NULL or an empty string for any one of the fixed parameters that is to be defaulted.

If the dbName contains an = sign, it is taken as a conninfo string in exactly the same way as if it had been passed to PQconnectdb, and the remaining parameters are then applied as above.

PQsetdb

> Makes a new connection to the database server.

```
PGconn *PQsetdb(char *pghost,
                char *pgport,
                char *pgoptions,
                char *pgtty,
                char *dbName);
```

> This is a macro that calls PQsetdbLogin with null pointers for the login and pwd parameters. It is provided for backward compatibility with very old programs.

PQconnectStart
PQconnectPoll

> Make a connection to the database server in a nonblocking manner.

```
PGconn *PQconnectStart(const char *conninfo);
PostgresPollingStatusType PQconnectPoll(PGconn *conn);
```

These two functions are used to open a connection to a database server such that your application's thread of execution is not blocked on remote I/O whilst doing so. The point of this approach is that the waits for I/O to complete can occur in the application's main loop, rather than down inside PQconnectdb, and so the application can manage this operation in parallel with other activities.

The database connection is made using the parameters taken from the string conninfo, passed to PQconnectStart. This string is in the same format as described above for PQconnectdb.

Neither PQconnectStart nor PQconnectPoll will block, so long as a number of restrictions are met:

- The hostaddr and host parameters are used appropriately to ensure that name and reverse name queries are not made. See the documentation of these parameters under PQconnectdb above for details.

- If you call PQtrace, ensure that the stream object into which you trace will not block.

- You ensure that the socket is in the appropriate state before calling PQconnectPoll, as described below.

To begin a nonblocking connection request, call conn = PQconnectStart ("*connection_info_string*"). If conn is null, then libpq has been unable to allocate a new PGconn structure. Otherwise, a valid PGconn pointer is returned (though not yet representing a valid connection to the database). On return from PQconnectStart, call status = PQstatus(conn). If status equals CONNECTION_BAD, PQconnectStart has failed.

If PQconnectStart succeeds, the next stage is to poll libpq so that it can proceed with the connection sequence. Use PQsocket(conn) to obtain the descriptor of the socket underlying the database connection. Loop thus: If PQconnectPoll(conn) last returned PGRES_POLLING_READING, wait until the socket is ready to read (as indicated by select(), poll(), or similar system function). Then call PQconnectPoll(conn) again. Conversely, if PQconnectPoll(conn) last returned PGRES_POLLING_WRITING, wait until the socket is ready to write, then call PQconnectPoll(conn) again. If you have yet to call PQconnectPoll, i.e., just after the call to PQconnectStart, behave as if it last returned PGRES_POLLING_WRITING. Continue this loop until PQconnectPoll(conn) returns PGRES_POLLING_FAILED, indicating the connection procedure has failed, or PGRES_POLLING_OK, indicating the connection has been successfully made.

At any time during connection, the status of the connection can be checked by calling PQstatus. If this gives CONNECTION_BAD, then the connection procedure has failed; if it gives CONNECTION_OK, then the connection is ready. Both of these states are equally detectable from the return value of PQconnectPoll, described above. Other states might also occur during (and only during) an asynchronous connection procedure. These indicate the current stage of the connection procedure and might be useful to provide feedback to the user for example. These statuses are:

CONNECTION_STARTED

> Waiting for connection to be made.

CONNECTION_MADE

> Connection OK; waiting to send.

CONNECTION_AWAITING_RESPONSE

> Waiting for a response from the server.

CONNECTION_AUTH_OK

> Received authentication; waiting for backend start-up to finish.

CONNECTION_SSL_STARTUP

> Negotiating SSL encryption.

CONNECTION_SETENV

> Negotiating environment-driven parameter settings.

Note that, although these constants will remain (in order to maintain compatibility), an application should never rely upon these occurring in a particular order, or at all, or on the status always being one of these documented values. An application might do something like this:

```
switch(PQstatus(conn))
{
        case CONNECTION_STARTED:
            feedback = "Connecting...";
            break;

        case CONNECTION_MADE:
            feedback = "Connected to server...";
            break;
        .
        .
        .

        default:
            feedback = "Connecting...";
}
```

The connect_timeout connection parameter is ignored when using PQconnectPoll; it is the application's responsibility to decide whether an excessive amount of time has elapsed. Otherwise, PQconnectStart followed by a PQconnectPoll loop is equivalent to PQconnectdb.

Note that if PQconnectStart returns a non-null pointer, you must call PQfinish when you are finished with it, in order to dispose of the structure and any associated memory blocks. This must be done even if the connection attempt fails or is abandoned.

PQconndefaults

Returns the default connection options.

```
PQconninfoOption *PQconndefaults(void);

typedef struct
{
    char    *keyword;    /* The keyword of the option */
    char    *envvar;     /* Fallback environment variable name */
    char    *compiled;   /* Fallback compiled in default value */
    char    *val;        /* Option's current value, or NULL */
    char    *label;      /* Label for field in connect dialog */
    char    *dispchar;   /* Indicates how to display this field
                            in a connect dialog. Values are:
                            ""          Display entered value as is
                            "*"         Password field - hide value
                            "D"         Debug option - don't show by default */
    int     dispsize;    /* Field size in characters for dialog */
} PQconninfoOption;
```

Returns a connection options array. This can be used to determine all possible PQconnectdb options and their current default values. The return value points to an array of PQconninfoOption structures, which ends with an entry having a null keyword pointer. The null pointer is returned if memory could not be allocated. Note that the current default values (val fields) will depend on environment variables and other context. Callers must treat the connection options data as read-only.

After processing the options array, free it by passing it to PQconninfoFree. If this is not done, a small amount of memory is leaked for each call to PQconndefaults.

PQconninfoParse

Returns parsed connection options from the provided connection string.

```
PQconninfoOption *PQconninfoParse(const char *conninfo, char **errmsg);
```

Parses a connection string and returns the resulting options as an array; or returns NULL if there is a problem with the connection string. This can be used to determine the PQconnectdb options in the provided connection string. The return value points to an array of PQconninfoOption structures, which ends with an entry having a null keyword pointer.

Note that only options explicitly specified in the string will have values set in the result array; no defaults are inserted.

If errmsg is not NULL, then *errmsg is set to NULL on success, else to a malloc'd error string explaining the problem. (It is also possible for *errmsg to be set to NULL even when NULL is returned; this indicates an out-of-memory situation.)

After processing the options array, free it by passing it to PQconninfoFree. If this is not done, some memory is leaked for each call to PQconninfoParse. Conversely, if an error occurs and errmsg is not NULL, be sure to free the error string using PQfreemem.

PQfinish

Closes the connection to the server. Also frees memory used by the PGconn object.

```
void PQfinish(PGconn *conn);
```

Note that even if the server connection attempt fails (as indicated by PQstatus), the application should call PQfinish to free the memory used by the PGconn object. The PGconn pointer must not be used again after PQfinish has been called.

PQreset

Resets the communication channel to the server.

```
void PQreset(PGconn *conn);
```

This function will close the connection to the server and attempt to reestablish a new connection to the same server, using all the same parameters previously used. This might be useful for error recovery if a working connection is lost.

PQresetStart
PQresetPoll

Reset the communication channel to the server, in a nonblocking manner.

```
int PQresetStart(PGconn *conn);
PostgresPollingStatusType PQresetPoll(PGconn *conn);
```

These functions will close the connection to the server and attempt to reestablish a new connection to the same server, using all the same parameters previously used. This can be useful for error recovery if a working connection is lost. They differ from PQreset (above) in that they act in a nonblocking manner. These functions suffer from the same restrictions as PQconnectStart and PQconnectPoll.

To initiate a connection reset, call PQresetStart. If it returns 0, the reset has failed. If it returns 1, poll the reset using PQresetPoll in exactly the same way as you would create the connection using PQconnectPoll.

30.2. Connection Status Functions

These functions can be used to interrogate the status of an existing database connection object.

 Tip

> libpq application programmers should be careful to maintain the PGconn abstraction. Use the accessor functions described below to get at the contents of PGconn. Reference to internal PGconn fields using libpq-int.h is not recommended because they are subject to change in the future.

The following functions return parameter values established at connection. These values are fixed for the life of the PGconn object.

PQdb

> Returns the database name of the connection.
>
>   char *PQdb(const PGconn *conn);

PQuser

> Returns the user name of the connection.
>
>   char *PQuser(const PGconn *conn);

PQpass

> Returns the password of the connection.
>
>   char *PQpass(const PGconn *conn);

PQhost

> Returns the server host name of the connection.
>
>   char *PQhost(const PGconn *conn);

PQport

> Returns the port of the connection.
>
>   char *PQport(const PGconn *conn);

PQtty

Returns the debug TTY of the connection. (This is obsolete, since the server no longer pays attention to the TTY setting, but the function remains for backwards compatibility.)

```
char *PQtty(const PGconn *conn);
```

PQoptions

Returns the command-line options passed in the connection request.

```
char *PQoptions(const PGconn *conn);
```

The following functions return status data that can change as operations are executed on the PGconn object.

PQstatus

Returns the status of the connection.

```
ConnStatusType PQstatus(const PGconn *conn);
```

The status can be one of a number of values. However, only two of these are seen outside of an asynchronous connection procedure: CONNECTION_OK and CONNECTION_BAD. A good connection to the database has the status CONNECTION_OK. A failed connection attempt is signaled by status CONNECTION_BAD. Ordinarily, an OK status will remain so until PQfinish, but a communications failure might result in the status changing to CONNECTION_BAD prematurely. In that case the application could try to recover by calling PQreset.

See the entry for PQconnectStart and PQconnectPoll with regards to other status codes that might be seen.

PQtransactionStatus

Returns the current in-transaction status of the server.

```
PGTransactionStatusType PQtransactionStatus(const PGconn *conn);
```

The status can be PQTRANS_IDLE (currently idle), PQTRANS_ACTIVE (a command is in progress), PQTRANS_INTRANS (idle, in a valid transaction block), or PQTRANS_INERROR (idle, in a failed transaction block). PQTRANS_UNKNOWN is reported if the connection is bad. PQTRANS_ACTIVE is reported only when a query has been sent to the server and not yet completed.

Caution

PQtransactionStatus will give incorrect results when using a PostgreSQL 7.3 server that has the parameter autocommit set to off. The server-side autocommit feature has been deprecated and does not exist in later server versions.

PQparameterStatus

Looks up a current parameter setting of the server.

```
const char *PQparameterStatus(const PGconn *conn, const char *paramName);
```

Certain parameter values are reported by the server automatically at connection startup or whenever their values change. PQparameterStatus can be used to interrogate these settings. It returns the current value of a parameter if known, or NULL if the parameter is not known.

Parameters reported as of the current release include server_version, server_encoding, client_encoding, is_superuser, session_authorization, DateStyle, IntervalStyle, TimeZone, integer_datetimes, and standard_conforming_strings. (server_encoding, TimeZone, and integer_datetimes were not reported by releases before 8.0; standard_conforming_strings was not reported by releases before 8.1; IntervalStyle was not reported by releases before 8.4.) Note that server_version, server_encoding and integer_datetimes cannot change after startup.

Pre-3.0-protocol servers do not report parameter settings, but libpq includes logic to obtain values for server_version and client_encoding anyway. Applications are encouraged to use PQparameterStatus rather than *ad hoc* code to determine these values. (Beware however that on a pre-3.0 connection, changing client_encoding via SET after connection startup will not be reflected by PQparameterStatus.) For server_version, see also PQserverVersion, which returns the information in a numeric form that is much easier to compare against.

If no value for standard_conforming_strings is reported, applications can assume it is off, that is, backslashes are treated as escapes in string literals. Also, the presence of this parameter can be taken as an indication that the escape string syntax (E'...') is accepted.

Although the returned pointer is declared const, it in fact points to mutable storage associated with the PGconn structure. It is unwise to assume the pointer will remain valid across queries.

PQprotocolVersion

Interrogates the frontend/backend protocol being used.

```
int PQprotocolVersion(const PGconn *conn);
```

Applications might wish to use this to determine whether certain features are supported. Currently, the possible values are 2 (2.0 protocol), 3 (3.0 protocol), or zero (connection bad). This will not change after connection startup is complete, but it could theoretically change during a connection reset. The 3.0 protocol will normally be used when communicating with PostgreSQL 7.4 or later servers; pre-7.4 servers support only protocol 2.0. (Protocol 1.0 is obsolete and not supported by libpq.)

PQserverVersion

Returns an integer representing the backend version.

```
int PQserverVersion(const PGconn *conn);
```

Applications might use this to determine the version of the database server they are connected to. The number is formed by converting the major, minor, and revision numbers into two-decimal-digit numbers and appending them together. For example, version 8.1.5 will be returned as 80105, and version 8.2 will be returned as 80200 (leading zeroes are not shown). Zero is returned if the connection is bad.

PQerrorMessage

Returns the error message most recently generated by an operation on the connection.

```
char *PQerrorMessage(const PGconn *conn);
```

Nearly all libpq functions will set a message for PQerrorMessage if they fail. Note that by libpq convention, a nonempty PQerrorMessage result can be multiple lines, and will include a trailing newline. The caller should not free the result directly. It will be freed when the associated PGconn handle is passed to PQfinish. The result string should not be expected to remain the same across operations on the PGconn structure.

PQsocket

Obtains the file descriptor number of the connection socket to the server. A valid descriptor will be greater than or equal to 0; a result of -1 indicates that no server connection is currently open. (This will not change during normal operation, but could change during connection setup or reset.)

```
int PQsocket(const PGconn *conn);
```

PQbackendPID

Returns the process ID (PID) of the backend server process handling this connection.

```
int PQbackendPID(const PGconn *conn);
```

The backend PID is useful for debugging purposes and for comparison to NOTIFY messages (which include the PID of the notifying backend process). Note that the PID belongs to a process executing on the database server host, not the local host!

PQconnectionNeedsPassword

Returns true (1) if the connection authentication method required a password, but none was available. Returns false (0) if not.

```
int PQconnectionNeedsPassword(const PGconn *conn);
```

This function can be applied after a failed connection attempt to decide whether to prompt the user for a password.

PQconnectionUsedPassword

> Returns true (1) if the connection authentication method used a password. Returns false (0) if not.
>
> ```
> int PQconnectionUsedPassword(const PGconn *conn);
> ```
>
> This function can be applied after either a failed or successful connection attempt to detect whether the server demanded a password.

PQgetssl

> Returns the SSL structure used in the connection, or null if SSL is not in use.
>
> ```
> SSL *PQgetssl(const PGconn *conn);
> ```
>
> This structure can be used to verify encryption levels, check server certificates, and more. Refer to the OpenSSL documentation for information about this structure.
>
> You must define USE_SSL in order to get the correct prototype for this function. Doing this will also automatically include ssl.h from OpenSSL.

30.3. Command Execution Functions

Once a connection to a database server has been successfully established, the functions described here are used to perform SQL queries and commands.

30.3.1. Main Functions

PQexec

> Submits a command to the server and waits for the result.
>
> ```
> PGresult *PQexec(PGconn *conn, const char *command);
> ```
>
> Returns a PGresult pointer or possibly a null pointer. A non-null pointer will generally be returned except in out-of-memory conditions or serious errors such as inability to send the command to the server. If a null pointer is returned, it should be treated like a PGRES_FATAL_ERROR result. Use PQerrorMessage to get more information about such errors.

It is allowed to include multiple SQL commands (separated by semicolons) in the command string. Multiple queries sent in a single PQexec call are processed in a single transaction, unless there are explicit BEGIN/COMMIT commands included in the query string to divide it into multiple transactions. Note however that the returned PGresult structure describes only the result of the last command executed from the string. Should one of the commands fail, processing of the string stops with it and the returned PGresult describes the error condition.

PQexecParams

Submits a command to the server and waits for the result, with the ability to pass parameters separately from the SQL command text.

```
PGresult *PQexecParams(PGconn *conn,
                       const char *command,
                       int nParams,
                       const Oid *paramTypes,
                       const char * const *paramValues,
                       const int *paramLengths,
                       const int *paramFormats,
                       int resultFormat);
```

PQexecParams is like PQexec, but offers additional functionality: parameter values can be specified separately from the command string proper, and query results can be requested in either text or binary format. PQexecParams is supported only in protocol 3.0 and later connections; it will fail when using protocol 2.0.

The function arguments are:

conn

The connection object to send the command through.

command

The SQL command string to be executed. If parameters are used, they are referred to in the command string as $1, $2, etc.

nParams

The number of parameters supplied; it is the length of the arrays paramTypes[], paramValues[], paramLengths[], and paramFormats[]. (The array pointers can be NULL when nParams is zero.)

paramTypes[]

Specifies, by OID, the data types to be assigned to the parameter symbols. If paramTypes is NULL, or any particular element in the array is zero, the server infers a data type for the parameter symbol in the same way it would do for an untyped literal string.

paramValues[]

Specifies the actual values of the parameters. A null pointer in this array means the corresponding parameter is null; otherwise the pointer points to a zero-terminated text string (for text format) or binary data in the format expected by the server (for binary format).

`paramLengths[]`

Specifies the actual data lengths of binary-format parameters. It is ignored for null parameters and text-format parameters. The array pointer can be null when there are no binary parameters.

`paramFormats[]`

Specifies whether parameters are text (put a zero in the array entry for the corresponding parameter) or binary (put a one in the array entry for the corresponding parameter). If the array pointer is null then all parameters are presumed to be text strings.

Values passed in binary format require knowlege of the internal representation expected by the backend. For example, integers must be passed in network byte order. Passing `numeric` values requires knowledge of the server storage format, as implemented in `src/backend/utils/adt/numeric.c::numeric_send()` and `src/backend/utils/adt/numeric.c::numeric_recv()`.

`resultFormat`

Specify zero to obtain results in text format, or one to obtain results in binary format. (There is not currently a provision to obtain different result columns in different formats, although that is possible in the underlying protocol.)

The primary advantage of PQexecParams over PQexec is that parameter values can be separated from the command string, thus avoiding the need for tedious and error-prone quoting and escaping.

Unlike PQexec, PQexecParams allows at most one SQL command in the given string. (There can be semicolons in it, but not more than one nonempty command.) This is a limitation of the underlying protocol, but has some usefulness as an extra defense against SQL-injection attacks.

 Tip

Specifying parameter types via OIDs is tedious, particularly if you prefer not to hard-wire particular OID values into your program. However, you can avoid doing so even in cases where the server by itself cannot determine the type of the parameter, or chooses a different type than you want. In the SQL command text, attach an explicit cast to the parameter symbol to show what data type you will send. For example:

```
SELECT * FROM mytable WHERE x = $1::bigint;
```

This forces parameter $1 to be treated as `bigint`, whereas by default it would be assigned the same type as x. Forcing the parameter type decision, either this way or by specifying a numeric type OID, is strongly recommended when sending parameter values in binary format, because binary format has less redundancy than text format and so there is less chance that the server will detect a type mismatch mistake for you.

PQprepare

Submits a request to create a prepared statement with the given parameters, and waits for completion.

```
PGresult *PQprepare(PGconn *conn,
                    const char *stmtName,
                    const char *query,
                    int nParams,
                    const Oid *paramTypes);
```

PQprepare creates a prepared statement for later execution with PQexecPrepared. This feature allows commands that will be used repeatedly to be parsed and planned just once, rather than each time they are executed. PQprepare is supported only in protocol 3.0 and later connections; it will fail when using protocol 2.0.

The function creates a prepared statement named stmtName from the query string, which must contain a single SQL command. stmtName can be "" to create an unnamed statement, in which case any pre-existing unnamed statement is automatically replaced; otherwise it is an error if the statement name is already defined in the current session. If any parameters are used, they are referred to in the query as $1, $2, etc. nParams is the number of parameters for which types are pre-specified in the array paramTypes[]. (The array pointer can be NULL when nParams is zero.) paramTypes[] specifies, by OID, the data types to be assigned to the parameter symbols. If paramTypes is NULL, or any particular element in the array is zero, the server assigns a data type to the parameter symbol in the same way it would do for an untyped literal string. Also, the query can use parameter symbols with numbers higher than nParams; data types will be inferred for these symbols as well. (See PQdescribePrepared for a means to find out what data types were inferred.)

As with PQexec, the result is normally a PGresult object whose contents indicate server-side success or failure. A null result indicates out-of-memory or inability to send the command at all. Use PQerrorMessage to get more information about such errors.

Prepared statements for use with PQexecPrepared can also be created by executing SQL PREPARE statements. (But PQprepare is more flexible since it does not require parameter types to be pre-specified.) Also, although there is no libpq function for deleting a prepared statement, the SQL DEALLOCATE statement can be used for that purpose.

PQexecPrepared

Sends a request to execute a prepared statement with given parameters, and waits for the result.

```
PGresult *PQexecPrepared(PGconn *conn,
                         const char *stmtName,
                         int nParams,
                         const char * const *paramValues,
                         const int *paramLengths,
                         const int *paramFormats,
                         int resultFormat);
```

PQexecPrepared is like PQexecParams, but the command to be executed is specified by naming a previously-prepared statement, instead of giving a query string. This feature allows commands that will be used repeatedly to be parsed and planned just once, rather than each time they are executed. The statement must have been prepared previously in the current session. PQexecPrepared is supported only in protocol 3.0 and later connections; it will fail when using protocol 2.0.

The parameters are identical to PQexecParams, except that the name of a prepared statement is given instead of a query string, and the paramTypes[] parameter is not present (it is not needed since the prepared statement's parameter types were determined when it was created).

PQdescribePrepared

Submits a request to obtain information about the specified prepared statement, and waits for completion.

```
PGresult *PQdescribePrepared(PGconn *conn, const char *stmtName);
```

PQdescribePrepared allows an application to obtain information about a previously prepared statement. PQdescribePrepared is supported only in protocol 3.0 and later connections; it will fail when using protocol 2.0.

stmtName can be "" or NULL to reference the unnamed statement, otherwise it must be the name of an existing prepared statement. On success, a PGresult with status PGRES_COMMAND_OK is returned. The functions PQnparams and PQparamtype can be applied to this PGresult to obtain information about the parameters of the prepared statement, and the functions PQnfields, PQfname, PQftype, etc provide information about the result columns (if any) of the statement.

PQdescribePortal

Submits a request to obtain information about the specified portal, and waits for completion.

```
PGresult *PQdescribePortal(PGconn *conn, const char *portalName);
```

PQdescribePortal allows an application to obtain information about a previously created portal. (libpq does not provide any direct access to portals, but you can use this function to inspect the properties of a cursor created with a DECLARE CURSOR SQL command.) PQdescribePortal is supported only in protocol 3.0 and later connections; it will fail when using protocol 2.0.

portalName can be "" or NULL to reference the unnamed portal, otherwise it must be the name of an existing portal. On success, a PGresult with status PGRES_COMMAND_OK is returned. The functions PQnfields, PQfname, PQftype, etc can be applied to the PGresult to obtain information about the result columns (if any) of the portal.

The PGresult structure encapsulates the result returned by the server. libpq application programmers should be careful to maintain the PGresult abstraction. Use the accessor functions below to get at the contents of PGresult. Avoid directly referencing the fields of the PGresult structure because they are subject to change in the future.

PQresultStatus

Returns the result status of the command.

```
ExecStatusType PQresultStatus(const PGresult *res);
```

PQresultStatus can return one of the following values:

PGRES_EMPTY_QUERY

The string sent to the server was empty.

PGRES_COMMAND_OK

Successful completion of a command returning no data.

PGRES_TUPLES_OK

Successful completion of a command returning data (such as a SELECT or SHOW).

PGRES_COPY_OUT

Copy Out (from server) data transfer started.

PGRES_COPY_IN

Copy In (to server) data transfer started.

PGRES_BAD_RESPONSE

The server's response was not understood.

PGRES_NONFATAL_ERROR

A nonfatal error (a notice or warning) occurred.

PGRES_FATAL_ERROR

A fatal error occurred.

If the result status is PGRES_TUPLES_OK, then the functions described below can be used to retrieve the rows returned by the query. Note that a SELECT command that happens to retrieve zero rows still shows PGRES_TUPLES_OK. PGRES_COMMAND_OK is for commands that can never return rows (INSERT, UPDATE, etc.). A response of PGRES_EMPTY_QUERY might indicate a bug in the client software.

A result of status PGRES_NONFATAL_ERROR will never be returned directly by PQexec or other query execution functions; results of this kind are instead passed to the notice processor (see *Section 30.11* - page 292).

PQresStatus

Converts the enumerated type returned by PQresultStatus into a string constant describing the status code. The caller should not free the result.

```
char *PQresStatus(ExecStatusType status);
```

PQresultErrorMessage

Returns the error message associated with the command, or an empty string if there was no error.

```
char *PQresultErrorMessage(const PGresult *res);
```

If there was an error, the returned string will include a trailing newline. The caller should not free the result directly. It will be freed when the associated PGresult handle is passed to PQclear.

Immediately following a PQexec or PQgetResult call, PQerrorMessage (on the connection) will return the same string as PQresultErrorMessage (on the result). However, a PGresult will retain its error message until destroyed, whereas the connection's error message will change when subsequent operations are done. Use PQresultErrorMessage when you want to know the status associated with a particular PGresult; use PQerrorMessage when you want to know the status from the latest operation on the connection.

PQresultErrorField

Returns an individual field of an error report.

```
char *PQresultErrorField(const PGresult *res, int fieldcode);
```

fieldcode is an error field identifier; see the symbols listed below. NULL is returned if the PGresult is not an error or warning result, or does not include the specified field. Field values will normally not include a trailing newline. The caller should not free the result directly. It will be freed when the associated PGresult handle is passed to PQclear.

The following field codes are available:

PG_DIAG_SEVERITY

The severity; the field contents are ERROR, FATAL, or PANIC (in an error message), or WARNING, NOTICE, DEBUG, INFO, or LOG (in a notice message), or a localized translation of one of these. Always present.

PG_DIAG_SQLSTATE

> The SQLSTATE code for the error. The SQLSTATE code identifies the type of error that has occurred; it can be used by front-end applications to perform specific operations (such as error handling) in response to a particular database error. For a list of the possible SQLSTATE codes, see *Appendix A*. This field is not localizable, and is always present.

PG_DIAG_MESSAGE_PRIMARY

> The primary human-readable error message (typically one line). Always present.

PG_DIAG_MESSAGE_DETAIL

> Detail: an optional secondary error message carrying more detail about the problem. Might run to multiple lines.

PG_DIAG_MESSAGE_HINT

> Hint: an optional suggestion what to do about the problem. This is intended to differ from detail in that it offers advice (potentially inappropriate) rather than hard facts. Might run to multiple lines.

PG_DIAG_STATEMENT_POSITION

> A string containing a decimal integer indicating an error cursor position as an index into the original statement string. The first character has index 1, and positions are measured in characters not bytes.

PG_DIAG_INTERNAL_POSITION

> This is defined the same as the PG_DIAG_STATEMENT_POSITION field, but it is used when the cursor position refers to an internally generated command rather than the one submitted by the client. The PG_DIAG_INTERNAL_QUERY field will always appear when this field appears.

PG_DIAG_INTERNAL_QUERY

> The text of a failed internally-generated command. This could be, for example, a SQL query issued by a PL/pgSQL function.

PG_DIAG_CONTEXT

> An indication of the context in which the error occurred. Presently this includes a call stack traceback of active procedural language functions and internally-generated queries. The trace is one entry per line, most recent first.

PG_DIAG_SOURCE_FILE

> The file name of the source-code location where the error was reported.

PG_DIAG_SOURCE_LINE

>   The line number of the source-code location where the error was reported.

PG_DIAG_SOURCE_FUNCTION

>   The name of the source-code function reporting the error.

The client is responsible for formatting displayed information to meet its needs; in particular it should break long lines as needed. Newline characters appearing in the error message fields should be treated as paragraph breaks, not line breaks.

Errors generated internally by libpq will have severity and primary message, but typically no other fields. Errors returned by a pre-3.0-protocol server will include severity and primary message, and sometimes a detail message, but no other fields.

Note that error fields are only available from PGresult objects, not PGconn objects; there is no PQerrorField function.

PQclear

>   Frees the storage associated with a PGresult. Every command result should be freed via PQclear when it is no longer needed.
>
>    ```
>    void PQclear(PGresult *res);
>    ```

You can keep a PGresult object around for as long as you need it; it does not go away when you issue a new command, nor even if you close the connection. To get rid of it, you must call PQclear. Failure to do this will result in memory leaks in your application.

30.3.2. Retrieving Query Result Information

These functions are used to extract information from a PGresult object that represents a successful query result (that is, one that has status PGRES_TUPLES_OK). They can also be used to extract information from a successful Describe operation: a Describe's result has all the same column information that actual execution of the query would provide, but it has zero rows. For objects with other status values, these functions will act as though the result has zero rows and zero columns.

PQntuples

>   Returns the number of rows (tuples) in the query result. Because it returns an integer result, large result sets might overflow the return value on 32-bit operating systems.
>
>    ```
>    int PQntuples(const PGresult *res);
>    ```

PQnfields

>   Returns the number of columns (fields) in each row of the query result.
>
>    ```
>    int PQnfields(const PGresult *res);
>    ```

PQfname

Returns the column name associated with the given column number. Column numbers start at 0. The caller should not free the result directly. It will be freed when the associated PGresult handle is passed to PQclear.

```
char *PQfname(const PGresult *res,
              int column_number);
```

NULL is returned if the column number is out of range.

PQfnumber

Returns the column number associated with the given column name.

```
int PQfnumber(const PGresult *res,
              const char *column_name);
```

-1 is returned if the given name does not match any column.

The given name is treated like an identifier in an SQL command, that is, it is downcased unless double-quoted. For example, given a query result generated from the SQL command:

```
SELECT 1 AS FOO, 2 AS "BAR";
```

we would have the results:

```
PQfname(res, 0)              foo
PQfname(res, 1)              BAR
PQfnumber(res, "FOO")        0
PQfnumber(res, "foo")        0
PQfnumber(res, "BAR")        -1
PQfnumber(res, "\"BAR\"")    1
```

PQftable

Returns the OID of the table from which the given column was fetched. Column numbers start at 0.

```
Oid PQftable(const PGresult *res,
             int column_number);
```

InvalidOid is returned if the column number is out of range, or if the specified column is not a simple reference to a table column, or when using pre-3.0 protocol. You can query the system table pg_class to determine exactly which table is referenced.

The type Oid and the constant InvalidOid will be defined when you include the libpq header file. They will both be some integer type.

PQftablecol

Returns the column number (within its table) of the column making up the specified query result column. Query-result column numbers start at 0, but table columns have nonzero numbers.

```
int PQftablecol(const PGresult *res,
                int column_number);
```

Zero is returned if the column number is out of range, or if the specified column is not a simple reference to a table column, or when using pre-3.0 protocol.

PQfformat

Returns the format code indicating the format of the given column. Column numbers start at 0.

```
int PQfformat(const PGresult *res,
              int column_number);
```

Format code zero indicates textual data representation, while format code one indicates binary representation. (Other codes are reserved for future definition.)

PQftype

Returns the data type associated with the given column number. The integer returned is the internal OID number of the type. Column numbers start at 0.

```
Oid PQftype(const PGresult *res,
            int column_number);
```

You can query the system table pg_type to obtain the names and properties of the various data types. The OIDs of the built-in data types are defined in the file src/include/catalog/pg_type.h in the source tree.

PQfmod

Returns the type modifier of the column associated with the given column number. Column numbers start at 0.

```
int PQfmod(const PGresult *res,
           int column_number);
```

The interpretation of modifier values is type-specific; they typically indicate precision or size limits. The value -1 is used to indicate "no information available". Most data types do not use modifiers, in which case the value is always -1.

PQfsize

Returns the size in bytes of the column associated with the given column number. Column numbers start at 0.

```
int PQfsize(const PGresult *res,
            int column_number);
```

PQfsize returns the space allocated for this column in a database row, in other words the size of the server's internal representation of the data type. (Accordingly, it is not really very useful to clients.) A negative value indicates the data type is variable-length.

PQbinaryTuples

Returns 1 if the PGresult contains binary data and 0 if it contains text data.

```
int PQbinaryTuples(const PGresult *res);
```

This function is deprecated (except for its use in connection with COPY), because it is possible for a single PGresult to contain text data in some columns and binary data in others. PQfformat is preferred. PQbinaryTuples returns 1 only if all columns of the result are binary (format 1).

PQgetvalue

Returns a single field value of one row of a PGresult. Row and column numbers start at 0. The caller should not free the result directly. It will be freed when the associated PGresult handle is passed to PQclear.

```
char *PQgetvalue(const PGresult *res,
                 int row_number,
                 int column_number);
```

For data in text format, the value returned by PQgetvalue is a null-terminated character string representation of the field value. For data in binary format, the value is in the binary representation determined by the data type's typsend and typreceive functions. (The value is actually followed by a zero byte in this case too, but that is not ordinarily useful, since the value is likely to contain embedded nulls.)

An empty string is returned if the field value is null. See PQgetisnull to distinguish null values from empty-string values.

The pointer returned by PQgetvalue points to storage that is part of the PGresult structure. One should not modify the data it points to, and one must explicitly copy the data into other storage if it is to be used past the lifetime of the PGresult structure itself.

PQgetisnull

Tests a field for a null value. Row and column numbers start at 0.

```
int PQgetisnull(const PGresult *res,
                int row_number,
                int column_number);
```

This function returns 1 if the field is null and 0 if it contains a non-null value. (Note that PQgetvalue will return an empty string, not a null pointer, for a null field.)

PQgetlength

Returns the actual length of a field value in bytes. Row and column numbers start at 0.

```
int PQgetlength(const PGresult *res,
                int row_number,
                int column_number);
```

This is the actual data length for the particular data value, that is, the size of the object pointed to by PQgetvalue. For text data format this is the same as strlen(). For binary format this is essential information. Note that one should *not* rely on PQfsize to obtain the actual data length.

PQnparams

Returns the number of parameters of a prepared statement.

```
int PQnparams(const PGresult *res);
```

This function is only useful when inspecting the result of PQdescribePrepared. For other types of queries it will return zero.

PQparamtype

Returns the data type of the indicated statement parameter. Parameter numbers start at 0.

```
Oid PQparamtype(const PGresult *res, int param_number);
```

This function is only useful when inspecting the result of PQdescribePrepared. For other types of queries it will return zero.

PQprint

Prints out all the rows and, optionally, the column names to the specified output stream.

```
void PQprint(FILE *fout,        /* output stream */
             const PGresult *res,
             const PQprintOpt *po);
typedef struct {
  pqbool header;        /* print output field headings and row count */
  pqbool align;         /* fill align the fields */
  pqbool standard;      /* old brain dead format */
  pqbool html3;         /* output HTML tables */
  pqbool expanded;      /* expand tables */
  pqbool pager;         /* use pager for output if needed */
  char   *fieldSep;     /* field separator */
  char   *tableOpt;     /* attributes for HTML table element */
  char   *caption;      /* HTML table caption */
  char   **fieldName;   /* null-terminated array of replacement field names */
} PQprintOpt;
```

This function was formerly used by psql to print query results, but this is no longer the case. Note that it assumes all the data is in text format.

30.3.3. Retrieving Result Information for Other Commands

These functions are used to extract information from PGresult objects that are not SELECT results.

PQcmdStatus

Returns the command status tag from the SQL command that generated the PGresult.

```
char *PQcmdStatus(PGresult *res);
```

Commonly this is just the name of the command, but it might include additional data such as the number of rows processed. The caller should not free the result directly. It will be freed when the associated PGresult handle is passed to PQclear.

PQcmdTuples

Returns the number of rows affected by the SQL command.

```
char *PQcmdTuples(PGresult *res);
```

This function returns a string containing the number of rows affected by the SQL statement that generated the PGresult. This function can only be used following the execution of an INSERT, UPDATE, DELETE, MOVE, FETCH, or COPY statement, or an EXECUTE of a prepared query that contains an INSERT, UPDATE, or DELETE statement. If the command that generated the PGresult was anything else, PQcmdTuples returns an empty string. The caller should not free the return value directly. It will be freed when the associated PGresult handle is passed to PQclear.

PQoidValue

Returns the OID of the inserted row, if the SQL command was an INSERT that inserted exactly one row into a table that has OIDs, or a EXECUTE of a prepared query containing a suitable INSERT statement. Otherwise, this function returns InvalidOid. This function will also return InvalidOid if the table affected by the INSERT statement does not contain OIDs.

```
Oid PQoidValue(const PGresult *res);
```

PQoidStatus

Returns a string with the OID of the inserted row, if the SQL command was an INSERT that inserted exactly one row, or a EXECUTE of a prepared statement consisting of a suitable INSERT. (The string will be 0 if the INSERT did not insert exactly one row, or if the target table does not have OIDs.) If the command was not an INSERT, returns an empty string.

```
char *PQoidStatus(const PGresult *res);
```

This function is deprecated in favor of PQoidValue. It is not thread-safe.

30.3.4. Escaping Strings for Inclusion in SQL Commands

PQescapeStringConn escapes a string for use within an SQL command. This is useful when inserting data values as literal constants in SQL commands. Certain characters (such as quotes and backslashes) must be escaped to prevent them from being interpreted specially by the SQL parser. PQescapeStringConn performs this operation.

Tip

> It is especially important to do proper escaping when handling strings that were received from an untrustworthy source. Otherwise there is a security risk: you are vulnerable to "SQL injection" attacks wherein unwanted SQL commands are fed to your database.

Note that it is not necessary nor correct to do escaping when a data value is passed as a separate parameter in PQexecParams or its sibling routines.

```
size_t PQescapeStringConn (PGconn *conn,
                           char *to, const char *from, size_t length,
                           int *error);
```

PQescapeStringConn writes an escaped version of the from string to the to buffer, escaping special characters so that they cannot cause any harm, and adding a terminating zero byte. The single quotes that must surround PostgreSQL string literals are not included in the result string; they should be provided in the SQL command that the result is inserted into. The parameter from points to the first character of the string that is to be escaped, and the length parameter gives the number of bytes in this string. A terminating zero byte is not required, and should not be counted in length. (If a terminating zero byte is found before length bytes are processed, PQescapeStringConn stops at the zero; the behavior is thus rather like strncpy.) to shall point to a buffer that is able to hold at least one more byte than twice the value of length, otherwise the behavior is undefined. Behavior is likewise undefined if the to and from strings overlap.

If the error parameter is not NULL, then *error is set to zero on success, nonzero on error. Presently the only possible error conditions involve invalid multibyte encoding in the source string. The output string is still generated on error, but it can be expected that the server will reject it as malformed. On error, a suitable message is stored in the conn object, whether or not error is NULL.

PQescapeStringConn returns the number of bytes written to to, not including the terminating zero byte.

```
size_t PQescapeString (char *to, const char *from, size_t length);
```

PQescapeString is an older, deprecated version of PQescapeStringConn; the difference is that it does not take conn or error parameters. Because of this, it cannot adjust its behavior depending on the connection properties (such as character encoding) and therefore *it might give the wrong results*. Also, it has no way to report error conditions.

PQescapeString can be used safely in single-threaded client programs that work with only one PostgreSQL connection at a time (in this case it can find out what it needs to know "behind the scenes"). In other contexts it is a security hazard and should be avoided in favor of PQescapeStringConn.

30.3.5. Escaping Binary Strings for Inclusion in SQL Commands

PQescapeByteaConn

Escapes binary data for use within an SQL command with the type bytea. As with PQescapeStringConn, this is only used when inserting data directly into an SQL command string.

```
unsigned char *PQescapeByteaConn(PGconn *conn,
                                 const unsigned char *from,
                                 size_t from_length,
                                 size_t *to_length);
```

Certain byte values *must* be escaped (but all byte values *can* be escaped) when used as part of a bytea literal in an SQL statement. In general, to escape a byte, it is converted into the three digit octal number equal to the octet value, and preceded by usually two backslashes. The single quote (') and backslash (\) characters have special alternative escape sequences. See *Section 8.4* - Vol.I page 146 for more information. PQescapeByteaConn performs this operation, escaping only the minimally required bytes.

The from parameter points to the first byte of the string that is to be escaped, and the from_length parameter gives the number of bytes in this binary string. (A terminating zero byte is neither necessary nor counted.) The to_length parameter points to a variable that will hold the resultant escaped string length. This result string length includes the terminating zero byte of the result.

PQescapeByteaConn returns an escaped version of the from parameter binary string in memory allocated with malloc(). This memory must be freed using PQfreemem() when the result is no longer needed. The return string has all special characters replaced so that they can be properly processed by the PostgreSQL string literal parser, and the bytea input function. A terminating zero byte is also added. The single quotes that must surround PostgreSQL string literals are not part of the result string.

On error, a NULL pointer is returned, and a suitable error message is stored in the conn object. Currently, the only possible error is insufficient memory for the result string.

PQescapeBytea

PQescapeBytea is an older, deprecated version of PQescapeByteaConn.

```
unsigned char *PQescapeBytea(const unsigned char *from,
                             size_t from_length,
                             size_t *to_length);
```

The only difference from PQescapeByteaConn is that PQescapeBytea does not take a PGconn parameter. Because of this, it cannot adjust its behavior depending on the connection properties (in particular, whether standard-conforming strings are enabled) and therefore *it might give the wrong results*. Also, it has no way to return an error message on failure.

PQescapeBytea can be used safely in single-threaded client programs that work with only one PostgreSQL connection at a time (in this case it can find out what it needs to know "behind the scenes"). In other contexts it is a security hazard and should be avoided in favor of PQescapeByteaConn.

PQunescapeBytea

Converts a string representation of binary data into binary data — the reverse of PQescapeBytea. This is needed when retrieving bytea data in text format, but not when retrieving it in binary format.

```
unsigned char *PQunescapeBytea(const unsigned char *from, size_t *to_length);
```

The from parameter points to a string such as might be returned by PQgetvalue when applied to a bytea column. PQunescapeBytea converts this string representation into its binary representation. It returns a pointer to a buffer allocated with malloc(), or null on error, and puts the size of the buffer in to_length. The result must be freed using PQfreemem when it is no longer needed.

This conversion is not exactly the inverse of PQescapeBytea, because the string is not expected to be "escaped" when received from PQgetvalue. In particular this means there is no need for string quoting considerations, and so no need for a PGconn parameter.

30.4. Asynchronous Command Processing

The PQexec function is adequate for submitting commands in normal, synchronous applications. It has a couple of deficiencies, however, that can be of importance to some users:

- PQexec waits for the command to be completed. The application might have other work to do (such as maintaining a user interface), in which case it won't want to block waiting for the response.

- Since the execution of the client application is suspended while it waits for the result, it is hard for the application to decide that it would like to try to cancel the ongoing command. (It can be done from a signal handler, but not otherwise.)

- PQexec can return only one PGresult structure. If the submitted command string contains multiple SQL commands, all but the last PGresult are discarded by PQexec.

Applications that do not like these limitations can instead use the underlying functions that PQexec is built from: PQsendQuery and PQgetResult. There are also PQsendQueryParams, PQsendPrepare, PQsendQueryPrepared, PQsendDescribePrepared, and PQsendDescribePortal, which can be used with PQgetResult to duplicate the functionality of PQexecParams, PQprepare, PQexecPrepared, PQdescribePrepared, and PQdescribePortal respectively.

PQsendQuery

> Submits a command to the server without waiting for the result(s). 1 is returned if the command was successfully dispatched and 0 if not (in which case, use PQerrorMessage to get more information about the failure).
>
> ```
> int PQsendQuery(PGconn *conn, const char *command);
> ```
>
> After successfully calling PQsendQuery, call PQgetResult one or more times to obtain the results. PQsendQuery cannot be called again (on the same connection) until PQgetResult has returned a null pointer, indicating that the command is done.

PQsendQueryParams

> Submits a command and separate parameters to the server without waiting for the result(s).
>
> ```
> int PQsendQueryParams(PGconn *conn,
>                       const char *command,
>                       int nParams,
>                       const Oid *paramTypes,
>                       const char * const *paramValues,
>                       const int *paramLengths,
>                       const int *paramFormats,
>                       int resultFormat);
> ```
>
> This is equivalent to PQsendQuery except that query parameters can be specified separately from the query string. The function's parameters are handled identically to PQexecParams. Like PQexecParams, it will not work on 2.0-protocol connections, and it allows only one command in the query string.

PQsendPrepare

> Sends a request to create a prepared statement with the given parameters, without waiting for completion.
>
> ```
> int PQsendPrepare(PGconn *conn,
>                   const char *stmtName,
>                   const char *query,
>                   int nParams,
>                   const Oid *paramTypes);
> ```
>
> This is an asynchronous version of PQprepare: it returns 1 if it was able to dispatch the request, and 0 if not. After a successful call, call PQgetResult to determine whether the

server successfully created the prepared statement. The function's parameters are handled identically to PQprepare. Like PQprepare, it will not work on 2.0-protocol connections.

PQsendQueryPrepared

Sends a request to execute a prepared statement with given parameters, without waiting for the result(s).

```
int PQsendQueryPrepared(PGconn *conn,
                        const char *stmtName,
                        int nParams,
                        const char * const *paramValues,
                        const int *paramLengths,
                        const int *paramFormats,
                        int resultFormat);
```

This is similar to PQsendQueryParams, but the command to be executed is specified by naming a previously-prepared statement, instead of giving a query string. The function's parameters are handled identically to PQexecPrepared. Like PQexecPrepared, it will not work on 2.0-protocol connections.

PQsendDescribePrepared

Submits a request to obtain information about the specified prepared statement, without waiting for completion.

```
int PQsendDescribePrepared(PGconn *conn, const char *stmtName);
```

This is an asynchronous version of PQdescribePrepared: it returns 1 if it was able to dispatch the request, and 0 if not. After a successful call, call PQgetResult to obtain the results. The function's parameters are handled identically to PQdescribePrepared. Like PQdescribePrepared, it will not work on 2.0-protocol connections.

PQsendDescribePortal

Submits a request to obtain information about the specified portal, without waiting for completion.

```
int PQsendDescribePortal(PGconn *conn, const char *portalName);
```

This is an asynchronous version of PQdescribePortal: it returns 1 if it was able to dispatch the request, and 0 if not. After a successful call, call PQgetResult to obtain the results. The function's parameters are handled identically to PQdescribePortal. Like PQdescribePortal, it will not work on 2.0-protocol connections.

PQgetResult

Waits for the next result from a prior PQsendQuery, PQsendQueryParams, PQsendPrepare, or PQsendQueryPrepared call, and returns it. A null pointer is returned when the command is complete and there will be no more results.

```
PGresult *PQgetResult(PGconn *conn);
```

PQgetResult must be called repeatedly until it returns a null pointer, indicating that the command is done. (If called when no command is active, PQgetResult will just return a null pointer at once.) Each non-null result from PQgetResult should be processed using the same PGresult accessor functions previously described. Don't forget to free each result object with PQclear when done with it. Note that PQgetResult will block only if a command is active and the necessary response data has not yet been read by PQconsumeInput.

Using PQsendQuery and PQgetResult solves one of PQexec's problems: If a command string contains multiple SQL commands, the results of those commands can be obtained individually. (This allows a simple form of overlapped processing, by the way: the client can be handling the results of one command while the server is still working on later queries in the same command string.) However, calling PQgetResult will still cause the client to block until the server completes the next SQL command. This can be avoided by proper use of two more functions:

PQconsumeInput

> If input is available from the server, consume it.
>
>   int PQconsumeInput(PGconn *conn);
>
> PQconsumeInput normally returns 1 indicating "no error", but returns 0 if there was some kind of trouble (in which case PQerrorMessage can be consulted). Note that the result does not say whether any input data was actually collected. After calling PQconsumeInput, the application can check PQisBusy and/or PQnotifies to see if their state has changed.
>
> PQconsumeInput can be called even if the application is not prepared to deal with a result or notification just yet. The function will read available data and save it in a buffer, thereby causing a select() read-ready indication to go away. The application can thus use PQconsumeInput to clear the select() condition immediately, and then examine the results at leisure.

PQisBusy

> Returns 1 if a command is busy, that is, PQgetResult would block waiting for input. A 0 return indicates that PQgetResult can be called with assurance of not blocking.
>
>   int PQisBusy(PGconn *conn);
>
> PQisBusy will not itself attempt to read data from the server; therefore PQconsumeInput must be invoked first, or the busy state will never end.

A typical application using these functions will have a main loop that uses select() or poll() to wait for all the conditions that it must respond to. One of the conditions will be input available from the server, which in terms of select() means readable data on the file descriptor identified by PQsocket. When the main loop detects input ready, it should call PQconsumeInput to read the input. It can then call PQisBusy, followed by PQgetResult if PQisBusy returns false (0). It can also call PQnotifies to detect NOTIFY messages (see *Section 30.7* - page 282).

A client that uses PQsendQuery/PQgetResult can also attempt to cancel a command that is still being processed by the server; see *Section 30.5* - page 280. But regardless of the return value of PQcancel, the application must continue with the normal result-reading sequence using PQgetResult. A successful cancellation will simply cause the command to terminate sooner than it would have otherwise.

By using the functions described above, it is possible to avoid blocking while waiting for input from the database server. However, it is still possible that the application will block waiting to send output to the server. This is relatively uncommon but can happen if very long SQL commands or data values are sent. (It is much more probable if the application sends data via COPY IN, however.) To prevent this possibility and achieve completely nonblocking database operation, the following additional functions can be used.

PQsetnonblocking

> Sets the nonblocking status of the connection.
>
> ```
> int PQsetnonblocking(PGconn *conn, int arg);
> ```
>
> Sets the state of the connection to nonblocking if arg is 1, or blocking if arg is 0. Returns 0 if OK, -1 if error.
>
> In the nonblocking state, calls to PQsendQuery, PQputline, PQputnbytes, and PQendcopy will not block but instead return an error if they need to be called again.
>
> Note that PQexec does not honor nonblocking mode; if it is called, it will act in blocking fashion anyway.

PQisnonblocking

> Returns the blocking status of the database connection.
>
> ```
> int PQisnonblocking(const PGconn *conn);
> ```
>
> Returns 1 if the connection is set to nonblocking mode and 0 if blocking.

PQflush

> Attempts to flush any queued output data to the server. Returns 0 if successful (or if the send queue is empty), -1 if it failed for some reason, or 1 if it was unable to send all the data in the send queue yet (this case can only occur if the connection is nonblocking).
>
> ```
> int PQflush(PGconn *conn);
> ```

After sending any command or data on a nonblocking connection, call PQflush. If it returns 1, wait for the socket to be write-ready and call it again; repeat until it returns 0. Once

PQflush returns 0, wait for the socket to be read-ready and then read the response as described above.

30.5. Cancelling Queries in Progress

A client application can request cancellation of a command that is still being processed by the server, using the functions described in this section.

PQgetCancel

Creates a data structure containing the information needed to cancel a command issued through a particular database connection.

```
PGcancel *PQgetCancel(PGconn *conn);
```

PQgetCancel creates a PGcancel object given a PGconn connection object. It will return NULL if the given conn is NULL or an invalid connection. The PGcancel object is an opaque structure that is not meant to be accessed directly by the application; it can only be passed to PQcancel or PQfreeCancel.

PQfreeCancel

Frees a data structure created by PQgetCancel.

```
void PQfreeCancel(PGcancel *cancel);
```

PQfreeCancel frees a data object previously created by PQgetCancel.

PQcancel

Requests that the server abandon processing of the current command.

```
int PQcancel(PGcancel *cancel, char *errbuf, int errbufsize);
```

The return value is 1 if the cancel request was successfully dispatched and 0 if not. If not, errbuf is filled with an error message explaining why not. errbuf must be a char array of size errbufsize (the recommended size is 256 bytes).

Successful dispatch is no guarantee that the request will have any effect, however. If the cancellation is effective, the current command will terminate early and return an error result. If the cancellation fails (say, because the server was already done processing the command), then there will be no visible result at all.

PQcancel can safely be invoked from a signal handler, if the errbuf is a local variable in the signal handler. The PGcancel object is read-only as far as PQcancel is concerned, so it can also be invoked from a thread that is separate from the one manipulating the PGconn object.

PQrequestCancel

Requests that the server abandon processing of the current command.

```
int PQrequestCancel(PGconn *conn);
```

PQrequestCancel is a deprecated variant of PQcancel. It operates directly on the PGconn object, and in case of failure stores the error message in the PGconn object (whence it can be retrieved by PQerrorMessage). Although the functionality is the same, this approach creates hazards for multiple-thread programs and signal handlers, since it is possible that overwriting the PGconn's error message will mess up the operation currently in progress on the connection.

30.6. The Fast-Path Interface

PostgreSQL provides a fast-path interface to send simple function calls to the server.

 Tip

This interface is somewhat obsolete, as one can achieve similar performance and greater functionality by setting up a prepared statement to define the function call. Then, executing the statement with binary transmission of parameters and results substitutes for a fast-path function call.

The function PQfn requests execution of a server function via the fast-path interface:

```
PGresult *PQfn(PGconn *conn,
               int fnid,
               int *result_buf,
               int *result_len,
               int result_is_int,
               const PQArgBlock *args,
               int nargs);

typedef struct {
    int len;
    int isint;
    union {
        int *ptr;
        int integer;
    } u;
} PQArgBlock;
```

The fnid argument is the OID of the function to be executed. args and nargs define the parameters to be passed to the function; they must match the declared function argument list. When the isint field of a parameter structure is true, the u.integer value is sent to the server as an integer of the indicated length (this must be 1, 2, or 4 bytes); proper byte-swapping occurs. When isint is false, the indicated number of bytes at *u.ptr are sent with no processing; the data must be in the format expected by the server for binary transmission of the function's argument data type. result_buf is the buffer in which to place the return value. The caller must have allocated sufficient space to store the return value. (There is no check!) The actual result length will be returned in the integer pointed to by result_len. If a 1, 2, or 4-byte integer result is expected, set result_is_int to 1, otherwise set it to 0. Setting result_is_int to 1 causes libpq to byte-swap the value if necessary, so that it is delivered as a proper int value for the client machine. When result_is_int is 0, the binary-format byte string sent by the server is returned unmodified.

PQfn always returns a valid PGresult pointer. The result status should be checked before the result is used. The caller is responsible for freeing the PGresult with PQclear when it is no longer needed.

Note that it is not possible to handle null arguments, null results, nor set-valued results when using this interface.

30.7. Asynchronous Notification

PostgreSQL offers asynchronous notification via the LISTEN and NOTIFY commands. A client session registers its interest in a particular notification condition with the LISTEN command (and can stop listening with the UNLISTEN command). All sessions listening on a particular condition will be notified asynchronously when a NOTIFY command with that condition name is executed by any session. No additional information is passed from the notifier to the listener. Thus, typically, any actual data that needs to be communicated is transferred through a database table. Commonly, the condition name is the same as the associated table, but it is not necessary for there to be any associated table.

libpq applications submit LISTEN and UNLISTEN commands as ordinary SQL commands. The arrival of NOTIFY messages can subsequently be detected by calling PQnotifies.

The function PQnotifies returns the next notification from a list of unhandled notification messages received from the server. It returns a null pointer if there are no pending notifications. Once a notification is returned from PQnotifies, it is considered handled and will be removed from the list of notifications.

```
PGnotify *PQnotifies(PGconn *conn);

typedef struct pgNotify {
    char *relname;              /* notification condition name */
    int  be_pid;                /* process ID of notifying server process */
    char *extra;                /* notification parameter */
} PGnotify;
```

After processing a PGnotify object returned by PQnotifies, be sure to free it with PQfreemem. It is sufficient to free the PGnotify pointer; the relname and extra fields do not represent separate allocations. (At present, the extra field is unused and will always point to an empty string.)

Example 30-2 gives a sample program that illustrates the use of asynchronous notification.

PQnotifies does not actually read data from the server; it just returns messages previously absorbed by another libpq function. In prior releases of libpq, the only way to ensure timely receipt of NOTIFY messages was to constantly submit commands, even empty ones, and then check PQnotifies after each PQexec. While this still works, it is deprecated as a waste of processing power.

A better way to check for NOTIFY messages when you have no useful commands to execute is to call PQconsumeInput, then check PQnotifies. You can use select() to wait for data to arrive from the server, thereby using no CPU power unless there is something to do. (See PQsocket to obtain the file descriptor number to use with select().) Note that this will work OK whether you submit commands with PQsendQuery/PQgetResult or simply use PQexec. You should, however, remember to check PQnotifies after each PQgetResult or PQexec, to see if any notifications came in during the processing of the command.

30.8. Functions Associated with the COPY Command

The COPY command in PostgreSQL has options to read from or write to the network connection used by libpq. The functions described in this section allow applications to take advantage of this capability by supplying or consuming copied data.

The overall process is that the application first issues the SQL COPY command via PQexec or one of the equivalent functions. The response to this (if there is no error in the command) will be a PGresult object bearing a status code of PGRES_COPY_OUT or PGRES_COPY_IN (depending on the specified copy direction). The application should then use the functions of this section to receive or transmit data rows. When the data transfer is complete, another PGresult object is returned to indicate success or failure of the transfer. Its status will be PGRES_COMMAND_OK for success or PGRES_FATAL_ERROR if some problem was encountered. At this point further SQL commands can be issued via PQexec. (It is not possible to execute other SQL commands using the same connection while the COPY operation is in progress.)

If a COPY command is issued via PQexec in a string that could contain additional commands, the application must continue fetching results via PQgetResult after completing the COPY sequence. Only when PQgetResult returns NULL is it certain that the PQexec command string is done and it is safe to issue more commands.

The functions of this section should be executed only after obtaining a result status of PGRES_COPY_OUT or PGRES_COPY_IN from PQexec or PQgetResult.

A PGresult object bearing one of these status values carries some additional data about the COPY operation that is starting. This additional data is available using functions that are also used in connection with query results:

PQnfields

Returns the number of columns (fields) to be copied.

PQbinaryTuples

> 0 indicates the overall copy format is textual (rows separated by newlines, columns separated by separator characters, etc). 1 indicates the overall copy format is binary. See COPY for more information.

PQfformat

> Returns the format code (0 for text, 1 for binary) associated with each column of the copy operation. The per-column format codes will always be zero when the overall copy format is textual, but the binary format can support both text and binary columns. (However, as of the current implementation of COPY, only binary columns appear in a binary copy; so the per-column formats always match the overall format at present.)

 Note

> These additional data values are only available when using protocol 3.0. When using protocol 2.0, all these functions will return 0.

30.8.1. Functions for Sending COPY Data

These functions are used to send data during COPY FROM STDIN. They will fail if called when the connection is not in COPY_IN state.

PQputCopyData

> Sends data to the server during COPY_IN state.

```
int PQputCopyData(PGconn *conn,
                  const char *buffer,
                  int nbytes);
```

> Transmits the COPY data in the specified buffer, of length nbytes, to the server. The result is 1 if the data was sent, zero if it was not sent because the attempt would block (this case is only possible if the connection is in nonblocking mode), or -1 if an error occurred. (Use PQerrorMessage to retrieve details if the return value is -1. If the value is zero, wait for write-ready and try again.)

> The application can divide the COPY data stream into buffer loads of any convenient size. Buffer-load boundaries have no semantic significance when sending. The contents of the data stream must match the data format expected by the COPY command; see COPY for details.

PQputCopyEnd

> Sends end-of-data indication to the server during COPY_IN state.

```
int PQputCopyEnd(PGconn *conn,
                 const char *errormsg);
```

Ends the COPY_IN operation successfully if errormsg is NULL. If errormsg is not NULL then the COPY is forced to fail, with the string pointed to by errormsg used as the error message. (One should not assume that this exact error message will come back from the server, however, as the server might have already failed the COPY for its own reasons. Also note that the option to force failure does not work when using pre-3.0-protocol connections.)

The result is 1 if the termination data was sent, zero if it was not sent because the attempt would block (this case is only possible if the connection is in nonblocking mode), or -1 if an error occurred. (Use PQerrorMessage to retrieve details if the return value is -1. If the value is zero, wait for write-ready and try again.)

After successfully calling PQputCopyEnd, call PQgetResult to obtain the final result status of the COPY command. One can wait for this result to be available in the usual way. Then return to normal operation.

30.8.2. Functions for Receiving COPY Data

These functions are used to receive data during COPY TO STDOUT. They will fail if called when the connection is not in COPY_OUT state.

PQgetCopyData

Receives data from the server during COPY_OUT state.

```
int PQgetCopyData(PGconn *conn,
                  char **buffer,
                  int async);
```

Attempts to obtain another row of data from the server during a COPY. Data is always returned one data row at a time; if only a partial row is available, it is not returned. Successful return of a data row involves allocating a chunk of memory to hold the data. The buffer parameter must be non-NULL. *buffer is set to point to the allocated memory, or to NULL in cases where no buffer is returned. A non-NULL result buffer must be freed using PQfreemem when no longer needed.

When a row is successfully returned, the return value is the number of data bytes in the row (this will always be greater than zero). The returned string is always null-terminated, though this is probably only useful for textual COPY. A result of zero indicates that the COPY is still in progress, but no row is yet available (this is only possible when async is true). A result of -1 indicates that the COPY is done. A result of -2 indicates that an error occurred (consult PQerrorMessage for the reason).

When async is true (not zero), PQgetCopyData will not block waiting for input; it will return zero if the COPY is still in progress but no complete row is available. (In this case wait for read-ready and then call PQconsumeInput before calling PQgetCopyData again.)

When async is false (zero), PQgetCopyData will block until data is available or the operation completes.

After PQgetCopyData returns -1, call PQgetResult to obtain the final result status of the COPY command. One can wait for this result to be available in the usual way. Then return to normal operation.

30.8.3. Obsolete Functions for COPY

These functions represent older methods of handling COPY. Although they still work, they are deprecated due to poor error handling, inconvenient methods of detecting end-of-data, and lack of support for binary or nonblocking transfers.

PQgetline

Reads a newline-terminated line of characters (transmitted by the server) into a buffer string of size length.

```
int PQgetline(PGconn *conn,
              char *buffer,
              int length);
```

This function copies up to length-1 characters into the buffer and converts the terminating newline into a zero byte. PQgetline returns EOF at the end of input, 0 if the entire line has been read, and 1 if the buffer is full but the terminating newline has not yet been read.

Note that the application must check to see if a new line consists of the two characters \., which indicates that the server has finished sending the results of the COPY command. If the application might receive lines that are more than length-1 characters long, care is needed to be sure it recognizes the \. line correctly (and does not, for example, mistake the end of a long data line for a terminator line).

PQgetlineAsync

Reads a row of COPY data (transmitted by the server) into a buffer without blocking.

```
int PQgetlineAsync(PGconn *conn,
                   char *buffer,
                   int bufsize);
```

This function is similar to PQgetline, but it can be used by applications that must read COPY data asynchronously, that is, without blocking. Having issued the COPY command and gotten a PGRES_COPY_OUT response, the application should call PQconsumeInput and PQgetlineAsync until the end-of-data signal is detected.

Unlike PQgetline, this function takes responsibility for detecting end-of-data.

On each call, PQgetlineAsync will return data if a complete data row is available in libpq's input buffer. Otherwise, no data is returned until the rest of the row arrives. The function returns -1 if the end-of-copy-data marker has been recognized, or 0 if no data is available, or a positive number giving the number of bytes of data returned. If -1 is returned, the caller must next call PQendcopy, and then return to normal processing.

The data returned will not extend beyond a data-row boundary. If possible a whole row will be returned at one time. But if the buffer offered by the caller is too small to hold a row sent by the server, then a partial data row will be returned. With textual data this can be detected by testing whether the last returned byte is \n or not. (In a binary COPY, actual parsing of the COPY data format will be needed to make the equivalent determination.) The returned string is not null-terminated. (If you want to add a terminating null, be sure to pass a bufsize one smaller than the room actually available.)

PQputline

Sends a null-terminated string to the server. Returns 0 if OK and EOF if unable to send the string.

```
int PQputline(PGconn *conn,
              const char *string);
```

The COPY data stream sent by a series of calls to PQputline has the same format as that returned by PQgetlineAsync, except that applications are not obliged to send exactly one data row per PQputline call; it is okay to send a partial line or multiple lines per call.

Note

Before PostgreSQL protocol 3.0, it was necessary for the application to explicitly send the two characters \. as a final line to indicate to the server that it had finished sending COPY data. While this still works, it is deprecated and the special meaning of \. can be expected to be removed in a future release. It is sufficient to call PQendcopy after having sent the actual data.

PQputnbytes

Sends a non-null-terminated string to the server. Returns 0 if OK and EOF if unable to send the string.

```
int PQputnbytes(PGconn *conn,
                const char *buffer,
                int nbytes);
```

This is exactly like PQputline, except that the data buffer need not be null-terminated since the number of bytes to send is specified directly. Use this procedure when sending binary data.

PQendcopy

Synchronizes with the server.

```
int PQendcopy(PGconn *conn);
```

This function waits until the server has finished the copying. It should either be issued when the last string has been sent to the server using PQputline or when the last string has been received from the server using PGgetline. It must be issued or the server will get "out of sync" with the client. Upon return from this function, the server is ready to receive the next SQL command. The return value is 0 on successful completion, nonzero otherwise. (Use PQerrorMessage to retrieve details if the return value is nonzero.)

When using PQgetResult, the application should respond to a PGRES_COPY_OUT result by executing PQgetline repeatedly, followed by PQendcopy after the terminator line is seen. It should then return to the PQgetResult loop until PQgetResult returns a null pointer. Similarly a PGRES_COPY_IN result is processed by a series of PQputline calls followed by PQendcopy, then return to the PQgetResult loop. This arrangement will ensure that a COPY command embedded in a series of SQL commands will be executed correctly.

Older applications are likely to submit a COPY via PQexec and assume that the transaction is done after PQendcopy. This will work correctly only if the COPY is the only SQL command in the command string.

30.9. Control Functions

These functions control miscellaneous details of libpq's behavior.

PQclientEncoding

> Returns the client encoding.
>
>   int PQclientEncoding(const PGconn *conn);
>
> Note that it returns the encoding ID, not a symbolic string such as EUC_JP. To convert an encoding ID to an encoding name, you can use:
>
> char *pg_encoding_to_char(int encoding_id);

PQsetClientEncoding

> Sets the client encoding.
>
>   int PQsetClientEncoding(PGconn *conn, const char *encoding);
>
> conn is a connection to the server, and encoding is the encoding you want to use. If the function successfully sets the encoding, it returns 0, otherwise -1. The current encoding for this connection can be determined by using PQclientEncoding.

PQsetErrorVerbosity

> Determines the verbosity of messages returned by PQerrorMessage and PQresultErrorMessage.

```
typedef enum {
    PQERRORS_TERSE,
    PQERRORS_DEFAULT,
    PQERRORS_VERBOSE
} PGVerbosity;
```

```
PGVerbosity PQsetErrorVerbosity(PGconn *conn, PGVerbosity verbosity);
```

PQsetErrorVerbosity sets the verbosity mode, returning the connection's previous setting. In *TERSE* mode, returned messages include severity, primary text, and position only; this will normally fit on a single line. The default mode produces messages that include the above plus any detail, hint, or context fields (these might span multiple lines). The *VERBOSE* mode includes all available fields. Changing the verbosity does not affect the messages available from already-existing PGresult objects, only subsequently-created ones.

PQtrace

Enables tracing of the client/server communication to a debugging file stream.

```
void PQtrace(PGconn *conn, FILE *stream);
```

Note

On Windows, if the libpq library and an application are compiled with different flags, this function call will crash the application because the internal representation of the FILE pointers differ. Specifically, multithreaded/single-threaded, release/debug, and static/dynamic flags should be the same for the library and all applications using that library.

PQuntrace

Disables tracing started by PQtrace.

```
void PQuntrace(PGconn *conn);
```

30.10. Miscellaneous Functions

As always, there are some functions that just don't fit anywhere.

PQfreemem

Frees memory allocated by libpq.

```
void PQfreemem(void *ptr);
```

Frees memory allocated by libpq, particularly PQescapeByteaConn, PQescapeBytea, PQunescapeBytea, and PQnotifies. It is particularly important that this function, rather than free(), be used on Microsoft Windows. This is because allocating memory in a DLL and releasing it in the application works only if multithreaded/single-threaded, release/debug, and static/dynamic flags are the same for the DLL and the application.

On non-Microsoft Windows platforms, this function is the same as the standard library function free().

PQconninfoFree

Frees the data structures allocated by PQconndefaults or PQconninfoParse.

```
void PQconninfoFree(PQconninfoOption *connOptions);
```

A simple PQfreemem will not do for this, since the array contains references to subsidiary strings.

PQencryptPassword

Prepares the encrypted form of a PostgreSQL password.

```
char * PQencryptPassword(const char *passwd, const char *user);
```

This function is intended to be used by client applications that wish to send commands like ALTER USER joe PASSWORD 'pwd'. It is good practice not to send the original cleartext password in such a command, because it might be exposed in command logs, activity displays, and so on. Instead, use this function to convert the password to encrypted form before it is sent. The arguments are the cleartext password, and the SQL name of the user it is for. The return value is a string allocated by malloc, or NULL if out of memory. The caller can assume the string doesn't contain any special characters that would require escaping. Use PQfreemem to free the result when done with it.

PQmakeEmptyPGresult

Constructs an empty PGresult object with the given status.

```
PGresult *PQmakeEmptyPGresult(PGconn *conn, ExecStatusType status);
```

This is libpq's internal function to allocate and initialize an empty PGresult object. This function returns NULL if memory could not be allocated. It is exported because some applications find it useful to generate result objects (particularly objects with error status) themselves. If conn is not null and status indicates an error, the current error message of the specified connection is copied into the PGresult. Also, if conn is not null, any event procedures registered in the connection are copied into the PGresult. (They do not get PGEVT_RESULTCREATE calls, but see PQfireResultCreateEvents.) Note that PQclear should eventually be called on the object, just as with a PGresult returned by libpq itself.

PQfireResultCreateEvents

Fires a PGEVT_RESULTCREATE event (see *Section 30.12* - page 293) for each event procedure registered in the PGresult object. Returns non-zero for success, zero if any event procedure fails.

```
int PQfireResultCreateEvents(PGconn *conn, PGresult *res);
```

The `conn` argument is passed through to event procedures but not used directly. It can be NULL if the event procedures won't use it.

Event procedures that have already received a `PGEVT_RESULTCREATE` or `PGEVT_RESULTCOPY` event for this object are not fired again.

The main reason that this function is separate from PQmakeEmptyPGResult is that it is often appropriate to create a PGresult and fill it with data before invoking the event procedures.

PQcopyResult

Makes a copy of a PGresult object. The copy is not linked to the source result in any way and PQclear must be called when the copy is no longer needed. If the function fails, NULL is returned.

```
PGresult *PQcopyResult(const PGresult *src, int flags);
```

This is not intended to make an exact copy. The returned result is always put into PGRES_TUPLES_OK status, and does not copy any error message in the source. (It does copy the command status string, however.) The flags argument determines what else is copied. It is a bitwise OR of several flags. PG_COPYRES_ATTRS specifies copying the source result's attributes (column definitions). PG_COPYRES_TUPLES specifies copying the source result's tuples. (This implies copying the attributes, too.) PG_COPYRES_NOTICEHOOKS specifies copying the source result's notify hooks. PG_COPYRES_EVENTS specifies copying the source result's events. (But any instance data associated with the source is not copied.)

PQsetResultAttrs

Sets the attributes of a PGresult object.

```
int PQsetResultAttrs(PGresult *res, int numAttributes, PGresAttDesc *attDescs);
```

The provided attDescs are copied into the result. If the attDescs pointer is NULL or numAttributes is less than one, the request is ignored and the function succeeds. If res already contains attributes, the function will fail. If the function fails, the return value is zero. If the function succeeds, the return value is non-zero.

PQsetvalue

Sets a tuple field value of a PGresult object.

```
int PQsetvalue(PGresult *res, int tup_num, int field_num, char *value, int len);
```

The function will automatically grow the result's internal tuples array as needed. However, the tup_num argument must be less than or equal to PQntuples, meaning this function can only grow the tuples array one tuple at a time. But any field of any existing tuple can be modified in any order. If a value at field_num already exists, it will be overwritten. If len is -1 or value is NULL, the field value will be set to an SQL NULL. The value is copied into the result's private storage, thus is no longer needed after the function returns. If the function fails, the return value is zero. If the function succeeds, the return value is non-zero.

PQresultAlloc

Allocate subsidiary storage for a PGresult object.

```
void *PQresultAlloc(PGresult *res, size_t nBytes);
```

Any memory allocated with this function will be freed when res is cleared. If the function fails, the return value is NULL. The result is guaranteed to be adequately aligned for any type of data, just as for malloc.

30.11. Notice Processing

Notice and warning messages generated by the server are not returned by the query execution functions, since they do not imply failure of the query. Instead they are passed to a notice handling function, and execution continues normally after the handler returns. The default notice handling function prints the message on stderr, but the application can override this behavior by supplying its own handling function.

For historical reasons, there are two levels of notice handling, called the notice receiver and notice processor. The default behavior is for the notice receiver to format the notice and pass a string to the notice processor for printing. However, an application that chooses to provide its own notice receiver will typically ignore the notice processor layer and just do all the work in the notice receiver.

The function PQsetNoticeReceiver sets or examines the current notice receiver for a connection object. Similarly, PQsetNoticeProcessor sets or examines the current notice processor.

```
typedef void (*PQnoticeReceiver) (void *arg, const PGresult *res);

PQnoticeReceiver
PQsetNoticeReceiver(PGconn *conn,
                    PQnoticeReceiver proc,
                    void *arg);

typedef void (*PQnoticeProcessor) (void *arg, const char *message);

PQnoticeProcessor
PQsetNoticeProcessor(PGconn *conn,
                    PQnoticeProcessor proc,
                    void *arg);
```

Each of these functions returns the previous notice receiver or processor function pointer, and sets the new value. If you supply a null function pointer, no action is taken, but the current pointer is returned.

When a notice or warning message is received from the server, or generated internally by libpq, the notice receiver function is called. It is passed the message in the form of a PGRES_NONFATAL_ERROR PGresult. (This allows the receiver to extract individual fields using PQresultErrorField, or the complete preformatted message using PQresultErrorMessage.) The same void pointer passed to PQsetNoticeReceiver is also passed. (This pointer can be used to access application-specific state if needed.)

The default notice receiver simply extracts the message (using PQresultErrorMessage) and passes it to the notice processor.

The notice processor is responsible for handling a notice or warning message given in text form. It is passed the string text of the message (including a trailing newline), plus a void pointer that is the same one passed to PQsetNoticeProcessor. (This pointer can be used to access application-specific state if needed.)

The default notice processor is simply:

```
static void
defaultNoticeProcessor(void *arg, const char *message)
{
    fprintf(stderr, "%s", message);
}
```

Once you have set a notice receiver or processor, you should expect that that function could be called as long as either the PGconn object or PGresult objects made from it exist. At creation of a PGresult, the PGconn's current notice handling pointers are copied into the PGresult for possible use by functions like PQgetvalue.

30.12. Event System

libpq's event system is designed to notify registered event handlers about interesting libpq events, such as the creation or destruction of PGconn and PGresult objects. A principal use case is that this allows applications to associate their own data with a PGconn or PGresult and ensure that that data is freed at an appropriate time.

Each registered event handler is associated with two pieces of data, known to libpq only as opaque void * pointers. There is a *passthrough* pointer that is provided by the application when the event handler is registered with a PGconn. The passthrough pointer never changes for the life of the PGconn and all PGresults generated from it; so if used, it must point to long-lived data. In addition there is an *instance data* pointer, which starts out NULL in every PGconn and PGresult. This pointer can be manipulated using the PQinstanceData, PQsetInstanceData, PQresultInstanceData and PQsetResultInstanceData functions. Note that unlike the passthrough pointer, instance data of a PGconn is not automatically inherited by PGresults created from it. libpq does not know what passthrough and instance data pointers point to (if anything) and will never attempt to free them — that is the responsibility of the event handler.

30.12.1. Event Types

The enum PGEventId names the types of events handled by the event system. All its values have names beginning with PGEVT. For each event type, there is a corresponding event info structure that carries the parameters passed to the event handlers. The event types are:

PGEVT_REGISTER

> The register event occurs when PQregisterEventProc is called. It is the ideal time to initialize any instanceData an event procedure may need. Only one register event will be fired per event handler per connection. If the event procedure fails, the registration is aborted.

```
typedef struct
{
    PGconn *conn;
} PGEventRegister;
```

> When a PGEVT_REGISTER event is received, the evtInfo pointer should be cast to a PGEventRegister *. This structure contains a PGconn that should be in the CONNECTION_OK status; guaranteed if one calls PQregisterEventProc right after obtaining a good PGconn. When returning a failure code, all cleanup must be performed as no PGEVT_CONNDESTROY event will be sent.

PGEVT_CONNRESET

> The connection reset event is fired on completion of PQreset or PQresetPoll. In both cases, the event is only fired if the reset was successful. If the event procedure fails, the entire connection reset will fail; the PGconn is put into CONNECTION_BAD status and PQresetPoll will return PGRES_POLLING_FAILED.

```
typedef struct
{
    PGconn *conn;
} PGEventConnReset;
```

> When a PGEVT_CONNRESET event is received, the evtInfo pointer should be cast to a PGEventConnReset *. Although the contained PGconn was just reset, all event data remains unchanged. This event should be used to reset/reload/requery any associated instanceData. Note that even if the event procedure fails to process PGEVT_CONNRESET, it will still receive a PGEVT_CONNDESTROY event when the connection is closed.

PGEVT_CONNDESTROY

> The connection destroy event is fired in response to PQfinish. It is the event procedure's responsibility to properly clean up its event data as libpq has no ability to manage this memory. Failure to clean up will lead to memory leaks.

```
typedef struct
{
    PGconn *conn;
} PGEventConnDestroy;
```

When a PGEVT_CONNDESTROY event is received, the evtInfo pointer should be cast to a PGEventConnDestroy *. This event is fired prior to PQfinish performing any other cleanup. The return value of the event procedure is ignored since there is no way of indicating a failure from PQfinish. Also, an event procedure failure should not abort the process of cleaning up unwanted memory.

PGEVT_RESULTCREATE

The result creation event is fired in response to any query execution function that generates a result, including PQgetResult. This event will only be fired after the result has been created successfully.

```
typedef struct
{
    PGconn *conn;
    PGresult *result;
} PGEventResultCreate;
```

When a PGEVT_RESULTCREATE event is received, the evtInfo pointer should be cast to a PGEventResultCreate *. The conn is the connection used to generate the result. This is the ideal place to initialize any instanceData that needs to be associated with the result. If the event procedure fails, the result will be cleared and the failure will be propagated. The event procedure must not try to PQclear the result object for itself. When returning a failure code, all cleanup must be performed as no PGEVT_RESULTDESTROY event will be sent.

PGEVT_RESULTCOPY

The result copy event is fired in response to PQcopyResult. This event will only be fired after the copy is complete. Only event procedures that have successfully handled the PGEVT_RESULTCREATE or PGEVT_RESULTCOPY event for the source result will receive PGEVT_RESULTCOPY events.

```
typedef struct
{
    const PGresult *src;
    PGresult *dest;
} PGEventResultCopy;
```

When a PGEVT_RESULTCOPY event is received, the evtInfo pointer should be cast to a PGEventResultCopy *. The src result is what was copied while the dest result is the copy destination. This event can be used to provide a deep copy of instanceData, since PQcopyResult cannot do that. If the event procedure fails, the entire copy operation will fail and the dest result will be cleared. When returning a failure code, all cleanup must be performed as no PGEVT_RESULTDESTROY event will be sent for the destination result.

PGEVT_RESULTDESTROY

The result destroy event is fired in response to a PQclear. It is the event procedure's responsibility to properly clean up its event data as libpq has no ability to manage this memory. Failure to clean up will lead to memory leaks.

```
typedef struct
{
    PGresult *result;
} PGEventResultDestroy;
```

When a PGEVT_RESULTDESTROY event is received, the evtInfo pointer should be cast to a PGEventResultDestroy *. This event is fired prior to PQclear performing any other cleanup. The return value of the event procedure is ignored since there is no way of indicating a failure from PQclear. Also, an event procedure failure should not abort the process of cleaning up unwanted memory.

30.12.2. Event Callback Procedure

PGEventProc

PGEventProc is a typedef for a pointer to an event procedure, that is, the user callback function that receives events from libpq. The signature of an event procedure must be

```
int eventproc(PGEventId evtId, void *evtInfo, void *passThrough)
```

The evtId parameter indicates which PGEVT event occurred. The evtInfo pointer must be cast to the appropriate structure type to obtain further information about the event. The passThrough parameter is the pointer provided to PQregisterEventProc when the event procedure was registered. The function should return a non-zero value if it succeeds and zero if it fails.

A particular event procedure can be registered only once in any PGconn. This is because the address of the procedure is used as a lookup key to identify the associated instance data.

 Caution

On Windows, functions can have two different addresses: one visible from outside a DLL and another visible from inside the DLL. One should be careful that only one of these addresses is used with libpq's event-procedure functions, else confusion will result. The simplest rule for writing code that will work is to ensure that event procedures are declared static. If the procedure's address must be available outside its own source file, expose a separate function to return the address.

30.12.3. Event Support Functions

PQregisterEventProc

Registers an event callback procedure with libpq.

```
int PQregisterEventProc(PGconn *conn, PGEventProc proc,
                        const char *name, void *passThrough);
```

An event procedure must be registered once on each PGconn you want to receive events about. There is no limit, other than memory, on the number of event procedures that can be registered with a connection. The function returns a non-zero value if it succeeds and zero if it fails.

The proc argument will be called when a libpq event is fired. Its memory address is also used to lookup instanceData. The name argument is used to refer to the event procedure in error messages. This value cannot be NULL or a zero-length string. The name string is copied into the PGconn, so what is passed need not be long-lived. The passThrough pointer is passed to the proc whenever an event occurs. This argument can be NULL.

PQsetInstanceData

Sets the conn's instanceData for proc to data. This returns non-zero for success and zero for failure. (Failure is only possible if the proc has not been properly registered in the conn.)

```
int PQsetInstanceData(PGconn *conn, PGEventProc proc, void *data);
```

PQinstanceData

Returns the conn's instanceData associated with proc, or NULL if there is none.

```
void *PQinstanceData(const PGconn *conn, PGEventProc proc);
```

PQresultSetInstanceData

Sets the result's instanceData for proc to data. This returns non-zero for success and zero for failure. (Failure is only possible if the proc has not been properly registered in the result.)

```
int PQresultSetInstanceData(PGresult *res, PGEventProc proc, void *data);
```

PQresultInstanceData

Returns the result's instanceData associated with proc, or NULL if there is none.

```
void *PQresultInstanceData(const PGresult *res, PGEventProc proc);
```

30.12.4. Event Example

Here is a skeleton example of managing private data associated with libpq connections and results.

```
/* required header for libpq events (note: includes libpq-fe.h) */
#include <libpq-events.h>

/* The instanceData */
typedef struct
{
    int n;
    char *str;
} mydata;

/* PGEventProc */
static int myEventProc(PGEventId evtId, void *evtInfo, void *passThrough);

int
main(void)
{
    mydata *data;
    PGresult *res;
    PGconn *conn = PQconnectdb("dbname = postgres");

    if (PQstatus(conn) != CONNECTION_OK)
    {
        fprintf(stderr, "Connection to database failed: %s",
                PQerrorMessage(conn));
        PQfinish(conn);
        return 1;
    }

    /* called once on any connection that should receive events.
     * Sends a PGEVT_REGISTER to myEventProc.
     */
    if (!PQregisterEventProc(conn, myEventProc, "mydata_proc", NULL))
    {
        fprintf(stderr, "Cannot register PGEventProc\n");
        PQfinish(conn);
        return 1;
    }

    /* conn instanceData is available */
    data = PQinstanceData(conn, myEventProc);

    /* Sends a PGEVT_RESULTCREATE to myEventProc */
    res = PQexec(conn, "SELECT 1 + 1");

    /* result instanceData is available */
    data = PQresultInstanceData(res, myEventProc);

    /* If PG_COPYRES_EVENTS is used, sends a PGEVT_RESULTCOPY to myEventProc */
    res_copy = PQcopyResult(res, PG_COPYRES_TUPLES | PG_COPYRES_EVENTS);

    /* result instanceData is available if PG_COPYRES_EVENTS was
     * used during the PQcopyResult call.
     */
```

```
    data = PQresultInstanceData(res_copy, myEventProc);

    /* Both clears send a PGEVT_RESULTDESTROY to myEventProc */
    PQclear(res);
    PQclear(res_copy);

    /* Sends a PGEVT_CONNDESTROY to myEventProc */
    PQfinish(conn);

    return 0;
}

static int
myEventProc(PGEventId evtId, void *evtInfo, void *passThrough)
{
    switch (evtId)
    {
        case PGEVT_REGISTER:
        {
            PGEventRegister *e = (PGEventRegister *)evtInfo;
            mydata *data = get_mydata(e->conn);

            /* associate app specific data with connection */
            PQsetInstanceData(e->conn, myEventProc, data);
            break;
        }

        case PGEVT_CONNRESET:
        {
            PGEventConnReset *e = (PGEventConnReset *)evtInfo;
            mydata *data = PQinstanceData(e->conn, myEventProc);

            if (data)
              memset(data, 0, sizeof(mydata));
            break;
        }

        case PGEVT_CONNDESTROY:
        {
            PGEventConnDestroy *e = (PGEventConnDestroy *)evtInfo;
            mydata *data = PQinstanceData(e->conn, myEventProc);

            /* free instance data because the conn is being destroyed */
            if (data)
              free_mydata(data);
            break;
        }

        case PGEVT_RESULTCREATE:
        {
            PGEventResultCreate *e = (PGEventResultCreate *)evtInfo;
            mydata *conn_data = PQinstanceData(e->conn, myEventProc);
            mydata *res_data = dup_mydata(conn_data);
```

```
            /* associate app specific data with result (copy it from conn) */
            PQsetResultInstanceData(e->result, myEventProc, res_data);
            break;
        }

        case PGEVT_RESULTCOPY:
        {
            PGEventResultCopy *e = (PGEventResultCopy *)evtInfo;
            mydata *src_data = PQresultInstanceData(e->src, myEventProc);
            mydata *dest_data = dup_mydata(src_data);

            /* associate app specific data with result (copy it from a result) */
            PQsetResultInstanceData(e->dest, myEventProc, dest_data);
            break;
        }

        case PGEVT_RESULTDESTROY:
        {
            PGEventResultDestroy *e = (PGEventResultDestroy *)evtInfo;
            mydata *data = PQresultInstanceData(e->result, myEventProc);

            /* free instance data because the result is being destroyed */
            if (data)
              free_mydata(data);
            break;
        }

        /* unknown event id, just return TRUE. */
        default:
            break;
    }

    return TRUE; /* event processing succeeded */
}
```

30.13. Environment Variables

The following environment variables can be used to select default connection parameter values, which will be used by PQconnectdb, PQsetdbLogin and PQsetdb if no value is directly specified by the calling code. These are useful to avoid hard-coding database connection information into simple client applications, for example.

- PGHOST behaves the same as *host* connection parameter.
- PGHOSTADDR behaves the same as *hostaddr* connection parameter. This can be set instead of or in addition to PGHOST to avoid DNS lookup overhead.
- PGPORT behaves the same as *port* connection parameter.
- PGDATABASE behaves the same as *dbname* connection parameter.
- PGUSER behaves the same as *user* connection parameter. database.

- PGPASSWORD behaves the same as *password* connection parameter. Use of this environment variable is not recommended for security reasons (some operating systems allow non-root users to see process environment variables via ps); instead consider using the ~/.pgpass file (see *Section 30.14* - page 302).

- PGPASSFILE specifies the name of the password file to use for lookups. If not set, it defaults to ~/.pgpass (see *Section 30.14* - page 302).

- PGSERVICE behaves the same as *service* connection parameter.

- PGREALM sets the Kerberos realm to use with PostgreSQL, if it is different from the local realm. If PGREALM is set, libpq applications will attempt authentication with servers for this realm and use separate ticket files to avoid conflicts with local ticket files. This environment variable is only used if Kerberos authentication is selected by the server.

- PGOPTIONS behaves the same as *options* connection parameter.

- PGSSLMODE behaves the same as *sslmode* connection parameter.

- PGREQUIRESSL behaves the same as *requiressl* connection parameter.

- PGSSLCERT behaves the same as *sslcert* connection parameter.

- PGSSLKEY behaves the same as *sslkey* connection parameter.

- PGSSLROOTCERT behaves the same as *sslrootcert* connection parameter.

- PGSSLCRL behaves the same as *sslcrl* connection parameter.

- PGKRBSRVNAME behaves the same as *krbsrvname* connection parameter.

- PGGSSLIB behaves the same as *gsslib* connection parameter.

- PGCONNECT_TIMEOUT behaves the same as *connect_timeout* connection parameter.

The following environment variables can be used to specify default behavior for each PostgreSQL session. (See also the ALTER USER and ALTER DATABASE commands for ways to set default behavior on a per-user or per-database basis.)

- PGDATESTYLE sets the default style of date/time representation. (Equivalent to SET datestyle TO ....)

- PGTZ sets the default time zone. (Equivalent to SET timezone TO ....)

- PGCLIENTENCODING sets the default client character set encoding. (Equivalent to SET client_encoding TO ....)

- PGGEQO sets the default mode for the genetic query optimizer. (Equivalent to SET geqo TO ....)

Refer to the SQL command SET for information on correct values for these environment variables.

The following environment variables determine internal behavior of libpq; they override compiled-in defaults.

- PGSYSCONFDIR sets the directory containing the pg_service.conf file.
- PGLOCALEDIR sets the directory containing the locale files for message internationalization.

30.14. The Password File

The file .pgpass in a user's home directory or the file referenced by PGPASSFILE can contain passwords to be used if the connection requires a password (and no password has been specified otherwise). On Microsoft Windows the file is named %APPDATA%\postgresql\pgpass.conf (where %APPDATA% refers to the Application Data subdirectory in the user's profile).

This file should contain lines of the following format:

```
hostname:port:database:username:password
```

Each of the first four fields can be a literal value, or *, which matches anything. The password field from the first line that matches the current connection parameters will be used. (Therefore, put more-specific entries first when you are using wildcards.) If an entry needs to contain : or \, escape this character with \. A host name of localhost matches both TCP (host name localhost) and Unix domain socket (pghost empty or the default socket directory) connections coming from the local machine.

On Unix systems, the permissions on .pgpass must disallow any access to world or group; achieve this by the command chmod 0600 ~/.pgpass. If the permissions are less strict than this, the file will be ignored. On Microsoft Windows, it is assumed that the file is stored in a directory that is secure, so no special permissions check is made.

30.15. The Connection Service File

The connection service file allows libpq connection parameters to be associated with a single service name. That service name can then be specified by a libpq connection, and the associated settings will be used. This allows connection parameters to be modified without requiring a recompile of the libpq application. The service name can also be specified using the PGSERVICE environment variable.

To use this feature, copy share/pg_service.conf.sample to etc/pg_service.conf and edit the file to add service names and parameters. This file can be used for client-only installs too. The file's location can also be specified by the PGSYSCONFDIR environment variable.

30.16. LDAP Lookup of Connection Parameters

If libpq has been compiled with LDAP support (option --with-ldap for configure) it is possible to retrieve connection options like host or dbname via LDAP from a central server. The advantage is that if the connection parameters for a database change, the connection information doesn't have to be updated on all client machines.

LDAP connection parameter lookup uses the connection service file pg_service.conf (see *Section 30.15* - page 302). A line in a pg_service.conf stanza that starts with ldap:// will be recognized as an LDAP URL and an LDAP query will be performed. The result must be a list of keyword = value pairs which will be used to set connection options. The URL must conform to RFC 1959 and be of the form

```
ldap://[hostname[:port]]/search_base?attribute?search_scope?filter
```

where *hostname* defaults to localhost and *port* defaults to 389.

Processing of pg_service.conf is terminated after a successful LDAP lookup, but is continued if the LDAP server cannot be contacted. This is to provide a fallback with further LDAP URL lines that point to different LDAP servers, classical keyword = value pairs, or default connection options. If you would rather get an error message in this case, add a syntactically incorrect line after the LDAP URL.

A sample LDAP entry that has been created with the LDIF file

```
version:1
dn:cn=mydatabase,dc=mycompany,dc=com
changetype:add
objectclass:top
objectclass:groupOfUniqueNames
cn:mydatabase
uniqueMember:host=dbserver.mycompany.com
uniqueMember:port=5439
uniqueMember:dbname=mydb
uniqueMember:user=mydb_user
uniqueMember:sslmode=require
```

might be queried with the following LDAP URL:

```
ldap://ldap.mycompany.com/dc=mycompany,dc=com?uniqueMember?one?(cn=mydatabase)
```

You can also mix regular service file entries with LDAP lookups. A complete example for a stanza in pg_service.conf would be:

```
# only host and port are stored in LDAP, specify dbname and user explicitly
[customerdb]
dbname=customer
user=appuser
ldap://ldap.acme.com/cn=dbserver,cn=hosts?pgconnectinfo?base?(objectclass=*)
```

30.17. SSL Support

PostgreSQL has native support for using SSL connections to encrypt client/server communications for increased security. See *Section 17.8* - page 73 for details about the server-side SSL functionality.

libpq reads the system-wide OpenSSL configuration file. By default, this file is named openssl.cnf and is located in the directory reported by openssl version -d. This default can be overridden by setting environment variable OPENSSL_CONF to the name of the desired configuration file.

30.17.1. Certificate verification

By default, PostgreSQL will not perform any verification of the server certificate. This means that it is possible to spoof the server identity (for example by modifying a DNS record or by taking over the server IP address) without the client knowing. In order to prevent this, SSL certificate verification must be used.

If the parameter sslmode is set to verify-ca libpq will verify that the server is trustworthy by checking the certificate chain up to a trusted CA. If sslmode is set to verify-full, libpq will *also* verify that the server hostname matches that of the certificate. The SSL connection will fail if the server certificate cannot be verified. verify-full is recommended in most security sensitive environments.

In verify-full mode, the cn attribute of the certificate is matched against the hostname. If the cn attribute starts with an asterisk (*), it will be treated as a wildcard, and will match all characters *except* a dot (.). This means the certificate will not match subdomains. If the connection is made using an IP address instead of a hostname, the IP address will be matched (without doing any DNS lookups).

To allow verification, the certificate of a trusted CA must be placed in the file ~/.postgresql/root.crt in the user's home directory. (On Microsoft Windows the file is named %APPDATA%\postgresql\root.crt.)

Certificate Revocation List (CRL) entries are also checked if the file ~/.postgresql/root.crl exists (%APPDATA%\postgresql\root.crl on Microsoft Windows).

The location of the root certificate store and the CRL can be overridden by the connection parameters sslrootcert and sslcrl or the environment variables PGSSLROOTCERT and PGSSLCRL.

30.17.2. Client certificates

If the server requests a trusted client certificate, libpq will send the certificate stored in file ~/.postgresql/postgresql.crt in the user's home directory. The certificate must be signed by one of the certificate authorities (CA) trusted by the server. A matching private key file ~/.postgresql/postgresql.key must also be present. The private key file must not allow any access to world or group; achieve this by the command chmod 0600 ~/.postgresql/postgresql.key. On Microsoft Windows these files are named %APPDATA%\postgresql\postgresql.crt and %APPDATA%\postgresql\postgresql.key, and there is no special permissions check since the directory is presumed secure. The location of the certificate and key files can be overridden by the connection parameters sslcert and sslkey or the environment variables PGSSLCERT and PGSSLKEY.

30.17.3. Protection provided in different modes

The different values for the sslmode parameter provide different levels of protection, in different environments. SSL itself provides protection against three different types of attacks:

Type	Description
Eavesdropping	If a third party can listen to the network traffic between the client and the server, it can read both connection information (including the username and password) and the data that is passed. SSL uses encryption to prevent this.
Man in the middle (MITM)	If a third party can modify the data while passing between the client and server, it can pretend to be the server and therefore see and modify data *even if it is encrypted*. The third party can then forward the connection information and data to the original server, making it impossible to detect this attack. Common vectors to do this include DNS poisoning and address hijacking, whereby the client is directed to a different server than intended. There are also several other attack methods that can accomplish this. SSL uses certificate verification to prevent this, by authenticating the server to the client.
Impersonation	If a third party can pretend to be an authorized client, it can simply access data it should not have access to. Typically this can happen through insecure password management. SSL uses client certificates to prevent this, by making sure that only holders of valid certificates can access the server.

Table 30-2. SSL attacks

For a connection to be known secure, the two first of these have to be set up on *both the client and the server* before the connection is made. If it is only configured on the server, the client may end up sending sensitive information (e.g. passwords) before it knows that the server requires high security. In libpq, this is controlled by setting the sslmode parameter to verify-full or verify-ca, and providing the system with a root certificate to verify against. This is analogous to using a https URL for encrypted web browsing.

Once the server has been authenticated, the client can pass sensitive data. This means that up until this point, the client does not need to know if certificates will be used for authentication, making it safe to specify this only in the server configuration.

All SSL options carry overhead in the form of encryption and key-exchange, and it is a tradeoff that has to be made between performance and security. The following table illustrates the risks the different sslmode values protect against, and what statement they make about security and overhead:

sslmode	Eavesdropping protection	MITM protection	Statement
disabled	No	No	I don't care about security, and I don't want to pay the overhead of encryption.
allow	Maybe	No	I don't care about security, but I will pay the overhead of encryption if the server insists on it.
prefer	Maybe	No	I don't care about encryption, but I wish to pay the overhead of encryption if the server supports it.
require	Yes	No	I want my data to be encrypted, and I accept the overhead. I trust that the network will make sure I always connect to the server I want.
verify-ca	Yes	Depends on CA-policy	I want my data encrypted, and I accept the overhead. I want to be sure that I connect to a server that I trust.
verify-full	Yes	Yes	I want my data encrypted, and I accept the overhead. I want to be sure that I connect to a server I trust, and that it's the one I specify.

Table 30-3. SSL mode descriptions

The difference between verify-ca and verify-full depends on the policy of the root CA. If a public CA is used, verify-ca allows connections to a server that *somebody else* may have registered with the CA to succeed. In this case, verify-full should always be used. If a local CA is used, or even a self-signed certificate, using verify-ca often provides enough protection.

The default value for sslmode is prefer. As is shown in the table, this makes no sense from a security point of view, and it only promises performance overhead if possible. It is only provided as the default for backwards compatiblity, and not recommended in secure deployments.

30.17.4. SSL File Usage

File	Contents	Effect
~/.postgresql/postgresql.crt	client certificate	requested by server
~/.postgresql/postgresql.key	client private key	proves client certificate sent by owner; does not indicate certificate owner is trustworthy
~/.postgresql/root.crt	trusted certificate authorities	checks server certificate is signed by a trusted certificate authority

File	Contents	Effect
`~/.postgresql/root.crl`	certificates revoked by certificate authorities	server certificate must not be on this list

Table 30-4. Libpq/Client SSL File Usage

30.17.5. SSL library initialization

If your application initializes libssl and/or libcrypto libraries and libpq is built with SSL support, you should call PQinitOpenSSL to tell libpq that the libssl and/or libcrypto libraries have been initialized by your application, so that libpq will not also initialize those libraries. See *http://h71000.www7.hp.com/doc/83final/BA554_90007/ch04.html* for details on the SSL API.

PQinitOpenSSL

Allows applications to select which security libraries to initialize.

```
void PQinitOpenSSL(int do_ssl, init do_crypto);
```

When do_ssl is non-zero, libpq will initialize the OpenSSL library before first opening a database connection. When do_crypto is non-zero, the libcrypto library will be initialized. By default (if PQinitOpenSSL is not called), both libraries are initialized. When SSL support is not compiled in, this function is present but does nothing.

If your application uses and initializes either OpenSSL or its underlying libcrypto library, you *must* call this function with zeroes for the appropriate parameter(s) before first opening a database connection. Also be sure that you have done that initialization before opening a database connection.

PQinitSSL

Allows applications to select which security libraries to initialize.

```
void PQinitSSL(int do_ssl);
```

This function is equivalent to PQinitOpenSSL(do_ssl, do_ssl). It is sufficient for applications that initialize both or neither of OpenSSL and libcrypto.

PQinitSSL has been present since PostgreSQL 8.0, while PQinitOpenSSL was added in PostgreSQL 8.4, so PQinitSSL might be preferable for applications that need to work with older versions of libpq.

30.18. Behavior in Threaded Programs

libpq is reentrant and thread-safe if the configure command-line option --enable-thread-safety was used when the PostgreSQL distribution was built. In addition, you might need to use additional compiler command-line options when you compile your application code.

Refer to your system's documentation for information about how to build thread-enabled applications, or look in src/Makefile.global for PTHREAD_CFLAGS and PTHREAD_LIBS. This function allows the querying of libpq's thread-safe status:

PQisthreadsafe

> Returns the thread safety status of the libpq library.
>
> ```
> int PQisthreadsafe();
> ```
>
> Returns 1 if the libpq is thread-safe and 0 if it is not.

One thread restriction is that no two threads attempt to manipulate the same PGconn object at the same time. In particular, you cannot issue concurrent commands from different threads through the same connection object. (If you need to run concurrent commands, use multiple connections.)

PGresult objects are read-only after creation, and so can be passed around freely between threads.

The deprecated functions PQrequestCancel and PQoidStatus are not thread-safe and should not be used in multithread programs. PQrequestCancel can be replaced by PQcancel. PQoidStatus can be replaced by PQoidValue.

If you are using Kerberos inside your application (in addition to inside libpq), you will need to do locking around Kerberos calls because Kerberos functions are not thread-safe. See function PQregisterThreadLock in the libpq source code for a way to do cooperative locking between libpq and your application.

If you experience problems with threaded applications, run the program in src/tools/thread to see if your platform has thread-unsafe functions. This program is run by configure, but for binary distributions your library might not match the library used to build the binaries.

30.19. Building libpq Programs

To build (i.e., compile and link) a program using libpq you need to do all of the following things:

- Include the libpq-fe.h header file:
  ```
  #include <libpq-fe.h>
  ```

  If you failed to do that then you will normally get error messages from your compiler similar to:
  ```
  foo.c: In function `main':
  foo.c:34: `PGconn' undeclared (first use in this function)
  foo.c:35: `PGresult' undeclared (first use in this function)
  ```

```
foo.c:54: `CONNECTION_BAD' undeclared (first use in this function)
foo.c:68: `PGRES_COMMAND_OK' undeclared (first use in this function)
foo.c:95: `PGRES_TUPLES_OK' undeclared (first use in this function)
```

- Point your compiler to the directory where the PostgreSQL header files were installed, by supplying the -I*directory* option to your compiler. (In some cases the compiler will look into the directory in question by default, so you can omit this option.) For instance, your compile command line could look like:

```
cc -c -I/usr/local/pgsql/include testprog.c
```

If you are using makefiles then add the option to the CPPFLAGS variable:

```
CPPFLAGS += -I/usr/local/pgsql/include
```

If there is any chance that your program might be compiled by other users then you should not hardcode the directory location like that. Instead, you can run the utility pg_config to find out where the header files are on the local system:

```
$ pg_config --includedir
/usr/local/include
```

Failure to specify the correct option to the compiler will result in an error message such as:

```
testlibpq.c:8:22: libpq-fe.h: No such file or directory
```

- When linking the final program, specify the option -lpq so that the libpq library gets pulled in, as well as the option -L*directory* to point the compiler to the directory where the libpq library resides. (Again, the compiler will search some directories by default.) For maximum portability, put the -L option before the -lpq option. For example:

```
cc -o testprog testprog1.o testprog2.o -L/usr/local/pgsql/lib -lpq
```

You can find out the library directory using pg_config as well:

```
$ pg_config --libdir
/usr/local/pgsql/lib
```

Error messages that point to problems in this area could look like the following:

```
testlibpq.o: In function `main':
testlibpq.o(.text+0x60): undefined reference to `PQsetdbLogin'
testlibpq.o(.text+0x71): undefined reference to `PQstatus'
testlibpq.o(.text+0xa4): undefined reference to `PQerrorMessage'
```

This means you forgot -lpq.

```
/usr/bin/ld: cannot find -lpq
```

This means you forgot the -L option or did not specify the right directory.

30.20. Example Programs

These examples and others can be found in the directory src/test/examples in the source code distribution.

```c
/*
 * testlibpq.c
 *
 *        Test the C version of libpq, the PostgreSQL frontend library.
 */
#include <stdio.h>
#include <stdlib.h>
#include "libpq-fe.h"

static void
exit_nicely(PGconn *conn)
{
    PQfinish(conn);
    exit(1);
}

int
main(int argc, char **argv)
{
    const char *conninfo;
    PGconn      *conn;
    PGresult    *res;
    int          nFields;
    int          i,
                 j;

    /*
     * If the user supplies a parameter on the command line, use it as the
     * conninfo string; otherwise default to setting dbname=postgres and using
     * environment variables or defaults for all other connection parameters.
     */
    if (argc > 1)
        conninfo = argv[1];
    else
        conninfo = "dbname = postgres";

    /* Make a connection to the database */
    conn = PQconnectdb(conninfo);

    /* Check to see that the backend connection was successfully made */
    if (PQstatus(conn) != CONNECTION_OK)
    {
        fprintf(stderr, "Connection to database failed: %s",
                PQerrorMessage(conn));
        exit_nicely(conn);
    }
```

```
 /*
  * Our test case here involves using a cursor, for which we must be inside
  * a transaction block.  We could do the whole thing with a single
  * PQexec() of "select * from pg_database", but that's too trivial to make
  * a good example.
  */

 /* Start a transaction block */
 res = PQexec(conn, "BEGIN");
 if (PQresultStatus(res) != PGRES_COMMAND_OK)
 {
     fprintf(stderr, "BEGIN command failed: %s", PQerrorMessage(conn));
     PQclear(res);
     exit_nicely(conn);
 }

 /*
  * Should PQclear PGresult whenever it is no longer needed to avoid memory
  * leaks
  */
 PQclear(res);

 /*
  * Fetch rows from pg_database, the system catalog of databases
  */
 res = PQexec(conn, "DECLARE myportal CURSOR FOR select * from pg_database");
 if (PQresultStatus(res) != PGRES_COMMAND_OK)
 {
     fprintf(stderr, "DECLARE CURSOR failed: %s", PQerrorMessage(conn));
     PQclear(res);
     exit_nicely(conn);
 }
 PQclear(res);

 res = PQexec(conn, "FETCH ALL in myportal");
 if (PQresultStatus(res) != PGRES_TUPLES_OK)
 {
     fprintf(stderr, "FETCH ALL failed: %s", PQerrorMessage(conn));
     PQclear(res);
     exit_nicely(conn);
 }

 /* first, print out the attribute names */
 nFields = PQnfields(res);
 for (i = 0; i < nFields; i++)
     printf("%-15s", PQfname(res, i));
 printf("\n\n");

 /* next, print out the rows */
 for (i = 0; i < PQntuples(res); i++)
 {
     for (j = 0; j < nFields; j++)
         printf("%-15s", PQgetvalue(res, i, j));
```

```
            printf("\n");
    }

    PQclear(res);

    /* close the portal ... we don't bother to check for errors ... */
    res = PQexec(conn, "CLOSE myportal");
    PQclear(res);

    /* end the transaction */
    res = PQexec(conn, "END");
    PQclear(res);

    /* close the connection to the database and cleanup */
    PQfinish(conn);

    return 0;
}
```

Example 30-1. libpq Example Program 1

```
/*
 * testlibpq2.c
 *      Test of the asynchronous notification interface
 *
 * Start this program, then from psql in another window do
 *   NOTIFY TBL2;
 * Repeat four times to get this program to exit.
 *
 * Or, if you want to get fancy, try this:
 * populate a database with the following commands
 * (provided in src/test/examples/testlibpq2.sql):
 *
 *   CREATE TABLE TBL1 (i int4);
 *
 *   CREATE TABLE TBL2 (i int4);
 *
 *   CREATE RULE r1 AS ON INSERT TO TBL1 DO
 *     (INSERT INTO TBL2 VALUES (new.i); NOTIFY TBL2);
 *
 * and do this four times:
 *
 *   INSERT INTO TBL1 VALUES (10);
 */
#include <stdio.h>
#include <stdlib.h>
#include <string.h>
#include <errno.h>
#include <sys/time.h>
#include "libpq-fe.h"

static void
```

```
exit_nicely(PGconn *conn)
{
    PQfinish(conn);
    exit(1);
}

int
main(int argc, char **argv)
{
    const char *conninfo;
    PGconn     *conn;
    PGresult   *res;
    PGnotify   *notify;
    int         nnotifies;

    /*
     * If the user supplies a parameter on the command line, use it as the
     * conninfo string; otherwise default to setting dbname=postgres and using
     * environment variables or defaults for all other connection parameters.
     */
    if (argc > 1)
        conninfo = argv[1];
    else
        conninfo = "dbname = postgres";

    /* Make a connection to the database */
    conn = PQconnectdb(conninfo);

    /* Check to see that the backend connection was successfully made */
    if (PQstatus(conn) != CONNECTION_OK)
    {
        fprintf(stderr, "Connection to database failed: %s",
                PQerrorMessage(conn));
        exit_nicely(conn);
    }

    /*
     * Issue LISTEN command to enable notifications from the rule's NOTIFY.
     */
    res = PQexec(conn, "LISTEN TBL2");
    if (PQresultStatus(res) != PGRES_COMMAND_OK)
    {
        fprintf(stderr, "LISTEN command failed: %s", PQerrorMessage(conn));
        PQclear(res);
        exit_nicely(conn);
    }

    /*
     * should PQclear PGresult whenever it is no longer needed to avoid memory
     * leaks
     */
    PQclear(res);
```

```
    /* Quit after four notifies are received. */
    nnotifies = 0;
    while (nnotifies < 4)
    {
        /*
         * Sleep until something happens on the connection.  We use select(2)
         * to wait for input, but you could also use poll() or similar
         * facilities.
         */
        int         sock;
        fd_set      input_mask;

        sock = PQsocket(conn);

        if (sock < 0)
            break;                  /* shouldn't happen */

        FD_ZERO(&input_mask);
        FD_SET(sock, &input_mask);

        if (select(sock + 1, &input_mask, NULL, NULL, NULL) < 0)
        {
            fprintf(stderr, "select() failed: %s\n", strerror(errno));
            exit_nicely(conn);
        }

        /* Now check for input */
        PQconsumeInput(conn);
        while ((notify = PQnotifies(conn)) != NULL)
        {
            fprintf(stderr,
                    "ASYNC NOTIFY of '%s' received from backend pid %d\n",
                    notify->relname, notify->be_pid);
            PQfreemem(notify);
            nnotifies++;
        }
    }

    fprintf(stderr, "Done.\n");

    /* close the connection to the database and cleanup */
    PQfinish(conn);

    return 0;
}
```

Example 30-2. libpq Example Program 2

```
/*
 * testlibpq3.c
 *      Test out-of-line parameters and binary I/O.
 *
```

```
 * Before running this, populate a database with the following commands
 * (provided in src/test/examples/testlibpq3.sql):
 *
 * CREATE TABLE test1 (i int4, t text, b bytea);
 *
 * INSERT INTO test1 values (1, 'joe''s place', '\\000\\001\\002\\003\\004');
 * INSERT INTO test1 values (2, 'ho there', '\\004\\003\\002\\001\\000');
 *
 * The expected output is:
 *
 * tuple 0: got
 *  i = (4 bytes) 1
 *  t = (11 bytes) 'joe's place'
 *  b = (5 bytes) \000\001\002\003\004
 *
 * tuple 0: got
 *  i = (4 bytes) 2
 *  t = (8 bytes) 'ho there'
 *  b = (5 bytes) \004\003\002\001\000
 */
#include <stdio.h>
#include <stdlib.h>
#include <string.h>
#include <sys/types.h>
#include "libpq-fe.h"

/* for ntohl/htonl */
#include <netinet/in.h>
#include <arpa/inet.h>


static void
exit_nicely(PGconn *conn)
{
    PQfinish(conn);
    exit(1);
}

/*
 * This function prints a query result that is a binary-format fetch from
 * a table defined as in the comment above.  We split it out because the
 * main() function uses it twice.
 */
static void
show_binary_results(PGresult *res)
{
    int         i,
                j;
    int         i_fnum,
                t_fnum,
                b_fnum;

    /* Use PQfnumber to avoid assumptions about field order in result */
```

```
        i_fnum = PQfnumber(res, "i");
        t_fnum = PQfnumber(res, "t");
        b_fnum = PQfnumber(res, "b");

    for (i = 0; i < PQntuples(res); i++)
    {
        char        *iptr;
        char        *tptr;
        char        *bptr;
        int          blen;
        int          ival;

        /* Get the field values (we ignore possibility they are null!) */
        iptr = PQgetvalue(res, i, i_fnum);
        tptr = PQgetvalue(res, i, t_fnum);
        bptr = PQgetvalue(res, i, b_fnum);

        /*
         * The binary representation of INT4 is in network byte order, which
         * we'd better coerce to the local byte order.
         */
        ival = ntohl(*((uint32_t *) iptr));

        /*
         * The binary representation of TEXT is, well, text, and since libpq
         * was nice enough to append a zero byte to it, it'll work just fine
         * as a C string.
         *
         * The binary representation of BYTEA is a bunch of bytes, which could
         * include embedded nulls so we have to pay attention to field length.
         */
        blen = PQgetlength(res, i, b_fnum);

        printf("tuple %d: got\n", i);
        printf(" i = (%d bytes) %d\n",
                PQgetlength(res, i, i_fnum), ival);
        printf(" t = (%d bytes) '%s'\n",
                PQgetlength(res, i, t_fnum), tptr);
        printf(" b = (%d bytes) ", blen);
        for (j = 0; j < blen; j++)
            printf("\\%03o", bptr[j]);
        printf("\n\n");
    }
}

int
main(int argc, char **argv)
{
    const char *conninfo;
    PGconn      *conn;
    PGresult    *res;
    const char *paramValues[1];
    int          paramLengths[1];
```

```
    int         paramFormats[1];
    uint32_t    binaryIntVal;

    /*
     * If the user supplies a parameter on the command line, use it as the
     * conninfo string; otherwise default to setting dbname=postgres and using
     * environment variables or defaults for all other connection parameters.
     */
    if (argc > 1)
        conninfo = argv[1];
    else
        conninfo = "dbname = postgres";

    /* Make a connection to the database */
    conn = PQconnectdb(conninfo);

    /* Check to see that the backend connection was successfully made */
    if (PQstatus(conn) != CONNECTION_OK)
    {
        fprintf(stderr, "Connection to database failed: %s",
                PQerrorMessage(conn));
        exit_nicely(conn);
    }

    /*
     * The point of this program is to illustrate use of PQexecParams() with
     * out-of-line parameters, as well as binary transmission of data.
     *
     * This first example transmits the parameters as text, but receives the
     * results in binary format.  By using out-of-line parameters we can
     * avoid a lot of tedious mucking about with quoting and escaping, even
     * though the data is text.  Notice how we don't have to do anything
     * special with the quote mark in the parameter value.
     */

    /* Here is our out-of-line parameter value */
    paramValues[0] = "joe's place";

    res = PQexecParams(conn,
                    "SELECT * FROM test1 WHERE t = $1",
                    1,       /* one param */
                    NULL,    /* let the backend deduce param type */
                    paramValues,
                    NULL,    /* don't need param lengths since text */
                    NULL,    /* default to all text params */
                    1);      /* ask for binary results */

    if (PQresultStatus(res) != PGRES_TUPLES_OK)
    {
        fprintf(stderr, "SELECT failed: %s", PQerrorMessage(conn));
        PQclear(res);
        exit_nicely(conn);
    }
```

```
    show_binary_results(res);

    PQclear(res);

    /*
     * In this second example we transmit an integer parameter in binary
     * form, and again retrieve the results in binary form.
     *
     * Although we tell PQexecParams we are letting the backend deduce
     * parameter type, we really force the decision by casting the parameter
     * symbol in the query text.  This is a good safety measure when sending
     * binary parameters.
     */

    /* Convert integer value "2" to network byte order */
    binaryIntVal = htonl((uint32_t) 2);

    /* Set up parameter arrays for PQexecParams */
    paramValues[0] = (char *) &binaryIntVal;
    paramLengths[0] = sizeof(binaryIntVal);
    paramFormats[0] = 1;          /* binary */

    res = PQexecParams(conn,
                   "SELECT * FROM test1 WHERE i = $1::int4",
                   1,           /* one param */
                   NULL,        /* let the backend deduce param type */
                   paramValues,
                   paramLengths,
                   paramFormats,
                   1);          /* ask for binary results */

    if (PQresultStatus(res) != PGRES_TUPLES_OK)
    {
        fprintf(stderr, "SELECT failed: %s", PQerrorMessage(conn));
        PQclear(res);
        exit_nicely(conn);
    }

    show_binary_results(res);

    PQclear(res);

    /* close the connection to the database and cleanup */
    PQfinish(conn);

    return 0;
}
```

Example 30-3. libpq Example Program 3

Chapter 31.
Large Objects

PostgreSQL has a *large object* facility, which provides stream-style access to user data that is stored in a special large-object structure. Streaming access is useful when working with data values that are too large to manipulate conveniently as a whole.

This chapter describes the implementation and the programming and query language interfaces to PostgreSQL large object data. We use the libpq C library for the examples in this chapter, but most programming interfaces native to PostgreSQL support equivalent functionality. Other interfaces might use the large object interface internally to provide generic support for large values. This is not described here.

31.1. Introduction

All large objects are placed in a single system table called pg_largeobject. PostgreSQL also supports a storage system called "TOAST" that automatically stores values larger than a single database page into a secondary storage area per table. This makes the large object facility partially obsolete. One remaining advantage of the large object facility is that it allows values up to 2 GB in size, whereas TOASTed fields can be at most 1 GB. Also, large objects can be randomly modified using a read/write API that is more efficient than performing such operations using TOAST.

31.2. Implementation Features

The large object implementation breaks large objects up into "chunks" and stores the chunks in rows in the database. A B-tree index guarantees fast searches for the correct chunk number when doing random access reads and writes.

31.3. Client Interfaces

This section describes the facilities that PostgreSQL client interface libraries provide for accessing large objects. All large object manipulation using these functions *must* take place within an SQL transaction block. The PostgreSQL large object interface is modeled after the Unix file-system interface, with analogues of open, read, write, lseek, etc.

Client applications which use the large object interface in libpq should include the header file libpq/libpq-fs.h and link with the libpq library.

31.3.1. Creating a Large Object

The function

```
Oid lo_creat(PGconn *conn, int mode);
```

creates a new large object. The return value is the OID that was assigned to the new large object, or InvalidOid (zero) on failure. *mode* is unused and ignored as of PostgreSQL 8.1; however, for backwards compatibility with earlier releases it is best to set it to INV_READ, INV_WRITE, or INV_READ | INV_WRITE. (These symbolic constants are defined in the header file libpq/libpq-fs.h.)

An example:

```
inv_oid = lo_creat(conn, INV_READ|INV_WRITE);
```

The function

```
Oid lo_create(PGconn *conn, Oid lobjId);
```

also creates a new large object. The OID to be assigned can be specified by *lobjId*; if so, failure occurs if that OID is already in use for some large object. If *lobjId* is InvalidOid (zero) then lo_create assigns an unused OID (this is the same behavior as lo_creat). The return value is the OID that was assigned to the new large object, or InvalidOid (zero) on failure.

lo_create is new as of PostgreSQL 8.1; if this function is run against an older server version, it will fail and return InvalidOid.

An example:

```
inv_oid = lo_create(conn, desired_oid);
```

31.3.2. Importing a Large Object

To import an operating system file as a large object, call

```
Oid lo_import(PGconn *conn, const char *filename);
```

filename specifies the operating system name of the file to be imported as a large object. The return value is the OID that was assigned to the new large object, or InvalidOid (zero) on failure. Note that the file is read by the client interface library, not by the server; so it must exist in the client file system and be readable by the client application.

The function

```
Oid lo_import_with_oid(PGconn *conn, const char *filename, Oid lobjId);
```

also imports a new large object. The OID to be assigned can be specified by *lobjId*; if so, failure occurs if that OID is already in use for some large object. If *lobjId* is InvalidOid (zero) then lo_import_with_oid assigns an unused OID (this is the same behavior as lo_import). The return value is the OID that was assigned to the new large object, or InvalidOid (zero) on failure.

lo_import_with_oid is new as of PostgreSQL 8.4 and uses lo_create internally which is new in 8.1; if this function is run against 8.0 or before, it will fail and return InvalidOid.

31.3.3. Exporting a Large Object

To export a large object into an operating system file, call

```
int lo_export(PGconn *conn, Oid lobjId, const char *filename);
```

The lobjId argument specifies the OID of the large object to export and the filename argument specifies the operating system name of the file. Note that the file is written by the client interface library, not by the server. Returns 1 on success, -1 on failure.

31.3.4. Opening an Existing Large Object

To open an existing large object for reading or writing, call

```
int lo_open(PGconn *conn, Oid lobjId, int mode);
```

The lobjId argument specifies the OID of the large object to open. The mode bits control whether the object is opened for reading (INV_READ), writing (INV_WRITE), or both. (These symbolic constants are defined in the header file libpq/libpq-fs.h.) A large object cannot be opened before it is created. lo_open returns a (non-negative) large object descriptor for later use in lo_read, lo_write, lo_lseek, lo_tell, and lo_close. The descriptor is only valid for the duration of the current transaction. On failure, -1 is returned.

The server currently does not distinguish between modes INV_WRITE and INV_READ | INV_WRITE: you are allowed to read from the descriptor in either case. However there is a significant difference between these modes and INV_READ alone: with INV_READ you cannot write on the descriptor, and the data read from it will reflect the contents of the large object at the time of the transaction snapshot that was active when lo_open was executed, regardless of later writes by this or other transactions. Reading from a descriptor opened with INV_WRITE returns data that reflects all writes of other committed transactions as well as writes of the current transaction. This is similar to the behavior of SERIALIZABLE versus READ COMMITTED transaction modes for ordinary SQL SELECT commands.

An example:

```
inv_fd = lo_open(conn, inv_oid, INV_READ|INV_WRITE);
```

31.3.5. Writing Data to a Large Object

The function

```
int lo_write(PGconn *conn, int fd, const char *buf, size_t len);
```

writes len bytes from buf to large object descriptor fd. The fd argument must have been returned by a previous lo_open. The number of bytes actually written is returned. In the event of an error, the return value is negative.

31.3.6. Reading Data from a Large Object

The function

```
int lo_read(PGconn *conn, int fd, char *buf, size_t len);
```

reads len bytes from large object descriptor fd into buf. The fd argument must have been returned by a previous lo_open. The number of bytes actually read is returned. In the event of an error, the return value is negative.

31.3.7. Seeking in a Large Object

To change the current read or write location associated with a large object descriptor, call

```
int lo_lseek(PGconn *conn, int fd, int offset, int whence);
```

This function moves the current location pointer for the large object descriptor identified by fd to the new location specified by offset. The valid values for whence are SEEK_SET (seek from object start), SEEK_CUR (seek from current position), and SEEK_END (seek from object end). The return value is the new location pointer, or -1 on error.

31.3.8. Obtaining the Seek Position of a Large Object

To obtain the current read or write location of a large object descriptor, call

```
int lo_tell(PGconn *conn, int fd);
```

If there is an error, the return value is negative.

31.3.9. Truncating a Large Object

To truncate a large object to a given length, call

```
int lo_truncate(PGcon *conn, int fd, size_t len);
```

truncates the large object descriptor fd to length len. The fd argument must have been returned by a previous lo_open. If len is greater than the current large object length, the large object is extended with null bytes ('\0').

The file offset is not changed.

On success lo_truncate returns zero. On error, the return value is negative.

lo_truncate is new as of PostgreSQL 8.3; if this function is run against an older server version, it will fail and return a negative value.

31.3.10. Closing a Large Object Descriptor

A large object descriptor can be closed by calling

```
int lo_close(PGconn *conn, int fd);
```

where fd is a large object descriptor returned by lo_open. On success, lo_close returns zero. On error, the return value is negative.

Any large object descriptors that remain open at the end of a transaction will be closed automatically.

31.3.11. Removing a Large Object

To remove a large object from the database, call

```
int lo_unlink(PGconn *conn, Oid lobjId);
```

The lobjId argument specifies the OID of the large object to remove. Returns 1 if successful, -1 on failure.

31.4. Server-Side Functions

There are server-side functions callable from SQL that correspond to each of the client-side functions described above; indeed, for the most part the client-side functions are simply interfaces to the equivalent server-side functions. The ones that are actually useful to call via SQL commands are lo_creat, lo_create, lo_unlink, lo_import, and lo_export. Here are examples of their use:

```
CREATE TABLE image (
    name            text,
    raster          oid
);

SELECT lo_creat(-1);        -- returns OID of new, empty large object

SELECT lo_create(43213);    -- attempts to create large object with OID 43213

SELECT lo_unlink(173454);   -- deletes large object with OID 173454

INSERT INTO image (name, raster)
    VALUES ('beautiful image', lo_import('/etc/motd'));

INSERT INTO image (name, raster)   -- same as above, but specify OID to use
    VALUES ('beautiful image', lo_import('/etc/motd', 68583));

SELECT lo_export(image.raster, '/tmp/motd') FROM image
    WHERE name = 'beautiful image';
```

The server-side lo_import and lo_export functions behave considerably differently from their client-side analogs. These two functions read and write files in the server's file system, using the permissions of the database's owning user. Therefore, their use is restricted to superusers. In contrast, the client-side import and export functions read and write files in the client's file system, using the permissions of the client program. The client-side functions can be used by any PostgreSQL user.

31.5. Example Program

Example 31-1 is a sample program which shows how the large object interface in libpq can be used. Parts of the program are commented out but are left in the source for the reader's benefit. This program can also be found in src/test/examples/testlo.c in the source distribution.

```c
/*-------------------------------------------------------------
 *
 * testlo.c--
 *    test using large objects with libpq
 *
 * Copyright (c) 1994, Regents of the University of California
 *
 *-------------------------------------------------------------
 */
#include <stdio.h>
#include "libpq-fe.h"
#include "libpq/libpq-fs.h"

#define BUFSIZE         1024

/*
 * importFile
 *    import file "in_filename" into database as large object "lobjOid"
 *
 */
Oid
importFile(PGconn *conn, char *filename)
{
    Oid         lobjId;
    int         lobj_fd;
    char        buf[BUFSIZE];
    int         nbytes,
                tmp;
    int         fd;

    /*
     * open the file to be read in
     */
    fd = open(filename, O_RDONLY, 0666);
    if (fd < 0)
    {                               /* error */
        fprintf(stderr, "cannot open unix file %s\n", filename);
    }

    /*
     * create the large object
     */
    lobjId = lo_creat(conn, INV_READ | INV_WRITE);
    if (lobjId == 0)
        fprintf(stderr, "cannot create large object\n");
```

```
        lobj_fd = lo_open(conn, lobjId, INV_WRITE);

        /*
         * read in from the Unix file and write to the inversion file
         */
        while ((nbytes = read(fd, buf, BUFSIZE)) > 0)
        {
            tmp = lo_write(conn, lobj_fd, buf, nbytes);
            if (tmp < nbytes)
                fprintf(stderr, "error while reading large object\n");
        }

        (void) close(fd);
        (void) lo_close(conn, lobj_fd);

        return lobjId;
}

void
pickout(PGconn *conn, Oid lobjId, int start, int len)
{
    int         lobj_fd;
    char        *buf;
    int         nbytes;
    int         nread;

    lobj_fd = lo_open(conn, lobjId, INV_READ);
    if (lobj_fd < 0)
    {
        fprintf(stderr, "cannot open large object %d\n",
                lobjId);
    }

    lo_lseek(conn, lobj_fd, start, SEEK_SET);
    buf = malloc(len + 1);

    nread = 0;
    while (len - nread > 0)
    {
        nbytes = lo_read(conn, lobj_fd, buf, len - nread);
        buf[nbytes] = ' ';
        fprintf(stderr, ">>> %s", buf);
        nread += nbytes;
    }
    free(buf);
    fprintf(stderr, "\n");
    lo_close(conn, lobj_fd);
}

void
overwrite(PGconn *conn, Oid lobjId, int start, int len)
{
```

```
    int         lobj_fd;
    char        *buf;
    int         nbytes;
    int         nwritten;
    int         i;

    lobj_fd = lo_open(conn, lobjId, INV_WRITE);
    if (lobj_fd < 0)
    {
        fprintf(stderr, "cannot open large object %d\n",
                lobjId);
    }

    lo_lseek(conn, lobj_fd, start, SEEK_SET);
    buf = malloc(len + 1);

    for (i = 0; i < len; i++)
        buf[i] = 'X';
    buf[i] = ' ';

    nwritten = 0;
    while (len - nwritten > 0)
    {
        nbytes = lo_write(conn, lobj_fd, buf + nwritten, len - nwritten);
        nwritten += nbytes;
    }
    free(buf);
    fprintf(stderr, "\n");
    lo_close(conn, lobj_fd);
}

/*
 * exportFile
 *    export large object "lobjOid" to file "out_filename"
 *
 */
void
exportFile(PGconn *conn, Oid lobjId, char *filename)
{
    int         lobj_fd;
    char        buf[BUFSIZE];
    int         nbytes,
                tmp;
    int         fd;

    /*
     * open the large object
     */
    lobj_fd = lo_open(conn, lobjId, INV_READ);
    if (lobj_fd < 0)
    {
        fprintf(stderr, "cannot open large object %d\n",
                lobjId);
```

```
    }

    /*
     * open the file to be written to
     */
    fd = open(filename, O_CREAT | O_WRONLY, 0666);
    if (fd < 0)
    {                               /* error */
        fprintf(stderr, "cannot open unix file %s\n",
                filename);
    }

    /*
     * read in from the inversion file and write to the Unix file
     */
    while ((nbytes = lo_read(conn, lobj_fd, buf, BUFSIZE)) > 0)
    {
        tmp = write(fd, buf, nbytes);
        if (tmp < nbytes)
        {
            fprintf(stderr, "error while writing %s\n",
                    filename);
        }
    }

    (void) lo_close(conn, lobj_fd);
    (void) close(fd);

    return;
}

void
exit_nicely(PGconn *conn)
{
    PQfinish(conn);
    exit(1);
}

int
main(int argc, char **argv)
{
    char        *in_filename,
                *out_filename;
    char        *database;
    Oid          lobjOid;
    PGconn      *conn;
    PGresult    *res;

    if (argc != 4)
    {
        fprintf(stderr, "Usage: %s database_name in_filename out_filename\n",
                argv[0]);
        exit(1);
```

```
    }

    database = argv[1];
    in_filename = argv[2];
    out_filename = argv[3];

    /*
     * set up the connection
     */
    conn = PQsetdb(NULL, NULL, NULL, NULL, database);

    /* check to see that the backend connection was successfully made */
    if (PQstatus(conn) == CONNECTION_BAD)
    {
        fprintf(stderr, "Connection to database '%s' failed.\n", database);
        fprintf(stderr, "%s", PQerrorMessage(conn));
        exit_nicely(conn);
    }

    res = PQexec(conn, "begin");
    PQclear(res);

    printf("importing file %s\n", in_filename);
/*  lobjOid = importFile(conn, in_filename); */
    lobjOid = lo_import(conn, in_filename);
/*
    printf("as large object %d.\n", lobjOid);

    printf("picking out bytes 1000-2000 of the large object\n");
    pickout(conn, lobjOid, 1000, 1000);

    printf("overwriting bytes 1000-2000 of the large object with X's\n");
    overwrite(conn, lobjOid, 1000, 1000);
*/

    printf("exporting large object to file %s\n", out_filename);
/*    exportFile(conn, lobjOid, out_filename); */
    lo_export(conn, lobjOid, out_filename);

    res = PQexec(conn, "end");
    PQclear(res);
    PQfinish(conn);
    exit(0);
}
```

Example 31-1. Large Objects with libpq Example Program

Chapter 32.
ECPG - Embedded SQL in C

This chapter describes the embedded SQL package for PostgreSQL. It was written by Linus Tolke (*<linus@epact.se>*) and Michael Meskes (*<meskes@postgresql.org>*). Originally it was written to work with C. It also works with C++, but it does not recognize all C++ constructs yet.

This documentation is quite incomplete. But since this interface is standardized, additional information can be found in many resources about SQL.

32.1. The Concept

An embedded SQL program consists of code written in an ordinary programming language, in this case C, mixed with SQL commands in specially marked sections. To build the program, the source code is first passed through the embedded SQL preprocessor, which converts it to an ordinary C program, and afterwards it can be processed by a C compiler.

Embedded SQL has advantages over other methods for handling SQL commands from C code. First, it takes care of the tedious passing of information to and from variables in your C program. Second, the SQL code in the program is checked at build time for syntactical correctness. Third, embedded SQL in C is specified in the SQL standard and supported by many other SQL database systems. The PostgreSQL implementation is designed to match this standard as much as possible, and it is usually possible to port embedded SQL programs written for other SQL databases to PostgreSQL with relative ease.

As already stated, programs written for the embedded SQL interface are normal C programs with special code inserted to perform database-related actions. This special code always has the form:

```
EXEC SQL ...;
```

These statements syntactically take the place of a C statement. Depending on the particular statement, they can appear at the global level or within a function. Embedded SQL statements follow the case-sensitivity rules of normal SQL code, and not those of C.

The following sections explain all the embedded SQL statements.

32.2. Connecting to the Database Server

One connects to a database using the following statement:

```
EXEC SQL CONNECT TO target [AS connection-name] [USER user-name];
```

The *target* can be specified in the following ways:

- `dbname[@hostname][:port]`
- `tcp:postgresql://hostname[:port][/dbname][?options]`
- `unix:postgresql://hostname[:port][/dbname][?options]`
- an SQL string literal containing one of the above forms
- a reference to a character variable containing one of the above forms (see examples)
- `DEFAULT`

If you specify the connection target literally (that is, not through a variable reference) and you don't quote the value, then the case-insensitivity rules of normal SQL are applied. In that case you can also double-quote the individual parameters separately as needed. In practice, it is probably less error-prone to use a (single-quoted) string literal or a variable reference. The connection target DEFAULT initiates a connection to the default database under the default user name. No separate user name or connection name can be specified in that case.

There are also different ways to specify the user name:

- `username`
- `username/password`
- `username IDENTIFIED BY password`
- `username USING password`

As above, the parameters `username` and `password` can be an SQL identifier, an SQL string literal, or a reference to a character variable.

The `connection-name` is used to handle multiple connections in one program. It can be omitted if a program uses only one connection. The most recently opened connection becomes the current connection, which is used by default when an SQL statement is to be executed (see later in this chapter).

Here are some examples of CONNECT statements:

```
EXEC SQL CONNECT TO mydb@sql.mydomain.com;

EXEC SQL CONNECT TO unix:postgresql://sql.mydomain.com/mydb AS myconnection USER john;
```

```
EXEC SQL BEGIN DECLARE SECTION;
const char *target = "mydb@sql.mydomain.com";
const char *user = "john";
EXEC SQL END DECLARE SECTION;
  ...
EXEC SQL CONNECT TO :target USER :user;
```

The last form makes use of the variant referred to above as character variable reference. You will see in later sections how C variables can be used in SQL statements when you prefix them with a colon.

Be advised that the format of the connection target is not specified in the SQL standard. So if you want to develop portable applications, you might want to use something based on the last example above to encapsulate the connection target string somewhere.

32.3. Closing a Connection

To close a connection, use the following statement:

```
EXEC SQL DISCONNECT [connection];
```

The *connection* can be specified in the following ways:

- `connection-name`
- `DEFAULT`
- `CURRENT`
- `ALL`

If no connection name is specified, the current connection is closed.

It is good style that an application always explicitly disconnect from every connection it opened.

32.4. Running SQL Commands

Any SQL command can be run from within an embedded SQL application. Below are some examples of how to do that.

Creating a table:

```
EXEC SQL CREATE TABLE foo (number integer, ascii char(16));
EXEC SQL CREATE UNIQUE INDEX num1 ON foo(number);
EXEC SQL COMMIT;
```

Inserting rows:

```
EXEC SQL INSERT INTO foo (number, ascii) VALUES (9999, 'doodad');
EXEC SQL COMMIT;
```

Deleting rows:

```
EXEC SQL DELETE FROM foo WHERE number = 9999;
EXEC SQL COMMIT;
```

Single-row select:

```
EXEC SQL SELECT foo INTO :FooBar FROM table1 WHERE ascii = 'doodad';
```

Select using cursors:

```
EXEC SQL DECLARE foo_bar CURSOR FOR
    SELECT number, ascii FROM foo
    ORDER BY ascii;
EXEC SQL OPEN foo_bar;
EXEC SQL FETCH foo_bar INTO :FooBar, DooDad;
...
EXEC SQL CLOSE foo_bar;
EXEC SQL COMMIT;
```

Updates:

```
EXEC SQL UPDATE foo
    SET ascii = 'foobar'
    WHERE number = 9999;
EXEC SQL COMMIT;
```

The tokens of the form :*something* are *host variables*, that is, they refer to variables in the C program. They are explained in *Section 32.6* - page 333.

In the default mode, statements are committed only when EXEC SQL COMMIT is issued. The embedded SQL interface also supports autocommit of transactions (similar to libpq behavior) via the -t command-line option to ecpg (see below) or via the EXEC SQL SET AUTOCOMMIT TO ON statement. In autocommit mode, each command is automatically committed unless it is inside an explicit transaction block. This mode can be explicitly turned off using EXEC SQL SET AUTOCOMMIT TO OFF.

32.5. Choosing a Connection

The SQL statements shown in the previous section are executed on the current connection, that is, the most recently opened one. If an application needs to manage multiple connections, then there are two ways to handle this.

The first option is to explicitly choose a connection for each SQL statement, for example:

```
EXEC SQL AT connection-name SELECT ...;
```

This option is particularly suitable if the application needs to use several connections in mixed order.

If your application uses multiple threads of execution, they cannot share a connection concurrently. You must either explicitly control access to the connection (using mutexes) or use a connection for each thread. If each thread uses its own connection, you will need to use the AT clause to specify which connection the thread will use.

The second option is to execute a statement to switch the current connection. That statement is:

```
EXEC SQL SET CONNECTION connection-name;
```

This option is particularly convenient if many statements are to be executed on the same connection. It is not thread-aware.

32.6. Using Host Variables

In *Section 32.4* - page 331 you saw how you can execute SQL statements from an embedded SQL program. Some of those statements only used fixed values and did not provide a way to insert user-supplied values into statements or have the program process the values returned by the query. Those kinds of statements are not really useful in real applications. This section explains in detail how you can pass data between your C program and the embedded SQL statements using a simple mechanism called *host variables*. In an embedded SQL program we consider the SQL statements to be *guests* in the C program code which is the *host language*. Therefore the variables of the C program are called *host variables*.

32.6.1. Overview

Passing data between the C program and the SQL statements is particularly simple in embedded SQL. Instead of having the program paste the data into the statement, which entails various complications, such as properly quoting the value, you can simply write the name of a C variable into the SQL statement, prefixed by a colon. For example:

```
EXEC SQL INSERT INTO sometable VALUES (:v1, 'foo', :v2);
```

This statements refers to two C variables named v1 and v2 and also uses a regular SQL string literal, to illustrate that you are not restricted to use one kind of data or the other.

This style of inserting C variables in SQL statements works anywhere a value expression is expected in an SQL statement.

32.6.2. Declare Sections

To pass data from the program to the database, for example as parameters in a query, or to pass data from the database back to the program, the C variables that are intended to contain this data need to be declared in specially marked sections, so the embedded SQL preprocessor is made aware of them.

This section starts with:

```
EXEC SQL BEGIN DECLARE SECTION;
```

and ends with:

```
EXEC SQL END DECLARE SECTION;
```

Between those lines, there must be normal C variable declarations, such as:

```
int    x = 4;
char   foo[16], bar[16];
```

As you can see, you can optionally assign an initial value to the variable. The variable's scope is determined by the location of its declaring section within the program. You can also declare variables with the following syntax which implicitly creates a declare section:

```
EXEC SQL int i = 4;
```

You can have as many declare sections in a program as you like.

The declarations are also echoed to the output file as normal C variables, so there's no need to declare them again. Variables that are not intended to be used in SQL commands can be declared normally outside these special sections.

The definition of a structure or union also must be listed inside a DECLARE section. Otherwise the preprocessor cannot handle these types since it does not know the definition.

32.6.3. Different types of host variables

As a host variable you can also use arrays, typedefs, structs and pointers. Moreover there are special types of host variables that exist only in ECPG.

A few examples on host variables:

Arrays

> One of the most common uses of an array declaration is probably the allocation of a char array as in:
>
> ```
> EXEC SQL BEGIN DECLARE SECTION;
>     char str[50];
> EXEC SQL END DECLARE SECTION;
> ```
>
> Note that you have to take care of the length for yourself. If you use this host variable as the target variable of a query which returns a string with more than 49 characters, a buffer overflow occurs.

Typedefs

> Use the typedef keyword to map new types to already existing types.
>
> ```
> EXEC SQL BEGIN DECLARE SECTION;
>     typedef char mychartype[40];
>     typedef long serial_t;
> EXEC SQL END DECLARE SECTION;
> ```

Note that you could also use:

```
EXEC SQL TYPE serial_t IS long;
```

This declaration does not need to be part of a declare section.

Pointers

You can declare pointers to the most common types. Note however that you cannot use pointers as target variables of queries without auto-allocation. See *Section 32.10* - page 365 for more information on auto-allocation.

```
EXEC SQL BEGIN DECLARE SECTION;
    int   *intp;
    char **charp;
EXEC SQL END DECLARE SECTION;
```

Special types of variables

ECPG contains some special types that help you to interact easily with data from the SQL server. For example it has implemented support for the varchar, numeric, date, timestamp, and interval types. *Section 32.8* - page 338 contains basic functions to deal with those types, such that you do not need to send a query to the SQL server just for adding an interval to a timestamp for example.

The special type VARCHAR is converted into a named struct for every variable. A declaration like:

```
VARCHAR var[180];
```

is converted into:

```
struct varchar_var { int len; char arr[180]; } var;
```

This structure is suitable for interfacing with SQL datums of type varchar.

32.6.4. SELECT INTO and FETCH INTO

Now you should be able to pass data generated by your program into an SQL command. But how do you retrieve the results of a query? For that purpose, embedded SQL provides special variants of the usual commands SELECT and FETCH. These commands have a special INTO clause that specifies which host variables the retrieved values are to be stored in.

Here is an example:

```
/*
 * assume this table:
 * CREATE TABLE test1 (a int, b varchar(50));
 */

EXEC SQL BEGIN DECLARE SECTION;
int v1;
VARCHAR v2;
EXEC SQL END DECLARE SECTION;
```

```
. . .
EXEC SQL SELECT a, b INTO :v1, :v2 FROM test;
```

So the INTO clause appears between the select list and the FROM clause. The number of elements in the select list and the list after INTO (also called the target list) must be equal.

Here is an example using the command FETCH:

```
EXEC SQL BEGIN DECLARE SECTION;
int v1;
VARCHAR v2;
EXEC SQL END DECLARE SECTION;

    . . .

EXEC SQL DECLARE foo CURSOR FOR SELECT a, b FROM test;

    . . .

do {
    . . .
    EXEC SQL FETCH NEXT FROM foo INTO :v1, :v2;
    . . .
} while (...);
```

Here the INTO clause appears after all the normal clauses.

Both of these methods only allow retrieving one row at a time. If you need to process result sets that potentially contain more than one row, you need to use a cursor, as shown in the second example.

32.6.5. Indicators

The examples above do not handle null values. In fact, the retrieval examples will raise an error if they fetch a null value from the database. To be able to pass null values to the database or retrieve null values from the database, you need to append a second host variable specification to each host variable that contains data. This second host variable is called the *indicator* and contains a flag that tells whether the datum is null, in which case the value of the real host variable is ignored. Here is an example that handles the retrieval of null values correctly:

```
EXEC SQL BEGIN DECLARE SECTION;
VARCHAR val;
int val_ind;
EXEC SQL END DECLARE SECTION:

    . . .

EXEC SQL SELECT b INTO :val :val_ind FROM test1;
```

The indicator variable `val_ind` will be zero if the value was not null, and it will be negative if the value was null.

The indicator has another function: if the indicator value is positive, it means that the value is not null, but it was truncated when it was stored in the host variable.

32.7. Dynamic SQL

In many cases, the particular SQL statements that an application has to execute are known at the time the application is written. In some cases, however, the SQL statements are composed at run time or provided by an external source. In these cases you cannot embed the SQL statements directly into the C source code, but there is a facility that allows you to call arbitrary SQL statements that you provide in a string variable.

The simplest way to execute an arbitrary SQL statement is to use the command EXECUTE IMMEDIATE. For example:

```
EXEC SQL BEGIN DECLARE SECTION;
const char *stmt = "CREATE TABLE test1 (...);";
EXEC SQL END DECLARE SECTION;

EXEC SQL EXECUTE IMMEDIATE :stmt;
```

You cannot execute statements that retrieve data (e.g., SELECT) this way.

A more powerful way to execute arbitrary SQL statements is to prepare them once and execute the prepared statement as often as you like. It is also possible to prepare a generalized version of a statement and then execute specific versions of it by substituting parameters. When preparing the statement, write question marks where you want to substitute parameters later. For example:

```
EXEC SQL BEGIN DECLARE SECTION;
const char *stmt = "INSERT INTO test1 VALUES(?, ?);";
EXEC SQL END DECLARE SECTION;

EXEC SQL PREPARE mystmt FROM :stmt;
 ...
EXEC SQL EXECUTE mystmt USING 42, 'foobar';
```

If the statement you are executing returns values, then add an INTO clause:

```
EXEC SQL BEGIN DECLARE SECTION;
const char *stmt = "SELECT a, b, c FROM test1 WHERE a > ?";
int v1, v2;
VARCHAR v3;
EXEC SQL END DECLARE SECTION;

EXEC SQL PREPARE mystmt FROM :stmt;
 ...
EXEC SQL EXECUTE mystmt INTO v1, v2, v3 USING 37;
```

An EXECUTE command can have an INTO clause, a USING clause, both, or neither.

When you don't need the prepared statement anymore, you should deallocate it:

```
EXEC SQL DEALLOCATE PREPARE name;
```

32.8. pgtypes library

The pgtypes library maps PostgreSQL database types to C equivalents that can be used in C programs. It also offers functions to do basic calculations with those types within C, i.e., without the help of the PostgreSQL server. See the following example:

```
EXEC SQL BEGIN DECLARE SECTION;
    date date1;
    timestamp ts1, tsout;
    interval iv1;
    char *out;
EXEC SQL END DECLARE SECTION;

PGTYPESdate_today(&date1);
EXEC SQL SELECT started, duration INTO :ts1, :iv1 FROM datetbl WHERE d=:date1;
PGTYPEStimestamp_add_interval(&ts1, &iv1, &tsout);
out = PGTYPEStimestamp_to_asc(&tsout);
printf("Started + duration: %s\n", out);
free(out);
```

32.8.1. The numeric type

The numeric type offers to do calculations with arbitrary precision. See *Section 8.1 - Vol.I* page 138 for the equivalent type in the PostgreSQL server. Because of the arbitrary precision this variable needs to be able to expand and shrink dynamically. That's why you can only create variables on the heap by means of the PGTYPESnumeric_new and PGTYPESnumeric_free functions. The decimal type, which is similar but limited in the precision, can be created on the stack as well as on the heap.

The following functions can be used to work with the numeric type:

PGTYPESnumeric_new

> Request a pointer to a newly allocated numeric variable.

> ```
> numeric *PGTYPESnumeric_new(void);
> ```

PGTYPESnumeric_free

> Free a numeric type, release all of its memory.

> ```
> void PGTYPESnumeric_free(numeric *var);
> ```

PGTYPESnumeric_from_asc

> Parse a numeric type from its string notation.

> ```
> numeric *PGTYPESnumeric_from_asc(char *str, char **endptr);
> ```

Valid formats are for example: -2, .794, +3.44, 592.49E07 or -32.84e-4. If the value could be parsed successfully, a valid pointer is returned, else the NULL pointer. At the moment ecpg always parses the complete string and so it currently does not support to store the address of the first invalid character in *endptr. You can safely set endptr to NULL.

PGTYPESnumeric_to_asc

Returns a pointer to a string allocated by malloc that contains the string representation of the numeric type num.

```
char *PGTYPESnumeric_to_asc(numeric *num, int dscale);
```

The numeric value will be printed with dscale decimal digits, with rounding applied if necessary.

PGTYPESnumeric_add

Add two numeric variables into a third one.

```
int PGTYPESnumeric_add(numeric *var1, numeric *var2, numeric *result);
```

The function adds the variables var1 and var2 into the result variable result. The function returns 0 on success and -1 in case of error.

PGTYPESnumeric_sub

Subtract two numeric variables and return the result in a third one.

```
int PGTYPESnumeric_sub(numeric *var1, numeric *var2, numeric *result);
```

The function subtracts the variable var2 from the variable var1. The result of the operation is stored in the variable result. The function returns 0 on success and -1 in case of error.

PGTYPESnumeric_mul

Multiply two numeric variables and return the result in a third one.

```
int PGTYPESnumeric_mul(numeric *var1, numeric *var2, numeric *result);
```

The function multiplies the variables var1 and var2. The result of the operation is stored in the variable result. The function returns 0 on success and -1 in case of error.

PGTYPESnumeric_div

Divide two numeric variables and return the result in a third one.

```
int PGTYPESnumeric_div(numeric *var1, numeric *var2, numeric *result);
```

The function divides the variables var1 by var2. The result of the operation is stored in the variable result. The function returns 0 on success and -1 in case of error.

`PGTYPESnumeric_cmp`

Compare two numeric variables.

```
int PGTYPESnumeric_cmp(numeric *var1, numeric *var2)
```

This function compares two numeric variables. In case of error, INT_MAX is returned. On success, the function returns one of three possible results:

- 1, if var1 is bigger than var2
- -1, if var1 is smaller than var2
- 0, if var1 and var2 are equal

`PGTYPESnumeric_from_int`

Convert an int variable to a numeric variable.

```
int PGTYPESnumeric_from_int(signed int int_val, numeric *var);
```

This function accepts a variable of type signed int and stores it in the numeric variable var. Upon success, 0 is returned and -1 in case of a failure.

`PGTYPESnumeric_from_long`

Convert a long int variable to a numeric variable.

```
int PGTYPESnumeric_from_long(signed long int long_val, numeric *var);
```

This function accepts a variable of type signed long int and stores it in the numeric variable var. Upon success, 0 is returned and -1 in case of a failure.

`PGTYPESnumeric_copy`

Copy over one numeric variable into another one.

```
int PGTYPESnumeric_copy(numeric *src, numeric *dst);
```

This function copies over the value of the variable that src points to into the variable that dst points to. It returns 0 on success and -1 if an error occurs.

`PGTYPESnumeric_from_double`

Convert a variable of type double to a numeric.

```
int  PGTYPESnumeric_from_double(double d, numeric *dst);
```

This function accepts a variable of type double and stores the result in the variable that dst points to. It returns 0 on success and -1 if an error occurs.

`PGTYPESnumeric_to_double`

Convert a variable of type numeric to double.

```
int PGTYPESnumeric_to_double(numeric *nv, double *dp)
```

The function converts the numeric value from the variable that nv points to into the double variable that dp points to. It returns 0 on success and -1 if an error occurs, including overflow. On overflow, the global variable errno will be set to PGTYPES_NUM_OVERFLOW additionally.

PGTYPESnumeric_to_int

Convert a variable of type numeric to int.

```
int PGTYPESnumeric_to_int(numeric *nv, int *ip);
```

The function converts the numeric value from the variable that nv points to into the integer variable that ip points to. It returns 0 on success and -1 if an error occurs, including overflow. On overflow, the global variable errno will be set to PGTYPES_NUM_OVERFLOW additionally.

PGTYPESnumeric_to_long

Convert a variable of type numeric to long.

```
int PGTYPESnumeric_to_long(numeric *nv, long *lp);
```

The function converts the numeric value from the variable that nv points to into the long integer variable that lp points to. It returns 0 on success and -1 if an error occurs, including overflow. On overflow, the global variable errno will be set to PGTYPES_NUM_OVERFLOW additionally.

PGTYPESnumeric_to_decimal

Convert a variable of type numeric to decimal.

```
int PGTYPESnumeric_to_decimal(numeric *src, decimal *dst);
```

The function converts the numeric value from the variable that src points to into the decimal variable that dst points to. It returns 0 on success and -1 if an error occurs, including overflow. On overflow, the global variable errno will be set to PGTYPES_NUM_OVERFLOW additionally.

PGTYPESnumeric_from_decimal

Convert a variable of type decimal to numeric.

```
int PGTYPESnumeric_from_decimal(decimal *src, numeric *dst);
```

The function converts the decimal value from the variable that src points to into the numeric variable that dst points to. It returns 0 on success and -1 if an error occurs. Since the decimal type is implemented as a limited version of the numeric type, overflow cannot occur with this conversion.

32.8.2. The date type

The date type in C enables your programs to deal with data of the SQL type date. See *Section 8.5 - Vol.I page 148* for the equivalent type in the PostgreSQL server.

The following functions can be used to work with the date type:

PGTYPESdate_from_timestamp

> Extract the date part from a timestamp.
>
> ```
> date PGTYPESdate_from_timestamp(timestamp dt);
> ```
>
> The function receives a timestamp as its only argument and returns the extracted date part from this timestamp.

PGTYPESdate_from_asc

> Parse a date from its textual representation.
>
> ```
> date PGTYPESdate_from_asc(char *str, char **endptr);
> ```
>
> The function receives a C char* string str and a pointer to a C char* string endptr. At the moment ecpg always parses the complete string and so it currently does not support to store the address of the first invalid character in *endptr. You can safely set endptr to NULL.
>
> Note that the function always assumes MDY-formatted dates and there is currently no variable to change that within ecpg.

Table 32-1 shows the allowed input formats.

Input	Result
January 8, 1999	January 8, 1999
1999-01-08	January 8, 1999
1/8/1999	January 8, 1999
1/18/1999	January 18, 1999
01/02/03	February 1, 2003
1999-Jan-08	January 8, 1999
Jan-08-1999	January 8, 1999
08-Jan-1999	January 8, 1999
99-Jan-08	January 8, 1999
08-Jan-99	January 8, 1999
08-Jan-06	January 8, 2006
Jan-08-99	January 8, 1999
19990108	ISO 8601; January 8, 1999

Input	Result
990108	ISO 8601; January 8, 1999
1999.008	year and day of year
J2451187	Julian day
January 8, 99 BC	year 99 before the Common Era

Table 32-1. Valid input formats for PGTYPESdate_from_asc

PGTYPESdate_to_asc

Return the textual representation of a date variable.

```
char *PGTYPESdate_to_asc(date dDate);
```

The function receives the date dDate as its only parameter. It will output the date in the form 1999-01-18, i.e., in the YYYY-MM-DD format.

PGTYPESdate_julmdy

Extract the values for the day, the month and the year from a variable of type date.

```
void PGTYPESdate_julmdy(date d, int *mdy);
```

The function receives the date d and a pointer to an array of 3 integer values mdy. The variable name indicates the sequential order: mdy[0] will be set to contain the number of the month, mdy[1] will be set to the value of the day and mdy[2] will contain the year.

PGTYPESdate_mdyjul

Create a date value from an array of 3 integers that specify the day, the month and the year of the date.

```
void PGTYPESdate_mdyjul(int *mdy, date *jdate);
```

The function receives the array of the 3 integers (mdy) as its first argument and as its second argument a pointer to a variable of type date that should hold the result of the operation.

PGTYPESdate_dayofweek

Return a number representing the day of the week for a date value.

```
int PGTYPESdate_dayofweek(date d);
```

The function receives the date variable d as its only argument and returns an integer that indicates the day of the week for this date.

- 0 - Sunday
- 1 - Monday
- 2 - Tuesday
- 3 - Wednesday

- 4 - Thursday
- 5 - Friday
- 6 - Saturday

`PGTYPESdate_today`

Get the current date.

`void PGTYPESdate_today(date *d);`

The function receives a pointer to a date variable (d) that it sets to the current date.

`PGTYPESdate_fmt_asc`

Convert a variable of type date to its textual representation using a format mask.

`int PGTYPESdate_fmt_asc(date dDate, char *fmtstring, char *outbuf);`

The function receives the date to convert (dDate), the format mask (fmtstring) and the string that will hold the textual representation of the date (outbuf).

On success, 0 is returned and a negative value if an error occurred.

The following literals are the field specifiers you can use:

- dd - The number of the day of the month.
- mm - The number of the month of the year.
- yy - The number of the year as a two digit number.
- yyyy - The number of the year as a four digit number.
- ddd - The name of the day (abbreviated).
- mmm - The name of the month (abbreviated).

All other characters are copied 1:1 to the output string.

Table 32-2 indicates a few possible formats. This will give you an idea of how to use this function. All output lines are based on the same date: November 23, 1959.

fmt	result
mmddyy	112359
ddmmyy	231159
yymmdd	591123
yy/mm/dd	59/11/23
yy mm dd	59 11 23
yy.mm.dd	59.11.23
.mm.yyyy.dd.	.11.1959.23.
mmm. dd, yyyy	Nov. 23, 1959

fmt	result
mmm dd yyyy	Nov 23 1959
yyyy dd mm	1959 23 11
ddd, mmm. dd, yyyy	Mon, Nov. 23, 1959
(ddd) mmm. dd, yyyy	(Mon) Nov. 23, 1959

Table 32-2. Valid input formats for PGTYPESdate_fmt_asc

PGTYPESdate_defmt_asc

Use a format mask to convert a C char* string to a value of type date.

```
int PGTYPESdate_defmt_asc(date *d, char *fmt, char *str);
```

The function receives a pointer to the date value that should hold the result of the operation (d), the format mask to use for parsing the date (fmt) and the C char* string containing the textual representation of the date (str). The textual representation is expected to match the format mask. However you do not need to have a 1:1 mapping of the string to the format mask. The function only analyzes the sequential order and looks for the literals yy or yyyy that indicate the position of the year, mm to indicate the position of the month and dd to indicate the position of the day.

Table 32-3 indicates a few possible formats. This will give you an idea of how to use this function.

fmt	str	result
ddmmyy	21-2-54	1954-02-21
ddmmyy	2-12-54	1954-12-02
ddmmyy	20111954	1954-11-20
ddmmyy	130464	1964-04-13
mmm.dd.yyyy	MAR-12-1967	1967-03-12
yy/mm/dd	1954, February 3rd	1954-02-03
mmm.dd.yyyy	041269	1969-04-12
yy/mm/dd	In the year 2525, in the month of July, mankind will be alive on the 28th day	2525-07-28
dd-mm-yy	I said on the 28th of July in the year 2525	2525-07-28
mmm.dd.yyyy	9/14/58	1958-09-14
yy/mm/dd	47/03/29	1947-03-^
mmm.dd.yyyy	oct 28 1975	197^
mmddyy	Nov 14th, 1985	

Table 32-3. Valid input formats for rdefmtdate

346

32.8.3. The timestamp type

The timestamp type in C enables your programs to deal with data of the SQL type timestamp. See *Section 8.5* - Vol.I page 148 for the equivalent type in the PostgreSQL server.

The following functions can be used to work with the timestamp type:

PGTYPEStimestamp_from_asc

Parse a timestamp from its textual representation into a timestamp variable.

timestamp PGTYPEStimestamp_from_asc(char *str, char **endptr);

The function receives the string to parse (str) and a pointer to a C char* (endptr). At the moment ecpg always parses the complete string and so it currently does not support to store the address of the first invalid character in *endptr. You can safely set endptr to NULL.

The function returns the parsed timestamp on success. On error, PGTYPESInvalidTimestamp is returned and errno is set to PGTYPES_TS_BAD_TIMESTAMP. See *PGTYPESInvalidTimestamp* - page 352 for important notes on this value.

In general, the input string can contain any combination of an allowed date specification, a whitespace character and an allowed time specification. Note that timezones are not supported by ecpg. It can parse them but does not apply any calculation as the PostgreSQL server does for example. Timezone specifiers are silently discarded.

Table 32-4 contains a few examples for input strings.

Input	Result
1999-01-08 04:05:06	1999-01-08 04:05:06
January 8 04:05:06 1999 PST	1999-01-08 04:05:06
1999-Jan-08 04:05:06.789-8	1999-01-08 04:05:06.789 (time zone specifier ignored)
J2451187 04:05-08:00	1999-01-08 04:05:00 (time zone specifier ignored)

Table 32-4. Valid input formats for PGTYPEStimestamp_from_asc

PGTYPEStimestamp_to_asc

Converts a date to a C char* string.

char *PGTYPEStimestamp_to_asc(timestamp tstamp);

The function receives the timestamp tstamp as its only argument and returns an allocated string that contains the textual representation of the timestamp.

`PGTYPEStimestamp_current`

Retrieve the current timestamp.

`void PGTYPEStimestamp_current(timestamp *ts);`

The function retrieves the current timestamp and saves it into the timestamp variable that ts points to.

`PGTYPEStimestamp_fmt_asc`

Convert a timestamp variable to a C char* using a format mask.

`int PGTYPEStimestamp_fmt_asc(timestamp *ts, char *output, int str_len, char *fmtstr);`

The function receives a pointer to the timestamp to convert as its first argument (ts), a pointer to the output buffer (output), the maximal length that has been allocated for the output buffer (str_len) and the format mask to use for the conversion (fmtstr).

Upon success, the function returns 0 and a negative value if an error occurred.

You can use the following format specifiers for the format mask. The format specifiers are the same ones that are used in the strftime function in libc. Any non-format specifier will be copied into the output buffer.

- `%A` - is replaced by national representation of the full weekday name.
- `%a` - is replaced by national representation of the abbreviated weekday name.
- `%B` - is replaced by national representation of the full month name.
- `%b` - is replaced by national representation of the abbreviated month name.
- `%C` - is replaced by (year / 100) as decimal number; single digits are preceded by a zero.
- `%c` - is replaced by national representation of time and date.
- `%D` - is equivalent to `%m/%d/%y`.
- `%d` - is replaced by the day of the month as a decimal number (01-31).
- `%E*` `%O*` - POSIX locale extensions. The sequences `%Ec` `%EC` `%Ex` `%EX` `%Ey` `%EY` `%Od` `%Oe` `%OH` `%OI` `%Om` `%OM` `%OS` `%Ou` `%OU` `%OV` `%Ow` `%OW` `%Oy` are supposed to provide alternative representations.
- Additionally `%OB` implemented to represent alternative months names (used standalone, without day mentioned).
- `%e` - is replaced by the day of month as a decimal number (1-31); single digits are preceded by a blank.
- `%F` - is equivalent to `%Y-%m-%d`.
- `%G` - is replaced by a year as a decimal number with century. This year is the one that contains the greater part of the week (Monday as the first day of the week).

- %g - is replaced by the same year as in %G, but as a decimal number without century (00-99).
- %H - is replaced by the hour (24-hour clock) as a decimal number (00-23).
- %h - the same as %b.
- %I - is replaced by the hour (12-hour clock) as a decimal number (01-12).
- %j - is replaced by the day of the year as a decimal number (001-366).
- %k - is replaced by the hour (24-hour clock) as a decimal number (0-23); single digits are preceded by a blank.
- %l - is replaced by the hour (12-hour clock) as a decimal number (1-12); single digits are preceded by a blank.
- %M - is replaced by the minute as a decimal number (00-59).
- %m - is replaced by the month as a decimal number (01-12).
- %n - is replaced by a newline.
- %O* - the same as %E*.
- %p - is replaced by national representation of either "ante meridiem" or "post meridiem" as appropriate.
- %R - is equivalent to %H:%M.
- %r - is equivalent to %I:%M:%S %p.
- %S - is replaced by the second as a decimal number (00-60).
- %s - is replaced by the number of seconds since the Epoch, UTC.
- %T - is equivalent to %H:%M:%S
- %t - is replaced by a tab.
- %U - is replaced by the week number of the year (Sunday as the first day of the week) as a decimal number (00-53).
- %u - is replaced by the weekday (Monday as the first day of the week) as a decimal number (1-7).
- %V - is replaced by the week number of the year (Monday as the first day of the week) as a decimal number (01-53). If the week containing January 1 has four or more days in the new year, then it is week 1; otherwise it is the last week of the previous year, and the next week is week 1.
- %v - is equivalent to %e-%b-%Y.
- %W - is replaced by the week number of the year (Monday as the first day of the week) as a decimal number (00-53).
- %w - is replaced by the weekday (Sunday as the first day of the week) as a decimal number (0-6).

- %X - is replaced by national representation of the time.
- %x - is replaced by national representation of the date.
- %Y - is replaced by the year with century as a decimal number.
- %y - is replaced by the year without century as a decimal number (00-99).
- %Z - is replaced by the time zone name.
- %z - is replaced by the time zone offset from UTC; a leading plus sign stands for east of UTC, a minus sign for west of UTC, hours and minutes follow with two digits each and no delimiter between them (common form for RFC 822 date headers).
- %+ - is replaced by national representation of the date and time.
- %-* - GNU libc extension. Do not do any padding when performing numerical outputs.
- $_* - GNU libc extension. Explicitly specify space for padding.
- %0* - GNU libc extension. Explicitly specify zero for padding.
- %% - is replaced by %.

PGTYPEStimestamp_sub

Subtract one timestamp from another one and save the result in a variable of type interval.

```
int PGTYPEStimestamp_sub(timestamp *ts1, timestamp *ts2, interval *iv);
```

The function will subtract the timestamp variable that ts2 points to from the timestamp variable that ts1 points to and will store the result in the interval variable that iv points to.

Upon success, the function returns 0 and a negative value if an error occurred.

PGTYPEStimestamp_defmt_asc

Parse a timestamp value from its textual representation using a formatting mask.

```
int PGTYPEStimestamp_defmt_asc(char *str, char *fmt, timestamp *d);
```

The function receives the textual representation of a timestamp in the variable str as well as the formatting mask to use in the variable fmt. The result will be stored in the variable that d points to.

If the formatting mask fmt is NULL, the function will fall back to the default formatting mask which is %Y-%m-%d %H:%M:%S.

This is the reverse function to *PGTYPEStimestamp_fmt_asc* - page 346. See the documentation there in order to find out about the possible formatting mask entries.

PGTYPEStimestamp_add_interval

>   Add an interval variable to a timestamp variable.

>   int PGTYPEStimestamp_add_interval(timestamp *tin, interval *span, timestamp *tout);

>   The function receives a pointer to a timestamp variable tin and a pointer to an interval variable span. It adds the interval to the timestamp and saves the resulting timestamp in the variable that tout points to.

>   Upon success, the function returns 0 and a negative value if an error occurred.

PGTYPEStimestamp_sub_interval

>   Subtract an interval variable from a timestamp variable.

>   int PGTYPEStimestamp_sub_interval(timestamp *tin, interval *span, timestamp *tout);

>   The function subtracts the interval variable that span points to from the timestamp variable that tin points to and saves the result into the variable that tout points to.

>   Upon success, the function returns 0 and a negative value if an error occurred.

32.8.4. The interval type

The interval type in C enables your programs to deal with data of the SQL type interval. See *Section 8.5 - Vol.I page 148* for the equivalent type in the PostgreSQL server.

The following functions can be used to work with the interval type:

PGTYPESinterval_new

>   Return a pointer to a newly allocated interval variable.

>   >   interval *PGTYPESinterval_new(void);

PGTYPESinterval_free

>   Release the memory of a previously allocated interval variable.

>   >   void PGTYPESinterval_new(interval *intvl);

PGTYPESinterval_from_asc

>   Parse an interval from its textual representation.

>   >   interval *PGTYPESinterval_from_asc(char *str, char **endptr);

>   The function parses the input string str and returns a pointer to an allocated interval variable. At the moment ecpg always parses the complete string and so it currently does not support to store the address of the first invalid character in *endptr. You can safely set endptr to NULL.

PGTYPESinterval_to_asc

>   Convert a variable of type interval to its textual representation.

>   >   char *PGTYPESinterval_to_asc(interval *span);

The function converts the interval variable that span points to into a C char*. The output looks like this example: @ 1 day 12 hours 59 mins 10 secs.

PGTYPESinterval_copy

Copy a variable of type interval.

```
int PGTYPESinterval_copy(interval *intvlsrc, interval *intvldest);
```

The function copies the interval variable that intvlsrc points to into the variable that intvldest points to. Note that you need to allocate the memory for the destination variable before.

32.8.5. The decimal type

The decimal type is similar to the numeric type. However it is limited to a maximal precision of 30 significant digits. In contrast to the numeric type which can be created on the heap only, the decimal type can be created either on the stack or on the heap (by means of the functions PGTYPESdecimal_new() and PGTYPESdecimal_free(). There are a lot of other functions that deal with the decimal type in the Informix compatibility mode described in *Section 32.9* - page 352.

The following functions can be used to work with the decimal type and are not only contained in the libcompat library.

PGTYPESdecimal_new

Request a pointer to a newly allocated decimal variable.

```
decimal *PGTYPESdecimal_new(void);
```

PGTYPESdecimal_free

Free a decimal type, release all of its memory.

```
void PGTYPESdecimal_free(decimal *var);
```

32.8.6. errno values of pgtypeslib

PGTYPES_NUM_BAD_NUMERIC

An argument should contain a numeric variable (or point to a numeric variable) but in fact its in-memory representation was invalid.

PGTYPES_NUM_OVERFLOW

An overflow occurred. Since the numeric type can deal with almost arbitrary precision, converting a numeric variable into other types might cause overflow.

PGTYPES_NUM_OVERFLOW

An underflow occurred. Since the numeric type can deal with almost arbitrary precision, converting a numeric variable into other types might cause underflow.

PGTYPES_NUM_DIVIDE_ZERO

A division by zero has been attempted.

PGTYPES_DATE_BAD_DATE

PGTYPES_DATE_ERR_EARGS

PGTYPES_DATE_ERR_ENOSHORTDATE

PGTYPES_INTVL_BAD_INTERVAL

PGTYPES_DATE_ERR_ENOTDMY

PGTYPES_DATE_BAD_DAY

PGTYPES_DATE_BAD_MONTH

PGTYPES_TS_BAD_TIMESTAMP

32.8.7. Special constants of pgtypeslib

PGTYPESInvalidTimestamp

A value of type timestamp representing an invalid time stamp. This is returned by the function PGTYPEStimestamp_from_asc on parse error. Note that due to the internal representation of the timestamp datatype, PGTYPESInvalidTimestamp is also a valid timestamp at the same time. It is set to 1899-12-31 23:59:59. In order to detect errors, make sure that your application does not only test for PGTYPESInvalidTimestamp but also for errno != 0 after each call to PGTYPEStimestamp_from_asc.

32.9. Informix compatibility mode

ecpg can be run in a so-called *Informix compatibility mode*. If this mode is active, it tries to behave as if it were the Informix precompiler for Informix E/SQL. Generally spoken this will allow you to use the dollar sign instead of the EXEC SQL primitive to introduce embedded SQL commands.:

```
$int j = 3;
$CONNECT TO :dbname;
$CREATE TABLE test(i INT PRIMARY KEY, j INT);
$INSERT INTO test(i, j) VALUES (7, :j);
$COMMIT;
```

There are two compatiblity modes: INFORMIX, INFORMIX_SE

When linking programs that use this compatibility mode, remember to link against libcompat that is shipped with ecpg.

Besides the previously explained syntactic sugar, the Informix compatibility mode ports some functions for input, output and transformation of data as well as embedded SQL statements known from E/SQL to ecpg.

Informix compatibility mode is closely connected to the pgtypeslib library of ecpg. pgtypeslib maps SQL data types to data types within the C host program and most of the additional functions of the Informix compatibility mode allow you to operate on those C host program types. Note however that the extent of the compatibility is limited. It does not try to copy Informix behaviour; it allows you to do more or less the same operations and gives you functions that have the same name and the same basic behavior but it is no drop-in replacement if you are using Informix at the moment. Moreover, some of the data types are different. For example, PostgreSQL's datetime and interval types do not know about ranges like for example YEAR TO MINUTE so you won't find support in ecpg for that either.

32.9.1. Additional embedded SQL statements

CLOSE DATABASE

This statement closes the current connection. In fact, this is a synonym for ecpg's DISCONNECT CURRENT.:

```
$CLOSE DATABASE;                          /* close the current connection */
EXEC SQL CLOSE DATABASE;
```

32.9.2. Additional functions

decadd

Add two decimal type values.

```
int decadd(decimal *arg1, decimal *arg2, decimal *sum);
```

The function receives a pointer to the first operand of type decimal (arg1), a pointer to the second operand of type decimal (arg2) and a pointer to a value of type decimal that will contain the sum (sum). On success, the function returns 0. ECPG_INFORMIX_NUM_OVERFLOW is returned in case of overflow and ECPG_INFORMIX_NUM_UNDERFLOW in case of underflow. -1 is returned for other failures and errno is set to the respective errno number of the pgtypeslib.

deccmp

Compare two variables of type decimal.

```
int deccmp(decimal *arg1, decimal *arg2);
```

The function receives a pointer to the first decimal value (arg1), a pointer to the second decimal value (arg2) and returns an integer value that indicates which is the bigger value.

- 1, if the value that arg1 points to is bigger than the value that var2 points to
- -1, if the value that arg1 points to is smaller than the value that arg2 points to
- 0, if the value that arg1 points to and the value that arg2 points to are equal

deccopy

Copy a decimal value.

```
void deccopy(decimal *src, decimal *target);
```

The function receives a pointer to the decimal value that should be copied as the first argument (src) and a pointer to the target structure of type decimal (target) as the second argument.

deccvasc

Convert a value from its ASCII representation into a decimal type.

```
int deccvasc(char *cp, int len, decimal *np);
```

The function receives a pointer to string that contains the string representation of the number to be converted (cp) as well as its length len. np is a pointer to the decimal value that saves the result of the operation.

Valid formats are for example: -2, .794, +3.44, 592.49E07 or -32.84e-4.

The function returns 0 on success. If overflow or underflow occurred, ECPG_INFORMIX_NUM_OVERFLOW or ECPG_INFORMIX_NUM_UNDERFLOW is returned. If the ASCII representation could not be parsed, ECPG_INFORMIX_BAD_NUMERIC is returned or ECPG_INFORMIX_BAD_EXPONENT if this problem occurred while parsing the exponent.

deccvdbl

Convert a value of type double to a value of type decimal.

```
int deccvdbl(double dbl, decimal *np);
```

The function receives the variable of type double that should be converted as its first argument (dbl). As the second argument (np), the function receives a pointer to the decimal variable that should hold the result of the operation.

The function returns 0 on success and a negative value if the conversion failed.

deccvint

Convert a value of type int to a value of type decimal.

```
int deccvint(int in, decimal *np);
```

The function receives the variable of type int that should be converted as its first argument (in). As the second argument (np), the function receives a pointer to the decimal variable that should hold the result of the operation.

The function returns 0 on success and a negative value if the conversion failed.

deccvlong

Convert a value of type long to a value of type decimal.

```
int deccvlong(long lng, decimal *np);
```

The function receives the variable of type long that should be converted as its first argument (lng). As the second argument (np), the function receives a pointer to the decimal variable that should hold the result of the operation.

The function returns 0 on success and a negative value if the conversion failed.

decdiv

Divide two variables of type decimal.

```
int decdiv(decimal *n1, decimal *n2, decimal *result);
```

The function receives pointers to the variables that are the first (n1) and the second (n2) operands and calculates n1/n2. result is a pointer to the variable that should hold the result of the operation.

On success, 0 is returned and a negative value if the division fails. If overflow or underflow occurred, the function returns ECPG_INFORMIX_NUM_OVERFLOW or ECPG_INFORMIX_NUM_UNDERFLOW respectively. If an attempt to divide by zero is observed, the function returns ECPG_INFORMIX_DIVIDE_ZERO.

decmul

Multiply two decimal values.

```
int decmul(decimal *n1, decimal *n2, decimal *result);
```

The function receives pointers to the variables that are the first (n1) and the second (n2) operands and calculates n1*n2. result is a pointer to the variable that should hold the result of the operation.

On success, 0 is returned and a negative value if the multiplication fails. If overflow or underflow occurred, the function returns ECPG_INFORMIX_NUM_OVERFLOW or ECPG_INFORMIX_NUM_UNDERFLOW respectively.

decsub

Subtract one decimal value from another.

```
int decsub(decimal *n1, decimal *n2, decimal *result);
```

The function receives pointers to the variables that are the first (n1) and the second (n2) operands and calculates n1-n2. result is a pointer to the variable that should hold the result of the operation.

On success, 0 is returned and a negative value if the subtraction fails. If overflow or underflow occurred, the function returns ECPG_INFORMIX_NUM_OVERFLOW or ECPG_INFORMIX_NUM_UNDERFLOW respectively.

dectoasc

Convert a variable of type decimal to its ASCII representation in a C char* string.

```
int dectoasc(decimal *np, char *cp, int len, int right)
```

The function receives a pointer to a variable of type decimal (np) that it converts to its textual representation. cp is the buffer that should hold the result of the operation. The parameter right specifies, how many digits right of the decimal point should be included in the output. The result will be rounded to this number of decimal digits. Setting right to -1 indicates that all available decimal digits should be included in the output. If the length of the output buffer, which is indicated by len is not sufficient to hold the textual representation including the trailing NUL character, only a single * character is stored in the result and -1 is returned.

The function returns either -1 if the buffer cp was too small or ECPG_INFORMIX_OUT_OF_MEMORY if memory was exhausted.

dectodbl

Convert a variable of type decimal to a double.

```
int dectodbl(decimal *np, double *dblp);
```

The function receives a pointer to the decimal value to convert (np) and a pointer to the double variable that should hold the result of the operation (dblp).

On success, 0 is returned and a negative value if the conversion failed.

dectoint

Convert a variable to type decimal to an integer.

```
int dectoint(decimal *np, int *ip);
```

The function receives a pointer to the decimal value to convert (np) and a pointer to the integer variable that should hold the result of the operation (ip).

On success, 0 is returned and a negative value if the conversion failed. If an overflow occurred, ECPG_INFORMIX_NUM_OVERFLOW is returned.

Note that the ecpg implementation differs from the Informix implementation. Informix limits an integer to the range from -32767 to 32767, while the limits in the ecpg implementation depend on the architecture (-INT_MAX .. INT_MAX).

dectolong

Convert a variable to type decimal to a long integer.

```
int dectolong(decimal *np, long *lngp);
```

The function receives a pointer to the decimal value to convert (np) and a pointer to the long variable that should hold the result of the operation (lngp).

On success, 0 is returned and a negative value if the conversion failed. If an overflow occurred, ECPG_INFORMIX_NUM_OVERFLOW is returned.

Note that the ecpg implementation differs from the Informix implementation. Informix limits a long integer to the range from -2,147,483,647 to 2,147,483,647, while the limits in the ecpg implementation depend on the architecture (-LONG_MAX .. LONG_MAX).

rdatestr

Converts a date to a C char* string.

```
int rdatestr(date d, char *str);
```

The function receives two arguments, the first one is the date to convert (d and the second one is a pointer to the target string. The output format is always yyyy-mm-dd, so you need to allocate at least 11 bytes (including the NUL-terminator) for the string.

The function returns 0 on success and a negative value in case of error.

Note that ecpg's implementation differs from the Informix implementation. In Informix the format can be influenced by setting environment variables. In ecpg however, you cannot change the output format.

rstrdate

Parse the textual representation of a date.

```
int rstrdate(char *str, date *d);
```

The function receives the textual representation of the date to convert (str) and a pointer to a variable of type date (d). This function does not allow you to specify a format mask. It uses the default format mask of Informix which is mm/dd/yyyy. Internally, this function is implemented by means of rdefmtdate. Therefore, rstrdate is not faster and if you have the choice you should opt for rdefmtdate which allows you to specify the format mask explicitly.

The function returns the same values as rdefmtdate.

rtoday

Get the current date.

```
void rtoday(date *d);
```

The function receives a pointer to a date variable (d) that it sets to the current date.

Internally this function uses the *PGTYPESdate_today* - page 342 function.

rjulmdy

Extract the values for the day, the month and the year from a variable of type date.

```
int rjulmdy(date d, short mdy[3]);
```

The function receives the date d and a pointer to an array of 3 short integer values mdy. The variable name indicates the sequential order: mdy[0] will be set to contain the number of the month, mdy[1] will be set to the value of the day and mdy[2] will contain the year.

The function always returns 0 at the moment.

Internally the function uses the *PGTYPESdate_julmdy* - page 342 function.

rdefmtdate

Use a format mask to convert a character string to a value of type date.

```
int rdefmtdate(date *d, char *fmt, char *str);
```

The function receives a pointer to the date value that should hold the result of the operation (d), the format mask to use for parsing the date (fmt) and the C char* string containing the textual representation of the date (str). The textual representation is expected to match the format mask. However you do not need to have a 1:1 mapping of the string to the format mask. The function only analyzes the sequential order and looks for the literals yy or yyyy that indicate the position of the year, mm to indicate the position of the month and dd to indicate the position of the day.

The function returns the following values:

- 0 - The function terminated successfully.
- ECPG_INFORMIX_ENOSHORTDATE - The date does not contain delimiters between day, month and year. In this case the input string must be exactly 6 or 8 bytes long but isn't.
- ECPG_INFORMIX_ENOTDMY - The format string did not correctly indicate the sequential order of year, month and day.
- ECPG_INFORMIX_BAD_DAY - The input string does not contain a valid day.
- ECPG_INFORMIX_BAD_MONTH - The input string does not contain a valid month.
- ECPG_INFORMIX_BAD_YEAR - The input string does not contain a valid year.

Internally this function is implemented to use the *PGTYPESdate_defmt_asc* - page 342 function. See the reference there for a table of example input.

rfmtdate

Convert a variable of type date to its textual representation using a format mask.

```
int rfmtdate(date d, char *fmt, char *str);
```

The function receives the date to convert (d), the format mask (fmt) and the string that will hold the textual representation of the date (str).

On success, 0 is returned and a negative value if an error occurred.

Internally this function uses the *PGTYPESdate_fmt_asc* - page 342 function, see the reference there for examples.

rmdyjul

Create a date value from an array of 3 short integers that specify the day, the month and the year of the date.

```
int rmdyjul(short mdy[3], date *d);
```

The function receives the array of the 3 short integers (mdy) and a pointer to a variable of type date that should hold the result of the operation.

Currently the function returns always 0.

Internally the function is implemented to use the function *PGTYPESdate_mdyjul* - page 342.

rdayofweek

Return a number representing the day of the week for a date value.

```
int rdayofweek(date d);
```

The function receives the date variable d as its only argument and returns an integer that indicates the day of the week for this date.

- 0 - Sunday
- 1 - Monday
- 2 - Tuesday
- 3 - Wednesday
- 4 - Thursday
- 5 - Friday
- 6 - Saturday

Internally the function is implemented to use the function *PGTYPESdate_dayofweek* – page 342.

dtcurrent

Retrieve the current timestamp.

```
void dtcurrent(timestamp *ts);
```

The function retrieves the current timestamp and saves it into the timestamp variable that ts points to.

dtcvasc

Parses a timestamp from its textual representation in ANSI standard into a timestamp variable.

```
int dtcvasc(char *str, timestamp *ts);
```

The function receives the string to parse (str) and a pointer to the timestamp variable that should hold the result of the operation (ts).

The function returns 0 on success and a negative value in case of error.

Internally this function uses the *PGTYPEStimestamp_from_asc* - page 346 function. See the reference there for a table with example inputs.

dtcvfmtasc

Parses a timestamp from its textual representation in ANSI standard using a format mask into a timestamp variable.

```
dtcvfmtasc(char *inbuf, char *fmtstr, timestamp *dtvalue)
```

The function receives the string to parse (inbuf), the format mask to use (fmtstr) and a pointer to the timestamp variable that should hold the result of the operation (ts).

This functions is implemented by means of the *PGTYPEStimestamp_defmt_asc* - page 346. See the documentation there for a list of format specifiers that can be used.

The function returns 0 on success and a negative value in case of error.

dtsub

Subtract one timestamp from another and return a variable of type interval.

```
int dtsub(timestamp *ts1, timestamp *ts2, interval *iv);
```

The function will subtract the timestamp variable that ts2 points to from the timestamp variable that ts1 points to and will store the result in the interval variable that iv points to.

Upon success, the function returns 0 and a negative value if an error occurred.

dttoasc

Convert a timestamp variable to a C char* string.

```
int dttoasc(timestamp *ts, char *output);
```

The function receives a pointer to the timestamp variable to convert (ts) and the string that should hold the result of the operation output). It converts ts to its textual representation in the ANSI SQL standard which is defined to be YYYY-MM-DD HH:MM:SS.

Upon success, the function returns 0 and a negative value if an error occurred.

`dttofmtasc`

Convert a timestamp variable to a C char* using a format mask.

```
int dttofmtasc(timestamp *ts, char *output, int str_len, char *fmtstr);
```

The function receives a pointer to the timestamp to convert as its first argument (ts), a pointer to the output buffer (output), the maximal length that has been allocated for the output buffer (str_len) and the format mask to use for the conversion (fmtstr).

Upon success, the function returns 0 and a negative value if an error occurred.

Internally, this function uses the *PGTYPEStimestamp_fmt_asc* - page 346 function. See the reference there for information on what format mask specifiers can be used.

`intoasc`

Convert an interval variable to a C char* string.

```
int intoasc(interval *i, char *str);
```

The function receives a pointer to the interval variable to convert (i) and the string that should hold the result of the operation str). It converts i to its textual representation in the ANSI SQL standard which is defined to be YYYY-MM-DD HH:MM:SS.

Upon success, the function returns 0 and a negative value if an error occurred.

`rfmtlong`

Convert a long integer value to its textual representation using a format mask.

```
int rfmtlong(long lng_val, char *fmt, char *outbuf);
```

The function receives the long value lng_val, the format mask fmt and a pointer to the output buffer outbuf. It converts the long value according to the format mask to its textual representation.

The format mask can be composed of the following format specifying characters:

- * (asterisk) - if this position would be blank otherwise, fill it with an asterisk.
- & (ampersand) - if this position would be blank otherwise, fill it with a zero.
- # - turn leading zeroes into blanks.
- < - left-justify the number in the string.
- , (comma) - group numbers of four or more digits into groups of three digits separated by a comma.
- . (period) - this character separates the whole-number part of the number from the fractional part.
- - (minus) - the minus sign appears if the number is a negative value.

- + (plus) - the plus sign appears if the number is a positive value.
- (- this replaces the minus sign in front of the negative number. The minus sign will not appear.
-) - this character replaces the minus and is printed behind the negative value.
- $ - the currency symbol.

rupshift

Convert a string to upper case.

```
void rupshift(char *str);
```

The function receives a pointer to the string and transforms every lower case character to upper case.

byleng

Return the number of characters in a string without counting trailing blanks.

```
int byleng(char *str, int len);
```

The function expects a fixed-length string as its first argument (str) and its length as its second argument (len). It returns the number of significant characters, that is the length of the string without trailing blanks.

ldchar

Copy a fixed-length string into a null-terminated string.

```
void ldchar(char *src, int len, char *dest);
```

The function receives the fixed-length string to copy (src), its length (len) and a pointer to the destination memory (dest). Note that you need to reserve at least len+1 bytes for the string that dest points to. The function copies at most len bytes to the new location (less if the source string has trailing blanks) and adds the null-terminator.

rgetmsg

```
int rgetmsg(int msgnum, char *s, int maxsize);
```

This function exists but is not implemented at the moment!

rtypalign

```
int rtypalign(int offset, int type);
```

This function exists but is not implemented at the moment!

rtypmsize

```
int rtypmsize(int type, int len);
```

This function exists but is not implemented at the moment!

rtypwidth

```
int rtypwidth(int sqltype, int sqllen);
```

This function exists but is not implemented at the moment!

rsetnull

Set a variable to NULL.

```
int rsetnull(int t, char *ptr);
```

The function receives an integer that indicates the type of the variable and a pointer to the variable itself that is casted to a C char* pointer.

The following types exist:

- CCHARTYPE - For a variable of type char or char*
- CSHORTTYPE - For a variable of type short int
- CINTTYPE - For a variable of type int
- CBOOLTYPE - For a variable of type boolean
- CFLOATTYPE - For a variable of type float
- CLONGTYPE - For a variable of type long
- CDOUBLETYPE - For a variable of type double
- CDECIMALTYPE - For a variable of type decimal
- CDATETYPE - For a variable of type date
- CDTIMETYPE - For a variable of type timestamp

Here is an example of a call to this function:

```
$char c[] = "abc        ";
$short s = 17;
$int i = -74874;

rsetnull(CCHARTYPE, (char *) c);
rsetnull(CSHORTTYPE, (char *) &s);
rsetnull(CINTTYPE, (char *) &i);
```

risnull

Test if a variable is NULL.

```
int risnull(int t, char *ptr);
```

The function receives the type of the variable to test (t) as well a pointer to this variable (ptr). Note that the latter needs to be casted to a char*. See the function *rsetnull* - page 353 for a list of possible variable types.

Here is an example of how to use this function:

```
$char c[] = "abc        ";
$short s = 17;
$int i = -74874;

risnull(CCHARTYPE, (char *) c);
risnull(CSHORTTYPE, (char *) &s);
risnull(CINTTYPE, (char *) &i);
```

32.9.3. Additional constants

Note that all constants here describe errors and all of them are defined to represent negative values. In the descriptions of the different constants you can also find the value that the constants represent in the current implementation. However you should not rely on this number. You can however rely on the fact all of them are defined to represent negative values.

ECPG_INFORMIX_NUM_OVERFLOW

Functions return this value if an overflow occurred in a calculation. Internally it is defined to -1200 (the Informix definition).

ECPG_INFORMIX_NUM_UNDERFLOW

Functions return this value if an underflow occurred in a calculation. Internally it is defined to -1201 (the Informix definition).

ECPG_INFORMIX_DIVIDE_ZERO

Functions return this value if an attempt to divide by zero is observed. Internally it is defined to -1202 (the Informix definition).

ECPG_INFORMIX_BAD_YEAR

Functions return this value if a bad value for a year was found while parsing a date. Internally it is defined to -1204 (the Informix definition).

ECPG_INFORMIX_BAD_MONTH

Functions return this value if a bad value for a month was found while parsing a date. Internally it is defined to -1205 (the Informix definition).

ECPG_INFORMIX_BAD_DAY

Functions return this value if a bad value for a day was found while parsing a date. Internally it is defined to -1206 (the Informix definition).

ECPG_INFORMIX_ENOSHORTDATE

Functions return this value if a parsing routine needs a short date representation but did not get the date string in the right length. Internally it is defined to -1209 (the Informix definition).

ECPG_INFORMIX_DATE_CONVERT

Functions return this value if Internally it is defined to -1210 (the Informix definition).

ECPG_INFORMIX_OUT_OF_MEMORY

Functions return this value if Internally it is defined to -1211 (the Informix definition).

ECPG_INFORMIX_ENOTDMY

Functions return this value if a parsing routine was supposed to get a format mask (like mmddyy) but not all fields were listed correctly. Internally it is defined to -1212 (the Informix definition).

ECPG_INFORMIX_BAD_NUMERIC

Functions return this value either if a parsing routine cannot parse the textual representation for a numeric value because it contains errors or if a routine cannot complete a calculation involving numeric variables because at least one of the numeric variables is invalid. Internally it is defined to -1213 (the Informix definition).

ECPG_INFORMIX_BAD_EXPONENT

Functions return this value if Internally it is defined to -1216 (the Informix definition).

ECPG_INFORMIX_BAD_DATE

Functions return this value if Internally it is defined to -1218 (the Informix definition).

ECPG_INFORMIX_EXTRA_CHARS

Functions return this value if Internally it is defined to -1264 (the Informix definition).

32.10. Using SQL Descriptor Areas

An SQL descriptor area is a more sophisticated method for processing the result of a SELECT or FETCH statement. An SQL descriptor area groups the data of one row of data together with metadata items into one data structure. The metadata is particularly useful when executing dynamic SQL statements, where the nature of the result columns might not be known ahead of time.

An SQL descriptor area consists of a header, which contains information concerning the entire descriptor, and one or more item descriptor areas, which basically each describe one column in the result row.

Before you can use an SQL descriptor area, you need to allocate one:

```
EXEC SQL ALLOCATE DESCRIPTOR identifier;
```

The identifier serves as the "variable name" of the descriptor area. When you don't need the descriptor anymore, you should deallocate it:

```
EXEC SQL DEALLOCATE DESCRIPTOR identifier;
```

To use a descriptor area, specify it as the storage target in an INTO clause, instead of listing host variables:

```
EXEC SQL FETCH NEXT FROM mycursor INTO DESCRIPTOR mydesc;
```

Now how do you get the data out of the descriptor area? You can think of the descriptor area as a structure with named fields. To retrieve the value of a field from the header and store it into a host variable, use the following command:

```
EXEC SQL GET DESCRIPTOR name :hostvar = field;
```

Currently, there is only one header field defined: *COUNT*, which tells how many item descriptor areas exist (that is, how many columns are contained in the result). The host variable needs to be of an integer type. To get a field from the item descriptor area, use the following command:

```
EXEC SQL GET DESCRIPTOR name VALUE num :hostvar = field;
```

num can be a literal integer or a host variable containing an integer. Possible fields are:

CARDINALITY (integer)

>number of rows in the result set

DATA

>actual data item (therefore, the data type of this field depends on the query)

DATETIME_INTERVAL_CODE (integer)

>?

DATETIME_INTERVAL_PRECISION (integer)

>not implemented

INDICATOR (integer)

>the indicator (indicating a null value or a value truncation)

KEY_MEMBER (integer)

>not implemented

LENGTH (integer)

>length of the datum in characters

NAME (string)

>name of the column

NULLABLE (integer)

> not implemented

OCTET_LENGTH (integer)

> length of the character representation of the datum in bytes

PRECISION (integer)

> precision (for type numeric)

RETURNED_LENGTH (integer)

> length of the datum in characters

RETURNED_OCTET_LENGTH (integer)

> length of the character representation of the datum in bytes

SCALE (integer)

> scale (for type numeric)

TYPE (integer)

> numeric code of the data type of the column

32.11. Error Handling

This section describes how you can handle exceptional conditions and warnings in an embedded SQL program. There are several nonexclusive facilities for this.

32.11.1. Setting Callbacks

One simple method to catch errors and warnings is to set a specific action to be executed whenever a particular condition occurs. In general:

```
EXEC SQL WHENEVER condition action;
```

condition can be one of the following:

SQLERROR

> The specified action is called whenever an error occurs during the execution of an SQL statement.

SQLWARNING

> The specified action is called whenever a warning occurs during the execution of an SQL statement.

`NOT FOUND`

The specified action is called whenever an SQL statement retrieves or affects zero rows. (This condition is not an error, but you might be interested in handling it specially.)

action can be one of the following:

`CONTINUE`

This effectively means that the condition is ignored. This is the default.

`GOTO label`
`GO TO label`

Jump to the specified label (using a C goto statement).

`SQLPRINT`

Print a message to standard error. This is useful for simple programs or during prototyping. The details of the message cannot be configured.

`STOP`

Call exit(1), which will terminate the program.

`DO BREAK`

Execute the C statement break. This should only be used in loops or switch statements.

`CALL name (args)`
`DO name (args)`

Call the specified C functions with the specified arguments.

The SQL standard only provides for the actions CONTINUE and GOTO (and GO TO).

Here is an example that you might want to use in a simple program. It prints a simple message when a warning occurs and aborts the program when an error happens:

```
EXEC SQL WHENEVER SQLWARNING SQLPRINT;
EXEC SQL WHENEVER SQLERROR STOP;
```

The statement EXEC SQL WHENEVER is a directive of the SQL preprocessor, not a C statement. The error or warning actions that it sets apply to all embedded SQL statements that appear below the point where the handler is set, unless a different action was set for the same condition between the first EXEC SQL WHENEVER and the SQL statement causing the condition, regardless of the flow of control in the C program. So neither of the two following C program excerpts will have the desired effect:

```
/*
 * WRONG
 */
int main(int argc, char *argv[])
```

```
{
    ...
    if (verbose) {
        EXEC SQL WHENEVER SQLWARNING SQLPRINT;
    }
    ...
    EXEC SQL SELECT ...;
    ...
}
/*
 * WRONG
 */
int main(int argc, char *argv[])
{
    ...
    set_error_handler();
    ...
    EXEC SQL SELECT ...;
    ...
}

static void set_error_handler(void)
{
    EXEC SQL WHENEVER SQLERROR STOP;
}
```

32.11.2. sqlca

For more powerful error handling, the embedded SQL interface provides a global variable with the name sqlca that has the following structure:

```
struct
{
    char sqlcaid[8];
    long sqlabc;
    long sqlcode;
    struct
    {
        int sqlerrml;
        char sqlerrmc[SQLERRMC_LEN];
    } sqlerrm;
    char sqlerrp[8];
    long sqlerrd[6];
    char sqlwarn[8];
    char sqlstate[5];
} sqlca;
```

(In a multithreaded program, every thread automatically gets its own copy of sqlca. This works similarly to the handling of the standard C global variable errno.)

sqlca covers both warnings and errors. If multiple warnings or errors occur during the execution of a statement, then sqlca will only contain information about the last one.

If no error occurred in the last SQL statement, sqlca.sqlcode will be 0 and sqlca.sqlstate will be "00000". If a warning or error occurred, then sqlca.sqlcode will be negative and sqlca.sqlstate will be different from "00000". A positive sqlca.sqlcode indicates a harmless condition, such as that the last query returned zero rows. sqlcode and sqlstate are two different error code schemes; details appear below.

If the last SQL statement was successful, then sqlca.sqlerrd[1] contains the OID of the processed row, if applicable, and sqlca.sqlerrd[2] contains the number of processed or returned rows, if applicable to the command.

In case of an error or warning, sqlca.sqlerrm.sqlerrmc will contain a string that describes the error. The field sqlca.sqlerrm.sqlerrml contains the length of the error message that is stored in sqlca.sqlerrm.sqlerrmc (the result of strlen(), not really interesting for a C programmer). Note that some messages are too long to fit in the fixed-size sqlerrmc array; they will be truncated.

In case of a warning, sqlca.sqlwarn[2] is set to W. (In all other cases, it is set to something different from W.) If sqlca.sqlwarn[1] is set to W, then a value was truncated when it was stored in a host variable. sqlca.sqlwarn[0] is set to W if any of the other elements are set to indicate a warning.

The fields sqlcaid, sqlcabc, sqlerrp, and the remaining elements of sqlerrd and sqlwarn currently contain no useful information.

The structure sqlca is not defined in the SQL standard, but is implemented in several other SQL database systems. The definitions are similar at the core, but if you want to write portable applications, then you should investigate the different implementations carefully.

32.11.3. SQLSTATE vs SQLCODE

The fields sqlca.sqlstate and sqlca.sqlcode are two different schemes that provide error codes. Both are derived from the SQL standard, but SQLCODE has been marked deprecated in the SQL-92 edition of the standard and has been dropped in later editions. Therefore, new applications are strongly encouraged to use SQLSTATE.

SQLSTATE is a five-character array. The five characters contain digits or upper-case letters that represent codes of various error and warning conditions. SQLSTATE has a hierarchical scheme: the first two characters indicate the general class of the condition, the last three characters indicate a subclass of the general condition. A successful state is indicated by the code 00000. The SQLSTATE codes are for the most part defined in the SQL standard. The PostgreSQL server natively supports SQLSTATE error codes; therefore a high degree of consistency can be achieved by using this error code scheme throughout all applications. For further information see *Appendix A*.

SQLCODE, the deprecated error code scheme, is a simple integer. A value of 0 indicates success, a positive value indicates success with additional information, a negative value indicates an error. The SQL standard only defines the positive value +100, which indicates that the last command returned or affected zero rows, and no specific negative values. Therefore, this scheme can only achieve poor portability and does not have a hierarchical code assignment. Historically, the embedded SQL processor for PostgreSQL has assigned some specific SQLCODE values for its use, which are listed below with their numeric value and their symbolic name. Remember that these are not portable to other SQL implementations. To simplify the porting of applications to the SQLSTATE scheme, the corresponding SQLSTATE is also listed. There is, however, no one-to-one or one-to-many mapping between the two schemes (indeed it is many-to-many), so you should consult the global SQLSTATE listing in *Appendix A* in each case.

These are the assigned SQLCODE values:

-12 (ECPG_OUT_OF_MEMORY)

> Indicates that your virtual memory is exhausted. (SQLSTATE YE001)

-200 (ECPG_UNSUPPORTED)

> Indicates the preprocessor has generated something that the library does not know about. Perhaps you are running incompatible versions of the preprocessor and the library. (SQLSTATE YE002)

-201 (ECPG_TOO_MANY_ARGUMENTS)

> This means that the command specified more host variables than the command expected. (SQLSTATE 07001 or 07002)

-202 (ECPG_TOO_FEW_ARGUMENTS)

> This means that the command specified fewer host variables than the command expected. (SQLSTATE 07001 or 07002)

-203 (ECPG_TOO_MANY_MATCHES)

> This means a query has returned multiple rows but the statement was only prepared to store one result row (for example, because the specified variables are not arrays). (SQLSTATE 21000)

-204 (ECPG_INT_FORMAT)

> The host variable is of type int and the datum in the database is of a different type and contains a value that cannot be interpreted as an int. The library uses strtol() for this conversion. (SQLSTATE 42804)

-205 (`ECPG_UINT_FORMAT`)

The host variable is of type unsigned int and the datum in the database is of a different type and contains a value that cannot be interpreted as an unsigned int. The library uses strtoul() for this conversion. (SQLSTATE 42804)

-206 (`ECPG_FLOAT_FORMAT`)

The host variable is of type float and the datum in the database is of another type and contains a value that cannot be interpreted as a float. The library uses strtod() for this conversion. (SQLSTATE 42804)

-207 (`ECPG_CONVERT_BOOL`)

This means the host variable is of type bool and the datum in the database is neither 't' nor 'f'. (SQLSTATE 42804)

-208 (`ECPG_EMPTY`)

The statement sent to the PostgreSQL server was empty. (This cannot normally happen in an embedded SQL program, so it might point to an internal error.) (SQLSTATE YE002)

-209 (`ECPG_MISSING_INDICATOR`)

A null value was returned and no null indicator variable was supplied. (SQLSTATE 22002)

-210 (`ECPG_NO_ARRAY`)

An ordinary variable was used in a place that requires an array. (SQLSTATE 42804)

-211 (`ECPG_DATA_NOT_ARRAY`)

The database returned an ordinary variable in a place that requires array value. (SQLSTATE 42804)

-220 (`ECPG_NO_CONN`)

The program tried to access a connection that does not exist. (SQLSTATE 08003)

-221 (`ECPG_NOT_CONN`)

The program tried to access a connection that does exist but is not open. (This is an internal error.) (SQLSTATE YE002)

-230 (`ECPG_INVALID_STMT`)

The statement you are trying to use has not been prepared. (SQLSTATE 26000)

-240 (`ECPG_UNKNOWN_DESCRIPTOR`)

The descriptor specified was not found. The statement you are trying to use has not been prepared. (SQLSTATE 33000)

-241 (`ECPG_INVALID_DESCRIPTOR_INDEX`)

The descriptor index specified was out of range. (SQLSTATE 07009)

-242 (`ECPG_UNKNOWN_DESCRIPTOR_ITEM`)

An invalid descriptor item was requested. (This is an internal error.) (SQLSTATE YE002)

-243 (`ECPG_VAR_NOT_NUMERIC`)

During the execution of a dynamic statement, the database returned a numeric value and the host variable was not numeric. (SQLSTATE 07006)

-244 (`ECPG_VAR_NOT_CHAR`)

During the execution of a dynamic statement, the database returned a non-numeric value and the host variable was numeric. (SQLSTATE 07006)

-400 (`ECPG_PGSQL`)

Some error caused by the PostgreSQL server. The message contains the error message from the PostgreSQL server.

-401 (`ECPG_TRANS`)

The PostgreSQL server signaled that we cannot start, commit, or rollback the transaction. (SQLSTATE 08007)

-402 (`ECPG_CONNECT`)

The connection attempt to the database did not succeed. (SQLSTATE 08001)

100 (`ECPG_NOT_FOUND`)

This is a harmless condition indicating that the last command retrieved or processed zero rows, or that you are at the end of the cursor. (SQLSTATE 02000)

32.12. Preprocessor directives

32.12.1. Including files

To include an external file into your embedded SQL program, use:

```
EXEC SQL INCLUDE filename;
```

The embedded SQL preprocessor will look for a file named *filename*.h, preprocess it, and include it in the resulting C output. Thus, embedded SQL statements in the included file are handled correctly.

Note that this is *not* the same as:

```
#include <filename.h>
```

because this file would not be subject to SQL command preprocessing. Naturally, you can continue to use the C #include directive to include other header files.

Note

The include file name is case-sensitive, even though the rest of the EXEC SQL INCLUDE command follows the normal SQL case-sensitivity rules.

32.12.2. The #define and #undef directives

Similar to the directive #define that is known from C, embedded SQL has a similar concept:

```
EXEC SQL DEFINE name;
EXEC SQL DEFINE name value;
```

So you can define a name:

```
EXEC SQL DEFINE HAVE_FEATURE;
```

And you can also define constants:

```
EXEC SQL DEFINE MYNUMBER 12;
EXEC SQL DEFINE MYSTRING 'abc';
```

Use undef to remove a previous definition:

```
EXEC SQL UNDEF MYNUMBER;
```

Of course you can continue to use the C versions #define and #undef in your embedded SQL program. The difference is where your defined values get evaluated. If you use EXEC SQL DEFINE then the ecpg preprocessor evaluates the defines and substitutes the values. For example if you write:

```
EXEC SQL DEFINE MYNUMBER 12;
...
EXEC SQL UPDATE Tbl SET col = MYNUMBER;
```

then ecpg will already do the substitution and your C compiler will never see any name or identifier MYNUMBER. Note that you cannot use #define for a constant that you are going to use in an embedded SQL query because in this case the embedded SQL precompiler is not able to see this declaration.

32.12.3. ifdef, ifndef, else, elif and endif directives

You can use the following directives to compile code sections conditionally:

```
EXEC SQL ifdef name;
```

Checks a *name* and processes subsequent lines if *name* has been created with EXEC SQL define *name*.

```
EXEC SQL ifndef name;
```

Checks a *name* and processes subsequent lines if *name* has *not* been created with EXEC SQL define *name*.

```
EXEC SQL else;
```

Starts processing an alternative section to a section introduced by either EXEC SQL ifdef *name* or EXEC SQL ifndef *name*.

```
EXEC SQL elif name;
```

Checks *name* and starts an alternative section if *name* has been created with EXEC SQL define *name*.

```
EXEC SQL endif;
```

Ends an alternative section.

Example:

```
exec sql ifndef TZVAR;
exec sql SET TIMEZONE TO 'GMT';
exec sql elif TZNAME;
exec sql SET TIMEZONE TO TZNAME;
exec sql else;
exec sql SET TIMEZONE TO TZVAR;
exec sql endif;
```

32.13. Processing Embedded SQL Programs

Now that you have an idea how to form embedded SQL C programs, you probably want to know how to compile them. Before compiling you run the file through the embedded SQL C preprocessor, which converts the SQL statements you used to special function calls. After compiling, you must link with a special library that contains the needed functions. These functions fetch information from the arguments, perform the SQL command using the libpq interface, and put the result in the arguments specified for output.

The preprocessor program is called ecpg and is included in a normal PostgreSQL installation. Embedded SQL programs are typically named with an extension .pgc. If you have a program file called prog1.pgc, you can preprocess it by simply calling:

```
ecpg prog1.pgc
```

This will create a file called prog1.c. If your input files do not follow the suggested naming pattern, you can specify the output file explicitly using the -o option.

The preprocessed file can be compiled normally, for example:

```
cc -c prog1.c
```

The generated C source files include header files from the PostgreSQL installation, so if you installed PostgreSQL in a location that is not searched by default, you have to add an option such as -I/usr/local/pgsql/include to the compilation command line.

To link an embedded SQL program, you need to include the libecpg library, like so:

```
cc -o myprog prog1.o prog2.o ... -lecpg
```

Again, you might have to add an option like -L/usr/local/pgsql/lib to that command line.

If you manage the build process of a larger project using make, it might be convenient to include the following implicit rule to your makefiles:

```
ECPG = ecpg

%.c: %.pgc
        $(ECPG) $<
```

The complete syntax of the ecpg command is detailed in *ecpg* (see Vol.V).

The ecpg library is thread-safe if it is built using the --enable-thread-safety command-line option to configure. (You might need to use other threading command-line options to compile your client code.)

32.14. Library Functions

The libecpg library primarily contains "hidden" functions that are used to implement the functionality expressed by the embedded SQL commands. But there are some functions that can usefully be called directly. Note that this makes your code unportable.

- ECPGdebug(int *on*, FILE **stream*) turns on debug logging if called with the first argument non-zero. Debug logging is done on *stream*. The log contains all SQL statements with all the input variables inserted, and the results from the PostgreSQL server. This can be very useful when searching for errors in your SQL statements.

 Note

> On Windows, if the ecpg libraries and an application are compiled with different flags, this function call will crash the application because the internal representation of the FILE pointers differ. Specifically, multithreaded/single-threaded, release/debug, and static/dynamic flags should be the same for the library and all applications using that library.

- ECPGstatus(int *lineno*, const char* *connection_name*) returns true if you are connected to a database and false if not. *connection_name* can be NULL if a single connection is being used.

32.15. Internals

This section explains how ECPG works internally. This information can occasionally be useful to help users understand how to use ECPG.

The first four lines written by ecpg to the output are fixed lines. Two are comments and two are include lines necessary to interface to the library. Then the preprocessor reads through the file and writes output. Normally it just echoes everything to the output.

When it sees an EXEC SQL statement, it intervenes and changes it. The command starts with EXEC SQL and ends with ;. Everything in between is treated as an SQL statement and parsed for variable substitution.

Variable substitution occurs when a symbol starts with a colon (:). The variable with that name is looked up among the variables that were previously declared within a EXEC SQL DECLARE section.

The most important function in the library is ECPGdo, which takes care of executing most commands. It takes a variable number of arguments. This can easily add up to 50 or so arguments, and we hope this will not be a problem on any platform.

The arguments are:

A line number

This is the line number of the original line; used in error messages only.

A string

This is the SQL command that is to be issued. It is modified by the input variables, i.e., the variables that where not known at compile time but are to be entered in the command. Where the variables should go the string contains ?.

Input variables

Every input variable causes ten arguments to be created. (See below.)

ECPGt_EOIT

An enum telling that there are no more input variables.

Output variables

Every output variable causes ten arguments to be created. (See below.) These variables are filled by the function.

ECPGt_EORT

An enum telling that there are no more variables.

For every variable that is part of the SQL command, the function gets ten arguments:

1. The type as a special symbol.

2. A pointer to the value or a pointer to the pointer.

3. The size of the variable if it is a char or varchar.

4. The number of elements in the array (for array fetches).

5. The offset to the next element in the array (for array fetches).

6. The type of the indicator variable as a special symbol.

7. A pointer to the indicator variable.

8. 0

9. The number of elements in the indicator array (for array fetches).

10. The offset to the next element in the indicator array (for array fetches).

Note that not all SQL commands are treated in this way. For instance, an open cursor statement like:

```
EXEC SQL OPEN cursor;
```

is not copied to the output. Instead, the cursor's DECLARE command is used at the position of the OPEN command because it indeed opens the cursor.

Here is a complete example describing the output of the preprocessor of a file foo.pgc (details might change with each particular version of the preprocessor):

```
EXEC SQL BEGIN DECLARE SECTION;
int index;
int result;
EXEC SQL END DECLARE SECTION;
...
EXEC SQL SELECT res INTO :result FROM mytable WHERE index = :index;
```

is translated into:

```
/* Processed by ecpg (2.6.0) */
/* These two include files are added by the preprocessor */
#include <ecpgtype.h>;
#include <ecpglib.h>;

/* exec sql begin declare section */

#line 1 "foo.pgc"

  int index;
  int result;
/* exec sql end declare section */
```

```
...
ECPGdo(__LINE__, NULL, "SELECT res FROM mytable WHERE index = ?      ",
        ECPGt_int,&(index),1L,1L,sizeof(int),
        ECPGt_NO_INDICATOR, NULL , 0L, 0L, 0L, ECPGt_EOIT,
        ECPGt_int,&(result),1L,1L,sizeof(int),
        ECPGt_NO_INDICATOR, NULL , 0L, 0L, 0L, ECPGt_EORT);
#line 147 "foo.pgc"
```

(The indentation here is added for readability and not something the preprocessor does.)

Chapter 33.
The Information Schema

The information schema consists of a set of views that contain information about the objects defined in the current database. The information schema is defined in the SQL standard and can therefore be expected to be portable and remain stable — unlike the system catalogs, which are specific to PostgreSQL and are modelled after implementation concerns. The information schema views do not, however, contain information about PostgreSQL-specific features; to inquire about those you need to query the system catalogs or other PostgreSQL-specific views.

33.1. The Schema

The information schema itself is a schema named information_schema. This schema automatically exists in all databases. The owner of this schema is the initial database user in the cluster, and that user naturally has all the privileges on this schema, including the ability to drop it (but the space savings achieved by that are minuscule).

By default, the information schema is not in the schema search path, so you need to access all objects in it through qualified names. Since the names of some of the objects in the information schema are generic names that might occur in user applications, you should be careful if you want to put the information schema in the path.

33.2. Data Types

The columns of the information schema views use special data types that are defined in the information schema. These are defined as simple domains over ordinary built-in types. You should not use these types for work outside the information schema, but your applications must be prepared for them if they select from the information schema.

These types are:

cardinal_number

  A nonnegative integer.

character_data

  A character string (without specific maximum length).

`sql_identifier`

A character string. This type is used for SQL identifiers, the type character_data is used for any other kind of text data.

`time_stamp`

A domain over the type timestamp with time zone

Every column in the information schema has one of these four types.

Boolean (true/false) data is represented in the information schema by a column of type character_data that contains either YES or NO. (The information schema was invented before the type boolean was added to the SQL standard, so this convention is necessary to keep the information schema backward compatible.)

33.3. `information_schema_catalog_name`

information_schema_catalog_name is a table that always contains one row and one column containing the name of the current database (current catalog, in SQL terminology).

Name	Data Type	Description
catalog_name	sql_identifier	Name of the database that contains this information schema

Table 33-1. `information_schema_catalog_name` Columns

33.4. `administrable_role_authorizations`

The view administrable_role_authorizations identifies all roles that the current user has the admin option for.

Name	Data Type	Description
grantee	sql_identifier	Name of the role to which this role membership was granted (can be the current user, or a different role in case of nested role memberships)
role_name	sql_identifier	Name of a role
is_grantable	character_data	Always YES

Table 33-2. `administrable_role_authorizations` Columns

33.5. `applicable_roles`

The view applicable_roles identifies all roles whose privileges the current user can use. This means there is some chain of role grants from the current user to the role in question. The current user itself is also an applicable role. The set of applicable roles is generally used for permission checking.

Name	Data Type	Description
grantee	sql_identifier	Name of the role to which this role membership was granted (can be the current user, or a different role in case of nested role memberships)
role_name	sql_identifier	Name of a role
is_grantable	character_data	YES if the grantee has the admin option on the role, NO if not

Table 33-3. `applicable_roles` Columns

33.6. `attributes`

The view attributes contains information about the attributes of composite data types defined in the database. (Note that the view does not give information about table columns, which are sometimes called attributes in PostgreSQL contexts.)

Name	Data Type	Description
udt_catalog	sql_identifier	Name of the database containing the data type (always the current database)
udt_schema	sql_identifier	Name of the schema containing the data type
udt_name	sql_identifier	Name of the data type
attribute_name	sql_identifier	Name of the attribute
ordinal_position	cardinal_number	Ordinal position of the attribute within the data type (count starts at 1)
attribute_default	character_data	Default expression of the attribute
is_nullable	character_data	YES if the attribute is possibly nullable, NO if it is known not nullable.
data_type	character_data	Data type of the attribute, if it is a built-in type, or ARRAY if it is some array (in that case, see the view element_types), else USER-DEFINED (in that case, the type is identified in attribute_udt_name and associated columns).
character_maximum_length	cardinal_number	If data_type identifies a character or bit string type, the declared maximum length; null for all other data types or if no maximum length was declared.
character_octet_length	cardinal_number	If data_type identifies a character type, the maximum possible length in octets (bytes) of a datum (this should not be of concern to PostgreSQL users); null for all other data types.
numeric_precision	cardinal_number	If data_type identifies a numeric type, this column contains the (declared or implicit) precision of the type for this attribute. The

Name	Data Type	Description
		precision indicates the number of significant digits. It can be expressed in decimal (base 10) or binary (base 2) terms, as specified in the column `numeric_precision_radix`. For all other data types, this column is null.
numeric_precision_radix	cardinal_number	If `data_type` identifies a numeric type, this column indicates in which base the values in the columns `numeric_precision` and `numeric_scale` are expressed. The value is either 2 or 10. For all other data types, this column is null.
numeric_scale	cardinal_number	If `data_type` identifies an exact numeric type, this column contains the (declared or implicit) scale of the type for this attribute. The scale indicates the number of significant digits to the right of the decimal point. It can be expressed in decimal (base 10) or binary (base 2) terms, as specified in the column `numeric_precision_radix`. For all other data types, this column is null.
datetime_precision	cardinal_number	If `data_type` identifies a date, time, timestamp, or interval type, this column contains the (declared or implicit) fractional seconds precision of the type for this attribute, that is, the number of decimal digits maintained following the decimal point in the seconds value. For all other data types, this column is null.
interval_type	character_data	Not yet implemented
interval_precision	character_data	Not yet implemented
attribute_udt_catalog	sql_identifier	Name of the database that the attribute data type is defined in (always the current database)
attribute_udt_schema	sql_identifier	Name of the schema that the attribute data type is defined in
attribute_udt_name	sql_identifier	Name of the attribute data type
scope_catalog	sql_identifier	Applies to a feature not available in PostgreSQL
scope_schema	sql_identifier	Applies to a feature not available in PostgreSQL
scope_name	sql_identifier	Applies to a feature not available in PostgreSQL

Name	Data Type	Description
maximum_cardinality	cardinal_number	Always null, because arrays always have unlimited maximum cardinality in PostgreSQL
dtd_identifier	sql_identifier	An identifier of the data type descriptor of the column, unique among the data type descriptors pertaining to the table. This is mainly useful for joining with other instances of such identifiers. (The specific format of the identifier is not defined and not guaranteed to remain the same in future versions.)
is_derived_reference_attribute	character_data	Applies to a feature not available in PostgreSQL

Table 33-4. attributes Columns

See also under *Section 33.12* - page 386, a similarly structured view, for further information on some of the columns.

33.7. check_constraint_routine_usage

The view check_constraint_routine_usage identifies routines (functions and procedures) that are used by a check constraint. Only those routines are shown that are owned by a currently enabled role.

Name	Data Type	Description
constraint_catalog	sql_identifier	Name of the database containing the constraint (always the current database)
constraint_schema	sql_identifier	Name of the schema containing the constraint
constraint_name	sql_identifier	Name of the constraint
specific_catalog	sql_identifier	Name of the database containing the function (always the current database)
specific_schema	sql_identifier	Name of the schema containing the function
specific_name	sql_identifier	The "specific name" of the function. See *Section 33.33* - page 406 for more information.

Table 33-5. check_constraint_routine_usage Columns

33.8. check_constraints

The view check_constraints contains all check constraints, either defined on a table or on a domain, that are owned by a currently enabled role. (The owner of the table or domain is the owner of the constraint.)

Name	Data Type	Description
constraint_catalog	sql_identifier	Name of the database containing the constraint (always the current database)
constraint_schema	sql_identifier	Name of the schema containing the constraint
constraint_name	sql_identifier	Name of the constraint
check_clause	character_data	The check expression of the check constraint

Table 33-6. `check_constraints` Columns

33.9. `column_domain_usage`

The view column_domain_usage identifies all columns (of a table or a view) that make use of some domain defined in the current database and owned by a currently enabled role.

Name	Data Type	Description
domain_catalog	sql_identifier	Name of the database containing the domain (always the current database)
domain_schema	sql_identifier	Name of the schema containing the domain
domain_name	sql_identifier	Name of the domain
table_catalog	sql_identifier	Name of the database containing the table (always the current database)
table_schema	sql_identifier	Name of the schema containing the table
table_name	sql_identifier	Name of the table
column_name	sql_identifier	Name of the column

Table 33-7. `column_domain_usage` Columns

33.10. `column_privileges`

The view column_privileges identifies all privileges granted on columns to a currently enabled role or by a currently enabled role. There is one row for each combination of column, grantor, and grantee.

If a privilege has been granted on an entire table, it will show up in this view as a grant for each column, but only for the privilege types where column granularity is possible: SELECT, INSERT, UPDATE, REFERENCES.

Name	Data Type	Description
grantor	sql_identifier	Name of the role that granted the privilege
grantee	sql_identifier	Name of the role that the privilege was granted to

Name	Data Type	Description
table_catalog	sql_identifier	Name of the database that contains the table that contains the column (always the current database)
table_schema	sql_identifier	Name of the schema that contains the table that contains the column
table_name	sql_identifier	Name of the table that contains the column
column_name	sql_identifier	Name of the column
privilege_type	character_data	Type of the privilege: SELECT, INSERT, UPDATE, or REFERENCES
is_grantable	character_data	YES if the privilege is grantable, NO if not

Table 33-8. column_privileges Columns

33.11. column_udt_usage

The view column_udt_usage identifies all columns that use data types owned by a currently enabled role. Note that in PostgreSQL, built-in data types behave like user-defined types, so they are included here as well. See also *Section 33.12* - page 386 for details.

Name	Data Type	Description
udt_catalog	sql_identifier	Name of the database that the column data type (the underlying type of the domain, if applicable) is defined in (always the current database)
udt_schema	sql_identifier	Name of the schema that the column data type (the underlying type of the domain, if applicable) is defined in
udt_name	sql_identifier	Name of the column data type (the underlying type of the domain, if applicable)
table_catalog	sql_identifier	Name of the database containing the table (always the current database)
table_schema	sql_identifier	Name of the schema containing the table
table_name	sql_identifier	Name of the table
column_name	sql_identifier	Name of the column

Table 33-9. column_udt_usage Columns

33.12. columns

The view columns contains information about all table columns (or view columns) in the database. System columns (oid, etc.) are not included. Only those columns are shown that the current user has access to (by way of being the owner or having some privilege).

Name	Data Type	Description
table_catalog	sql_identifier	Name of the database containing the table (always the current database)
table_schema	sql_identifier	Name of the schema containing the table
table_name	sql_identifier	Name of the table
column_name	sql_identifier	Name of the column
ordinal_position	cardinal_number	Ordinal position of the column within the table (count starts at 1)
column_default	character_data	Default expression of the column
is_nullable	character_data	YES if the column is possibly nullable, NO if it is known not nullable. A not-null constraint is one way a column can be known not nullable, but there can be others.
data_type	character_data	Data type of the column, if it is a built-in type, or ARRAY if it is some array (in that case, see the view element_types), else USER-DEFINED (in that case, the type is identified in udt_name and associated columns). If the column is based on a domain, this column refers to the type underlying the domain (and the domain is identified in domain_name and associated columns).
character_maximum_length	cardinal_number	If data_type identifies a character or bit string type, the declared maximum length; null for all other data types or if no maximum length was declared.
character_octet_length	cardinal_number	If data_type identifies a character type, the maximum possible length in octets (bytes) of a datum (this should not be of concern to PostgreSQL users); null for all other data types.
numeric_precision	cardinal_number	If data_type identifies a numeric type, this column contains the (declared or implicit) precision of the type for this column. The precision indicates the number of significant digits. It can be expressed in decimal (base 10) or binary (base 2) terms, as specified in the column numeric_precision_radix. For all other data types, this column is null.
numeric_precision_radix	cardinal_number	If data_type identifies a numeric type, this column indicates in which base the values in the columns numeric_precision and numeric_scale are expressed. The value is either 2 or 10. For all other data types, this column is null.

Name	Data Type	Description
numeric_scale	cardinal_number	If data_type identifies an exact numeric type, this column contains the (declared or implicit) scale of the type for this column. The scale indicates the number of significant digits to the right of the decimal point. It can be expressed in decimal (base 10) or binary (base 2) terms, as specified in the column numeric_precision_radix. For all other data types, this column is null.
datetime_precision	cardinal_number	If data_type identifies a date, time, timestamp, or interval type, this column contains the (declared or implicit) fractional seconds precision of the type for this column, that is, the number of decimal digits maintained following the decimal point in the seconds value. For all other data types, this column is null.
interval_type	character_data	Not yet implemented
interval_precision	character_data	Not yet implemented
character_set_catalog	sql_identifier	Applies to a feature not available in PostgreSQL
character_set_schema	sql_identifier	Applies to a feature not available in PostgreSQL
character_set_name	sql_identifier	Applies to a feature not available in PostgreSQL
collation_catalog	sql_identifier	Applies to a feature not available in PostgreSQL
collation_schema	sql_identifier	Applies to a feature not available in PostgreSQL
collation_name	sql_identifier	Applies to a feature not available in PostgreSQL
domain_catalog	sql_identifier	If the column has a domain type, the name of the database that the domain is defined in (always the current database), else null.
domain_schema	sql_identifier	If the column has a domain type, the name of the schema that the domain is defined in, else null.
domain_name	sql_identifier	If the column has a domain type, the name of the domain, else null.
udt_catalog	sql_identifier	Name of the database that the column data type (the underlying type of the domain, if

Name	Data Type	Description
		applicable) is defined in (always the current database)
udt_schema	sql_identifier	Name of the schema that the column data type (the underlying type of the domain, if applicable) is defined in
udt_name	sql_identifier	Name of the column data type (the underlying type of the domain, if applicable)
scope_catalog	sql_identifier	Applies to a feature not available in PostgreSQL
scope_schema	sql_identifier	Applies to a feature not available in PostgreSQL
scope_name	sql_identifier	Applies to a feature not available in PostgreSQL
maximum_cardinality	cardinal_number	Always null, because arrays always have unlimited maximum cardinality in PostgreSQL
dtd_identifier	sql_identifier	An identifier of the data type descriptor of the column, unique among the data type descriptors pertaining to the table. This is mainly useful for joining with other instances of such identifiers. (The specific format of the identifier is not defined and not guaranteed to remain the same in future versions.)
is_self_referencing	character_data	Applies to a feature not available in PostgreSQL
is_identity	character_data	Applies to a feature not available in PostgreSQL
identity_generation	character_data	Applies to a feature not available in PostgreSQL
identity_start	character_data	Applies to a feature not available in PostgreSQL
identity_increment	character_data	Applies to a feature not available in PostgreSQL
identity_maximum	character_data	Applies to a feature not available in PostgreSQL
identity_minimum	character_data	Applies to a feature not available in PostgreSQL
identity_cycle	character_data	Applies to a feature not available in PostgreSQL
is_generated	character_data	Applies to a feature not available in PostgreSQL

Name	Data Type	Description
generation_expression	character_data	Applies to a feature not available in PostgreSQL
is_updatable	character_data	YES if the column is updatable, NO if not (Columns in base tables are always updatable, columns in views not necessarily)

Table 33-10. columns Columns

Since data types can be defined in a variety of ways in SQL, and PostgreSQL contains additional ways to define data types, their representation in the information schema can be somewhat difficult. The column data_type is supposed to identify the underlying built-in type of the column. In PostgreSQL, this means that the type is defined in the system catalog schema pg_catalog. This column might be useful if the application can handle the well-known built-in types specially (for example, format the numeric types differently or use the data in the precision columns). The columns udt_name, udt_schema, and udt_catalog always identify the underlying data type of the column, even if the column is based on a domain. (Since PostgreSQL treats built-in types like user-defined types, built-in types appear here as well. This is an extension of the SQL standard.) These columns should be used if an application wants to process data differently according to the type, because in that case it wouldn't matter if the column is really based on a domain. If the column is based on a domain, the identity of the domain is stored in the columns domain_name, domain_schema, and domain_catalog. If you want to pair up columns with their associated data types and treat domains as separate types, you could write coalesce(domain_name, udt_name), etc.

33.13. constraint_column_usage

The view constraint_column_usage identifies all columns in the current database that are used by some constraint. Only those columns are shown that are contained in a table owned by a currently enabled role. For a check constraint, this view identifies the columns that are used in the check expression. For a foreign key constraint, this view identifies the columns that the foreign key references. For a unique or primary key constraint, this view identifies the constrained columns.

Name	Data Type	Description
table_catalog	sql_identifier	Name of the database that contains the table that contains the column that is used by some constraint (always the current database)
table_schema	sql_identifier	Name of the schema that contains the table that contains the column that is used by some constraint

Name	Data Type	Description
table_name	sql_identifier	Name of the table that contains the column that is used by some constraint
column_name	sql_identifier	Name of the column that is used by some constraint
constraint_catalog	sql_identifier	Name of the database that contains the constraint (always the current database)
constraint_schema	sql_identifier	Name of the schema that contains the constraint
constraint_name	sql_identifier	Name of the constraint

Table 33-11. constraint_column_usage Columns

33.14. constraint_table_usage

The view constraint_table_usage identifies all tables in the current database that are used by some constraint and are owned by a currently enabled role. (This is different from the view table_constraints, which identifies all table constraints along with the table they are defined on.) For a foreign key constraint, this view identifies the table that the foreign key references. For a unique or primary key constraint, this view simply identifies the table the constraint belongs to. Check constraints and not-null constraints are not included in this view.

Name	Data Type	Description
table_catalog	sql_identifier	Name of the database that contains the table that is used by some constraint (always the current database)
table_schema	sql_identifier	Name of the schema that contains the table that is used by some constraint
table_name	sql_identifier	Name of the table that is used by some constraint
constraint_catalog	sql_identifier	Name of the database that contains the constraint (always the current database)
constraint_schema	sql_identifier	Name of the schema contains the constraint
constraint_name	sql_identifier	Name of the constraint

Table 33-12. constraint_table_usage Columns

33.15. data_type_privileges

The view data_type_privileges identifies all data type descriptors that the current user has access to, by way of being the owner of the described object or having some privilege for it. A data type descriptor is generated whenever a data type is used in the definition of a table column, a domain, or a function (as parameter or return type) and stores some information about how the data type is used in that instance (for example, the declared maximum length, if applicable). Each data type descriptor is assigned an arbitrary identifier that is unique among the data type descriptor identifiers assigned for one object (table, domain, function). This view is probably not useful for applications, but it is used to define some other views in the information schema.

Name	Data Type	Description
object_catalog	sql_identifier	Name of the database that contains the described object (always the current database)
object_schema	sql_identifier	Name of the schema that contains the described object
object_name	sql_identifier	Name of the described object
object_type	character_data	The type of the described object: one of TABLE (the data type descriptor pertains to a column of that table), DOMAIN (the data type descriptors pertains to that domain), ROUTINE (the data type descriptor pertains to a parameter or the return data type of that function).
dtd_identifier	sql_identifier	The identifier of the data type descriptor, which is unique among the data type descriptors for that same object.

Table 33-13. `data_type_privileges` Columns

33.16. `domain_constraints`

The view `domain_constraints` contains all constraints belonging to domains defined in the current database.

Name	Data Type	Description
constraint_catalog	sql_identifier	Name of the database that contains the constraint (always the current database)
constraint_schema	sql_identifier	Name of the schema that contains the constraint
constraint_name	sql_identifier	Name of the constraint
domain_catalog	sql_identifier	Name of the database that contains the domain (always the current database)
domain_schema	sql_identifier	Name of the schema that contains the domain
domain_name	sql_identifier	Name of the domain
is_deferrable	character_data	YES if the constraint is deferrable, NO if not

Name	Data Type	Description
initially_deferred	character_data	YES if the constraint is deferrable and initially deferred, NO if not

Table 33-14. `domain_constraints` Columns

33.17. `domain_udt_usage`

The view `domain_udt_usage` identifies all domains that are based on data types owned by a currently enabled role. Note that in PostgreSQL, built-in data types behave like user-defined types, so they are included here as well.

Name	Data Type	Description
udt_catalog	sql_identifier	Name of the database that the domain data type is defined in (always the current database)
udt_schema	sql_identifier	Name of the schema that the domain data type is defined in
udt_name	sql_identifier	Name of the domain data type
domain_catalog	sql_identifier	Name of the database that contains the domain (always the current database)
domain_schema	sql_identifier	Name of the schema that contains the domain
domain_name	sql_identifier	Name of the domain

Table 33-15. `domain_udt_usage` Columns

33.18. `domains`

The view `domains` contains all domains defined in the current database.

Name	Data Type	Description
domain_catalog	sql_identifier	Name of the database that contains the domain (always the current database)
domain_schema	sql_identifier	Name of the schema that contains the domain
domain_name	sql_identifier	Name of the domain
data_type	character_data	Data type of the domain, if it is a built-in type, or ARRAY if it is some array (in that case, see the view element_types), else USER-DEFINED (in that case, the type is identified in udt_name and associated columns).
character_maximum_length	cardinal_number	If the domain has a character or bit string type, the declared maximum length; null for all other data types or if no maximum length was declared.

Name	Data Type	Description
character_octet_length	cardinal_number	If the domain has a character type, the maximum possible length in octets (bytes) of a datum (this should not be of concern to PostgreSQL users); null for all other data types.
character_set_catalog	sql_identifier	Applies to a feature not available in PostgreSQL
character_set_schema	sql_identifier	Applies to a feature not available in PostgreSQL
character_set_name	sql_identifier	Applies to a feature not available in PostgreSQL
collation_catalog	sql_identifier	Applies to a feature not available in PostgreSQL
collation_schema	sql_identifier	Applies to a feature not available in PostgreSQL
collation_name	sql_identifier	Applies to a feature not available in PostgreSQL
numeric_precision	cardinal_number	If the domain has a numeric type, this column contains the (declared or implicit) precision of the type for this domain. The precision indicates the number of significant digits. It can be expressed in decimal (base 10) or binary (base 2) terms, as specified in the column numeric_precision_radix. For all other data types, this column is null.
numeric_precision_radix	cardinal_number	If the domain has a numeric type, this column indicates in which base the values in the columns numeric_precision and numeric_scale are expressed. The value is either 2 or 10. For all other data types, this column is null.
numeric_scale	cardinal_number	If the domain has an exact numeric type, this column contains the (declared or implicit) scale of the type for this domain. The scale indicates the number of significant digits to the right of the decimal point. It can be expressed in decimal (base 10) or binary (base 2) terms, as specified in the column numeric_precision_radix. For all other data types, this column is null.
datetime_precision	cardinal_number	If data_type identifies a date, time, timestamp, or interval type, this column contains the (declared or implicit) fractional

Name	Data Type	Description
		seconds precision of the type for this domain, that is, the number of decimal digits maintained following the decimal point in the seconds value. For all other data types, this column is null.
interval_type	character_data	Not yet implemented
interval_precision	character_data	Not yet implemented
domain_default	character_data	Default expression of the domain
udt_catalog	sql_identifier	Name of the database that the domain data type is defined in (always the current database)
udt_schema	sql_identifier	Name of the schema that the domain data type is defined in
udt_name	sql_identifier	Name of the domain data type
scope_catalog	sql_identifier	Applies to a feature not available in PostgreSQL
scope_schema	sql_identifier	Applies to a feature not available in PostgreSQL
scope_name	sql_identifier	Applies to a feature not available in PostgreSQL
maximum_cardinality	cardinal_number	Always null, because arrays always have unlimited maximum cardinality in PostgreSQL
dtd_identifier	sql_identifier	An identifier of the data type descriptor of the domain, unique among the data type descriptors pertaining to the domain (which is trivial, because a domain only contains one data type descriptor). This is mainly useful for joining with other instances of such identifiers. (The specific format of the identifier is not defined and not guaranteed to remain the same in future versions.)

Table 33-16. domains Columns

33.19. element_types

The view element_types contains the data type descriptors of the elements of arrays. When a table column, domain, function parameter, or function return value is defined to be of an array type, the respective information schema view only contains ARRAY in the column data_type. To obtain information on the element type of the array, you can join the respective view with this view. For example, to show the columns of a table with data types and array element types, if applicable, you could do:

```
SELECT c.column_name, c.data_type, e.data_type AS element_type
FROM information_schema.columns c LEFT JOIN information_schema.element_types e
  ON ((c.table_catalog, c.table_schema, c.table_name, 'TABLE', c.dtd_identifier)
    = (e.object_catalog, e.object_schema, e.object_name, e.object_type, e.dtd_identifier))
WHERE c.table_schema = '...' AND c.table_name = '...'
ORDER BY c.ordinal_position;
```

This view only includes objects that the current user has access to, by way of being the owner or having some privilege.

Name	Data Type	Description
object_catalog	sql_identifier	Name of the database that contains the object that uses the array being described (always the current database)
object_schema	sql_identifier	Name of the schema that contains the object that uses the array being described
object_name	sql_identifier	Name of the object that uses the array being described
object_type	character_data	The type of the object that uses the array being described: one of TABLE (the array is used by a column of that table), DOMAIN (the array is used by that domain), ROUTINE (the array is used by a parameter or the return data type of that function).
dtd_identifier	sql_identifier	The identifier of the data type descriptor of the array being described
data_type	character_data	Data type of the array elements, if it is a built-in type, else USER-DEFINED (in that case, the type is identified in udt_name and associated columns).
character_maximum_length	cardinal_number	Always null, since this information is not applied to array element data types in PostgreSQL
character_octet_length	cardinal_number	Always null, since this information is not applied to array element data types in PostgreSQL
character_set_catalog	sql_identifier	Applies to a feature not available in PostgreSQL
character_set_schema	sql_identifier	Applies to a feature not available in PostgreSQL
character_set_name	sql_identifier	Applies to a feature not available in PostgreSQL
collation_catalog	sql_identifier	Applies to a feature not available in PostgreSQL

Name	Data Type	Description
collation_schema	sql_identifier	Applies to a feature not available in PostgreSQL
collation_name	sql_identifier	Applies to a feature not available in PostgreSQL
numeric_precision	cardinal_number	Always null, since this information is not applied to array element data types in PostgreSQL
numeric_precision_radix	cardinal_number	Always null, since this information is not applied to array element data types in PostgreSQL
numeric_scale	cardinal_number	Always null, since this information is not applied to array element data types in PostgreSQL
datetime_precision	cardinal_number	Always null, since this information is not applied to array element data types in PostgreSQL
interval_type	character_data	Always null, since this information is not applied to array element data types in PostgreSQL
interval_precision	character_data	Always null, since this information is not applied to array element data types in PostgreSQL
domain_default	character_data	Not yet implemented
udt_catalog	sql_identifier	Name of the database that the data type of the elements is defined in (always the current database)
udt_schema	sql_identifier	Name of the schema that the data type of the elements is defined in
udt_name	sql_identifier	Name of the data type of the elements
scope_catalog	sql_identifier	Applies to a feature not available in PostgreSQL
scope_schema	sql_identifier	Applies to a feature not available in PostgreSQL
scope_name	sql_identifier	Applies to a feature not available in PostgreSQL
maximum_cardinality	cardinal_number	Always null, because arrays always have unlimited maximum cardinality in PostgreSQL

Table 33-17. element_types Columns

33.20. `enabled_roles`

The view `enabled_roles` identifies the currently "enabled roles". The enabled roles are recursively defined as the current user together with all roles that have been granted to the enabled roles with automatic inheritance. In other words, these are all roles that the current user has direct or indirect, automatically inheriting membership in.

For permission checking, the set of "applicable roles" is applied, which can be broader than the set of enabled roles. So generally, it is better to use the view `applicable_roles` instead of this one; see also there.

Name	Data Type	Description
role_name	sql_identifier	Name of a role

Table 33-18. `enabled_roles` Columns

33.21. `foreign_data_wrapper_options`

The view `foreign_data_wrapper_options` contains all the options defined for foreign-data wrappers in the current database. Only those foreign-data wrappers are shown that the current user has access to (by way of being the owner or having some privilege).

Name	Data Type	Description
foreign_data_wrapper_catalog	sql_identifier	Name of the database that the foreign-data wrapper is defined in (always the current database)
foreign_data_wrapper_name	sql_identifier	Name of the foreign-data wrapper
option_name	sql_identifier	Name of an option
option_value	character_data	Value of the option

Table 33-19. `foreign_data_wrapper_options` Columns

33.22. `foreign_data_wrappers`

The view `foreign_data_wrappers` contains all foreign-data wrappers defined in the current database. Only those foreign-data wrappers are shown that the current user has access to (by way of being the owner or having some privilege).

Name	Data Type	Description
foreign_data_wrapper_catalog	sql_identifier	Name of the database that contains the foreign-data wrapper (always the current database)
foreign_data_wrapper_name	sql_identifier	Name of the foreign-data wrapper
authorization_identifier	sql_identifier	Name of the owner of the foreign server

Name	Data Type	Description
library_name	character_data	File name of the library that implementing this foreign-data wrapper
foreign_data_wrapper_language	character_data	Language used to implement this foreign-data wrapper

Table 33-20. `foreign_data_wrappers` Columns

33.23. `foreign_server_options`

The view `foreign_server_options` contains all the options defined for foreign servers in the current database. Only those foreign servers are shown that the current user has access to (by way of being the owner or having some privilege).

Name	Data Type	Description
foreign_server_catalog	sql_identifier	Name of the database that the foreign server is defined in (always the current database)
foreign_server_name	sql_identifier	Name of the foreign server
option_name	sql_identifier	Name of an option
option_value	character_data	Value of the option

Table 33-21. `foreign_server_options` Columns

33.24. `foreign_servers`

The view `foreign_servers` contains all foreign servers defined in the current database. Only those foreign servers are shown that the current user has access to (by way of being the owner or having some privilege).

Name	Data Type	Description
foreign_server_catalog	sql_identifier	Name of the database that the foreign server is defined in (always the current database)
foreign_server_name	sql_identifier	Name of the foreign server
foreign_data_wrapper_catalog	sql_identifier	Name of the database that contains the foreign-data wrapper used by the foreign server (always the current database)
foreign_data_wrapper_name	sql_identifier	Name of the foreign-data wrapper used by the foreign server
foreign_server_type	character_data	Foreign server type information, if specified upon creation
foreign_server_version	character_data	Foreign server version information, if specified upon creation

Name	Data Type	Description
authorization_identifier	sql_identifier	Name of the owner of the foreign server

Table 33-22. `foreign_servers` Columns

33.25. `key_column_usage`

The view `key_column_usage` identifies all columns in the current database that are restricted by some unique, primary key, or foreign key constraint. Check constraints are not included in this view. Only those columns are shown that the current user has access to, by way of being the owner or having some privilege.

Name	Data Type	Description
constraint_catalog	sql_identifier	Name of the database that contains the constraint (always the current database)
constraint_schema	sql_identifier	Name of the schema that contains the constraint
constraint_name	sql_identifier	Name of the constraint
table_catalog	sql_identifier	Name of the database that contains the table that contains the column that is restricted by this constraint (always the current database)
table_schema	sql_identifier	Name of the schema that contains the table that contains the column that is restricted by this constraint
table_name	sql_identifier	Name of the table that contains the column that is restricted by this constraint
column_name	sql_identifier	Name of the column that is restricted by this constraint
ordinal_position	cardinal_number	Ordinal position of the column within the constraint key (count starts at 1)
position_in_unique_constraint	cardinal_number	For a foreign-key constraint, ordinal position of the referenced column within its unique constraint (count starts at 1); otherwise null

Table 33-23. `key_column_usage` Columns

33.26. `parameters`

The view `parameters` contains information about the parameters (arguments) of all functions in the current database. Only those functions are shown that the current user has access to (by way of being the owner or having some privilege).

Name	Data Type	Description
specific_catalog	sql_identifier	Name of the database containing the function (always the current database)
specific_schema	sql_identifier	Name of the schema containing the function
specific_name	sql_identifier	The "specific name" of the function. See *Section 33.33 - page 406* for more information.
ordinal_position	cardinal_number	Ordinal position of the parameter in the argument list of the function (count starts at 1)
parameter_mode	character_data	IN for input parameter, OUT for output parameter, and INOUT for input/output parameter.
is_result	character_data	Applies to a feature not available in PostgreSQL
as_locator	character_data	Applies to a feature not available in PostgreSQL
parameter_name	sql_identifier	Name of the parameter, or null if the parameter has no name
data_type	character_data	Data type of the parameter, if it is a built-in type, or ARRAY if it is some array (in that case, see the view element_types), else USER-DEFINED (in that case, the type is identified in udt_name and associated columns).
character_maximum_length	cardinal_number	Always null, since this information is not applied to parameter data types in PostgreSQL
character_octet_length	cardinal_number	Always null, since this information is not applied to parameter data types in PostgreSQL
character_set_catalog	sql_identifier	Applies to a feature not available in PostgreSQL
character_set_schema	sql_identifier	Applies to a feature not available in PostgreSQL
character_set_name	sql_identifier	Applies to a feature not available in PostgreSQL
collation_catalog	sql_identifier	Applies to a feature not available in PostgreSQL
collation_schema	sql_identifier	Applies to a feature not available in PostgreSQL
collation_name	sql_identifier	Applies to a feature not available in PostgreSQL
numeric_precision	cardinal_number	Always null, since this information is not applied to parameter data types in PostgreSQL

Name	Data Type	Description
numeric_precision_radix	cardinal_number	Always null, since this information is not applied to parameter data types in PostgreSQL
numeric_scale	cardinal_number	Always null, since this information is not applied to parameter data types in PostgreSQL
datetime_precision	cardinal_number	Always null, since this information is not applied to parameter data types in PostgreSQL
interval_type	character_data	Always null, since this information is not applied to parameter data types in PostgreSQL
interval_precision	character_data	Always null, since this information is not applied to parameter data types in PostgreSQL
udt_catalog	sql_identifier	Name of the database that the data type of the parameter is defined in (always the current database)
udt_schema	sql_identifier	Name of the schema that the data type of the parameter is defined in
udt_name	sql_identifier	Name of the data type of the parameter
scope_catalog	sql_identifier	Applies to a feature not available in PostgreSQL
scope_schema	sql_identifier	Applies to a feature not available in PostgreSQL
scope_name	sql_identifier	Applies to a feature not available in PostgreSQL
maximum_cardinality	cardinal_number	Always null, because arrays always have unlimited maximum cardinality in PostgreSQL
dtd_identifier	sql_identifier	An identifier of the data type descriptor of the parameter, unique among the data type descriptors pertaining to the function. This is mainly useful for joining with other instances of such identifiers. (The specific format of the identifier is not defined and not guaranteed to remain the same in future versions.)

Table 33-24. parameters Columns

33.27. referential_constraints

The view referential_constraints contains all referential (foreign key) constraints in the current database. Only those constraints are shown for which the current user has write access to the referencing table (by way of being the owner or having some privilege other than SELECT).

Name	Data Type	Description
constraint_catalog	sql_identifier	Name of the database containing the constraint (always the current database)
constraint_schema	sql_identifier	Name of the schema containing the constraint
constraint_name	sql_identifier	Name of the constraint
unique_constraint_catalog	sql_identifier	Name of the database that contains the unique or primary key constraint that the foreign key constraint references (always the current database)
unique_constraint_schema	sql_identifier	Name of the schema that contains the unique or primary key constraint that the foreign key constraint references
unique_constraint_name	sql_identifier	Name of the unique or primary key constraint that the foreign key constraint references
match_option	character_data	Match option of the foreign key constraint: FULL, PARTIAL, or NONE.
update_rule	character_data	Update rule of the foreign key constraint: CASCADE, SET NULL, SET DEFAULT, RESTRICT, or NO ACTION.
delete_rule	character_data	Delete rule of the foreign key constraint: CASCADE, SET NULL, SET DEFAULT, RESTRICT, or NO ACTION.

Table 33-25. `referential_constraints` Columns

33.28. `role_column_grants`

The view `role_column_grants` identifies all privileges granted on columns where the grantor or grantee is a currently enabled role. Further information can be found under `column_privileges`.

Name	Data Type	Description
grantor	sql_identifier	Name of the role that granted the privilege
grantee	sql_identifier	Name of the role that the privilege was granted to
table_catalog	sql_identifier	Name of the database that contains the table that contains the column (always the current database)
table_schema	sql_identifier	Name of the schema that contains the table that contains the column
table_name	sql_identifier	Name of the table that contains the column
column_name	sql_identifier	Name of the column

Name	Data Type	Description
privilege_type	character_data	Type of the privilege: SELECT, INSERT, UPDATE, or REFERENCES
is_grantable	character_data	YES if the privilege is grantable, NO if not

Table 33-26. `role_column_grants` Columns

33.29. `role_routine_grants`

The view `role_routine_grants` identifies all privileges granted on functions where the grantor or grantee is a currently enabled role. Further information can be found under `routine_privileges`.

Name	Data Type	Description
grantor	sql_identifier	Name of the role that granted the privilege
grantee	sql_identifier	Name of the role that the privilege was granted to
specific_catalog	sql_identifier	Name of the database containing the function (always the current database)
specific_schema	sql_identifier	Name of the schema containing the function
specific_name	sql_identifier	The "specific name" of the function. See *Section 33.33 - page 406* for more information.
routine_catalog	sql_identifier	Name of the database containing the function (always the current database)
routine_schema	sql_identifier	Name of the schema containing the function
routine_name	sql_identifier	Name of the function (might be duplicated in case of overloading)
privilege_type	character_data	Always EXECUTE (the only privilege type for functions)
is_grantable	character_data	YES if the privilege is grantable, NO if not

Table 33-27. `role_routine_grants` Columns

33.30. `role_table_grants`

The view `role_table_grants` identifies all privileges granted on tables or views where the grantor or grantee is a currently enabled role. Further information can be found under `table_privileges`.

Name	Data Type	Description
grantor	sql_identifier	Name of the role that granted the privilege

Name	Data Type	Description
grantee	sql_identifier	Name of the role that the privilege was granted to
table_catalog	sql_identifier	Name of the database that contains the table (always the current database)
table_schema	sql_identifier	Name of the schema that contains the table
table_name	sql_identifier	Name of the table
privilege_type	character_data	Type of the privilege: SELECT, INSERT, UPDATE, DELETE, TRUNCATE, REFERENCES, or TRIGGER
is_grantable	character_data	YES if the privilege is grantable, NO if not
with_hierarchy	character_data	Applies to a feature not available in PostgreSQL

Table 33-28. `role_table_grants` Columns

33.31. `role_usage_grants`

The view `role_usage_grants` identifies USAGE privileges granted on various kinds of objects where the grantor or grantee is a currently enabled role. Further information can be found under `usage_privileges`.

Name	Data Type	Description
grantor	sql_identifier	The name of the role that granted the privilege
grantee	sql_identifier	The name of the role that the privilege was granted to
object_catalog	sql_identifier	Name of the database containing the object (always the current database)
object_schema	sql_identifier	Name of the schema containing the object, if applicable, else an empty string
object_name	sql_identifier	Name of the object
object_type	character_data	DOMAIN or FOREIGN DATA WRAPPER or FOREIGN SERVER
privilege_type	character_data	Always USAGE
is_grantable	character_data	YES if the privilege is grantable, NO if not

Table 33-29. `role_usage_grants` Columns

33.32. `routine_privileges`

The view `routine_privileges` identifies all privileges granted on functions to a currently enabled role or by a currently enabled role. There is one row for each combination of function, grantor, and grantee.

Name	Data Type	Description
grantor	sql_identifier	Name of the role that granted the privilege
grantee	sql_identifier	Name of the role that the privilege was granted to
specific_catalog	sql_identifier	Name of the database containing the function (always the current database)
specific_schema	sql_identifier	Name of the schema containing the function
specific_name	sql_identifier	The "specific name" of the function. See *Section 33.33* - page 406 for more information.
routine_catalog	sql_identifier	Name of the database containing the function (always the current database)
routine_schema	sql_identifier	Name of the schema containing the function
routine_name	sql_identifier	Name of the function (might be duplicated in case of overloading)
privilege_type	character_data	Always EXECUTE (the only privilege type for functions)
is_grantable	character_data	YES if the privilege is grantable, NO if not

Table 33-30. `routine_privileges` Columns

33.33. `routines`

The view `routines` contains all functions in the current database. Only those functions are shown that the current user has access to (by way of being the owner or having some privilege).

Name	Data Type	Description
specific_catalog	sql_identifier	Name of the database containing the function (always the current database)
specific_schema	sql_identifier	Name of the schema containing the function
specific_name	sql_identifier	The "specific name" of the function. This is a name that uniquely identifies the function in the schema, even if the real name of the function is overloaded. The format of the specific name is not defined, it should only be used to compare it to other instances of specific routine names.
routine_catalog	sql_identifier	Name of the database containing the function (always the current database)
routine_schema	sql_identifier	Name of the schema containing the function
routine_name	sql_identifier	Name of the function (might be duplicated in case of overloading)

Name	Data Type	Description
routine_type	character_data	Always FUNCTION (In the future there might be other types of routines.)
module_catalog	sql_identifier	Applies to a feature not available in PostgreSQL
module_schema	sql_identifier	Applies to a feature not available in PostgreSQL
module_name	sql_identifier	Applies to a feature not available in PostgreSQL
udt_catalog	sql_identifier	Applies to a feature not available in PostgreSQL
udt_schema	sql_identifier	Applies to a feature not available in PostgreSQL
udt_name	sql_identifier	Applies to a feature not available in PostgreSQL
data_type	character_data	Return data type of the function, if it is a built-in type, or ARRAY if it is some array (in that case, see the view element_types), else USER-DEFINED (in that case, the type is identified in type_udt_name and associated columns).
character_maximum_length	cardinal_number	Always null, since this information is not applied to return data types in PostgreSQL
character_octet_length	cardinal_number	Always null, since this information is not applied to return data types in PostgreSQL
character_set_catalog	sql_identifier	Applies to a feature not available in PostgreSQL
character_set_schema	sql_identifier	Applies to a feature not available in PostgreSQL
character_set_name	sql_identifier	Applies to a feature not available in PostgreSQL
collation_catalog	sql_identifier	Applies to a feature not available in PostgreSQL
collation_schema	sql_identifier	Applies to a feature not available in PostgreSQL
collation_name	sql_identifier	Applies to a feature not available in PostgreSQL
numeric_precision	cardinal_number	Always null, since this information is not applied to return data types in PostgreSQL
numeric_precision_radix	cardinal_number	Always null, since this information is not applied to return data types in PostgreSQL

Name	Data Type	Description
numeric_scale	cardinal_number	Always null, since this information is not applied to return data types in PostgreSQL
datetime_precision	cardinal_number	Always null, since this information is not applied to return data types in PostgreSQL
interval_type	character_data	Always null, since this information is not applied to return data types in PostgreSQL
interval_precision	character_data	Always null, since this information is not applied to return data types in PostgreSQL
type_udt_catalog	sql_identifier	Name of the database that the return data type of the function is defined in (always the current database)
type_udt_schema	sql_identifier	Name of the schema that the return data type of the function is defined in
type_udt_name	sql_identifier	Name of the return data type of the function
scope_catalog	sql_identifier	Applies to a feature not available in PostgreSQL
scope_schema	sql_identifier	Applies to a feature not available in PostgreSQL
scope_name	sql_identifier	Applies to a feature not available in PostgreSQL
maximum_cardinality	cardinal_number	Always null, because arrays always have unlimited maximum cardinality in PostgreSQL
dtd_identifier	sql_identifier	An identifier of the data type descriptor of the return data type of this function, unique among the data type descriptors pertaining to the function. This is mainly useful for joining with other instances of such identifiers. (The specific format of the identifier is not defined and not guaranteed to remain the same in future versions.)
routine_body	character_data	If the function is an SQL function, then SQL, else EXTERNAL.
routine_definition	character_data	The source text of the function (null if the function is not owned by a currently enabled role). (According to the SQL standard, this column is only applicable if routine_body is SQL, but in PostgreSQL it will contain whatever source text was specified when the function was created.)
external_name	character_data	If this function is a C function, then the external name (link symbol) of the function; else null. (This works out to be the same value that is shown in routine_definition.)

Name	Data Type	Description
external_language	character_data	The language the function is written in
parameter_style	character_data	Always GENERAL (The SQL standard defines other parameter styles, which are not available in PostgreSQL.)
is_deterministic	character_data	If the function is declared immutable (called deterministic in the SQL standard), then YES, else NO. (You cannot query the other volatility levels available in PostgreSQL through the information schema.)
sql_data_access	character_data	Always MODIFIES, meaning that the function possibly modifies SQL data. This information is not useful for PostgreSQL.
is_null_call	character_data	If the function automatically returns null if any of its arguments are null, then YES, else NO.
sql_path	character_data	Applies to a feature not available in PostgreSQL
schema_level_routine	character_data	Always YES (The opposite would be a method of a user-defined type, which is a feature not available in PostgreSQL.)
max_dynamic_result_sets	cardinal_number	Applies to a feature not available in PostgreSQL
is_user_defined_cast	character_data	Applies to a feature not available in PostgreSQL
is_implicitly_invocable	character_data	Applies to a feature not available in PostgreSQL
security_type	character_data	If the function runs with the privileges of the current user, then INVOKER, if the function runs with the privileges of the user who defined it, then DEFINER.
to_sql_specific_catalog	sql_identifier	Applies to a feature not available in PostgreSQL
to_sql_specific_schema	sql_identifier	Applies to a feature not available in PostgreSQL
to_sql_specific_name	sql_identifier	Applies to a feature not available in PostgreSQL
as_locator	character_data	Applies to a feature not available in PostgreSQL
created	time_stamp	Applies to a feature not available in PostgreSQL

Name	Data Type	Description
last_altered	time_stamp	Applies to a feature not available in PostgreSQL
new_savepoint_level	character_data	Applies to a feature not available in PostgreSQL
is_udt_dependent	character_data	Applies to a feature not available in PostgreSQL
result_cast_from_data_type	character_data	Applies to a feature not available in PostgreSQL
result_cast_as_locator	character_data	Applies to a feature not available in PostgreSQL
result_cast_char_max_length	cardinal_number	Applies to a feature not available in PostgreSQL
result_cast_char_octet_length	character_data	Applies to a feature not available in PostgreSQL
result_cast_char_set_catalog	sql_identifier	Applies to a feature not available in PostgreSQL
result_cast_char_set_schema	sql_identifier	Applies to a feature not available in PostgreSQL
result_cast_char_set_name	sql_identifier	Applies to a feature not available in PostgreSQL
result_cast_collation_catalog	sql_identifier	Applies to a feature not available in PostgreSQL
result_cast_collation_schema	sql_identifier	Applies to a feature not available in PostgreSQL
result_cast_collation_name	sql_identifier	Applies to a feature not available in PostgreSQL
result_cast_numeric_precision	cardinal_number	Applies to a feature not available in PostgreSQL
result_cast_numeric_precision_radix	cardinal_number	Applies to a feature not available in PostgreSQL
result_cast_numeric_scale	cardinal_number	Applies to a feature not available in PostgreSQL
result_cast_datetime_precision	character_data	Applies to a feature not available in PostgreSQL
result_cast_interval_type	character_data	Applies to a feature not available in PostgreSQL
result_cast_interval_precision	character_data	Applies to a feature not available in PostgreSQL
result_cast_type_udt_catalog	sql_identifier	Applies to a feature not avail-ble in PostgreSQL

Name	Data Type	Description
result_cast_type_udt_schema	sql_identifier	Applies to a feature not available in PostgreSQL
result_cast_type_udt_name	sql_identifier	Applies to a feature not available in PostgreSQL
result_cast_scope_catalog	sql_identifier	Applies to a feature not available in PostgreSQL
result_cast_scope_schema	sql_identifier	Applies to a feature not available in PostgreSQL
result_cast_scope_name	sql_identifier	Applies to a feature not available in PostgreSQL
result_cast_maximum_cardinality	cardinal_number	Applies to a feature not available in PostgreSQL
result_cast_dtd_identifier	sql_identifier	Applies to a feature not available in PostgreSQL

Table 33-31. routines Columns

33.34. schemata

The view schemata contains all schemas in the current database that are owned by a currently enabled role.

Name	Data Type	Description
catalog_name	sql_identifier	Name of the database that the schema is contained in (always the current database)
schema_name	sql_identifier	Name of the schema
schema_owner	sql_identifier	Name of the owner of the schema
default_character_set_catalog	sql_identifier	Applies to a feature not available in PostgreSQL
default_character_set_schema	sql_identifier	Applies to a feature not available in PostgreSQL
default_character_set_name	sql_identifier	Applies to a feature not available in PostgreSQL
sql_path	character_data	Applies to a feature not avail-ble in PostgreSQL

Table 33-32. schemata Columns

33.35. sequences

The view sequences contains all sequences defined in the current database. Only those sequences are shown that the current user has access to (by way of being the owner or having some privilege).

Name	Data Type	Description
sequence_catalog	sql_identifier	Name of the database that contains the sequence (always the current database)
sequence_schema	sql_identifier	Name of the schema that contains the sequence
sequence_name	sql_identifier	Name of the sequence
data_type	character_data	The data type of the sequence. In PostgreSQL, this is currently always bigint.
numeric_precision	cardinal_number	This column contains the (declared or implicit) precision of the sequence data type (see above). The precision indicates the number of significant digits. It can be expressed in decimal (base 10) or binary (base 2) terms, as specified in the column numeric_precision_radix.
numeric_precision_radix	cardinal_number	This column indicates in which base the values in the columns numeric_precision and numeric_scale are expressed. The value is either 2 or 10.
numeric_scale	cardinal_number	This column contains the (declared or implicit) scale of the sequence data type (see above). The scale indicates the number of significant digits to the right of the decimal point. It can be expressed in decimal (base 10) or binary (base 2) terms, as specified in the column numeric_precision_radix.
maximum_value	cardinal_number	Not yet implemented
minimum_value	cardinal_number	Not yet implemented
increment	cardinal_number	Not yet implemented
cycle_option	character_data	Not yet implemented

Table 33-33. **sequences** Columns

33.36. sql_features

The table sql_features contains information about which formal features defined in the SQL standard are supported by PostgreSQL. This is the same information that is presented in *Appendix D*. There you can also find some additional background information.

Name	Data Type	Description
feature_id	character_data	Identifier string of the feature
feature_name	character_data	Descriptive name of the feature
sub_feature_id	character_data	Identifier string of the subfeature, or a zero-length string if not a subfeature

Name	Data Type	Description
sub_feature_name	character_data	Descriptive name of the subfeature, or a zero-length string if not a subfeature
is_supported	character_data	YES if the feature is fully supported by the current version of PostgreSQL, NO if not
is_verified_by	character_data	Always null, since the PostgreSQL development group does not perform formal testing of feature conformance
comments	character_data	Possibly a comment about the supported status of the feature

Table 33-34. `sql_features` Columns

33.37. `sql_implementation_info`

The table `sql_implementation_info` contains information about various aspects that are left implementation-defined by the SQL standard. This information is primarily intended for use in the context of the ODBC interface; users of other interfaces will probably find this information to be of little use. For this reason, the individual implementation information items are not described here; you will find them in the description of the ODBC interface.

Name	Data Type	Description
implementation_info_id	character_data	Identifier string of the implementation information item
implementation_info_name	character_data	Descriptive name of the implementation information item
integer_value	cardinal_number	Value of the implementation information item, or null if the value is contained in the column `character_value`
character_value	character_data	Value of the implementation information item, or null if the value is contained in the column `integer_value`
comments	character_data	Possibly a comment pertaining to the implementation information item

Table 33-35. `sql_implementation_info` Columns

33.38. `sql_languages`

The table `sql_languages` contains one row for each SQL language binding that is supported by PostgreSQL. PostgreSQL supports direct SQL and embedded SQL in C; that is all you will learn from this table.

Name	Data Type	Description
sql_language_source	character_data	The name of the source of the language definition; always ISO 9075, that is, the SQL standard
sql_language_year	character_data	The year the standard referenced in sql_language_source was approved; currently 2003
sql_language_conformance	character_data	The standard conformance level for the language binding. For ISO 9075:2003 this is always CORE.
sql_language_integrity	character_data	Always null (This value is relevant to an earlier version of the SQL standard.)
sql_language_implementation	character_data	Always null
sql_language_binding_style	character_data	The language binding style, either DIRECT or EMBEDDED
sql_language_programming_language	character_data	The programming language, if the binding style is EMBEDDED, else null. PostgreSQL only supports the language C.

Table 33-36. `sql_languages` Columns

33.39. `sql_packages`

The table `sql_packages` contains information about which feature packages defined in the SQL standard are supported by PostgreSQL. Refer to *Appendix D* for background information on feature packages.

Name	Data Type	Description
feature_id	character_data	Identifier string of the package
feature_name	character_data	Descriptive name of the package
is_supported	character_data	YES if the package is fully supported by the current version of PostgreSQL, NO if not
is_verified_by	character_data	Always null, since the PostgreSQL development group does not perform formal testing of feature conformance
comments	character_data	Possibly a comment about the supported status of the package

Table 33-37. `sql_packages` Columns

33.40. `sql_parts`

The table sql_parts contains information about which of the several parts of the SQL standard are supported by PostgreSQL.

Name	Data Type	Description
feature_id	character_data	An identifier string containing the number of the part
feature_name	character_data	Descriptive name of the part
is_supported	character_data	YES if the part is fully supported by the current version of PostgreSQL, NO if not
is_verified_by	character_data	Always null, since the PostgreSQL development group does not perform formal testing of feature conformance
comments	character_data	Possibly a comment about the supported status of the part

Table 33-38. `sql_parts` Columns

33.41. `sql_sizing`

The table `sql_sizing` contains information about various size limits and maximum values in PostgreSQL. This information is primarily intended for use in the context of the ODBC interface; users of other interfaces will probably find this information to be of little use. For this reason, the individual sizing items are not described here; you will find them in the description of the ODBC interface.

Name	Data Type	Description
sizing_id	cardinal_number	Identifier of the sizing item
sizing_name	character_data	Descriptive name of the sizing item
supported_value	cardinal_number	Value of the sizing item, or 0 if the size is unlimited or cannot be determined, or null if the features for which the sizing item is applicable are not supported
comments	character_data	Possibly a comment pertaining to the sizing item

Table 33-39. `sql_sizing` Columns

33.42. `sql_sizing_profiles`

The table `sql_sizing_profiles` contains information about the `sql_sizing` values that are required by various profiles of the SQL standard. PostgreSQL does not track any SQL profiles, so this table is empty.

Name	Data Type	Description
sizing_id	cardinal_number	Identifier of the sizing item
sizing_name	character_data	Descriptive name of the sizing item

Name	Data Type	Description
profile_id	character_data	Identifier string of a profile
required_value	cardinal_number	The value required by the SQL profile for the sizing item, or 0 if the profile places no limit on the sizing item, or null if the profile does not require any of the features for which the sizing item is applicable
comments	character_data	Possibly a comment pertaining to the sizing item within the profile

Table 33-40. `sql_sizing_profiles` Columns

33.43. `table_constraints`

The view `table_constraints` contains all constraints belonging to tables that the current user owns or has some non-SELECT privilege on.

Name	Data Type	Description
constraint_catalog	sql_identifier	Name of the database that contains the constraint (always the current database)
constraint_schema	sql_identifier	Name of the schema that contains the constraint
constraint_name	sql_identifier	Name of the constraint
table_catalog	sql_identifier	Name of the database that contains the table (always the current database)
table_schema	sql_identifier	Name of the schema that contains the table
table_name	sql_identifier	Name of the table
constraint_type	character_data	Type of the constraint: CHECK, FOREIGN KEY, PRIMARY KEY, or UNIQUE
is_deferrable	character_data	YES if the constraint is deferrable, NO if not
initially_deferred	character_data	YES if the constraint is deferrable and initially deferred, NO if not

Table 33-41. `table_constraints` Columns

33.44. `table_privileges`

The view `table_privileges` identifies all privileges granted on tables or views to a currently enabled role or by a currently enabled role. There is one row for each combination of table, grantor, and grantee.

Name	Data Type	Description
grantor	sql_identifier	Name of the role that granted the privilege

Name	Data Type	Description
grantee	sql_identifier	Name of the role that the privilege was granted to
table_catalog	sql_identifier	Name of the database that contains the table (always the current database)
table_schema	sql_identifier	Name of the schema that contains the table
table_name	sql_identifier	Name of the table
privilege_type	character_data	Type of the privilege: SELECT, INSERT, UPDATE, DELETE, TRUNCATE, REFERENCES, or TRIGGER
is_grantable	character_data	YES if the privilege is grantable, NO if not
with_hierarchy	character_data	Applies to a feature not available in PostgreSQL

Table 33-42. `table_privileges` Columns

33.45. `tables`

The view `tables` contains all tables and views defined in the current database. Only those tables and views are shown that the current user has access to (by way of being the owner or having some privilege).

Name	Data Type	Description
table_catalog	sql_identifier	Name of the database that contains the table (always the current database)
table_schema	sql_identifier	Name of the schema that contains the table
table_name	sql_identifier	Name of the table
table_type	character_data	Type of the table: BASE TABLE for a persistent base table (the normal table type), VIEW for a view, or LOCAL TEMPORARY for a temporary table
self_referencing_column_name	sql_identifier	Applies to a feature not available in PostgreSQL
reference_generation	character_data	Applies to a feature not available in PostgreSQL
user_defined_type_catalog	sql_identifier	Applies to a feature not available in PostgreSQL
user_defined_type_schema	sql_identifier	Applies to a feature not available in PostgreSQL
user_defined_type_name	sql_identifier	Applies to a feature not available in PostgreSQL

Name	Data Type	Description
is_insertable_into	character_data	YES if the table is insertable into, NO if not (Base tables are always insertable into, views not necessarily.)
is_typed	character_data	Applies to a feature not available in PostgreSQL
commit_action	character_data	If the table is a temporary table, then PRESERVE, else null. (The SQL standard defines other commit actions for temporary tables, which are not supported by PostgreSQL.)

Table 33-43. `tables` Columns

33.46. `triggers`

The view `triggers` contains all triggers defined in the current database on tables that the current user owns or has some non-SELECT privilege on.

Name	Data Type	Description
trigger_catalog	sql_identifier	Name of the database that contains the trigger (always the current database)
trigger_schema	sql_identifier	Name of the schema that contains the trigger
trigger_name	sql_identifier	Name of the trigger
event_manipulation	character_data	Event that fires the trigger (INSERT, UPDATE, or DELETE)
event_object_catalog	sql_identifier	Name of the database that contains the table that the trigger is defined on (always the current database)
event_object_schema	sql_identifier	Name of the schema that contains the table that the trigger is defined on
event_object_table	sql_identifier	Name of the table that the trigger is defined on
action_order	cardinal_number	Not yet implemented
action_condition	character_data	Applies to a feature not available in PostgreSQL
action_statement	character_data	Statement that is executed by the trigger (currently always EXECUTE PROCEDURE *function*(...))
action_orientation	character_data	Identifies whether the trigger fires once for each processed row or once for each statement (ROW or STATEMENT)

Name	Data Type	Description
condition_timing	character_data	Time at which the trigger fires (BEFORE or AFTER)
condition_reference_old_table	sql_identifier	Applies to a feature not available in PostgreSQL
condition_reference_new_table	sql_identifier	Applies to a feature not available in PostgreSQL
condition_reference_old_row	sql_identifier	Applies to a feature not available in PostgreSQL
condition_reference_new_row	sql_identifier	Applies to a feature not available in PostgreSQL
created	time_stamp	Applies to a feature not available in PostgreSQL

Table 33-44. `triggers` Columns

Triggers in PostgreSQL have two incompatibilities with the SQL standard that affect the representation in the information schema. First, trigger names are local to the table in PostgreSQL, rather than being independent schema objects. Therefore there can be duplicate trigger names defined in one schema, as long as they belong to different tables. (`trigger_catalog` and `trigger_schema` are really the values pertaining to the table that the trigger is defined on.) Second, triggers can be defined to fire on multiple events in PostgreSQL (e.g., ON INSERT OR UPDATE), whereas the SQL standard only allows one. If a trigger is defined to fire on multiple events, it is represented as multiple rows in the information schema, one for each type of event. As a consequence of these two issues, the primary key of the view `triggers` is really (`trigger_catalog`, `trigger_schema`, `trigger_name`, `event_object_table`, `event_manipulation`) instead of (`trigger_catalog`, `trigger_schema`, `trigger_name`), which is what the SQL standard specifies. Nonetheless, if you define your triggers in a manner that conforms with the SQL standard (trigger names unique in the schema and only one event type per trigger), this will not affect you.

33.47. `sage_privileges`

The view `usage_privileges` identifies USAGE privileges granted on various kinds of objects to a currently enabled role or by a currently enabled role. In PostgreSQL, this currently applies to domains, foreign-data wrappers, and foreign servers. There is one row for each combination of object, grantor, and grantee.

Since domains do not have real privileges in PostgreSQL, this view shows implicit non-grantable USAGE privileges granted by the owner to PUBLIC for all domains. The other object types, however, show real privileges.

Name	Data Type	Description
grantor	sql_identifier	Name of the role that granted the privilege
grantee	sql_identifier	Name of the role that the privilege was granted to
object_catalog	sql_identifier	Name of the database containing the object (always the current database)
object_schema	sql_identifier	Name of the schema containing the object, if applicable, else an empty string
object_name	sql_identifier	Name of the object
object_type	character_data	DOMAIN or FOREIGN DATA WRAPPER or FOREIGN SERVER
privilege_type	character_data	Always USAGE
is_grantable	character_data	YES if the privilege is grantable, NO if not

Table 33-45. usage_privileges Columns

33.48. user_mapping_options

The view user_mapping_options contains all the options defined for user mappings in the current database. Only those user mappings are shown where the current user has access to the corresponding foreign server (by way of being the owner or having some privilege).

Name	Data Type	Description
authorization_identifier	sql_identifier	Name of the user being mapped, or PUBLIC if the mapping is public
foreign_server_catalog	sql_identifier	Name of the database that the foreign server used by this mapping is defined in (always the current database)
foreign_server_name	sql_identifier	Name of the foreign server used by this mapping
option_name	sql_identifier	Name of an option
option_value	character_data	Value of the option. This column will show as null unless the current user is the user being mapped, or the mapping is for PUBLIC and the current user is the server owner, or the current user is a superuser. The intent is to protect password information stored as user mapping option.

Table 33-46. user_mapping_options Columns

33.49. `user_mappings`

The view `user_mappings` contains all user mappings defined in the current database. Only those user mappings are shown where the current user has access to the corresponding foreign server (by way of being the owner or having some privilege).

Name	Data Type	Description
`authorization_identifier`	`sql_identifier`	Name of the user being mapped, or PUBLIC if the mapping is public
`foreign_server_catalog`	`sql_identifier`	Name of the database that the foreign server used by this mapping is defined in (always the current database)
`foreign_server_name`	`sql_identifier`	Name of the foreign server used by this mapping

Table 33-47. `user_mappings` Columns

33.50. `view_column_usage`

The view `view_column_usage` identifies all columns that are used in the query expression of a view (the SELECT statement that defines the view). A column is only included if the table that contains the column is owned by a currently enabled role.

 Note

Columns of system tables are not included. This should be fixed sometime.

Name	Data Type	Description
`view_catalog`	`sql_identifier`	Name of the database that contains the view (always the current database)
`view_schema`	`sql_identifier`	Name of the schema that contains the view
`view_name`	`sql_identifier`	Name of the view
`table_catalog`	`sql_identifier`	Name of the database that contains the table that contains the column that is used by the view (always the current database)
`table_schema`	`sql_identifier`	Name of the schema that contains the table that contains the column that is used by the view
`table_name`	`sql_identifier`	Name of the table that contains the column that is used by the view
`column_name`	`sql_identifier`	Name of the column that is used by the view

Table 33-48. `view_column_usage` Columns

33.51. `view_routine_usage`

The view `view_routine_usage` identifies all routines (functions and procedures) that are used in the query expression of a view (the SELECT statement that defines the view). A routine is only included if that routine is owned by a currently enabled role.

Name	Data Type	Description
table_catalog	sql_identifier	Name of the database containing the view (always the current database)
table_schema	sql_identifier	Name of the schema containing the view
table_name	sql_identifier	Name of the view
specific_catalog	sql_identifier	Name of the database containing the function (always the current database)
specific_schema	sql_identifier	Name of the schema containing the function
specific_name	sql_identifier	The "specific name" of the function. See *Section 33.33* - page 406 for more information.

Table 33-49. `view_routine_usage` Columns

33.52. `view_table_usage`

The view `view_table_usage` identifies all tables that are used in the query expression of a view (the SELECT statement that defines the view). A table is only included if that table is owned by a currently enabled role.

 Note

System tables are not included. This should be fixed sometime.

Name	Data Type	Description
view_catalog	sql_identifier	Name of the database that contains the view (always the current database)
view_schema	sql_identifier	Name of the schema that contains the view
view_name	sql_identifier	Name of the view
table_catalog	sql_identifier	Name of the database that contains the table that is used by the view (always the current database)
table_schema	sql_identifier	Name of the schema that contains the table that is used by the view
table_name	sql_identifier	Name of the table that is used by the view

Table 33-50. `view_table_usage` Columns

33.53. views

The view `views` contains all views defined in the current database. Only those views are shown that the current user has access to (by way of being the owner or having some privilege).

Name	Data Type	Description
table_catalog	sql_identifier	Name of the database that contains the view (always the current database)
table_schema	sql_identifier	Name of the schema that contains the view
table_name	sql_identifier	Name of the view
view_definition	character_data	Query expression defining the view (null if the view is not owned by a currently enabled role)
check_option	character_data	Applies to a feature not available in PostgreSQL
is_updatable	character_data	YES if the view is updatable (allows UPDATE and DELETE), NO if not
is_insertable_into	character_data	YES if the view is insertable into (allows INSERT), NO if not

Table 33-51. `views` Columns

List of Volumes

Volume I. The SQL Language

Volume II. Server Administration

Volume III. Server Programming

Part V. Server Programming

Volume IV. Reference

Part VI. Reference

Volume II.

Volume V. Internals and Appendixes

Part VII. Internals

Part VIII. Appendixes

Bibliography

Index

Index

LaVergne, TN USA
11 February 2010

172673LV00005B/2/P